THE *UNAUTHORIZED*

X-

CYCLOPEDIA

THE *UNAUTHORIZED*

X-CYCLOPEDIA

The Definitive Reference Guide to The X-Files

JAMES HATFIELD
AND GEORGE "DOC" BURT

With Illustrations by
Edwin E. Echols

Kensington Books
http://www.kensingtonbooks.com

KENSINGTON BOOKS are published by

Kensington Publishing Corp.
850 Third Avenue
New York, NY 10022

ISBN 1-57566-233-7

First Kensington Trade Paperback Printing: December, 1997
10 9 8 7 6 5 4 3 2 1

Printed in the United States of America

For my wife, Nancy,
who understood completely that a book such as this one
required a twenty-four-hour-a-day commitment,
and for accepting everything that such a responsibility entailed,
things like using our weekends to write,
having more mood swings than Edith Bunker going through menopause
(I was truly a real pain in the ass),
and locking myself away in my office way too much
during our first year of marriage.
She put up with *all* of it . . . and I love her for it—*forever.*

—*J.H.*

X-Philes and sci-fi fans of all ages around the world,
who have shown their continuing support for all of our writing projects;
and to unpublished wordsmiths whose works have yet to be shared
and enjoyed by all of us, remember—
"The truth is out there" and that truth is that you can succeed,
but you must never give up or stop trying;
"Trust no one" who tells you that success is not within your reach;
and, if there is no wind to blow your sails—ROW!

— *"Doc"*

ACKNOWLEDGMENTS

Everyone helps. Sometimes it's a piece of information, sometimes it's an idea, but mostly it's knowing they would be there to help if you needed them. You should know who they are and our apologies to any whose names we may have inadvertently omitted: Amanda Drogan, Gerald Nately, John Swithen, Maureen Cowan, Pete Jacobs, Joe Newall, Emily Sidley, Tom Decker, Josh Brannigar, Sarah Boone, Alicia Parkette, Glen Bateman, Bonita Alvarez, Mike Kelleher, Andy Cocker, Billy Bellamy, Jack Crager, Sharon Ackerman, Monica Bowden, Ray Brower, Leigh Cabot, Bill Baterman, Minette Banberry, Georgia Deever, Bud Brown, Doc Abelson, Roger King, Geoffrey Alliburton, Bryce Bell, Bobbi Anderson, Edgar Box, Dinah Bellman, Larry Talman, and "Star Invader" Brock Callahan. Each of these dedicated people readily gave their time and energy to this book, never with an eye for their own benefit, but rather, always trying to help the progress of *The Unauthorized X-cyclopedia* in any way they could. We thank them from the bottom of our hearts. The usual caveat applies: If we screwed up their input, it is our fault, and certainly not theirs.

At the various bookstores, a very special thanks to those overworked and underpaid "publishing partners" who have always aggressively promoted our previous books beyond the call of duty: John Lindsay at Borders Bookstore in Dallas, Texas; Jon Dowdy at Hastings in Fayetteville, Arkansas; Marcia Harris at Barnes & Noble in Orlando, Florida; Shannon Smith and J.P. Toner at Barnes & Noble in Houston; Matt Broyles at Borders Bookstore in Ft. Worth, Texas; Kendall Spooner at the Borders Bookstore in Plano, Texas; Kris "RazorBattling" Swim at the Faytteville, Arkansas B. Dalton; Kenn Davis at the Barnes & Noble in Dallas; Yvonne Gordon and Marcia Bennett at Barnes & Noble in Oklahoma City, Oklahoma; Julie Hoover at the Northwest Arkansas Mall's Waldenbooks; Mike Hills at the Fayetteville, Arkansas Barnes & Noble; Amazon Books' Jeffrey Bezos; and especially, Doug Waterhouse, president of the premiere online sci-fi bookstore, Star-Books.

They have our deepest gratitude.

So does Tracy Bernstein, a redwood among mere sprouts (our apologies to Frohike for stealing his line), whose vast editorial skills, guidance, competence, and red pen got us through another book (thanks also, Tracy, for your unquestioning faith in us and our work and *especially* for the deadline extension); Marcia Amsterdam, our invaluable literary agent, who supported, encouraged and put up with us throughout the writing of this book; Laura Shatzkin, Debra Broide and Sue Razaire, publicists extraordinaire who could teach P.T. Barnum a few tricks of the trade; Ruby Jean Jensen ("Over two million copies of her novels in print"), who gave us a publisher, an agent, an accountant and the fulfillment of our dreams; and "Webmaster" Bryan Grayson, a truly unique soul and our "Texas Bubba," who created our cyberspace calling card and made our lives a hell of a lot simpler by showing us a shortcut to saving this immense body of work on the computer everyday.

Most of all, our heartfelt thanks go to artist Edwin Echols, who worked into the wee hours of most mornings and on weekends during this project's compressed schedule for nothing more than a pat on the back and in the process produced some of the most realistic artwork to ever grace the inside of a book. Let out a long, deep sigh of relief, Ed. This one's finally finished. It's margarita time! (And the man does know how to make a *mean* one on the rocks.) Also, we surely would be skinned alive if we didn't pass along a heartfelt thanks to Judith Echols, Ed's long-suffering wife, who covertly faxed us copies of his illustrations while he was at his real job, and kept us posted on his progress so we wouldn't have to nag him constantly about that damn fast-approaching deadline.

On a personal note, we are eternally grateful to WMC-FM's multi-talented morning crew Ron Olson, Steve Conley, and Karen Perrin in Memphis; Ruben Macias (editor of the premiere online sci-fi and fantasy newsletter, *Subspace Chatter*); Joyce Mason (co-host of the syndicated radio show *Talk Trek & Beyond*); Philly's Sunday morning voice of reason, WIP's Peter Solomon; T. Craig Jones (who valiantly fought the evil forces living in Missouri); film critic and frequent dinner companion, Kurt Johnston; Texas transplants and steadfast friends, Mike and Susan Bradshaw; swimming buddies and "wrap party" attendants Bob and Karla Elliot; El Torro's genetics specialist and all-around nice guy, Kendron Benham; Andrea Mihlhauser and Carl and Joyce Martin (our Houston connections); Sandy Haley (also, thanks for the most delicious banana pudding this side of paradise!); Teddy Kuan (for that first intro to *The X-Files*); Barbara Garrigus (for taking care of the taxes so that a certain writer could attempt to meet a deadline); two Texans that treated us like friends when friends were hard to come by— Billy Bob Walker and Harold Skidmore; Ronnie Mauldin, Nick Morrison, and Cecil Larney—"The Three Wisemen" who looked the other way when a book had to be written; Robert Bush Ph.D., a Texas college professor who saw a spark of imagination way back when; Jeanette and Tom Mentzel— who were *always* there in sunshine and rain; Tommy and Sue Isaac for the winter break away from the book to go skiing in the Rockies; and Colon and Dana Washburn for a summer break at the pool with plenty of food, cold beer, and lots of laughter; and once again our sincerest gratitude to the government guys—MIBs—Bill and Eddie. They know why. Boy, *do* they.

Special acknowledgments from "Doc" to the following group of cheerful, stalwart souls: my banker, Bill Garst; attorney Kimberly Killebrew and her always competent assistant, Tammy Garcia; Susan Pinabel, who came to the rescue and handled the travel arrangements on my end of the book signing tour; my CPA, Lynn Colby; and my colleagues and friends—Bobbi Sanchez, Dan and Tresa Deetz, Beth Robertson, Jeanie Yandell, Susan Stanley, and Joshua Rhoden, and last, but certainly not least, Ross Sivertsen, who deserves a *very* special thanks.

And, of course, a last, final thank you to Chris Carter, creator and executive producer of *The X-Files*. Our only hope is that the book that you now hold in your hands somehow expresses the admiration and respect we have for him and his creation. If it does that, we can truly hope for no more.

Oh, yeah, lest we forget, everyone we may have been rude to while working on this book. God only knows, there were *plenty!*

ABOUT THE ILLUSTRATOR

Edwin E. Echols is a senior designer for a marine engineer and naval architectural firm in Houston, Texas. Since the age of five, he has drawn everything from Bugs Bunny to his favorite *Playboy* centerfolds (those came a little later in life) and on everything from his bedroom walls to the dining room tablecloth. When he's not sketching, oil painting, or designing, Ed is in the garage repairing mechanical contraptions that seem to perplex other folks. Next on his agenda is to find the time to restore his old Austin-Healy so she'll once again take to the road with the grace of years gone by. Ed and his wife, Judith, and their three cats make their home in a quiet little town on the coast of Texas.

"I believe that what we're looking for is in the X-Files. I'm more certain than ever that the truth is in there."

—*Mulder*, "Paper Clip"

"The fans read into the show a whole lot more than we ever intend. They take it apart like a coroner."

—*X-Files* director and producer, Kim Manners

INTRODUCTION

The X-Files' complex dramatic arc now spans four television seasons and, at this writing, a fifth year is underway and the first *X-Files* motion picture is scheduled to make its highly anticipated debut in movie theaters around the world in the summer of 1998. Top 20 ratings, a cottage industry of related products, a foreign television market of at least sixty countries, a number of new *X-Files* clones popping up on other networks, and a fanatical following of inquisitive and intelligent fans (known as "X-Philes") are all proof of the continued success of this preternaturally compelling phenomenon. Like it or not, *The X-Files* has indeed become an icon of 20th-century popular culture (like its illustrious predecessor, *Star Trek*) and is growing in size and complexity with every passing year.

What follows is an attempt on our part to keep track of the enormous body of details that has been created for this modern television classic. Entries in this encyclopedia are presented in alphabetical order. They give a brief explanation of each person, place, and thing, but they are far from complete. There are many rich details that simply could not fit into the space allotted. Despite our publisher's considerable generosity in giving us several hundred pages, we still had to select material on the basis of what we felt would be of the most interest to the greatest number of readers. Entries preceded with a 📁 are episode titles and synopses. **Background Checks** indicate behind-the-scenes information, while **Classic Sound Bites** provide memorable lines of dialogue. Character name entries generally include the actor's name in parentheses, where applicable, and other pertinent information about their acting career. *Italics* highlights inside stories, in-jokes, and real-life inspirations.

Please note: Many fine and imaginative novels, comic books, and other stories based on *The X-Files* have been published over the last few years. Some of these are adaptations of previously shown episodes, while others are original works of fiction. We considered including key elements of some of these works in this *X-cyclopedia*, since many such stories detail fascinating events not depicted in the episodes themselves. We finally chose not to do so, not out of dislike for these stories, but because it became too difficult to choose which books and events to include. We instead fell back on our original purpose—to provide a reference for the aired versions of the show itself. We sincerely hope the *X-cyclopedia* will be useful both to the series' fan base, as well as to *X-Files* writers of scripts, novels and comic books.

So here it is! A comprehensive and illustrated encyclopedia encompassing the first four seasons of *The X-Files* that we hope will increase your understanding, enjoyment and appreciation of one of the most popular and entertaining series ever to appear on television. From the Amaru urn to Dr. Zama and beyond—the *X-cyclopedia* has everything you need to know about the expanding *X-Files* world of the paranormal, extraterrestrials, and all manner of shadowy government conspiracies.

The truth is still *out there,*
James Hatfield & George "Doc" Burt

A

Amaru

A & A Anderson Tank Cleaning Service Septic-tank cleaning company in Newark, New Jersey. The Flukeman creature escaped from deep inside a portable toilet at the Lake Betty campsite when an A & A Anderson sewage tanker sucked the contents of the porta-potty into the truck. The genetic mutant momentarily clogged the tanker's vacuum tube during the process. ("The Host")

Aaron, Brother Member of the mysterious and reclusive Kindred sect in Steveston, Massachusetts. During a communal dinner attended by agents Mulder and Scully, Brother Aaron began choking to death. Scully rushed to help, but Sister Abby had the man whisked away. Later on, the agents found the community gathered in a barn, amid a bizarre ritual in which the congregants marched Brother Aaron into a cellar. His body was slathered with white clay and placed into a strange catacomb, and began to morph into a female. ("Genderbender") *The actor who portrayed Brother Aaron was uncredited.*

Abductee Magazine dedicated to allegedly true accounts of those abducted by aliens. Scully found a copy while searching the residence of Michael Fazekas, a Providence, Rhode Island police officer and alleged abductee, who killed himself after undergoing a radical type of regression therapy. On the cover was a photo of sixty-two-year-old Amy Cassandra, another Rhode Island abductee, whose brutal murder Mulder had been charged with. ("Demons")

Abigail, Sister (Michelle Goodger) Member of the Amish-like Kindred sect, she acted as the main spokesperson when Mulder and Scully investigated their settlement in connection with a bizarre series of murders. She admonished Brother Wilton for angrily denouncing the "outsiders." ("Genderbender") *Actress Michelle Goodger also played Barbara Ausbury in "Die Hand Die Verletzt."*

Aboah, Samuel (Willie Amakye) A recent immigrant to Philadelphia from the West African country of Burkino Faso, the construction worker was arrested after the mysterious disappearances/deaths of a number of black men whose bodies lacked pigmentation. Although Scully believed Aboah was a mutant, without a melanin-producing pituitary gland, Mulder theorized that he was a Teliko, a metamorphic ghost creature with the ability to transmogrify into any size or shape, whose West African tribe had survived over the years by stealing pituitary glands from other humans. Later hospitalized, it remained uncertain if Aboah would live long enough to stand trial for the murder of the five African-American men. According to Scully's field report, Aboah's response to hormone therapy was poor and his deterioration progressive. ("Teliko"). *As an in-joke, the birthdate on Samuel Aboah's Resident Alien photo ID was 9/25, the same as Gillian Anderson's daughter, Piper Maru.*

AB Pizza The Connerville, Oklahoma company that employed pizza deliverer and town bully, Jack Hammond, the fifth victim of human lightning rod, Darin Peter Oswald. ("D.P.O.")

Abramowitz Plumbing Name on the side of a surveillance van used by Crew-Cut Man and other shadowy government operatives. ("The Erlenmeyer Flask")

Adams Inn Motel where Scully stayed in Philadelphia, Pennsylvania while investigating Vsevlod Pudovkin, a Russian immigrant Mulder suspected of possessing valuable information on two crashed UFOs. ("Never Again")

Adams, Mrs. (Diana Stevan) She was working at a blood-drive table at a department store in Franklin, Pennsylvania, where postal worker Ed Funsch was prompted to turn violent by the digitized words "BEHIND YOU" (referring to the gun department), followed by "DO IT." ("Blood")

Adult Video News The trade magazine of the adult movie industry and one of many pornographic publications Mulder was said to read in his free time. ("Beyond the Sea")

Advanced Research Project Agency The governmental agency responsible for the Arctic Ice Core Project and its team of researchers in Icy Cape, Alaska. ("Ice")

Aeschylus The Father of Greek Drama. According to Lone Gunman Frohike's speculative dossier on the Cigarette-Smoking Man, the shadowy operative was able to quote Aeschylus from memory. When Robert Kennedy read from an Aeschylus poem at the funeral of Martin Luther King, CSM recited the verses while watching the proceedings on TV. ("Musings of a Cigarette-Smoking Man")

Ahab Scully's pet name for her father, a Naval captain, taken from Herman Melville's classic novel *Moby Dick* ("Beyond the Sea"). Believing herself stranded on a rock in the middle of Heuvelman's Lake in Georgia, Scully compared the obsessive Mulder to Ahab. "The truth or the white whale—what difference does it make?" she wondered aloud ("Quagmire").

Aiklen, Staff Sgt. Kevin A soldier whose case was similar to that of Lt. Col. Victor Stans. Aiklen's family perished in a fire, and he tried to take his own life by throwing himself into a wood chipper. Like Stans, Aiklen claimed a phantom soldier refused to let him kill himself. Scully noted similar underreported circumstances in the case of each man, both of whom served under Gen. Thomas Callahan in the Gulf War. ("The Walk")

Al-Hadithi, Mohammed An Iraqi military officer who witnessed UFOs on radar, which apparently attacked a fighter pilot and his aircraft over the 37th parallel. ("E.B.E.") *The actor who portrayed this character went uncredited.*

Alice The name of one of the horses outside the feed store in Steveston, Massachusetts. ("Genderbender")

Alice in Wonderland Beloved classic of children's literature. Lewis Carroll's tale follows a little girl named Alice into the nonsensical world of Wonderland where she attends the tea party of the Mad Hatter and plays croquet in the court of the Queen of Hearts. In search of the cloth hearts that John Lee Roche, a convicted serial child abductor/killer, cut from the nightclothes of his victims, Mulder and Scully discovered a copy of *Alice in Wonderland* hidden in the camper shell of the El Camino he once owned. Scattered throughout the pages were sixteen hearts, forcing Mulder to realize there were two victims unaccounted for during Roche's reign of terror. ("Paper Hearts")

Alien Autopsy A mail order videotape "guaranteed authentic," which Mulder reportedly bought for $29.95, plus shipping and handling. Inside a train car in Knoxville, Tennessee, in a hospital setting, four Japanese doctors worked on an unseen figure, extracting a strange green fluid. Suddenly, black-clad soldiers brandishing automatic weapons burst in, murdering the doctors and zipping the autopsy subject—glimpsed to reveal a gray-skinned extraterrestrial—into a body bag. Mulder bought the purported alien autopsy videotape from Allentown, Pennsylvania resident and MUFON member Steven Zinnszer, who claimed to have intercepted the images off a satellite dish. After viewing the tape, Scully commented to Mulder that it was "even hokier than the one they aired on the Fox network." ("Nisei") *A ten-year-old boy played the part of the alien on the autopsy table, while his sister served as an extraterrestrial on the quarantined train car. Scully joked "This is even hokier than the one they ran on the Fox network!" and Fox repeated the special the following night.*

"All Along the Watchtower" Classic 1960s tune by Jimi Hendrix. A skeptical Agent Mulder asked alleged psychic Luther Lee Boggs to summon the musician's soul and then requested he sing "All Along the Watchtower." ("Beyond the Grave")

"ALL DONE. BYE BYE." Digital readout displayed on Mulder's cellular phone by whoever, or whatever, was subjecting the population of Franklin, Pennsylvania to an experiment involving insecticides and artificially heightened phobias. ("Blood")

Allegheny Catholic Hospital The Pennsylvania medical center where EMT Michele Wilkes encountered Leonard Betts, her highly respected former partner, previously decapitated in an ambulance wreck. ("Leonard Betts")

Allegiance, USS U.S. nuclear submarine, on a cartography mission at a cruising depth of 1,000 feet, that detected the alien Bounty Hunter's submerged craft emitting apparently random radio signals. Pacific Command ordered the *Allegiance* to torpedo it, but once at the crash site, a huge shock wave shut down the sub's reactor, stranding the crew below thirty-two feet of ice. Using Mr. X's coordinates, Mulder located the *Allegiance*'s conning tower above the ice in the Arctic wasteland. Inside, he found one survivor— in fact, the morphed alien Bounty Hunter. After throwing Mulder around like a child, the extraterrestrial submerged the submarine, nearly slicing Mulder with a tower fin. ("End Game")

Allentown-Bethlehem Medical Center Hospital in Allentown, Pennsylvania where Penny Northern was treated for an inoperable brain tumor by Dr. Kevin Scanlon. After Scully was similarly diagnosed, Northern persuaded her to check into the medical facility for experimental treatment by Scanlon, who had allegedly isolated the cause of the tumor. Mulder later determined that the physician was a co-conspirator in the Shadowy Syndicate's colonization project, and was responsible for accelerating the deaths of the MUFON abductees. After Northern died, Scully checked out of the hospital, telling Mulder she had decided to fight the insidious disease and continue her work with the X-Files. ("Memento Mori")

Allentown Medical Center Hospital in Pennsylvania where a tumor-ridden Betsy Hagopian was dying of a cancerous condition that wouldn't respond to treatment, a result, the MUFON women contended, of repeated alien-abduction and testing since her teens. Scully was visibly shaken when they suggested her fate would be the same as Hagopian's. ("Nisei")

Allentown Police Substation Law-enforcement facility in Pennsylvania where Mulder and Scully took Kazuo Sakurai, the Asian suspect who fled the scene of Steven Zinnszer's execution-style murder. To the agents' surprise, Assistant Director Skinner arrived on the scene, saying they would have to release Sakurai because he was allegedly a high-ranking Japanese diplomat, and that Zinnszer's murder would be investigated by another federal agency. ("Nisei")

"Alligator Man" SEE: **Glazebrook, Jerald**

All-Nighter Pharmacy The drugstore in which NICAP member and UFO-conspiracy theorist Max Fenig had his prescription for the schizophrenia-treatment mellaril filled. Scully took note of Fenig's prescription drugs when he escorted her and Mulder to his camper-trailer. ("Fallen Angel")

Alpert, Martin (Mike Puttonen) The director and administrator of the New Horizon Psychiatric Center in Washington, D.C. One of his staff, Nurse Innes, was a serial killer responsible for the deaths of several young women. ("Elegy") *Mike Puttonen also played a motel manager in "Deep Throat," Dr. Pilsson in "Sleepless," and the Conductor on the quarantine train in "731."*

Alta A Navy icecutter that observed an alien spacecraft crash land in the Beaufort Sea, eighty-seven miles north of the Arctic Circle. The *Alta*'s crew rescued the shapeshifting extraterrestrial Bounty Hunter, who led them to believe he was a downed Russian pilot. ("Colony")

Alt-Fuels, Inc. Dr. Jeff Eckerle's experimental methane research facility in Miller's Grove, Massachusetts. The scientist had been importing animal dung, which may have explained the town's infestation by a new breed of cockroach, since roaches are dung-eaters. The company's motto was "Waste is a terrible thing to waste." ("War of the Coprophages")

Alves, Paulette A name on an airline manifest Scully scrutinized, trying to determine Mulder's whereabouts when he flew to a possible alien contact site in Puerto Rico. ("Little Green men") *Paulette Alves is the name of a prominent online X-Phile.*

Amaru Ecuadorian female shaman, whose remains were unearthed in a sacred burial urn and shipped to Boston's Museum of Natural History, despite warnings from the native Secona Indians. As forewarned by the tribe, a series of mysterious mutilation murders occurred at the museum as a result of the Amaru's vengeful jaguar spirit. After five deaths, the U.S. State Department agreed to return the Amaru urn to Equador and its proper resting place. ("Teso dos Bichos")

Ambassador Hotel Washington, D.C. landmark where Assistant Director Skinner sought solace in the bar after being presented with final divorce papers by his attorney. After meeting Carina Sayles, an attractive prostitute, Skinner took her upstairs to a room where they went to bed together. A few hours later, he awoke from a nightmare and found the woman next to him dead, her head twisted around. ("Avatar")

Ambrose, Willa (Jayne Atkinson) A naturalist hired by the Board of Supervisors of the impoverished Fairfield, Idaho Zoo, whose animals were the subjects of alien conservationists. Ambrose and the zoo's operations chief, Ed Meecham, were charged with the manslaughter of anticaptivity activist, Kyle Lang of the Wild Again Organization (WAO), a group dedicated to liberating circus and zoo animals. ("Fearful Symmetry")

American Ronin Solider-of-fortune magazine Robert Modell (a.k.a. Pusher) used to advertise his talents as a masterless samurai ("Ronin") who had the ability to cloud the minds of his victims. Modell bragged in the ad: "I solve problems. OSU"—the Japanese word "osu" meaning "to push." The self-styled assassin was so anxious to make sure Mulder didn't miss the clue "RONIN" that he finger-painted the word in blood on the side of a police car at a crime scene. ("Pusher") *Danielle Faith Friedman, a production assistant on the series, appeared as a cover model on one of the* American Ronin *magazines Mulder waded through in hopes of finding clues regarding Modell.*

American University Nationally and internationally recognized school of higher learning in Washington, D.C. Scully requested Dr. Vitagliano of the university's paleoclimatology lab to examine core samples taken from a cave in the Canadian Yukon Territory's St. Elias Mountains, where a survey team discovered the alleged corpse of an alien, entombed in a block of ice. ("Gethsemane")

Amrith A viscous, honey-like liquid manifested during an exorcism. As a physical display of spiritual phenomena, Amrith oozed out of the walls of Charlie Holvey's Arlington, Virginia hospital room when the Calusari performed the Romanian Ritual of Separation. ("The Calusari")

Amrolli, Mohammed A terrorist with ties to the exiled, Philadelphia-based Middle Eastern extremist group, Isfahan. Amrolli and an accomplice attacked Lauren Kyte at an ATM machine, only to be killed themselves by the unseen spirit of Kyte's dead boss, Howard Graves. Mulder identified the terrorist's body after surreptitiously obtaining the corpse's thumbprints on his eyeglasses. ("Shadows") *The actor who portrayed Mohammed Amrolli was uncredited.*

Anaphylactic Shock Fatal reaction to an insect bite. Scully initially hypothesized that anaphylactic shock was the cause of several cockroach-related deaths in the small town of Miller's Grove, Massachusetts. ("War of the Coprophages")

Anasazi Native American tribe that disappeared from New Mexico six hundred years ago. Albert Hosteen, a World War II Navajo code-talker, told Mulder that Anasazi meant "the ancient aliens" and that he believed the tribe was abducted "by visitors who come here still." ("Anasazi") *Anthropolo-*

gists have discovered polished bone-ends, as if boiled in pots, in Chaco Canyon, New Mexico, where the Anasazi are believed to have lived. It is theorized that the tribe practiced cannibalism, believing it prolonged life.

📁 **"Anasazi (Part 1 of 3)"** Written by Chris Carter (based upon a story by David Duchovny and Chris Carter). Directed by R.W. Goodwin. File number 2X25. *First aired May 19, 1995. Agent Mulder creates far-reaching and international consequences when a computer hacker entrusts him with a digital tape copy of the highly classified MJ documents, which contain information detailing the government's knowledge of UFOs for the past 50 years. This cliffhanger episode, in which Mulder is last seen trapped in a burning boxcar in New Mexico, marked the conclusion of the second season.* **Classic Sound Bite:** *"I'll save the government the plane fare. I just want to know which government that is."* **Background Check:** *David Duchovny and Chris Carter worked closely on the episode's storyline, and then* The X-Files *creator penned the final script. Carter also made a cameo appearance in the episode as one of Scully's interrogators in Skinner's office. As Mulder perused the un-translated text of the MJ files on his computer screen, eagle-eyed viewers could make out "do-ray-me-fa-so-la-todo" (five lines under the Department of Defense heading). Producer R.W. Goodwin also made a cameo appearance as a gardener, but the scene ended up on the cutting room floor.*

Andrea (Laura Harris) One of four Crowley High School students who unintentionally summoned the demon Azazel to the small New Hampshire town of Milford Haven. ("Die Hand Die Verletzt")

Andrew, Brother (Brent Hinkley) Member of the mysterious Kindred sect in Steveston, Massachusetts, whose mesmerizing handshake left Scully visibly shaken. The best friend of genderbending killer, Marty, Brother Andrew attempted to seduce Scully with his pheromonic (and possibly fatal) powers, but she was saved by Mulder. ("Genderbender")

angelica An exotic Chinese medical item described to Scully by San Francisco police detective Glen Chao. The anti-inflammatory, antioxidant, and immunopotentiating actions of the compound make it specific in the treatment of rheumatoid arthritis, gout, and osteoarthritis. ("Hell Money")

Angie's Midnight Bowl Bowling alley in Washington, D.C. owned and operated by Angelo Pintero, who discovered a badly injured young woman wedged inside a lane's pinsetter carriage. Pintero rushed outside to get help and was shocked to see a crowd gathered around the corpse of the same woman. Mulder suspected that Pintero had encountered her disembodied soul, a ghost attempting to communicate for reasons unknown at the time. ("Elegy")

ankuses Poles used to control elephants by animal trainers. ("Fearful Symmetry")

Annapolis Savings and Loan On May 9, 1993, the first banking institution to be robbed by homicidal robber Warren James Dupre and his accomplice/wife Lula Philips. ("Lazarus")

anthropomancy The primitive art of foretelling future events by examining the entrails of an eviscerated human being. Mulder made reference to the ancient practice during the crime scene investigation of a doll collector and amateur tasseographer's murder in St. Paul, Minnesota. The Puppet serial killer had left part of the woman's intestines on a table next to her eyes. ("Clyde Bruckman's Final Repose")

Antonio (Aurelio Dinunzio) A worried-looking United Nations assistant who informed an Italian diplomat that someone had penetrated the top-secret MJ documents. ("Anasazi")

🗁 **"Apocrypha (Part 2 of 2)"** Written by Frank Spotnitz and Chris Carter. Directed by Kim Manners. File number 3X16. *First aired February 16, 1996. Mulder escorts an oily alien-possessed Alex Krycek back to the U.S. from Hong Kong to retrieve the missing DAT tape, while Scully coordinates the investigation into Assistant Director Skinner's attempted assassination, hoping it will bring her sister's murderer to justice.* **Classic Sound Bite:** *"We show a talent for these G-men activities."* **Background Check:** *The episode's title means "of doubtful origin" or "from a questionable source." The apocrypha usually refers to the books included in the Septuagint and Vulgate but excluded from the Jewish and Protestant canons of the Old Testament.*

Apollo 11 **key chain** A birthday gift Mulder gave Scully, which commemorated the first moon landing on July 20, 1969. Although she believed that the present symbolized "glorious struggle and survival of mankind," Mulder said he gave it to her because he thought it was "a pretty cool key chain." ("Tempus Fugit/Max") *One of the authors of this book (and we won't say which) bought an identical key chain at the National Air and Space Museum for $4.99. Shame on Mulder for giving Scully such a CHEAP and cheesy gift on her birthday, especially in light of the fact that she was dying from inoperable brain cancer at the time.*

"Apology Is Policy" The alternate tag line that replaced the usual "The Truth Is Out There" during the opening credits of "731." The phrase "Apology Is Policy" was based on a statement Scully made to Mulder while describing the government's willingness to knowingly cover up its shameful deeds and then simply apologize for them later. An angry Mulder said he didn't want the usual formulated responses, but rather "an apology for the truth." ("731")

APU Auxiliary power unit valve which malfunctioned on a space shuttle, forcing the launch to be aborted. NASA's Mission Control communications commander, Michelle Generoo, feared the APU had been sabotaged after examining X rays and other documents revealing deep-grooved marks on the piece of equipment. ("Space")

Arctic Ice Core Project (A.I.C.P.) Scientific research expedition dispatched to Icy Cape, Alaska to drill into the Arctic's ice fields. The scientists slaughtered one another after being exposed to a 250,000-year-old, parasitic alien they uncovered in the drilling depths of a meteor crater. The ice station was torched by the military forty-five minutes after Mulder and Scully and the survivors of an investigative team were airlifted out. ("Ice")

Arden, Hal (David Fresco) Seventy-four-year-old Alzheimer's patient at Excelsis Dei convalescent home in Worscester, Massachusetts, who was accused of rape by nurse Michelle Charters. The elderly Arden was choked to death by an invisible attacker after threatening to expose the truth about the "special" pills given to nursing home residents by Asian orderly Gung Bituen. ("Excelsius Dei")

Ardent, USS U.S. Navy destroyer escort reported as "lost" in the Norwegian Sea's 65th parallel, an area Mulder referred to as a second Bremuda Triangle. By the time Mulder and Scully relocated the "ghost ship," it had begun to exhibit advanced, multi-year corrosion, even though the destroyer had been commissioned in 1991. An hour after Mulder and Scully were rescued by Navy SEALS, the *Ardent*'s outer hull corroded through and the ship sank. ("Dod Kalm")

Arecibo Ionospheric Observatory Deserted, mothballed SETI (Search for Extraterrestrial Intelligence) facility in Puerto Rico. Once home of one of the largest radar-radio telescopes in the world, the ambitious Arecibo project's funding was canceled by Congress. The abandoned observatory's electronic equipment mysteriously sprang to life after receiving a transmission recorded from the *Voyager* spacecraft years after the unmanned probe left our solar system. ("Little Green Men") *Unlike the mothballed and deserted station portrayed, the Arecibo observatory, affiliated with Cornell University's National Astronomy and Ionosphere Center, is a real and thriving research facility, and home to the world's largest radio-telescope.*

Arens, Sheriff Tom (Gary Grubbs) Chief law enforcement officer in the cannibalistic town of Dudley, Arkansas. Mulder killed Arens with two gunshots when the masked sheriff attempted to decapitate Scully during a ritualistic bonfire ceremony attended by numerous townsfolk. ("Our Town")

argotypoline Highly flammable rocket-propulsion class-3 fuel that pyrokinetic assassin Cecil L'ively used to increase the damage caused by fires. ("Fire")

Arlington National Cemetery Landmark burial site in Washington, D.C. where Mulder "attended" Deep Throat's funeral, using eight-power binoculars from 1,000 feet away ("Little Green Men"). Although no physical evidence linked war veteran Sgt. Leonard "Rappo" Trimble to a series of murders at an Army hospital, his family's request for burial in Arlington National Cemetery was denied ("The Walk").

Arlinsky (Matthew Walker) Forensics anthropologist employed at the Smithsonian Institution who had been in contact with Mulder during the term of his assignment in the X-Files unit. Several years earlier, Arlinsky had been involved in an embarrassing UFO photo enhancement scandal, but continued to profess his innocence. Mulder was skeptical when Arlinsky called, claiming he had definitive proof of an alien corpse entombed in an ice cave in the Canadian Yukon Territory. Mulder arranged to meet Arlinsky at the Smithsonian with Scully, where the anthropologist said that, sediment and ice core samples retrieved from the site showed the perfectly intact extraterrestrial body to be over two hundred years old. Arlinsky was later murdered by an assassin known as Ostelhoff, after he and Mulder successfully transported the E.B.E. to the United States for authentication. ("Gethsemane") *Matthew Walker also played rocket scientist Dr.Ronald Surnow in the first season episode "Roland."*

Army Central Identification Lab Military facility where Dr. Benjamin Keyser examined the alleged physical remains of Nathaniel Teager, recovered after the Green Beret's helicopter was shot down in enemy territory during the Vietnam War. Dr. Keyser met Mulder at the lab and showed the agent the extent of Teager's remains: two teeth, stored at the Army Forensics Lab since recovery from the chopper crash site in 1971. Keyser noted "pronounced scoring" on each tooth, strongly suggesting extraction, and possibly a faked death. ("Unrequited")

Army Detention Center Military stockade at Ft. Evanston, Maryland. Denny Markham, leader of the Right Hand radical paramilitary group, was held in custody at the base's detention center under the new anti-terrorist law. Markham, an ex-Marine, was threatened with an assortment of conspiracy, homicide, treason, and illegal weapons possession charges, for his suspected complicity in the deaths of two high-ranking military officers. ("Unrequited")

Army Forensics Lab Military facility which housed Sgt. Nathaniel Teager's physicals remains after his chopper was shot down in North Vietnam in 1971 and he was officially reported as killed in action. ("Unrequited")

Arntzen An alias used by Alex Krycek. When he contacted Vassily Peskow, a former KGB assassin living in St. Petersburg, Krycek sent detailed mission orders from "Comrade Arntzen," telling him that the Cold War wasn't over. Extreme right-wing militia leader, Terry Edward Mayhew, told Mulder and Scully that Krycek had introduced himself to the revolutionary group as "Arntzen." ("Terma")

📁 **"Ascension (Part 2 of 2)"** Written by Paul Brown. Directed by Michael Lange. File number 2X06. *First aired October 21, 1994. In a chase through the Virginia mountains, Mulder desperately attempts to rescue the kidnapped Scully before escaped mental patient and former FBI agent Duane Barry turns her over to the aliens who previously abducted him.* **Classic Sound Bite:** *"There are no answers for you, Mr. Mulder. They have only one policy: Deny everything."* **Background Check:** *A character-enhancing scene was filmed but later cut in which Mulder said to the Cigarette-Smoking Man, "Smoking is slow suicide." CSM's response was, "That's the point."*

ASL American Sign Language, which Sophie the gorilla used to communicate with naturalist Willa Ambrose at the Fairfield, Idaho Zoo. ("Fearful Symmetry")

Astadourian Lightning Observatory A scientific facility located near Connerville, Oklahoma, where researchers used 100 ionized rods designed specifically to stimulate lightning and its effects. ("D.P.O.") *Mary Astadourian, chief researcher and office manager for Ten-Thirteen Productions, is also Chris Carter's executive assistant.*

astral projection The psychokinetic ability to project one's spirit out of the physical body. Astral projection is based upon the belief that the celestial body has greater strength than the corporeal one. Mulder speculated that quadruple amputee Sgt. Leonard "Rappo" Trimble (who lost both arms and legs in the Gulf War) managed to exact revenge against his enemies and their families through astral projection. ("The Walk").

Atsumi, Leza (Akiko Morison) Special agent at the FBI's Sioux City, Iowa office who told Mulder and Scully there was nothing affecting national security in eight-year-old Kevin Morris' binary code drawings. Atsumi explained that when loaded into a computer, the boy's zeros and ones formed snatches of Shakespeare's sonnets, the Holy Koran, and Bach's Brandenburg Concertos. ("Conduit")

📁 **"Aubrey"** Written by Sara Charno. Directed by Rob Bowman. File number 2X12. *First aired January 6, 1995. A pregnant policewoman's dreams of a murder leads to the body of an FBI agent killed 50 years earlier, reopening the serial homicide case he had been investigating. When the murderer strikes* *again, Agents Mulder and Scully question the connection between the police officer and the modern-day imitator.* **Classic Sound Bite:** *"I've often felt that dreams are answers to questions we haven't yet figured out how to ask."* **Background Check:** *Episode writer Sara Charno's first effort for* The X-Files *was "finely honed" because of the numerous contributions to the script by producers and frequent writers Glen Morgan and James Wong, who also suggested casting Morgan Woodward in the role of old Harry Cokely.*

Audrey County Morgue The temporary storage facility which housed the corpse of Jane Brody, a mail sorter fatally attacked by a swarm of bees in the Desmond, Virginia routing center of the overnight delivery company, Transcontinental Express. As part of a deal with the Cigarette-Smoking Man to save Scully from terminal cancer, Skinner stole Brody's body from the morgue and incinerated it in the basement furnace of a power plant. ("Zero Sum")

Auerbach, Dr. Simon (Morris Paynch) One of the conspiring Pinck Pharmaceutical doctors who used Cumberland State Correctional Facility prisoners as guinea pigs to circumvent FDA regulations. ("F. Emasculata"). *Morris Paynch also played in the recurring role of the Gray-Haired Man, a ruthless and relentless assassin for the Shadowy Syndicate.*

Aurora Project A secret Defense Department suborbital-spycraft. ("Deep Throat")

Ausbury, Barbara (Michelle Goodger) Defended husband, Jim, against allegations that he conducted unspeakable Satanic rites with his stepdaughter, Shannon, and her sister, whom he allegedly murdered at eight. ("Die Hand Die Verletzt") *Michelle Goodger also portrayed Sister Abigail, the spokesperson for the mysterious Kindred in "Genderbender."*

Ausbury, Jim (Dan Butler) Member of devil-worshipping coven in Milford Haven, New Hampshire. His sixteen-year-old stepdaughter, Shannon, told Mulder and Scully that Ausbury and his coven performed rituals in her home when her mother was away, making her and her sister pregnant and then sacrificing the babies. Ausbury admitted to Mulder that he forced Shannon to participate in watered-down rituals, but never hurt her, and hypnotized her to repress the memories. He was devoured by a huge snake and reduced to bones. ("Die Hand Die Verletzt") *Dan Butler played Bob "Bulldog" Briscoe on the NBC comedy series* Frasier.

Ausbury, Shannon (Heather McComb) She claimed to be the victim of her stepfather's black magic. She told Mulder and Scully that she had delivered three babies, all buried in the basement after being sacrificed to Satan. A demon, in the form of substitute teacher, Phyllis Paddock, took Shannon's bracelet, which she used as a talisman to enchant the teenager into fatally

```
#101  Sat Jul 24 1999 10:56AM  Item(
s) checked out to BRINKERHOFF, KATRI
NA M.


            TITLE
     BARCODE              DUEDATE
The unauthorized X-cyclopedia : the
de  33331002588671    Aug 21 1999

Consumer reports
     33330000537300    Aug 07 1999
```

slashing her wrists. ("Die Hand Die Verletzt") *Shannon Ausbury and her family were named in honor of die-hard* X-Files *fan Jill Ausbury, who reportedly shares episode co-writer Glen Morgan's morbid sense of humor and taste in rock groups (especially the Ramones).*

Austin, Dr. Ross Listed as one of the doctors on call at the Lombard Research Facility when Mulder and the Lone Gunmen infiltrated the building. ("Memento Mori")

autoerotic asphyxiation The "undignified" manner of Mulder's demise, as predicted by psychic Clyde Bruckman, who could foresee how people would die. ("Clyde Bruckman's Final Repose") *Episode writer Darin Morgan has gone on record as saying that he put the memorable exchange between Mulder and Bruckman in the script because he really believes that's how Mulder will eventually die.*

Avalon Foundation A cryogenics facility at the Washington Institute of Technology. The preserved head of rocket scientist Dr. Arthur Grable was suspended in a storage unit of liquid nitrogen at the cryolab after he was killed in an automobile accident. ("Roland")

⬚ **"Avatar"** Written by Howard Gordon (based upon a story by Howard Gordon and David Duchovny). Directed by James Charleston. File number 3X21. *First aired April 26, 1996. When Assistant Director Skinner wakes up in a hotel bed next to a murdered prostitute, Mulder and Scully join the investigation to prove their boss' innocence. As they unravel the threads of a conspiracy, Mulder also becomes convinced that Skinner has been haunted since his tour of duty in Vietnam by a haglike apparition known as a succubus.* **Classic Sound Bite:** *"I was no choirboy. I inhaled."* **Background Check:** *The episode title refers to the Sanskrit word meaning "the descent to Earth of a deity in human or animal form." A scene was filmed but later cut (due to time considerations) in which the Cigarette-Smoking Man went to see Skinner, questioning his allegiance.*

Awakening, The Feminist novel by Kate Chopin. Mulder kept a copy of *The Awakening* on a bookshelf in his apartment.

Azazel Demon unintentionally summoned to the town of Milford Haven, New Hampshire by four high school classmates reading from an occult book. The body of one of the teenagers, Jerry Stevens, was later found mutilated and displayed in accordance with the Rites of the Azazel. ("Die Hand Die Verletzt")

B

Big Blue

B-11 The Green Beret detachment known as the "Bloody Sabers" during the Vietnam war. Sgt. Nathaniel Teager, a "killing machine" with twenty-six confirmed solo enemy executions, was a member of the B-11 before his chopper was shot down over enemy territory in 1971. Officially reported as killed in action, Teager spent the next twenty-five years in a Vietnamese prison camp. ("Unrequited")

Babcock (James Sutorius) An anthropologist, and colleague of Arlinsky from the Smithsonian Institution. Babcock narrowly escaped death when the assassin Ostelhoff killed all other members of a survey team that had discovered a frozen alien corpse in the Yukon Territory. Mulder, Arlinsky and Babcock recovered the extraterrestrial's remains and transported the corpse to Washington, where Arlinsky conducted an autopsy. Mulder later discovered Babcock and Arlinsky murdered, and the alien corpse missing. Babcock and Ostelhoff (who executed the two anthropologists) were participants in the elaborate conspiracy which possibly manufactured the corpse, intent on duping Mulder. ("Gethsemane")

Babe Academy Award-nominated movie about a talking pig. When Mulder and Scully released the Peacocks' pigs from their pens to lure the deformed brothers from their house, Scully commented that she had spent the weekend baby-sitting her nephew who watched the movie fifteen times. ("Home")

Bailey, Dr. William (Peter Hanlon) Research scientist assigned by the U.S. Forestry Service to investigate rapid frog extinction near Heuvelman's Lake in the Blue Ridge Mountains of Georgia. After refusing to place the amphibian *Rana sphenocephala* on the endangered species list, Dr. Bailey, searching for his pager along the lake's shore, was dragged to a watery death by either an enormous alligator or the legendary serpentine monster known as Big Blue. ("Quagmire) *Peter Hanlon also had bit part as an aid in "Musings of a Cigarette-Smoking Man."*

Baker, Dr. Aaron (Dana Gladstone) A Syracuse, New York abortion clinic doctor killed by the alien Bounty Hunter as part of a major offensive to terminate colonization clones. ("Colony")

Balboa Naval Hospital San Diego military hospital in which the entire crew of the French salvage ship, the *Piper Maru*, were treated for disfiguring burns associated with radiation levels non-existent "on this planet." ("Piper Maru")

Baltimore Animal Regulation The employer of mutant serial killer Eugene Victor Tooms. Apprehended slithering down an air vent at the site of a previous murder, Tooms claimed that, as an animal control officer, he was looking for a dead cat in response to complaints of a foul odor ("Squeeze"). After his discharge from Druid Hill Sanitarium, Tooms was re-employed by the Baltimore Animal Regulation ("Tooms")

banana cream pie The dessert Agent Mulder stepped in while pursuing the fortune-teller and serial killer, the Puppet, through a hotel kitchen, as envisioned by prophetic insurance salesman Clyde Bruckman. ("Clyde Bruckman's Final Repose")

Banks, Derek (Channon Roe) One of three anti-Semitic youths who murdered Isaac Luria inside his Brooklyn market. Mulder and Scully discovered Banks' body hanging from a wooden beam in a Brooklyn synagogue, the victim of a golem, whose physical features matched those of Isaac Luria. ("Kaddish")

Banton, Dr. Chester Ray (Tony Shalhoub) Brilliant scientist employed by Polarity Magnetics. After experimenting with dark matter using a particle accelerator, his shadow behaved like a black hole, reducing matter to pure energy. Realizing his shadow had become an entity intent on killing, the mysterious Mr. X, along with two government agents disguised as paramedics, kidnapped Banton from a psychiatric hospital. Dr. Banton is reportedly locked away in a secret government facility where he is relentlessly subjected to a flashing light over and over again. ("Soft Light") *Tony Shalhoub is best known as Antonio Scarpacci on the long-running NBC comedy series* Wings. *His film credits include* The Big Night, Quick Change, Barton Fink, Honeymoon in Vegas, Addams Family Values, *and* Men in Black, *in which he played Jeebs, an alien turned pawnbroker who quickly regenerates his blown-off head.*

Barbala, Rudy (Dwight Koss) Buffalo, New York police detective who mysteriously plummeted to his death from a window at the 14th Precinct House after interrogating eight-year-old Michelle Bishop. The young girl was later discovered to be the reincarnated spirit of Charlie Morris, a police officer Barbala was responsible for murdering nine years earlier. ("Born Again")

Barber (Markus Hondro) Also known as El Barbera by the illegal immigrants working as migrant labor in California's San Joaquin Valley. Operating from a barber shop (where he habitually watched Spanish soap operas on Univision), the goateed Barber illegally smuggled Mexican immigrants to and from the United States "for a modest fee." The money-grubbing immigrant, who had seemingly forgotten his roots, was killed by a highly contagious and fatal fungus when he sold Eladio and Soledad Buente a ride back to Mexico. ("El Mundo Gira")

Barclay, Capt. Phillip (David Cubitt) Thirty-five-year-old Commander of U.S. Navy destroyer USS *Ardent* who died of old age. After failing to keep his crew from abandoning ship, a shriveled and terrified Barclay was discovered by Mulder and Scully aboard the corroded "ghost ship" *Ardent* clutching a bottle of Jack Daniels. Barclay was the last of his crew to die from the vessel's contaminated water supply, which apparently catalyzed body fluids to cause rapid, massive cellular degeneration. ("Dod Kalm")

Barnett, John Earvin (David Peterson) Extremely dangerous armed robber and murderer; Agent Mulder's first case with the FBI's Violent Crimes Unit. In 1989, Mulder apparently hesitated in firing his weapon, which permitted Barnett to kill his hostage and FBI agent Steve Wallenberg. Although Barnett reportedly died of cardiac failure at Tashmoo Federal Correctional Facility, Mulder and Scully's investigation revealed that Barnett had been the subject of a government-financed prison hospital experiment which reversed the aging process using reptile regenerative-cell morphegins. Several years later, a youthful and rejuvenated Barnett sought vengeance against Mulder, but the agent killed him during a hostage situation with a single shot. ("Young at Heart") *Actor Alan Boyce played the youthful John Barnett.*

Barney (Guyle Frazier) A Richmond, Virginia police officer vaporized by Dr. Chester Banton's shadow when he attempted to apprehend the research scientist at a train station. ("Soft Light") *Guyle Frazier also played a police officer in "3."*

Barney A purple TV dinosaur popular with children. Mulder, however, considers Barney to be the most heinous and evil force in the twentieth century. ("E.B.E.")

Baron, Det. Bradley (Nathaniel Deveaux) Detective Kelly Ryan's superior on the Richmond, Virginia police force. Bradley arranged for Dr. Chester Banton's transfer from the Yaloff Psychiatric Hospital to the county jail after being manipulated by a scheming Ryan. ("Roland")

Barrington, Dr. Lawrence (Dave Hurtubise) A doctor at the Avalon Foundation cryogenics facility where aeronautical scientist Arthur Grable's head was preserved after his death. Dr. Barrington telephoned Mulder and Scully to advise them that someone had surreptitiously raised the temperature on Grable's cryogenic storage capsule. ("Roland") *Dave Hurtubise also played an unnamed pathologist who determined that the decapitated head of an EMT was riddled with cancer in "Leonard Betts."*

Barry, Duane (Steve Railsback) Former FBI agent forced to resign in 1982 after being shot in the line of duty rendered him a violently delusional psychotic dependent on psychiatric treatment and hospitalization. Barry claimed to be the victim of numerous alien abductions and experimentation. In 1994, he escaped from the Davis Correctional Treatment Center and took several people hostage, including Agent Scully. Mulder pursued Barry to the top of Skyland Mountain in Virginia, site of his first alleged alien abduction, but was too late to rescue Scully, whom Barry insisted he traded to extraterrestrials. Barry died moments later while alone with nefarious double agent Alex Krycek, allegedly from asphyxiation, although Mulder suspected Krycek had poisoned him. Medical examinations conducted on Barry while he was hospitalized at the Jefferson Memorial facility in Richmond, Virginia revealed mysterious marked pieces of metal in his abdomen, sinuses, and gums, apparently lending credence to his claim of alien experimentation ("Duane Barry/Ascension"). In addition, Barry's name appeared adjacent to Scully's in the most recent entries of the Defense Department's secret MJ files, which contained documented proof of the existence of alien visitation and experimentation ("Anasazi") *The role of Duane Barry was written especially for Steve Railsback who portrayed the infamous mass murderer and cult leader Charles Manson in the acclaimed 1976 TV movie* Helter Skelter. *Railsback also appeared in* The Stunt Man, The Stars Fell on Henrietta, Barb Wire, *and in the vampire-from-outer-space movie,* Lifeforce.

Bartle, Sylvia A name on an airline manifest Scully examined, trying to determine Mulder's whereabouts when he flew to a possible alien contact site in Puerto Rico. ("Little Green Men") *Sylvia Bartle is the name of a prominent online X-Phile.*

Batter (Cory Fry) During a sandlot baseball game in a vacant field next to the Peacocks' farmhouse, the boy discovered a dead baby's hand and oozing blood as he dug in with his foot at home plate. ("Home")

Battleship A table-top game played by two people facing each other. When Scully complained that she didn't have a desk in the X-Files basement office, Mulder sarcastically remarked that because of the cramped space they could put desks face-to-face and play Battleship. ("Never Again")

Bauer, Eric A basketball player at Grover Cleveland Alexander High School in "the Perfect Harmony City" of Comity. During a practice game, Bauer inadvertently crashed into a table on the sidelines, spilling lemonade all over Terri Roberts and Margi Kleinjan. When Bauer went behind the bleachers to retrieve the ball, the lights went out and the motorized bleachers retracted, crushing the screaming teenager to death. ("Syzygy") *The young actor who played Eric Bauer was uncredited.*

Bauvais, Pierre (Bruce Young) Haitian witch doctor, voodoo high priest, and self-proclaimed revolutionary incarcerated by Col. Jacob Wharton at the

Folkstone, North Carolina INS processing center. After Bauvais warned the base commander that he'd take his soldiers "one by one . . . take their souls" if the refugees weren't repatriated, Col. Wharton ordered his men to beat him. When Mulder and Scully returned to question the Haitian, they were told Bauvais had committed suicide by cutting his wrists on a bedspring. At a municipal graveyard, Wharton was discovered performing a voodoo ritual over Bauvais' coffin. The Haitian suddenly appeared and downed the colonel with some dust blown from the palm of his hand. Although Bauvais was last seen lying peacefully in his casket, it is believed that Col. Wharton was buried alive, the victim of Bauvais' zombification ritual. ("Fresh Bones")

Bay Area Carpeteers The San Francisco employer of Chinese immigrant and carpet layer Shuyang Hsin, who gambled his own organs attempting to win money to pay for his leukemia-stricken daughter's medical needs. ("Hell Money")

Bayside Funeral Home Mortuary in San Francisco's Chinatown where an immigrant was burned alive in the crematory oven during the Chinese Festival of the Hungry Ghosts. ("Hell Money")

Beach Grove Motel Mulder and Scully's place of lodging when they traveled to Southwest Idaho to investigate the disappearance of a test pilot at Ellens Air Force Base. ("Deep Throat")

Beakman's World Saturday morning children's science show. After Mulder discovered a rocket scientist's head had been dunked in liquid nitrogen and then shattered on the floor, he commented, "I don't think you'll be seeing this experiment on *Beakman's World.*" ("Roland")

Bear (Jeff Kober) Nickname of the civilian pilot who flew Mulder, Scully and a group of doctors and scientists from Jimmy Doolittle Airfield in Nome, Alaska to Icy Cape to investigate the unexplained deaths of a research team sent to drill into the Arctic ice core. Bear was the sixth victim of a small, single-celled alien lifeform, over 200,000 years old, that penetrates the hypothalamus gland. ("Ice") *Jeff Kober co-starred as Dodger on the critically acclaimed ABC series* China Beach.

Bear Creek State Park The Virginia park where two escaped convicts infected with a highly contagious disease murdered a vacationing father in the men's rest room and hijacked his family's motor home. ("F. Emasculata")

Bearded Man (Ken Jones) Long-haired, bearded chain-smoker followed out of a bar and killed by Leonard Betts, a mutant in need of the Bearded Man's cancerous lung. Betts took the body to his storage locker, where he ingested the diseased tissue and regenerated a duplicate of himself. Scully's autopsy revealed that the Bearded Man died from massive blood loss due to the surgical removal of his left lung. ("Leonard Betts)

Bearfeld, Bruce (Robert Moloney) Hunting and fishing guide on Great Sacandaga Lake in Upstate New York. Mulder hired Bearfeld and his boat service when the agent went scuba diving into the lake's murky waters in search of a crashed UFO. ("Tempus Fugit/Max") *Robert Moloney appeared as a line worker at the Chaco Chicken processing plant in "Our Town."*

bear gallbladder An exotic Chinese medical item described to Scully by San Francisco police detective Glen Chao. It is usually prepared in soup or tea. ("Hell Money")

Beatty, Melvin (Duncan Fraser) Arson specialist assigned to the FBI's Washington office. Beatty did not believe that pyrokinetic assassin Cecil L'ively was capable of spontaneous combustion, and suggested to Mulder that the real culprit was rocket fuel, which burns almost completely. ("Fire")

"Believe the Lie" The tag line that replaced "The Truth Is Out There" during the opening credits of the fourth season finale, "Gethsemane." The credo was reflected in many different contexts: UFO sightings, the existence of extraterrestrials (including the frozen alien discovered in the Yukons), Scully's denouncement of Mulder and the "illegitimacy" of his work to the review board, and Mulder's alleged suicide by a gunshot to the head. ("Gethsemane") *Noticeably different from other episodes in which the opening tag line had been changed, "Believe the Lie" was mentioned and emphasized several times throughout "Gethsemane."*

belladonna. A poisonous European plant of the nightshade family with reddish bell-shaped flowers and shining back berries, whose roots and leaves yield atropine, a common medicinal extract. It is also known as "witches berry," and used in hexing rituals. Mulder discovered that belladonna was an active ingredient in a prescription antacid taken by Dr. Harrison Lloyd, a cosmetic surgeon who claimed demonic possession as his defense for killing a patient during a violent liposuction procedure. ("Sanguinarium")

Belt, Lt. Col. Marcus Aurelius (Ed Lauter) Former astronaut and later supervisor of NASA's *Viking* Orbiter shuttle program, Belt was responsible for the sabotage of several space missions after being possessed by a mysterious astral force during a space-walk. After unconsciously alerting communications commander Michelle Generoo to another attempt against a shuttle, Belt leapt to his death from a thirteenth-floor window while wrestling with the extraterrestrial "presence." ("Space") *Noted character actor, Ed Lauter, is best known for his tough-guy roles in such movies as* The Longest Yard *and* Born on the Fourth of July.

Bennett, Dr. Mike Listed as one of the doctors on call at the Lombard Research Facility when Mulder and the Lone Gunmen infiltrated the building. ("Memento Mori")

Benson, Judge Virginia magistrate who issued the arrest warrant for Eurisko founder, Brad Wilczek. ("Ghost in the Machine")

Ben Zion Cemetery A Jewish burial ground in Brooklyn, New York where mourners gathered to pay their last respects to Isaac Luria, a young Hasidic man brutally murdered by three teenage neo-Nazis. After nightfall, Luria's betrothed, Ariel, returned to the cemetery and fashioned a likeness of Luria, a golem, out of mud and clay. ("Kaddish")

Berenbaum, Dr. Bambi (Bobbie Phillips) A stunning entomologist employed by the USDA as a cockroach research specialist at a secret government facility in Miller's Grove, Massachusetts. Mulder was quite taken with her . . . eh, theory that UFOs were actually nocturnal insect swarms, but Dr. Berenbaum was apparently more attracted to artificial-intelligence researcher, Dr. Alexander Ivanov, especially after discovering they shared a love for the movie *Planet of the Apes*. Dr. Berenbaum's parents, both naturalists, named her "Bambi" in homage to the Disney movie. ("War of the Coprophages") *Dr. Berenbaum was named for Dr. May R. Berenbaum, head of the Entomology Department at the University of Illinois and author of several books on insects. Actress Bobbie Phillips, who portrayed Dr. Berenbaum in this episode, has previously appeared on* Murder One, The Cape, Stargate SG-1, *and on the Showtime anthology series* Red Shoe Diaries *which, of course, has also featured David Duchovny.*

Bernstein, Danny Agent Mulder's ever-helpful, unseen cryptologist friend at FBI headquarters, who has expedited fingerprint searches, test results and other quantitative data. Danny analyzed eight-year-old Kevin Morris' coded drawings of zeros and ones in exchange for Mulder's tickets to a Redskins-Giants game. ("Conduit")

Bertram, Ted (Mark Acheson) The owner and manager of Ted's Bait and Tackle shop on the shores of Heuvelman's Lake in the Blue Ridge Mountains of Georgia. Bertram cashed in on the folklore surrounding the legendary lake monster, Big Blue, selling T-shirts and other Southern Serpent merchandise in his store. A victim of his own greed, Bertram was brutally attacked by some type of creature while tromping through the woods in special boots to leave fake Big Blue dinosaur tracks. ("Quagmire")

Berube, Dr. Terrence Allen (Ken Kramer) Harvard graduate who worked on the Human Genome Project in the Molecular Research Lab at the EmGen Corporation in Gaithersburg, Maryland. Dr. Berube was part of a secret government experiment with alien DNA conducted on terminal patients.

The official ruling of Berube's death was suicide, but he was murdered by a government assassin known only as Crew-Cut Man. ("The Erlenmeyer Flask") *Ken Kramer also played Dr. Browning in "3" and Dr. Ivanov in "War of the Coprophages."*

Beta Team Military unit involved in Operation Falcon's search-and-destroy mission for the pilot of the downed alien spacecraft near Townsend, Wisconsin. Team leader, Lt. Fraser, and his soldiers were severely burned when they encountered the translucent extraterrestrial. ("Fallen Angel")

Bethany Medical Center Hospital in Aubrey, Missouri where pregnant police detective B.J. Morrow was taken after alleging she was attacked by seventy-seven-year-old ex-con Harry Cokely. ("Aubrey")

Bethesda Naval Hospital Renowned medical facility in Bethesda, Maryland, where Mulder and Scully examined two corpses which exhibited signs of residual electromagnetic charge, and appeared to have had their throats crushed from the inside ("Shadows"). FBI agent Jack Willis was also taken to Bethesda's emergency room and revived after being shot by homicidal robber Warren James Dupre during a bank heist ("Lazarus"). The USS *Ardent's* twenty-eight-year-old commander, Lt. Richard Harper, died at the hospital, a victim of contaminated water which accelerated aging. Agents Mulder and Scully almost suffered the same fate, but were successfully treated at Bethesda with dialysis and a course of synthetic hormones ("Dod Kalm")

Bethesda Sleep Disorder Center Facility where Assistant Director Skinner received psychiatric treatment for three months for REM sleep disorder prior to the mysterious murder of Washington, D.C. prostitute, Carina Sayles in his hotel bed. Skinner acknowledged that he had been experiencing recurring lurid nightmares in which an old woman suffocated him. ("Avatar")

Betts, Leonard (Paul McCrane) A highly evolved humanoid lifeform with the ability to regenerate body parts; also known as Albert Tanner and Truelove. A respected Emergency Medical Technician (EMT) at a hospital in Pittsburgh, Pennsylvania, the thirty-four-year-old Betts was decapitated in an ambulance wreck while saving a patient's life with his extraordinary ability to detect cancer. After Betts' headless corpse kicked its way out of a morgue freezer drawer and walked home, a tissue sample from the severed head showed that Betts' body was riddled with cancer. Mulder correctly theorized that Betts' condition was his normal state, and that his life-force retained a blueprint that guided rapid growth, not as cancer, but regeneration. The mutant, who needed to ingest tumors in order to survive, was able to generate an empty shell of himself, similar to a snake's shed skin, and use it to fake his death, as he had several times in the past. After removing cancerous tissue from his mother to sustain himself, a scalpel-wielding Betts attacked

Scully in the back of an ambulance. Scully killed him using defibrillation pads, but not before Betts told her she possessed something he needed, an obvious pronouncement that she was afflicted with cancer. ("Leonard Betts") *Paul McCrane was a regular on the short-lived Steven Bochco ABC-TV series,* Cop Rock. *He also played a prison guard in* The Shawshank Redemption *and lost his head in the first* RoboCop *film.*

"Betty" A Betty Page-like tattoo of a winking, seductive woman with a polka dot ribbon in her hair. After too many drinks at a neighborhood bar, Philadelphia stockbroker and recent divorcee, Ed Jerse, had "Betty" tattooed on his right arm. Within hours, he began to hear a female voice in his head, taunting and mocking him, calling him a "loser." "Betty," whose self-described beauty went "all the way to the bone," was extremely jealous and hated women, and urged Jerse to kill his downstairs neighbor and viciously attack Scully. It was later discovered that the Russian tattoo artist Jerse went to used a rye-based ink tainted with a psychoactive contaminant. ("Never Again") *The "Betty" tattoo was voiced by Jodie Foster, whose Academy Award-winning portrayal of FBI trainee Clarice Starling in the film* Silence of the Lambs *has been acknowledged by* X-Files *creator Chris Carter as a precursor to Special Agent Dana Scully. Foster also starred in the 1997 theatrical movie* Contact, *an* X-Files-*like film about an astronomer who picks up a radio signal from an extraterrestrial civilization.*

"Beyond the Sea" Popular 1960 Bobby Darin song played at Captain William Scully's seaside funeral. Death-row inmate Luther Lee Boggs, who claimed to have psychic abilities, "channeled" the tune and hummed it when he first encountered Captain Scully's daughter, FBI agent Dana Scully. ("Beyond the Sea") *"Beyond the Sea" spent eleven weeks on the* Billboard *Top 40 in 1960.*

📁 **"Beyond the Sea"** Written by Glen Morgan and James Wong. Directed by David Nutter. File number 1X12. *First aired January 7, 1994. After Scully's father dies, the grieving agent's usual skepticism is put to the test by a death-row convict who claims that he can assist in the apprehension of a psychopathic kidnapper of two North Carolina teenagers using recently acquired psychic abilities.* **Classic Sound Bite:** *"Last time you were that engrossed it turned out you were reading the* Adult Video News." **Background Check:** *Fox executives were originally against making "Beyond the Sea," believing that it resembled the theatrical thriller* Silence of the Lambs *too much.*

B HEALD The letters on Reverend Calvin Hartley's vanity license plates. His adopted son, Samuel, had the power to heal the sick and bring the recently deceased back to life. ("Miracle Man")

Big and Beautiful Online chat room where overweight and lonely Lauren Mackalvey (online handle: "Hugs") first met serial killer Virgil Incanto (online handle: "Timid"). ("2Shy")

Big Blue Also known as the Southern Serpent, a legendary Loch Ness-like leviathan residing in Heuvelman's Lake in Millikan County, Georgia. Following a rash of local deaths, Mulder theorized that the lake's depletion of frogs had forced the aquatic dinosaur to seek an alternative food supply—humans. Although an enormous alligator was eventually killed, Mulder just missed seeing a prehistoric-looking creature knife through the lake's moonlit waters. ("Quagmire") *Episode writer Kim Newton called the lake monster "Big Blue" as an in-joke reference to IBM's nickname, whose mainframe computers are now considered to be dinosaurs.*

Big Bopper Insurance salesman Clyde Bruckman's boyhood musical hero. The reluctant psychic explained to Mulder that his paranormal ability to foresee other people's deaths was triggered by his obsession with the fateful coin toss that won the Big Bopper (best known for his 50s smash hit "Chantilly Lace") a seat on the doomed airplane flight that also claimed the life of Buddy Holly and Ritchie Valens. ("Clyde Bruckman's Final Repose")

Bigfoot A large, hairy, man-like beast reportedly sighted by hundreds of American and Canadian citizens over 150 years. Bigfoot is generally described as an upright ape-like creature with no neck, and long brown hair or fur. It is approximately seven feet tall, seems unconcerned or curious about the presence of humans, and has often been described as having a pungent scent. Mulder is known to occasionally watch the famous 1967 film footage thought to show the hairy monster strolling through the California countryside. ("Jose Chung's 'From Outer Space'")

Bilac, Dr. Alonso (Vic Trevino) Brazilian-born archaeologist who opposed Dr. Carl Roosevelt's plans to ship an unearthed Amaru urn, reputed to hold the remains of a female shaman, from the Equadorian highlands to Boston's Museum of Natural History. Dr. Bilac was the chief suspect in a series of mysterious mutilation deaths, including Dr. Roosevelt's, after it was discovered that he may have been possessed by an ancient jaguar spirit sent to protect the shaman's disturbed bones. Dr. Bilac's mangled corpse was later found in the steam tunnels beneath the museum. ("Teso dos Bichos")

Billy (Scott Heindl) The boyfriend and partner-in-crime of Mary Louise LeFante, a North Michigan postal sorter who had stolen several credit cards. While his girlfriend went into a drugstore for a quick passport photo, the nervous Billy, chain-smoking in his yellow Volkswagen bug, was murdered by paranoid-schizophrenic kidnapper, Gerry Schnauz. The autopsy on Billy's body revealed he had died from a puncture wound through the left eardrum into the brain, possibly by a long needle. ("Unruhe")

Bilton's Photo Photographic equipment and supply store in Easton, Washington where kidnapper Carl Wade maintained an account. Mulder and

Scully were able to obtain the address of Wade's wooded cabin from the small storefront business. ("Oubliette")

Biodiversity Project The name of the Pinck Pharmaceuticals' research project that took entomologist Dr. Robert Torrence to the Costa Rican rain forest in search of the parasitoid (parasite carrier) *Faciphaga emasculata*. ("F. Emasculata")

Bishop, Jim Father of eight-year-old Michelle Bishop, and divorced husband of Judy. The little girl, possessed with the reincarnated spirit of a drowned policeman, screamed when Mr. Bishop tried to teach her to swim. ("Born Again")

Bishop, Judy (Dey Young) Mother of Michelle, she refused to allow her young daughter to be studied any further after the little girl was discovered to possess psychokinetic powers. ("Born Again")

Bishop, Michelle (Andre Libman) Eight-year-old Buffalo, New York girl in whom the reincarnated spirit of dead policeman Charlie Morris emerged and exacted his revenge against his murderous former colleagues. ("Born Again")

Bituen, Gung (Sab Shimono) A Malayasian orderly employed at the Excelsis Dei convalescent home in Worcester, Massachusetts. Gung admitted to treating the elderly Alzheimer's patients with ibotenic acid, a powerful hallucinogen he extracted from homegrown mushrooms. Gung was remanded to the INS for illegal medication activity, and was to be deported. ("Excelsius Dei") *Sci-fi fans will recall actor Sab Shimono from his stint as an elder in Kevin Costner's* Waterworld *(1995).*

Black Crow Missile Complex Allegedly deserted military site in North Dakota where the Cigarette-Smoking Man relocated a salvaged alien spacecraft. Also abandoned behind secured silo door No. 1013 by CSM was a trapped Alex Krycek ("Apocrypha"), who was supposedly later freed by a ring-wing militia group during a salvage operation. ("Tunguska/Terma")

Blaine, Lt. (Dean McKenzie) A Cleveland policeman who informed Mulder and Scully of Jesse Landis' 911 call that led the agents to mutant serial killer Virgil Incanto. ("2Shy")

Blake Towers Construction site in downtown Boise, Idaho where an escaped tiger from the Fairfield Zoo was discovered and killed by Ed Meecham. ("Fearful Symmetry") *Blake Towers was named after William Blake, author of the poem "The Tyger," which influenced the title of the episode.*

Bledsoe, Dr. Ellen (Lorena Gale) The Philadelphia county medical examiner who confirmed that Howard Graves was indeed dead and had not faked his demise as Scully suspected. However, the only identification of the body came from Lauren Kyte, Grave's secretary, and the corpse was cremated after its organs were donated. ("Shadows") *Lorena Gale also played Nurse Wilkins in "One Breath" and Harold Spuller's defense attorney in "Elegy."*

Blessing Way Chant, The A Navajo healing ceremony performed by a tribe's holy men for those near death. The Blessing Way Chant was used by Native Americans on a New Mexico reservation to bring a badly injured Mulder back to life after he was left for dead in the smoldering wreckage of a buried boxcar. ("The Blessing Way")

🗁 **"Blessing Way, The (Part 2 of 3)"** Written by Chris Carter. Directed by R.W. Goodwin. File number 3X01. *First aired September 22, 1995. While Mulder undergoes a traditional life-saving Navajo Blessing Way ceremony, Scully is suspended from the Bureau and tracked by the Syndicate's Cigarette-Smoking Man and the Well-Manicured Man, both trying to gain possession of the missing Defense Department DAT tape.* **Classic Sound Bite:** *"The best way to predict the future is to invent it."* **Background Check:** *This episode was dedicated to the memory of Larry Wells (1946–1995), a costume designer on* The X-Files.

Blevins, Scott (Charles Cioffi) FBI Section Chief who assigned Scully to the X-Files unit and asked her to provide an analytical perspective on Mulder's work. Chief Blevins' ambiguous association with the mysterious Cigarette-Smoking Man makes it unclear whether the two men are attempting to thwart Mulder and Scully, aid them or parry their moves ("The X-Files: Pilot," "Deep Throat," "Conduit," and "Shadows"). As part of an elaborate hoax four years later, Scully appeared before an FBI review board chaired by Section Chief Blevins, and reported on the "illegitimacy" of Mulder's work and announced that he died the night before from an apparently self-inflicted gunshot wound to the head ("Gethsemane"). *Charles Cioffi is best remembered for his 1971 signature role as Shaft's NYPD contact, Lt. Vic Androzzi.*

Bloch, Maj. Gen. Benjamin (Scott Hylands) A high-ranking military officer and member of a secret three-person commission that covertly disposed of South Vietnamese soldiers employed as spies and commandos for the U.S. during the war in Vietnam. At the Vietnam Veterans War Memorial rededication ceremony in 1997, Gen. Bloch (who gave the keynote address) became the target of two assassination attempts by Nathaniel Teager, a seemingly invisible assassin, home after twenty-five years in a Vietnamese prison camp to kill the officers who had abandoned him. Although Generals MacDougal and Steffan, the other members of the clandestine tribunal, were shot and killed by Teager at close range, Gen. Bloch survived thanks to the heroic efforts of Mulder and Scully. Mulder discovered, however, that the U.S.

government had wanted Teager to assassinate the three, in order to maintain a policy of denial regarding POWs by silencing the men who made that policy. ("Unrequited")

Blockhead, Dr. (Jim Rose) Thrill-seeking former circus freak who emerged from under Jerald Glazebrook's casket at his funeral and pounded a nail into his chest in honor of the deceased. A background search on Dr. Blockhead revealed his true identity as Jeffrey Swaim, born in Milwaukee (and not Yemen, as he claimed). ("Humbug") *Jim Rose owns and operates the Jim Rose Circus Sideshow, which began as a Venice, California street act and is currently a stalwart of the alternative entertainment world. Episode writer Darin Morgan watched a videotape of the traveling troupe, casting Rose and the Enigma (this episode's Conundrum) in key roles though neither one of them had ever acted before.*

📂 **"Blood"** Written by Glen Morgan and James Wong. Directed by David Nutter. File number 2X03. *First aired September 30, 1994. When several residents of a small Pennsylvania farm town display extreme homicidal behavior prompted by electronic digital displays on common household appliances, Agent Mulder begins to suspect government involvement and experimentation.* **Classic Sound Bite:** *"Fear. It's the oldest tool of power. If you're distracted by fear of those around you, it keeps you from seeing the actions of those above."* **Background Check:** *Darin Morgan, who would later pen such classic* X-Files *episodes as "Humbug" and the Emmy Award-winning "Clyde Bruckman's Final Repose," contributed the idea of subliminal messages to his brother, episode co-writer Glen Morgan.*

Bloodworth, Raul According to a speculative dossier on the Cigarette-Smoking Man compiled by Lone Gunman Frohike, Raul Bloodworth was CSM's pseudonym for the pulp spy novels and stories he wrote in his spare-time about an action-adventure hero named Jack Colquitt. ("Musings of a Cigarette-Smoking Man")

Blue Beret UFO Retrieval Team A covert government force sanctioned to use terminal force on unauthorized personnel discovered at an alien contact site. Senator Matheson urged Mulder to investigate evidence of extraterrestrial life at the Arecibo Ionospheric Observatory in Puerto Rico before a Blue Beret UFO Retrieval Team was dispatched. ("Little Green Men")

Blue Danube, The Classical composition by Strauss which was playing on the sound system at Capital Ice, the Maryland skating rink where the Lone Gunmen attempted to covertly retrieve a package for Mulder. ("Apocrypha")

Blue Devil Brewery The Morrisville, North Carolina site of serial murderer Lucas Jackson Henry's death after he was wounded and pursued by Scully.

As "channeled" in a vision by death-row inmate Luther Lee Boggs, Henry fell to his death under the sign of the devil, the abandoned brewery's trademark logo. ("Beyond the Sea")

Blue-Suited Man One of Alex Krycek's accomplices, seen lurking ominously in Melissa Scully's hospital room. A suspicious Skinner chased him into the stairwell, where the assistant director was ambushed and beaten by Blue-Suited Man, Luis Cardinal, and Krycek, who stole the DAT tape from Skinner. When the three men stopped for gas and beer and left Krycek in the car, the renegade agent realized Blue-Suited Man and Cardinal meant to eliminate him, and escaped just before the vehicle exploded. ("Paper Clip") *Although he was uncredited, Blue-Suited Man was played by X-Files stunt coordinator Tony Morelli.*

Bob The name of the murdered Cape Cod estate caretaker, assumed by pyrokinetic assassin Cecil L'ively during his attempt on the life of Sir Malcolm Marsden and his family when they vacationed in Massachusetts. ("Fire")

Bob (Tim Dixon) Middle-aged, balding employee of the Travel Time Travel Agency and hostage of Duane Barry, inadvertently wounded when the escaped mental patient panicked during a momentary electrical blackout. Barry exchanged Bob for Mulder, who impersonated a sympathetic EMS medic. ("Duane Barry") *Tim Dixon also played the cross-dressing Dr. Richard Godfrey in "Syzygy."*

Bocks, Moe (Bruce Weitz) Special Agent assigned to the FBI's Minneapolis, Minnesota office who told Mulder and Scully, "Anything slightly freakazoid, that's the drill, call Moe Bocks." A paranormal buff more extreme than Mulder, Bocks requested the X-Files team examine a local cemetery's desecrated grave, believing it was the work of extraterrestrials. ("Irresistible") *Bruce Weitz won a 1984 Emmy Award for his portrayal of the eccentric, suspect-biting Detective Belker on* Hill Street Blues.

Boggs, Luther Lee (Brad Dourif) A North Carolina death-row inmate condemned to the gas chamber, in part by the psychological profile Mulder compiled when with the Bureau's Violent Crimes Unit. Years later, Boggs attempted to negotiate a commutation of his sentence by offering to use his newly acquired psychic channeling abilities to help Mulder and Scully investigate a kidnapper/killer. Boggs' long list of heinous crimes included killing all the animals in his housing complex when he was six years old, and strangling five members of his family during a Thanksgiving meal when he was thirty. ("Beyond the Sea") *Brad Dourif, best known for his Oscar-nominated portrayal of the doomed, young mental patient Billy Bibbitt in* One Flew Over the Cuckoo's Nest, *has made a name for himself by playing characters with a dark side in a wide-range of horror-oriented roles, among them* Body Parts, Graveyard Shift, The Exorcist III, *and the* Child's Play *series on the* *big screen, and* Millennium, Star Trek: Voyager, Babylon 5 *and* Tales from the Crypt *on television. Dourif was seen most recently in the fourth installment of the* Alien *sci-fi franchise as Dr. Gediman.*

Bonaparte, Chester (Jamil Walker Smith) Ten-year-old Haitian refugee who sold Mulder a protective charm at the Folkstone INS Processing Center. The X-Files team discovered later that Chester was the ghost of a boy who died during a riot at the refugee camp, six weeks earlier. ("Fresh Bones")

Bonnecaze, Special Agent (Malcolm Stewart) FBI official interrupted by Mulder as he rifled through Skinner's desk after the Assistant Director became the suspect in a prostitute's murder. ("Avatar") *Malcolm Stewart also played Dr. Glass in the pilot episode, Commander Carver in "3," and Dr. Sacks in "Tunguska/Terma."*

📁 **"Born Again"** Written by Alex Gansa and Howard Gordon. Directed by Jerrold Freedman. File number 1X21. *First aired April 29, 1994. When two Buffalo cops' homicides are investigated by Mulder and Scully, the evidence points to an eight-year-old girl, who might be the reincarnated spirit of a policeman murdered by a trio of his colleagues nine years earlier.* **Classic Sound Bite:** *"Jumpers tend to open the window before they jump."* **Background Check:** *"Born Again" was the first episode in which Mulder was seen writing longhand in a field journal instead of Scully typing computer reports as a way to bring closure and summation to the X-File.*

Bosher's Run Park The Manassa, Virginia city recreational park where the long-buried skeletal remains of a pre-adolescent girl named Addie Sparks were discovered. Awakening from a vivid dream in which a small, red ball of light directed him to an unmarked grave, Mulder raced to the park and unearthed the shallow burial spot. The girl was a victim of John Lee Roche, a serial kidnapper and child killer Mulder helped put away in prison many years before. ("Paper Hearts")

Boston Mercy Hospital Medical facility where Miss Kotchik was treated for severe burns after pyrokinetic assassin Cecil L'ively/Bob set fire to his arm and burned down a bar. L'ively was later placed in a hyperbaric chamber at the hospital after sustaining fifth- and sixth-degree burns over his entire body. Medical specialists discovered phenomenally rapid regeneration of L'ively's fundamental, basal cell tissue, allowing him to completely recover in as little as a month. ("Fire")

Boston University Internationally recognized school of higher education and research with fifteen schools and colleges, thirteen of which offer advanced degrees. On November 20, 1972, the university hosted a NASA symposium on the possible existence of extraterrestrial life with Carl Sagan, Philip Morrison, Ashley Montagu, and other noted scientists participating in the conference. Twenty-five years later, Mulder was watching a videotape of the roundtable discussion when he allegedly killed himself with a gunshot to the head. ("Gethsemane")

Boulle, Peter (Michael MacRae) Soon-to-retire New Jersey park ranger who told Mulder that he discovered the body of the legendary "Jersey Devil," a Bigfoot-like evolutionary throwback living in the woods, and turned it over to the authorities. Mulder theorized that another creature, the dead man-beast's mate, was responsible for several recent murders in Atlantic City. ("The Jersey Devil")

Bounty Hunter (Brian Thompson) According to one of the "Samantha" clones, a ruthless and relentless extraterrestrial dispatched to Earth with a prime directive to terminate alien colonists. Originally seen as an unnamed Russian pilot whose aircraft crashed into the Beaufort Sea, the hulking Bounty Hunter possesses the ability to morph into any form or likeness instantly, and can only be killed by piercing the base of his skull. If wounded, the Bounty Hunter bleeds a toxic green fluid, apparently containing an airborne retrovirus fatal to humans. Although an unmerciful assassin, the extraterrestrial resists injuring or killing humans unless absolutely essential. When the renegade Jeremiah Smith threatened to expose The Project to Mulder and Scully, the Cigarette-Smoking Man dispatched the Bounty Hunter to assassinate him. Like Smith, the Bounty Hunter can heal with the touch of his hand. At the behest of the Cigarette-Smoking Man, the extraterrestrial saved Mrs. Mulder's life, because Mulder would be a fiercer enemy if his mother was allowed to die. ("Colony/End Game" and "Talitha Cumi/Herrenvolk")

Bozoff, Agent Relieved Mulder of "meaningless" surveillance work so that he could investigate a murder in the New Jersey sewer system. ("The Host") *The actor who played Agent Bozoff was uncredited.*

Bradsean, Antonia A young victim of the serial murderer The Slash Killer, she was raped and had the word SISTER carved into her chest with a razor. Bradsean, along with two other women, were murdered in Aubrey, Missouri in 1942. The Slash Killer was never caught. ("Aubrey")

Braidwood, Tom The name that was stenciled onto Howard Graves' parking spot at HTG Industrial Technologies after his apparent suicide ("Shadows"). False-name "Level 5" security pass for the "Northwest Facility, Mattawa, WA" which Mulder used to enter a government facility allegedly housing an Extraterrestrial Biological Entity ("E.B.E."). *Mulder received the phony security credentials from the Lone Gunmen, the trio of nerdy characters who publish a newsletter on government conspiracies. Tom Braidwood is the series' first assistant director, who also occasionally portrays Frohike, the photographic and special operations member of the Lone Gunmen.*

Brandenburg Concerto Number Two in F Composition by Johann Sebastian Bach, which Sen. Matheson played in his Capitol Hill office to prevent eavesdropping when he told Mulder of a possible alien contact site in Puerto Rico. The musical recording was also included on the two unmanned *Voyager* space probes launched August 20 and September 5, 1977. ("Little Green Men")

Brandt, Alice (Angela Donahue) Thirty-two-year-old secretary to a North Michigan certified public accountant. She was abducted and found dead, a victim of Gerry Schnauz, a paranoid-schizophrenic who performed transorbital lobotomies on young women he "saved" from the "howlers" that existed only in his dark fantasies. ("Unruhe")

Braun, Dr. Sheila (P. Lynn Johnson) Developmental psychologist on staff at Brylin Psychiatric Hospital in Buffalo, New York. Eight-year-old Michelle Bishop, who dismembered and disfigured her dolls, was a patient of Dr. Braun's twice a week. The psychologist asked Mulder to leave when he suggested the little girl possessed psychokinetic powers. ("Born Again") *Actress P. Lynn Johnson also played Deborah Brown, one of the evil PTC members in "Die Hand Die Verletzt" and a health department doctor in "Small Potatoes."*

Bray, Ansel (R. Nelson Brown) Obsessed with photographing Big Blue, the legendary Southern Serpent of Heuvelman's Lake, Bray was attacked and eaten by either the leviathan or a very large alligator, while setting up his equipment on the shoreline. ("Quagmire") *The photographer was named Ansel in homage to noted nature lensman Ansel Adams.*

Breakfast at Tiffany's Truman Capote novel that Scully was reading in her living room when Mulder called to say that cockroaches were "mortally attacking people" in Miller's Grove, Massachusetts. ("War of the Coprophages") Breakfast at Tiffany's *was an in-joke reference to David Duchovny, who holds a master's degree in English literature from Yale University, but guessed wrong about the book on* Celebrity Jeopardy! *and lost the game to best-selling horror author and* X-Files *fan Stephen King.*

Brenman One of thirty-eight academics suspected of being the serial "fat-sucking vampire" preying on lonely, insecure women via the Internet. Brenman, a graduate student in Cleveland, Ohio, was questioned by Scully before the real perpetrator, Virgil Incanto, was apprehended and confessed to forty-seven murders in five states ("2Shy") *The actor playing Brenman had no lines of dialogue and was uncredited.*

Brewer, Wesley (Tom Glass) A trucker who barely avoided hitting an escaped, ten-foot-tall zoo elephant as he sped down Route 7 near Fairfield, Idaho. ("Fearful Symmetry")

Briggs, Frank (Henry Beckman) Baltimore, Maryland police detective who originally investigated the 1933 Powhatten Mill murders committed by liver-eating shapeshifter Eugene Victor Tooms. Although Briggs was unable to bring the mutant serial killer to justice, he provided Scully with both official and unofficial evidence he had collected over the years, including a 1963 photograph of an un-aged Tooms. Briggs resigned from the police department in 1968 and spent his later years at the dilapidated Lynn Acres Retirement Home. ("Squeeze" and "Tooms")

Bright Angel Halfway House The Seattle, Washington residence of thirty-year-old Lucy Householder, a former kidnap victim with lingering emotional problems from her five-year ordeal. When she developed "some kind of empathic transference" with the young victim of another abduction, Householder became a suspected accomplice in the girl's kidnapping. ("Oubliette")

Bright White Place Where MUFON (Mutual UFO Network) members in Allentown, Pennsylvania told Scully they had been taken by extraterrestrial abductors. ("Nisei")

Brisentine, Agent (Marc Bauer) FBI agent who informed Mulder that his reassignment (courtesy of Assistant Director Skinner) involved the homicide investigation of "John Doe," an unidentified body which turned up in the sewers of Newark, New Jersey. ("The Host") *Marc Bauer also had bit parts in "Ghost in the Machine" and "Musings of a Cigarette-Smoking Man."*

Brodeur, Leo (J.T. Walsh) Eastpoint State Penitentiary warden who oversaw the electrocution of Napoleon "Neech" Manley. The murderer swore before dying that he'd return and five men would pay for "all the petty tyranny and cruelty" he suffered, but Warden Brodeur was convinced the grisly murders committed at the Florida prison after Manley's execution were the work of an accomplice. Brodeur beat another convict, Sammon Roque, to death, demanding the names of Manley's enemies list. The warden died in an automobile accident after Manley mysteriously appeared in the backseat and grabbed his throat. ("The List") *Tony Award-winner J.T. Walsh has made memorable acting contributions in such films as* Breakdown; Sling Blade; Hannah and Her Sisters; Good Morning, Vietnam; Tin Men; Hoffa; The Client; *and* A Few Good Men, *as well as in the starring role in the short-lived* X-Files *wannabe series,* Dark Skies.

Brody, Jane (Lisa Stewart) A young mail sorter at the Transcontinental Express Routing Center in Desmond, Virginia. After sneaking into the rest room to smoke, she was fatally attacked by a swarm of bees that escaped from a damaged overnight package in the adjoining room. As part of a deal to save Scully with the Cigarette-Smoking Man, Skinner erased evidence of the bee attack and incinerated Brody's body. After learning that the young woman had died of a virulent strain of smallpox, Skinner speculated that the Cigarette-Smoking Man and his associates had engineered a method of spreading the deadly contagion using bees. ("Zero Sum")

Brothers K Arlington, Virginia fast-food restaurant. A disturbed Galen Muntz shot several customers in a mad rage. Alien clone Jeremiah Smith healed the wounds of Muntz (shot by a police marksman) and his victims with the touch of his hands before fleeing the scene. ("Talitha Cumi") *The name of the fast-food restaurant was an in-joke Chris Carter dreamed up due to the episode's thematic ties to Dostoevsky's* The Brothers Karamozov. *The real-life A & W restaurant had been used before as the diner where Lucy Householder collapsed during the opening scene in "Oubliette."*

Brown, Deborah (P. Lynn Johnson) Member of Milford Haven's occult religion, which worshipped the "lord of darkness." Pete Calcagni killed Brown with a shotgun while possessed by a demon. ("Die Hand Die Verletzt") *The character "Deborah Brown" was named in honor of "Mrs. Spooky," prominent online X-Phile and co-host of the AOL X-Files forum. Actress P. Lynn Johnson also played Dr. Sheila Braun in "Born Again" and an eastern Appalachian health care physician in "Small Potatoes."*

Brown, Deborah Director of a music video titled "Mary Beth Clark I Love You," by The Rosemarys. The video appeared on the television screen after Darin Peter Oswald changed the channel from across the room without using the remote control. ("D.P.O.")

Browning, Dr (Ken Kramer) Los Angeles police pathologist who examined the blackened body of John, "The Son," one of The Trinity Killers. John believed himself a vampire and, when jailed, an unconvinced Mulder hoped exposure to sunlight would scare him into testifying against the other two murderers. The sun did indeed burn John to death, and Dr. Browning suggested a diagnosis of Gunther's disease, a congenital erythropietic porphyria which causes lesions and blisters. ("3") *Ken Kramer also played Dr. Berube in "The Erlenmeyer Flask" and Dr. Ivanov in "War of the Coprophages."*

Bruckman, Clyde (Peter Boyle) Aging insurance salesman and gifted clairvoyant who could see the way people were predestined to die. His greatest regret in life was his inability to pick winning Lotto numbers. Bruckman reluctantly assisted Mulder and Scully in the apprehension of the Puppet, a serial killer who preyed upon fortune-tellers simply because he was a "homicidal maniac." Bruckman committed suicide by ingesting sleeping pills and placing a plastic bag over his head. When Scully discovered his body, she was next to him, fulfilling his prediction that they would end up in bed together. ("Clyde Bruckman's Final Repose") *Peter Boyle, whose classic movie portrayals include the sympathetic monster in Mel Brooks'* Young Frankenstein *and the cab driver-guru Wizard in* Taxi Driver, *won a prestigious Emmy Award for the role of Clyde Bruckman. The real Clyde Bruckman was a 1920-30s* *screenwriter and director of numerous short films, starring W.C. Fields, Buster Keaton, Laurel and Hardy, the Three Stooges and many others. After borrowing a pistol from his old pal, Keaton (who had no idea what he was going to do with it), Bruckman shot and killed himself either in a phone booth or a restaurant on Santa Monica Boulevard, depending on which account you read. Episode writer Darin Morgan has called the real Clyde Bruckman's life the "ultimate Hollywood horror story." While named for Bruckman, the character of the psychic insurance salesman was based on Morgan's father, also an insurance salesman.*

Bruin, Dr. Simon (Bob Morrisey) A physician with the Philadelphia office of the Centers for Disease Control, Bruin requested Scully's assistance after the body of a missing African-American male was discovered and the cause of death proved to be an odd lack of pigmentation. Dr. Bruin and Scully later subjected Samuel Aboah, a suspected disease carrier, to a battery of tests and examinations which revealed that the West African immigrant was missing the hormone-producing pituitary gland. ("Teliko")

Brumfield, Ellen (Glynis Davies) Suburban housewife, and customer on Donnie Pfaster's delivery route for Ficicello Frozen Foods. Pfaster, a death fetishist fixated on Lisa, one of Brumfield's three daughters, pilfered some discarded hair from her bathroom wastebasket. ("Irresistible") *Actress Glynis Davies also portrayed Tooms' attorney, Nelson, in "Tooms," and Virgil Incanto's landlady Monica Landis in "2Shy."*

Brumfield, Lisa Teenage object of obsession for Donnie Pfaster, who delivered frozen food to her mother's suburban Minneapolis home. ("Irresistible") *The actress who played Lisa Brumfield was uncredited.*

Brummitt, Sen. Member of the Senate Select Subcommittee on Intelligence and Terrorism. During a hearing to investigate a mysterious death at Assistant Director Skinner's apartment building, Sen. Brummitt was noticeably quiet while Senators Romine and Sorenson questioned Scully concerning the whereabouts of Mulder. ("Tunguska/Terma") *The actor who portrayed Sen. Brummitt was uncredited.*

Brunjes Copy Shop Brooklyn print shop owned and operated by Curt Brunjes, an outspoken neo-Nazi who used the business to publish racist propaganda pamphlets such as *How AIDS Was Created by the Jews.* ("Kaddish")

Brunjes, Curt (Jonathan Whittaker) Paranoid racist whose anti-Semitic hate-mongering incited three teenagers to brutally murder Isaac Luria. Brunjes was strangled to death in his Brooklyn copy shop by a golem whose features matched those of Luria. ("Kaddish")

Bruno Comity high school student believed kidnapped and murdered by an unknown Satanic cult. Bruno's best friend, footfall quarterback Jay "Boom" DeBoom, eulogized him, only to be found dead himself the next morning, hanging from a cliff in the woods. ("Syzygy")

Bruskin, Phil (Jackson Davies) Older Bureau agent present at Tommy Philips' murder crime scene at the Desmond Arms Residence Hotel when a cleaned-up Willis/Dupre returned. Agent Bruskin tracked Willis/Dupre and Scully to Lula Phillips' apartment, only to discover the trio had disappeared. Bruskin, who had given up cigarettes for nicotine gum, stayed on the case with Mulder until the two agents saw closure. ("Lazarus")

Brylin Psychiatric Hospital Buffalo, New York facility where Dr. Sheila Braum counseled eight-year-old Michelle Bishop twice a week for emotional problems. ("Born Again")

Bryon, Sen. Richard First-term U.S. senator from Nevada who canceled congressional funding for the Search for Extraterrestrial Intelligence (SETI), effectively terminating the project. ("Little Green Men")

Buchanon, Dr. Harvey (Dana Goldstone) Teaneck, New Jersey doctor who died in an abortion clinic fire, obviously the victim of arson. Mulder anonymously received Dr. Buchanon's obituary (along with two others) via E-mail. The agent was perplexed to discover that the three deceased doctors could have been identical triplets, and there were no records of their birth or past. ("Colony")

Budahas, Anita (Gabrielle Rose) The desperate wife of test-pilot Lt. Col. Robert Budahas, who reported her husband's disappearance to the FBI as a kidnapping, hoping the military would disclose his location. Once Budahas was returned, he behaved unpredictably and his wife seemed unwilling to believe that it was actually him. Most likely due to governmental pressure, Mrs. Budahas finally accepted her husband's mysterious condition and refused to have any further communication with the FBI. ("Deep Throat") *Gabrielle Rose also played Dr. Zenzola in "The Host."*

Budahas, Josh The young son of Robert and Anita Budahas. ("Deep Throat") *The child actor who portrayed Josh was uncredited.*

Budahas, Leslie The young daughter of Robert and Anita Budahas. ("Deep Throat") *The young girl who portrayed Leslie was uncredited.*

Budahas, Lt. Col. Robert. (Andrew Johnston). Test-pilot and recipient of a presidential commendation, stationed at Ellens Air Force Base in Southwest Idaho, rumored to be one of six sites where Roswell UFO wreckage was taken after the 1947 crash. The sixth pilot to turn up missing from the military facility since 1963, Col. Budahas inexplicably reappeared and returned home to his wife and family. "That is not my husband," Mrs. Budahas told agents Mulder and Scully. "They've done something to him." He sprinkled fish-food flakes on his food at a dinner party, yelled at his children for no reason, and suddenly shook as if he were having a seizure. Budahas' memories of all things aeronautical had also been erased. Scully suspected amnesia, but Mulder believed that the pilot's brain had been "rewired" to make him forget certain things, lest he became a security leak. ("Deep Throat") *Actor Andrew Johnston also played FBI Agent Weiss in "Colony/End Game" and a medical examiner in "Demons."*

Budget-Rest Motel Townsend, Wisconsin place of lodging where Mulder stayed while investigating a UFO crash site and the subsequent government cover-up. In his room at the motel, Mulder watched a TV reporter state that the military was vague about a "toxic cargo" forcing the evacuation of 12,000 Townsend residents. ("Fallen Angel")

Buente, Eladio (Raymond Cruz) Migrant worker in California's San Joaquin Valley, romantically interested in the attractive girlfriend of his brother, Soledad. After the young woman's mutilated corpse was discovered, Soledad suspected Eladio of killing her out of jealousy, but other laborers at the migrant camp were convinced that he was the mythological Chupacabra creature. After escaping from INS custody, Eladio became the target of an intense manhunt by his brother, who wanted revenge against Eladio for stealing the heart of his lover, and Mulder and Scully, who discovered that the illegal immigrant was the carrier of a powerfully fatal and highly contagious fungus. When Soledad finally caught up with his brother back at the shantytown migrant camp where it all began, he believed that the horribly disfigured Eladio was truly El Chupacabra. The brothers, who possessed an abnormal tolerance to the enzyme that made the fungus fatal, fled together to Mexico, where they were last seen hitchhiking off into the night, their appearances radically and luridly transformed into the very image of El Chupacabra by the monstrous fungal infection. ("El Mundo Gira") *Actor Raymond Cruz has appeared in such movies as* Up Close and Personal *and as DiStephano in the fourth installment of the* Alien *movies.*

Buente, Gabrielle (Simi) The cousin of brothers Eladio and Soledad Buente, the Mexican immigrant worked at a market, and as a maid for an affluent family living in the Meadowview Estates. Gabrielle believed her cousin, Eladio, was a legendary Chupacabra after he showed up horribly disfigured, begging for money to flee to Mexico. ("El Mundo Gira")

Buente, Soledad (Jose Yenque) A migrant worker in California's San Joaquin Valley, who accused his envious brother, Eladio, of murdering his girlfriend, Maria Dorantes, and set out to exact revenge. When Soledad had the opportunity to kill him, though, he couldn't shoot his brother. Eladio, his face grotesquely deformed by the effects of a deadly and highly contagious fungus, appeared to be the very image of El Chupacabra of Mexican folklore. According to their cousin, Gabrielle, the brothers fled to their homeland, their bodies and faces disfigured into the semblance of the legendary creatures. ("El Mundo Gira")

Buffalo Bills Professional footfall team from Buffalo, New York. According to Lone Gunman Frohike's rather dubious account of the Cigarette-Smoking Man's life, during a Domestic Unrest Operations meeting in 1991 CSM told his aides that as long as he was alive the Buffalo Bills "would never win the Super Bowl." ("Musings of a Cigarette-Smoking Man")

Buffalo Mutual Life Employer of insurance salesman Leon Felder, a former partner of deceased Buffalo, New York police detective Rudy Barbala, a co-conspirator along with Felder and Tony Fiore in the murder of another cop, Charlie Morris. ("Born Again")

Bugger, Dr. (Alex Bruhanski) Professional insect exterminator who described cockroaches poetically before stomping on one and collapsing, an apparent victim of extraterrestrial coprophages infesting the panic-stricken town of Miller's Grove, Massachusetts. ("War of the Coprophages") *Alex Bruhanski also played the doomed bowling alley proprietor, Angelo Pintero, in "Elegy."*

Burkholder, P.F.C. Gus (Don McWilliams) Limousine driver for Lt. Gen. Peter MacDougal. Private Burkholder was held in custody for suspicion of murder after the high-ranking military officer was gunned down at close range while riding in the limo. Although FBI forensic tests confirmed that the private did not do the shooting, he was suspected of having an accomplice, based upon a Death Card found at the crime scene, and his ties to a radical paramilitary group called the Right Hand, whose stated aim was "violent revolution." Burkholder, who maintained his innocence, later passed a polygraph test. ("Unrequited")

Burkina Faso. The small West African homeland of American immigrant, Samuel Aboah, a member of the Teliko, a lost tribe who survived for generations by hunting down humans to steal what they lacked: hormones from the pituitary gland. After Aboah arrived in Philadelphia from Burkina Faso, several black men disappeared and were eventually found dead, their bodies drained of pigmentation. ("Teliko")

Burks, Dr. Charles "Chuck" (Bill Dow). Digital-imaging expert at the University of Maryland. Mulder requested Burk examine a photo of two-year-old Teddy Holvey taken seconds before he was killed in a freak accident at a kiddie park. Dr. Burk's digital-imaging software raised an image of electromagnetic concentration, otherwise a ghostly apparition, seemingly luring the little boy to his doom ("The Calusari"). A few years later, Dr. Burks examined a sample from Leonard Betts' decapitated head and, by applying high-frequency electricity, successfully photographed the mutant's coronal discharge, or lifeforce. ("Leonard Betts") *Bill Dow also appeared briefly as a father in "The Jersey Devil" and as Dr. Newton in "War of the Coprophages."*

Burst, Frank (Vic Polizos) FBI agent who initially captured Robert Patrick Modell, (a.k.a. Pusher), a self-confessed masterless samurai who possessed the persuasive power to bend people to his will and force them to commit suicide. An overweight Burst was "talked" into having a fatal heart attack by Modell while the federal agent attempted to stall him on the phone long enough to trace the origin of the call. ("Pusher")

Busch, Special Agent (Mark Saunders) Assigned to the Latent Fingerprint Analysis Lab at FBI Headquarters in Washington, D.C., Busch lifted a bloodstain print from a dead prostitute's nail polish which eventually led to the identification of Donnie Pfaster. ("Irresistible"). *Mark Saunders also played a doctor in "Lazarus."*

Businessman, The (Don Stewart). Middle-aged, bespectacled black man whose pigment-drained corpse was discovered by a flight attendant in the lavatory of a chartered plane from the West African country of Burkino Faso to the United States. Minister Diabira of the nation's U.S. embassy demanded that the businessman's body be returned before an autopsy could be conducted. The West African businessman had been a victim of fellow passenger Samuel Aboah, in reality a metamorphic ghost, able to squeeze into small, confined spaces. ("Teliko")

"buttmunch" A crude and irreverent pet name which eight-year-old Samantha Mulder called her older brother, Fox ("Little Green Men" and "Paper Hearts"). *Although several fans of the series have complained that the word was born in the* Beavis and Butthead-*era of the late 1980s and early '90s, X-Files producer and writer, Glen Morgan, stated on AOL that "buttmunch" was in use in the early '70s and he used it a lot himself as a kid.*

Buxton, Stan (Peter Anderson) The coroner of Johnston County, Oklahoma, where the "statistically improbable" deaths of four young men by lightning piqued Mulder and Scully's interest. ("D.P.O.")

Byers (Bruce Harwood) The neatly bearded, dapperly dressed, military and information systems expert of the Lone Gunmen. One of three operatives who form the editorial staff of the conspiracy-oriented newsletters known as *The Lone Gunman* and *The Magic Bullet*, Byers is basically the no-nonsense "mole" of the trio, spending all his time gathering bits of information about government activities. He tore out a magnetic strip from inside a twenty-dollar bill of Scully's, telling her that was how the covert-government-within-the-government tracked money carried through airport metal detectors. He also stated that Vladimir Zhirinovsky, the leader of the Russian Social Democrats, had been "put into power" by the CIA, "the most heinous and evil force in the twentieth century" ("E.B.E."). During Mulder's investigation into a controlled experiment on the townsfolk in the small farming community of Franklin, Pennsylvania, Byers told the agent about LSDM, an experimental synthetic insecticide which, acting as a pheromone, triggered a fear response in insects ("Blood"). During Mulder and Scully's investigation of animal disappearances at the Fairfield, Idaho Zoo, Byers told Mulder that nearby Mountain Home Air Base was a UFO hotspot ("Fearful Symmetry"). After Scully was discovered comatose in a Washington hospital, Byers unerringly recognized and described the bizarre recombinant chemistry at the heart of her health problems, and uploaded her medical file to The Thinker, the newest Lone Gunman, for analysis ("One Breath"). Byers also informed Mulder that The Thinker wanted to meet with him after he hacked into the Defense Department's computer system and stole the top-secret MJ files ("Anasazi"). Byers and Langly identified Nazi scientist and war criminal, Victor Klemper, in a 1970s photograph of Mulder's father and others ("Paper Clip") The Lone Gunman also assisted in identifying Japanese satellite photos of the *Talapus,* a salvage vessel out of San Diego which had supposedly been searching for a gold-carrying submarine sunk during World War II. Byers noted that the *Talapus* reported nothing found, yet did not return to its home port, but to a Naval yard in Newport News, Virginia ("Nisei"). After examining an amazingly sophisticated video emitting device used for mind control, Byers correctly ascertained that Mulder was immune because color was a factor and he was red-green color-blind ("Wetwired"). Although he stated that no electronic surveillance device could cut through the (aptly named) CSM-25 Counter-Measure Filter, the Cigarette-Smoking Man simply flipped a switch and was able to eavesdrop on Frohike's entire version of what the Lone Gunman believed was the chilling, secret past of the CSM ("Musings of a Cigarette-Smoking Man"). Obviously more comfortable conducting research in the group's clutter-filled office, an ice-skating Byers did join his colleagues in a clandestine package retrieval mission for Mulder at a Washington-area rink ("Apocrypha") and in the infiltration of a research facility via a subterranean tunnel to perhaps secure information on the origin of Scully's brain tumor. Once Mulder realized that Scully's cancer specialist was on staff at the facility and was probably enhancing her tumor's destructive effects, the agent instructed Byers to locate Scully and tell her to stop treatment immediately ("Memento Mori"). *Bruce Harwood originally conceived of his character as a university professor, "but then I decided he's technically smart, but he's not that smart. I decided he works for Xerox—he's the guy who comes around in a suit and a tie and fixes the photocopiers. His whole focus is on maintaining the Lone Gunmen office and the newsletter." Harwood has made appearances on the TV series* The Outer Limits, 21 Jump Street, MacGyver, *and* Wiseguy. *He even played a computer technician in the less-than-successful sequel* The Fly II. *The actor moonlights as a clerical worker in his local library ("Nobody recognizes me," he says).*

Covarrubias

"CA 519, 705, 950" The code Scully left on Mulder's answering machine after she suspected she was being tailed at the Miami International Airport. Deciphered, the code meant she was taking Caribbean Air flight 519, leaving at 7:05 for St. Croix. ("Little Green Men")

Cable Man Line repairman who was part of the conspiracy involving mind control through television signals in the small Maryland community of Braddock Heights. The Cable Man installed sophisticated signal emitters which converted the populace's fears into dementia. He was shot to death at close range, along with co-conspirator Dr. Stroman, by Mr. X, possibly on orders from the Cigarette-Smoking Man. ("Wetwired") *The actor who played the Cable Man was uncredited.*

Calcagni, Pete (Shawn Johnston) Crowley High School psychologist and member of the PTA-like group, the PTC. A demon-possessed Calcagni shot two of his companions before turning the rifle on himself. ("Die Hand Die Verletzt") *Pete Calcagni was named for the husband of a prominent X-Files fan.*

Calder One of the agents assigned by Bruskin to canvass the three square miles around Washington County Regional Airport in an effort to find a kidnapped Scully. ("Lazarus")

Caleca, Linda (Sue Matthew) Young FBI agent assigned to protect Assistant Director Skinner, who was hospitalized after being shot at point-blank range in a Washington coffee shop. Caleca, a recent graduate of Quantico Academy, was partnered with Agent Brian Fuller. ("Apocrypha") *Sue Matthew also played FBI handwriting expert, Lisa Dole, in "Roland."*

California Institute of Technology Pasadena location of the volcano observatory. Personnel at the facility managed to activate the Firewalker exploration robot remotely, revealing the body of chief seismologist of the Cascade Volcano Research Team, Phil Erikson, and a shadow moving in the 130 degrees Fahrenheit where nothing should have existed. ("Firewalker")

California State University School located in Fresno, where professor Dr. Larry Steen of the university's mycology lab isolated an enzyme that made common household fungus grow at an alarming and fatal rate. ("El Mundo Gira")

Caligari Candidate, The A novel by Jose Chung, which Scully considered one of the greatest thrillers ever written. ("Jose Chung's 'From Outer Space' "). The Caligari Candidate *is a nod to Richard Condon's* The Manchurian Candidate, *a best-selling novel (and motion picture) about a brainwashed soldier manipulated into believing in alternate versions of reality by political enemies. Chung's book title is also in homage to* The Cabinet of Dr. Caligari, *a German silent film also dealing with mind control.*

Callahan, Frances (Andrea Barclay) The wife of Gen. Thomas Callahan, the commanding officer of Fort Evanston, Maryland. Mrs. Callahan was murdered by Leonard "Rappo" Trimble, a quadraplegic Gulf War vet who exacted his revenge by projecting his spirit out of his body. ("The Walk")

Callahan, Gen. Thomas (Thomas Kopache) Fort Evanston base commander who attempted to obstruct Mulder and Scully's investigation of an alleged "phantom soldier." After his military aide and family were killed, Gen. Callahan learned that bitter quadruple amputee veteran, Leonard "Rappo" Trimble, who possessed the power of astral projection, was in reality the revenge-seeking murderer. ("The Walk")

Callahan, Trevor (Brennan Kotowich) Eight-year-old son of Gen. Callahan and wife, Frances. The boy was killed in his backyard when a ghostly image of a figure exploded out of a sandbox and buried the boy alive. ("The Walk")

Caltrop A piece of twisted metal used by eco-terrorists to ruin the tires of logging vehicles. ("Darkness Falls")

Calusari According to Romanian folklore, elders responsible for the correct observance of sacred rites, such as the Ritual of Separation. A group of the dark-suited exorcists were called in by Charley Holvey's grandmother Golda to perform the ritual dividing the souls of the Holvey boy and his twin who had died at birth. ("The Calusari") *The Romanian holy men were played by Bill Croft, Campbell Lane, George Josef, and Kay E. Kuter, a classically trained Shakespearean actor who is best remembered for his role as Newt Kiley on* Green Acres.

📁 **"Calusari, The"** Written by Sara Charno. Directed by Michael Vejar. File number 2X21. *First aired April 14, 1995. When a two-year-old boy is killed in a freak accident involving a kiddie park railroad ride, Mulder and a group of Romanian spiritualists determine that an evil spirit has to be exorcised from the dead boy's older brother.* **Classic Sound Bite:** *"It is over for now. But you must be careful. It knows you now."* **Background Check:** *Chris*

Carter believed that episode writer Sue Charno's second script for the series lacked something and added the Calusari, the Romanian exorcists.

Camouflage Man (Mitch Davies) A.k.a. Stealth Man, the apparent leader of a contingent of soldiers who, on orders from the Cigarette-Smoking Man, set fire to a buried train refrigeration car inhabited by Mulder and what appeared to be numerous alien bodies. While driving across the Navajo Reservation northwest of Los Alamos, New Mexico, Scully was stopped by Camouflage Man and his troops, who took her copy of the MJ files, which documented the government's knowledge of alien visitors since the 1940s. ("Anasazi/The Blessing Way")

Campbell (Sonny Surowiec) A member of the Arctic Ice Core Project research team in Icy Cape, Alaska. Campbell attacked team captain John Richter, then shot himself. As if in a silent pact, Richter committed suicide the same way, claiming earlier in a video transmission, "We are not who we are. It goes no further than this." ("Ice")

Cancer Man SEE: **Cigarette-Smoking Man**

Capital Ice Maryland's finest ice skating wonderland, where the Lone Gunmen attempted to covertly retrieve a package for Mulder. ("Apocrypha")

CarboBoost A high-carbohydrate body-building drink. Mulder theorized that a brain tumor may have given self-styled assassin Robert "Pusher" Modell psychokinetic powers and that drinking large quantities of the protein drink was a means of replenishing his energy. Mango-Kiwi-Tropical Swirl was Modell's flavor of preference. ("Pusher")

Cardinal, Luis (Lenno Bristos) Also known as the Hispanic Man. Cardinal and his partner, renegade agent Alex Krycek, mistakenly shot Scully's sister, Melissa, in the head when she entered Dana's apartment. Realizing their error, the two assassins quickly vanished ("The Blessing Way"). When Assistant Director Skinner ignored warnings by MIBs not to reopen Melissa Scully's murder investigation, Cardinal was dispatched to shoot Skinner at point-blank range in a Washington, D.C. coffee shop. Cardinal said in Spanish, *"Chupa dura, amigo"*—literally "Suck hard, friend"—spitting on Skinner before running away from the scene of the crime. A wounded and hospitalized Skinner told Scully he recognized Cardinal as Krycek's companion when they attacked him in a hospital stairwell and stole the DAT tape a few months earlier. DNA results indicated that Cardinal was not only responsible for Skinner's shooting, but for the murder of Scully's sister, Melissa. When he attempted to finish off Skinner during the assistant director's transfer by ambulance to another hospital, Cardinal was confronted in the street by an armed Scully. The frightened Hispanic Man informed her that Krycek was headed to an abandoned missile silo in North Dakota, the hidden location of a salvaged UFO. Cardinal was later found dead in his jail cell. A background check revealed that the Nicaragua-born Cardinal had formerly been involved in the Iran/Contra scandal. ("Apocrypha")

Carolinian, The A North Carolina newspaper that ran a bogus story claiming that two kidnapped Jackson University students had been rescued. Mulder used the newspaper prop to disprove death-row inmate Luther Lee Boggs' claims of psychic ability, but the plan backfired. ("Beyond the Sea")

Carpenter, Dr. Ann (Anne DeSalvo) A scientist who worked at the Georgetown University Microbiology Department. After analyzing Dr. Berube's liquid-filled flask labeled "Purity Control," Dr. Carpenter told Scully she discovered bacteria that contained chloroplasts, or plant cells, which Scully theorized was for gene therapy. Dr. Carpenter later informed Scully the DNA possessed a fifth and sixth nucleotide that existed "nowhere in nature" and were thus, by definition, of alien origin. ("The Erlenmeyer Flask") *Anne DeSalvo, one of television's most familiar faces, had memorable recurring roles on* Wiseguy *and* Taxi.

Carstensen, T.C. A name on an airline manifest Scully scrutinized, trying to determine Mulder's whereabouts when he flew to a possible alien contact site in Puerto Rico. ("Little Green Men") *T.C. Carstensen is the name of a prominent online X-Phile.*

Carver, Commander (Malcolm Stewart) Los Angeles Police Department crime scene officer who oversaw the investigation into the vampire-like murder of Garrett Lorre. Commander Carver was impressed with Mulder's knowledge of the killers and his explanation that there had been six similar murders in Memphis and Portland. ("3") *Actor Malcolm Stewart also portrayed Dr. Glass in the pilot episode, Agent Bonnecaze in "Avatar," and Dr. Sacks in "Tunguska/Terma."*

Carver, Rick (Mike Kopsa) A California construction site foreman, and associate of the mercenary and greedy Barber, he gave illegal Mexican immigrant Eladio Buente a job building houses. Mulder and INS agent Conrad Lozano discovered Culver's body in a port-a-potty, his body ravaged by the highly contagious and fatal fungus that Eladio carried. ("El Mundo Gira")

Caryl County Sheriff's Station Location of Mulder and Scully's interview with Terri Roberts and Margi Kleinjan, two high schoolers involved in a series of deaths in the small town of Comity. Interviewed separately, the teenage girls offered virtually identical word-for-word accounts of a satanic cult ceremony in which an infant was to be sacrificed. ("Syzygy")

Cascade Volcano Research Team A group of project scientists assigned to explore Mt. Avalon with the aid of Firewalker, a robot that could descend into the fiery depths of a volcano. ("Firewalker")

Cash, Joseph (Don McKay) The warden of Central Prison in Raleigh, North Carolina. He refused Scully's request for a stay of execution for death-row inmate Luther Lee Boggs in exchange for his psychic assistance in locating a kidnapped youth. ("Beyond the Sea") *Don McKay also played Charlie, the sewage plant engineer in "The Host" and the Loudoun County judge who was swayed by Robert Modell in "Pusher."*

Cassal, Jay "Jane" (Tasha Simms) Walter Skinner's attorney. She presented the Assistant Director with divorce papers from Sharon, his wife of seventeen years. ("Avatar") *The character was originally intended to be male, so when Tasha Simms was cast in the role, the character was renamed in the script "Jane Cassal," although the screen and print credits read "Jay Cassal." Actress Tasha Simms also portrayed Ellen Reardon in "Eve," and Stan Phillips' daughter, Laura, in "Excelsius Dei."*

Cassandra, Amy Sixty-two-year-old Rhode Island woman who claimed to be an alien-abductee. Amy introduced Mulder to Dr. Goldstein after undergoing the psychiatrist's aggressive and unconventional therapy to access buried and repressed memories. Mulder himself undertook the radical regression treatment in order to "exorcise his demons" and lay claim to his past, especially the events surrounding the disappearance of his sister, Samantha. However, Dr. Goldstein's injections of a rapid-acting anesthetic caused mental blackouts and violent hallucinogenic episodes for his patients, resulting in the murder-suicide of Amy and her husband, David (using Mulder's service weapon). Forensic evidence eventually cleared Mulder of their deaths. ("Demons") *Episode writer R.W. Goodwin called the character Cassandra as a reference to the prophet of Greek mythology, whose curse was that no one would believe her, the implication being that Amy Cassandra was right about alien abductions but no one would believe her, either.*

Cassandra, David Husband of former alien-abductee, Amy Cassandra. David was shot to death by his wife at close-range after she underwent a hallucinogenic unconventional type of regression therapy. ("Demons")

Castor, Nurse (Jacqueline Danieneau) Young nurse at St. Matthews Medical Center bludgeoned by the ghost of Charlie Holvey's twin when she attempted to give the boy an injection. ("The Calusari")

Catcher (Neil Denis) One of several boys who discovered a hideously deformed baby buried in a shallow grave when they played a game of sandlot baseball in a vacant field next to the reclusive Peacock family's farmhouse. ("Home")

CCDTH21-38 Fiber-Optic Lens Micro Video Camera Miniature surveillance device the Lone Gunmen described as being attached to the back of a fly. ("Blood")

CDC Atlanta-based Centers for Disease Control, the federal agencies with jurisdiction over infectious diseases. Dr. Hodge suspected the CDC was responsible for torching the Arctic Ice Core Project research station in Icy Cape, Alaska ("Ice"). Dr. Osborne and Dr. Auerbach claimed to have quarantined Cumberland State Correctional Facility at the request of the CDC after a plaguelike illness killed ten inmates, but an infected Osborne later confessed he was actually employed with Pinck Pharmaceuticals ("F. Emasculata"). Dr. Simon Bruin of the CDC's Philadelphia office requested Scully's assistance when it was believed that a pathogen was responsible for the deaths of several African-American men whose bodies completely lacked pigmentation. ("Teliko")

Celebrity Skin Pornographic publication Mulder said kept him from reading the August edition of the conspiracy-oriented magazine *The Lone Gunman*. ("Blood")

cellular hypoxia A lack of oxygen to the cells. Margaret Hohman, who went into a seizure after young faith healer Samuel Hartley touched her, was believed by Scully to have died from cellular hypoxia caused by arsenic or by sodium or potassium cyanide. ("Miracle Man")

Center for Reproductive Medicine Federally operated fertility clinic located thirty miles outside of Allentown, Pennsylvania. After searching through hard-copy files in the basement of Betsy Hagopian's house, Mulder discovered that Hagopian and the other women belonging to the MUFON group of alleged alien-abductees were treated at the center. Mulder and one of the Kurt Crawford clones broke into the clinic separately, but then combined their efforts to hack into the facility's computer system and download a file directory containing a list of patients, including Scully, who had never been treated for infertility. ("Memento Mori")

Center for Special Warfare According to Lone Gunman Frohike's speculative dossier on the Cigarette-Smoking Man, the Army captain was stationed at the military facility in October 1962, where he was recruited to assassinate President Kennedy by a shadowy cabal. While stationed at the Fort Bragg, North Carolina base, the young military officer was a bunkmate to Bill Mulder. ("Musings of a Cigarette-Smoking Man")

Central Prison The state correctional facility in Raleigh, North Carolina where death-row inmate Luther Lee Boggs was imprisoned and later executed. ("Beyond the Sea")

Cerulean Hauling Transport company whose truck crashed into a police car carrying the apprehended Robert Modell (a.k.a. Pusher), enabling him to escape. Modell talked to the driver of the car in a soothing voice about cerulean blue until the truck the driver was looking at simply vanished. The driver then pulled forward, allowing the Cerulean Hauling truck to crash into them as Modell braced himself against the door. ("Pusher")

Chaco Chicken Founded by Walter "Chic" Chaco, poultry processing plant and sole employer in the small Arkansas town of Dudley. Bodies from the town's bonfire cannibal rituals were occasionally disposed of in the feed grinder at the company's processing plant. Ironically, the slogan for Chaco Chicken was "Good People, Good Food." ("Our Town")

Chaco, Walter "Chic" (John Milford) Founder of Dudley, Arkansas' Chaco Chicken. Born in 1902, he was ninety-three-years-old when he died, although physically he appeared to be thirty years younger. When his transport plane was shot down over New Guinea in 1944, he spent six months with the Jale tribe, which practiced cannibalism with the belief that it prolonged life. He founded Chaco Chicken in Dudley after he returned from World War II and evidently introduced the townsfolk to ritualistic cannibalism. Chaco was beheaded by a masked executioner during a torch-lit ceremony when he was accused of bringing in "the outsider," a federal poultry inspector suffering from the fatal Creutzfeldt-Jakob disease. Although Chaco's remains were never found, a workman found a wisp of gray hair similar to Chaco's in the chicken feed. ("Our Town") *John Milford played LAPD Captain Dempsey in the* Dukes of Hazzard *spinoff series,* Enos.

Chadwick's Washington coffee shop where Assistant Director Skinner ordered the blue plate special, and was shot at point-blank range by the Hispanic Man (later identified as mercenary Luis Cardinal). ("Piper Maru")

Challenger American space shuttle that exploded seventy-three seconds after launch on January 28, 1986, killing the entire crew. Mulder and Scully examined records which showed that alien-possessed Lt. Col. Aurelius Belt, supervisor of the shuttle program, possibly sabotaged the *Challenger*. ("Space")

Chamberlain, Michelle Young, blonde woman murdered by a Washington, D.C. serial killer, whose victims were all approximately the same age, height, weight, hair and eye color, and all found within six-blocks of each other. A ghost of each victim was encountered by someone only moments before their corpses were discovered, leading Mulder to suspect that the apparitions were attempting to communicate with the living for reasons unknown at the time. ("Elegy")

Chandler, Agent Eugene (Mark Holden) One of several FBI agents assigned to an anti-terrorist unit responsible for the protection of dozens of high-ranking military officials in Washington, D.C. for the rededication of the Vietnam Veterans Memorial. ("Unrequited")

Chaney, Sam Legendary FBI agent who disappeared, along with his partner, Tim Ledbetter, while investigating three serial homicides in Aubrey, Missouri in 1942. Considered an expert in "stranger killings," Chaney was on the trail of The Slash Killer, a murderer who carved the word SISTER into the chests of female victims and painted on the walls with their blood. The serial killer was never caught. Agent Chaney's skeletal remains were unearthed by pregnant police officer, B.J. Morrow, in a shallow grave in a vacant lot in 1995. ("Aubrey")

Chantal A 1-900 phone sex operator who left a message for "Marty" on Mulder's answering machine, advising him of new "lower rates." Marty Mulder was one of the agent's aliases. ("Small Potatoes")

Chao, Glen (B.D. Wong) A young Chinese-American police detective with the San Francisco Police Department. Assigned to aid Mulder and Scully in their investigation of several mysterious deaths involving Chinese immigrants, Det. Chao was actually providing protection for a Chinatown lottery where bettors risked losing their organs to black marketeers. After breaking up the fixed game and saving an older immigrant from having his heart removed, Chao disappeared "like a ghost." In retaliation for breaking a code of silence within the Chinese community and for dismantling the pyramid scheme, Chao was burned alive in a crematorium oven. ("Hell Money") *Tony Award-winning actor B.D. Wong also co-starred with Martin Short as the off-the-wall wedding coordinators in the Steve Martin comedy* Father of the Bride *and its sequel.*

Chapel, Ambrose (Tom Butler) CIA agent who approached Mulder with information that the identical doctors being killed in arson fires were in reality Soviet clones known as Gregors. Chapel was actually the shapeshifting alien Bounty Hunter dispatched to terminate extraterrestrial colonists who had genetically merged with humans. ("Colony") *The name "Ambrose Chapel" was in homage to Alfred Hitchcock and the movie,* The Man Who Knew Too Much. *In the film, the phrase "Ambrose Chapel" was incorrectly assumed to be the name of a person, but was in reality a church. Actor Tom Butler also portrayed Eurisko CEO Benjamin Drake in "Ghost in the Machine."*

Charez, Daniel (Greg Rogers) Executed death-row inmate Napoleon "Neech" Manley's twenty-six-year-old court-appointed lawyer, who represented the convict eleven years earlier. Manley always blamed the young and inexperienced Charez for his conviction and, during the two-month period before his scheduled execution, he telephoned Charez thirty times. Charez was smothered to death with a pillow, a victim of the reincarnated Manley's promise to return from the dead and avenge those who had wronged him. ("The List")

Charlie (Don McKay) The plant engineer at the Newark County Sewage Processing Plant. Charlie heard something splashing in a sewer reservoir.

When he backflushed the system, he caught sight of the Flukeman creature. ("The Host") *Don McKay also portrayed Warden Joseph Cash in "Beyond the Sea" and the Loudoun County judge who was swayed by Robert Modell in "Pusher."*

Charlotte's Diner A roadside café off Route 320A in Craiger, Maryland that specialized in "home-cooked meals." After barely escaping from "a small army" at the Strughold mines, Mulder and Scully secretly met Skinner at the diner to discuss turning over the DAT tape in exchange for their safety and reinstatement to the Bureau. ("Paper Clip")

Charne–Sayre, Dr. Bonita (Jessica Schreier) Prominent physician and virologist who had treated U.S. presidents. A well-known member of the World Health Organization, she was a leading authority on smallpox and had become a vocal proponent of eliminating the last storage vials of the virus in the U.S. and the former Soviet Union. She was also the Well-Manicured Man's personal physician and (it was implied) his lover. A former KGB assassin, dispatched to kill Dr. Charne-Sayre, choked her to death inside one of the stables at the Well-Manicured Man's horse farm in Charlottesville, Virginia. Charne-Sayre had been the intended recipient of a diplomatic pouch Scully and Mulder intercepted at the airport. Inside was a meteor fragment from Tunguska, Siberia, containing an alien biotoxin ("black cancer") that killed anyone who came into contact with it. ("Tunguska/Terma")

Charters, Michelle (Teryl Rothery) A nurse at the Excelsis Dei convalescent home who was pinned down and raped by an invisible entity. She accused Hal Arden, a seventy-four-year-old resident, of being her attacker. Mulder and Scully were called in to investigate nurse Charter's rape claim after she sued the federal government, alleging she couldn't get Social Security disability or workman's compensation, and was forced to work around the man who assaulted her. ("Excelsius Dei")

Charyn, Dr. Penelope (Anna Hagan) A doctor employed at the Grissom Sleep Disorder Center in Stamford, Connecticut. Dr. Charyn described to Mulder experimental modification of brain-wave patterns by electrical stimulation to alter dreams. ("Sleepless")

Checkpoint Alpha Military security station Mulder bypassed during his infiltration of a government-protected UFO crash site near Lake Michigan in Townsend, Wisconsin. After photographing the alien spacecraft's wreckage, Mulder was rifle-butted unconscious and placed in the brig alongside NICAP member Max Fenig. ("Fallen Angel")

Chen, Cliff A name on an airline manifest Scully examined, trying to ascertain Mulder's location when he flew to a potential extraterrestrial contact site in

Puerto Rico. ("Little Green Men") *Cliff Chen is a prominent online X-Phile who maintains a complete episode guide to the series.*

Chesapeake Lounge The bar in the Ambassador Hotel where Assistant Director Walter Skinner sought solace after being served final divorce papers from his wife of seventeen years. Over drinks, Skinner met Carina Sayles, an attractive prostitute whom he picked up and took to a room. He awakened from a nightmare to find her lying dead next to him. ("Avatar")

Chick (Nicole Parker) A teenage girl who, along with her friend Stoner, witnessed the cockroach attack on Dude while they were doing drugs. Dude hacked himself to death with a razor blade in an attempt to rid himself of the burrowing insects ("War of the Coprophages"). Chick and Stoner turned up again on a Heuvelman's Lake dock, where they observed a diver suddenly attacked, blood coloring the water before his head slowly bobbed to the surface. ("Quagmire")

Choc-o-saurus Insurance salesman and reluctant psychic Clyde Bruckman's favorite chocolate confection, which was shaped in the form of a dinosaur. ("Clyde Bruckman's Final Repose")

Chung, Jose (Charles Nelson Reilly) Novelist who authored *The Lonely Buddha* and *The Caligarian Candidate*. Chung's publisher assigned him the task of writing a book about alien abduction—in the process creating a new genre ("nonfiction science-fiction")—which he felt would assure him a spot on the best-seller list. Although Mulder was reluctant to speak to him, Chung interviewed Scully about a rumored UFO abduction of two Klass County, Washington teenagers. In return she asked that he only report the truth in his book. Chung scoffed, stating, "Truth is as subjective as reality." Mulder eventually met with the author, requesting that he not write the book, which would do a disservice to a field of inquiry that had struggled to achieve respectability. After spending several months in Klass County, Chung wrote the book *From Outer Space,* which detailed interviewees' conflicting stories of government cover-ups, mysterious Men in Black, and a monstrous red alien called Lord Kinbote of the Earth's Core. ("Jose Chung's 'From Outer Space'") *The Jose Chung character was named in honor of noted psychologist Carl Gustav Jung, who wrote a monograph entitled,* "Flying Saucers: A Modern Myth of Things Seen in the Skies." *Episode writer Darin Morgan considered only two actors for the role of the eccentric Chung—Rip Taylor or Charles Nelson Reilly.*

Chupacabra, El Also known as the Goatsucker, a legendary gray, hairless creature out of Mexican folklore with a small gray body, a large head, a tiny mouth, and prominent, bulging black eyes. Illegal immigrants living in a migrant workers' shantytown in California's San Joaquin Valley were convinced that a young woman, Maria Dorantes, was killed by Eladio Buente, whom they believed to be El Chupacabra. Cynical INS agent, Conrad Lozano, called the mythological creature "a fantastic tale." ("El Mundo Gira") *The Chupacabra myth started in 1993 in Puerto Rico and since that time has spread to Texas, Mexico, and Central and South America. Various reports of sightings have described El Chupacabra as being everything from a black bird-like monster that flew down and snatched goats off the ground to a dangerous strain of felines.*

Church of the Red Museum. A mysterious religious cult which relocated from California to a ranch in rural Delta Glen, Wisconsin. Followers of vegetarianism guru Richard Odin, the church's white-robed and red-turbaned acolytes believed in soul transference and eschewed eating meat, treating their five hundred head of cattle as pets. ("Red Museum")

Cigarette-Smoking Man (William B. Davis) A.k.a. Cancer Man, enigmatic, chain-smoking government insider with "no wife, no children, some power," who is "in the game" because he believes in it ("One Breath"). According to Lone Gunman Frohike's speculative dossier of "the most dangerous man alive," Cigarette-Smoking Man was born on August 20, 1940 in Baton Rouge, Louisiana (on the same day that Trotsky was assassinated). His father was an ardent Communist activist and Soviet spy executed for passing information to the Nazis on America's entry into World War II. His mother (a smoker) died of lung cancer while he was still a baby, which explained his early aversion to cigarettes. With no surviving family, he became a ward of the state and was sent to various orphanages throughout the Midwest. A lonely child that didn't make friends, he read extensively ("I'd rather read the worst novel ever written than sit through the best movie ever made"). Then, according to Frohike, he appeared to have vanished until a year-and-a-half after the Bay of Pigs invasion. In October 1962, he was evidently a captain in the U.S. Army, serving alongside William Mulder at the Center for Special Warfare at Fort Bragg, North Carolina. Although he denied having been involved in covert action in the Congo in 1961 and training Cuban nationals for Operation Zapata (the Bay of Pigs), the right-wing conspiracy that operated within the labyrinth of the official government recognized his unique capabilities and recruited the young officer for his first assignment: the assassination of John F. Kennedy. In its successful aftermath, he lit his first smoke (given to him by the "patsy" Lee Harvey Oswald) and became the Cigarette-Smoking Man. By 1968, CSM was in such a powerful position that he gave orders to FBI Director J. Edgar Hoover, and "worked hard to keep any President from knowing" he even existed. He respected Martin Luther King, Jr. ("an extraordinary man") and supported his civil rights stance, but personally took charge of his assassination because of King's perceived communist leanings. But even the Cigarette-Smoking Man had a dream. In his spare-time he wrote an action-adventure novel titled *Take a Chance* (under the pen name Raul Bloodworth), which was brutally rejected by publishers. By Christmas 1991, CSM had covertly started wars, assassinated world leaders, rigged elections, the Oscars, the Olympics, the Super Bowl, and moved the Rodney King trial to Simi Valley. Despite all his power, he still couldn't get one of his Jack Colquitt secret agent novels published. Then his mysterious associate (known to Mulder and Scully as the graying, trench-coated informant, Deep Throat) exterminated the only survivor of a crashed UFO and the Cigarette-Smoking Man had a revitalized purpose for living, and new truths to conceal. Although initially jubilant in 1996 after a magazine bought one of his books and planned to serialize it (he even prepared his resignation and lit his last cigarette), his old frustration and bitterness returned upon discovering that the periodical was a cheap salacious rag whose editors even had the audacity to alter the ending as he had written it ("Musings of a Cigarette-Smoking Man"). *Note: Much of Frohike's version of the Cigarette-Smoking Man's life contradicts other episodes and* The X-Files' *previously established timeline such as "Apocrypha," which had CSM working with Deep Throat and Bill Mulder in 1953 (and already chain-smoking). William Davis has repeatedly told fans at conventions that he believed the episode was about his character's* alleged *background. "I don't think we know if some of it is Frohike's imagination or his sense of what the CSM might be. Some of it may well be the CSM's imagination regarding what his life might have been."* The Cigarette-Smoking Man has been actively involved in the X-Files unit and its unorthodox cases ever since Section Chief Scott Blevins assigned Scully to "assist" Mulder, even going so far as to hide away evidence of the existence of UFOs and aliens in a huge storage room deep within the Pentagon ("The X-Files: Pilot"). CSM, who Mulder at one time believed was "probably CIA," unsuccessfully tried to get a homicidal bank robber to provide the location of Dr. Ridley's age-reversal research documents before he died ("Young at Heart"). The Cigarette-Smoking Man's silent presence in FBI Assistant Director Skinner's office provided no hint of who he represented, but Skinner seemed to defer to him. After reading Mulder's field report on the death of Eugene Tooms, the Assistant Director asked CSM if he believed it. "Of course I do," he replied, breaking his long silence ("Tooms"). The tension between Mulder and the Cigarette-Smoking Man increased steadily as the nameless man with the pack of Morleys consistently involved himself in Mulder's work. After the X-Files unit was shut down, Skinner chastised Mulder for abandoning his surveillance assignment and travelling to Puerto Rico to a possible alien contact site. During the discussion, the Cigarette-Smoking Man barked at Mulder, "Your time is over," but Skinner intervened and threw him out of the office ("Little Green Men"). While the X-Files unit was still disbanded and Scully transferred to a teaching post at Quantico Academy (where she still assisted Mulder unofficially), the Cigarette-Smoking Man arranged to have rookie agent Alex Krycek assigned as Mulder's new partner. After the two agents completed their investigation of a secret Vietnam-era sleep deprivation experiment on soldiers, Krycek met with CSM and told him that Mulder had "found another source" to replace Deep Throat and that Scully was "a much larger problem than you described." Not to worry, the

CSM assured him as he stubbed out a cigarette. "Every problem has a solution" ("Sleepless"). He apparently pulled Krycek's strings throughout the Duane Barry incident and the abduction of Scully. At a meeting in the garage at FBI headquarters, Krycek asked the Cigarette-Smoking Man why they didn't simply kill Mulder. "You risk turning one man's religion into a crusade" ("Duane Barry/Ascension"). After Scully turned up mysteriously at a Washington, D.C. hospital, alive but comatose, Mulder accused "Cancer Man" of being the one responsible. After CSM warned Skinner to "sit" on Mulder or "they would," a stranger provided Mulder with the means to find the Cigarette-Smoking Man, who he confronted at gunpoint. "I've watched presidents die," CSM scoffed, when Mulder threatened to kill him. "I have more respect for you, Mulder. You've become a player" ("One Breath"). CSM tried to set up Mulder and discredit him during the deadly *F. emasculata* outbreak, although he claimed no knowledge of the disease. If Mulder had gone public with the information on the contagion, he would have had no corroboration ("F. Emasculata"). After Mulder obtained the DAT tape containing the stolen MJ files, the Cigarette-Smoking Man visited the agent's father, addressing him as "Bill." When the elder Mulder asked CSM if he could protect his son, he said, "I've protected him this long, haven't I?" Shortly thereafter, Krycek fatally shot Mulder's father (most likely on orders from CSM) and the younger Mulder was left for dead in the New Mexico desert by the Cigarette-Smoking Man and a contingent of soldiers ("Anasazi"). CSM met with the Shadowy Syndicate at their private club in New York City and, unwilling to admit failure to the international consortium of conspirators, assured them that the matter of the stolen MJ documents was being handled and that the media attention would amount to "nothing more than a few scattered obituaries." Apparently CSM is a member of the group (their "Washington associate"), but he is obviously answerable to higher-ranking members such as the 1st Elder and the Well-Manicured Man ("The Blessing Way"). But Krycek's accidental murder of Scully's sister forced the Syndicate to grill CSM for committing "a horrible mistake" in shooting the wrong woman, demanding that he produce the missing tape, which he said he would do by the next day. He later claimed that the DAT was destroyed in the car bomb that "killed" Krycek, even though the renegade agent was very much alive and had the tape in his possession, promising CSM exposure if he was ever threatened again. The Cigarette-Smoking Man met with Skinner, telling him that the tape was gone and that his own life was in jeopardy, but the Assistant Director informed him that Albert Hosteen, a World War II Navajo code-talker, had memorized the encrypted MJ files and related them to twenty other Indians schooled in his tribe's narrative tradition ("Paper Clip"). The Cigarette-Smoking Man eventually retrieved the DAT tape from an alien-possessed Krycek and had the man sealed inside an abandoned missile silo in North Dakota ("Apocrypha"). Mrs. Mulder (Fox's mother) went to the family's deserted summer home in Rhode Island, where she met the Cigarette-Smoking Man, who reminisced about the good times of years past. He noted that he was a better water-skier than her husband, "but that could be said about so many things . . . couldn't it?" Mrs. Mulder snapped back that she had "repressed it all," but CSM needed her to remember something, and they argued heatedly. Mrs. Mulder, becoming violently angry, suffered a severe and debilitating stroke after he left. Only because Mr. X had been covertly observing her, and made an anonymous 911 call, did she receive immediate paramedic assistance. After learning his mother might not recover, Mulder discovered the Cigarette-Smoking Man lighting up a Morley in a hospital hallway. "Are you going to smoke that, or do you want to smoke this?" Mulder demanded, grabbing him and sticking a gun in his face. CSM noted that he had known Mulder's mother since "before you were born, Fox" ("Talitha Cumi"). The alien Bounty Hunter, who CSM had dispatched to terminate Jeremiah Smith, a extraterrestrial shapeshifter threatening the colonization project, was ordered to Mrs. Mulder's hospital bedside. Fearing that her son could become a fierce enemy with "nothing left to lose" if his mother died, the Cigarette-Smoking Man directed the alien to heal her with his paranormal powers ("Herrenvolk"). After Scully was diagnosed with inoperable brain cancer, Mulder approached Skinner and attempted to arrange a meeting with the Cigarette-Smoking Man. The Assistant Director refused, insisting that CSM only dealt in lies, but nonetheless, Skinner secretly enlisted the Cigarette-Smoking Man's help on his own in an effort to have Scully cured ("Memento Mori"). As part of his "deal with the Devil," Skinner obstructed justice and covered up the murderous attack of a small-pox-carrying swarm of bees. To insure his participation, a Virginia police detective was shot to death with a gun stolen from Skinner. The Assistant Director, angry at being framed and increasingly uncomfortable with his actions as dictated by the Cigarette-Smoking Man, confronted him with a gun. After CSM alluded to the fact that only he could save Scully's life, Skinner backed down, but fired several shots over the Cigarette-Smoking Man's shoulder into the wall, leaving him visibly shaken ("Zero Sum"). *William B. Davis is a drama teacher and still serves as director of Vancouver's William Davis Centre for Actor's Study. In addition to his recurring role on* The X-Files, *his resume includes* Stephen King's It, Airwolf, MacGyver, The Outer Limits, *and* Sliders *as well as the theatrical films* Looking Who's Talking *and* The Dead Zone. *Although he doesn't like to advertise it, he also appeared in a Canadian horror movie in the late '80s called* Midnight Matinee, *in which he spent a great deal of time dangling from chains. Although Davis' Smoking-Man character was originally intended to remain silent but deadly, CSM evolved as the conspiracy mythology became more prominent. Chris Carter was once asked if he would ever kill "Cancer Man," to which he replied, "You can't kill the Devil." Craig Warkentin played the young Cigarette-Smoking Man in the pre-credits sequence of "Apocrypha" and Chris Owens played him in "Musings of a Cigarette-Smoking Man" and in Fox Mulder's flashback scenes in "Demons."*

Clay's BBQ Diner in Delta Glen, Wisconsin. While Mulder and Scully were having dinner, four teenagers, including the sheriff's son, harassed a member of the local cult religion, the Church of the Red Museum, until Mulder intervened. ("Red Museum")

Clean-Suited Man (David Hay) A scientist clad in an anti-contamination suit at the High Containment Facility in Winthrop, Washington who told a quarantined Mulder that the government would use pesticides and controlled burning as "eradication procedures" to end the swarm of prehistoric mites in the Olympia National Forest. ("Darkness Falls")

clinazopam Anti-psychotic drug used to treat severe schizophrenia. New Horizon Psychiatric Hospital staff Nurse Innes had been ingesting mentally challenged patient Harold Spuller's doses of clinazopam, the effects of which were violence and unpredictable behavior, resulting in the murders of several young women in the Washington, D.C. area. ("Elegy")

Cline, Andrea (Laura Harris) One of four Crowley High School teenagers who used a Satanic ritual book, and unintentionally summon a demon. ("Die Hand Die Verletzt")

Cline, Det. (Frank Cassini) One of the St. Paul, Minnesota police detectives who investigated a series of killings involving fortune-tellers. Det. Cline requested the rather unorthodox assistance of TV psychic the Stupendous Yappi to help solve the string of serial murders. ("Clyde Bruckman's Final Repose") *Det. Cline was named in honor of Eddie Cline, a director of comedies of the silent era (much like the real-life Clyde Bruckman).*

Club Tepes Los Angeles nightclub named after the fifteenth-century Romanian, Vlad "the Impaler" Tepes. The majority of the patrons who frequented the after-sunset club were pale-skinned and wore black clothing. A stamp on a murder suspect's arm led Mulder to the Hollywood club where he met Kristen, a mysterious woman who practically confessed to a series of vampiric murders. ("3")

Clyde (Theodore Thomas) A building security guard at the Eurisko World Headquarters in Crystal City, Virginia. ("Ghost in the Machine")

🗁 **"Clyde Bruckman's Final Repose"** Written by Darin Morgan. Directed by David Nutter. File number 3X04. *First aired October 13, 1995. Agents Mulder and Scully enlist the reluctant assistance of a genuine clairvoyant when fortune-tellers who cannot predict their own deaths fall victim to a serial killer.* **Classic Sound Bite:** *"You know, there are worse ways to go, but I can't think of a more undignified one than autoerotic asphyxiation."* **Background**

Check: *As part of his research on the subject of "psychic detectives," episode writer Darin Morgan read dozens of books on the subject, including his main source, a book called* Psychic Sleuths, *for which eleven researchers spent a year investigating well-known psychics such as Noreen Renier, who foresaw the assassination attempt on President Reagan.*

Coast Guard Officer (Paul McLean) An official at a Naval shipyard in Newport News, Virginia, who told Mulder that the DEA wouldn't let the salvage vessel *Talapus* into port and put the ship back out to the sea the next morning. After distracting the Coast Guard officer, Mulder found a ship in the harbor which he discovered to be the *Talapus*. ("Nisei") *Paul McLean also played Dr. Josephs in "Shapes" and FBI ballistics expert Agent Kautz in "Anasazi."*

Cokely, Harry (Morgan Woodward) A seventy-seven-year-old ex-con sentenced to prison in 1945 for raping Linda Thibedeaux and carving the word SISTER on her chest with a strap razor before she escaped. Although Cokely was believed to be The Slash Killer, a serial murderer responsible for three young women's rapes and mutilation deaths in 1942 in Aubrey, Missouri, law enforcement agents could not connect him to the crimes at the time. However, Cokely served almost fifty years in McCallister Penitentiary for the 1945 crime. After his release from prison in December 1994, a feeble Cokely was dependent on an oxygen machine and lived in a rundown house. He was killed by pregnant police officer, B.J. Morrow, who Mulder and Scully discovered was Cokely's granddaughter, perhaps the victim of genetic transference of personality from one generation to another. ("Aubrey") *Morgan Woodward, who portrayed the pathetic Cokely, is best remembered in the sci-fi genre for two classic* Star Trek *episodes, "Dagger of Mind," and "The Omega Glory."*

Cole, Cpl. Augustus D. (Tony Todd) Also known as "Preacher." One of the experimental subjects of Dr. Saul Grissom's secret Vietnam-era project to create the perfect soldier by eradicating the need for sleep, since wakefulness dulled fear and heightened aggression. The Bible-quoting Cole, who hadn't slept in twenty-four years, had developed the psychic ability to create dreams so real they could kill. Twenty-four years after his Special Forces Recon Squad J-7 had gone AWOL and massacred three-hundred Vietnamese children outside Phu Bai, Cole decided to avenge the atrocities by using telepathic imagery to murder those he blamed for the project. Mulder caught up with Cole and asked him to testify about what the Army had done, but double-agent Alex Krycek, saying he saw a gun in Coles' hand instead of a Bible, shot and killed him. ("Sleepless") *Actor Tony Todd, who also played a soldier in the action-adventure thriller* The Rock, *is best remembered as Worf's brother, Kurn, on* Star Trek: The Next Generation *and the sympathetic monster in Clive Barker's* Candyman *movie and its sequel,* Farewell to the Flesh.

Collins, Agent (Steve Bacic) FBI agent on Frank Burst's team who doused himself in gasoline and set himself ablaze while under the influence of Robert "Pusher" Modell. Agents Mulder, Scully and Burst were able to extinguish the flames before Collins was killed. ("Pusher") *Steve Bacic also appeared as a police officer in "Soft Light."*

Collins, Dr. Richard (Frank C. Turner) A witness at Eugene Tooms' psychiatric hearing and sanitarium commitment review. Dr. Collins testified that Tooms' attack on Scully was simply frustration due to losing his job and being falsely arrested by the FBI. The panel elected to discharge Tooms from the Druid Hill Sanitarium in Baltimore, Maryland despite Mulder's warning that the mutant serial killer was a dangerous threat to society. ("Tooms") *Frank C. Turner also played Dr. Hakkie in "Duane Barry."*

Collum National Forest Northwest Oregon wooded area near the town of Bellefleur where several high school classmates were found dead, possibly the victims of alien abduction and experimentation. ("The X-Files: Pilot")

📁 **"Colony (Part 1 of 2)"** Written by Chris Carter (based upon a story by David Duchovny and Chris Carter). Directed by Nick Marck. File number 2X16. *First aired February 10, 1995. The search for a morphing alien Bounty Hunter responsible for the deaths of extraterrestrial clones sent to colonize Earth is interrupted when Mulder is contacted by his father, who tells him that his abducted sister, Samantha, has finally returned home.* **Classic Sound Bite:** *"You've got to wonder about a country where even the President has to worry about drive-by shootings."* **Background Check:** *"Colony" was the first X-Files episode to be told in flashback, an inspiration Chris Carter took from the original* Frankenstein *movie, which was told the same way.*

Colquitt, Jack The action-adventure hero and main character of Tom Clancy-esque spy novels written by Raul Bloodworth, the pseudonym of the Cigarette-Smoking Man, according to Lone Gunman Frohike's conjectural dossier on the nefarious chain-smoker. ("Musings of a Cigarette-Smoking Man") *Jack Colquitt was also the name of a Marine in an episode titled, "Who Monitors the Birds?" from Glen Morgan and James Wong's short-lived sci-fi series,* Space: Above and Beyond.

Colton, Tom (Donal Logue) An ambitious FBI agent assigned to the Bureau's Violent Crimes Section and an Academy classmate of Scully's. Over lunch, Colton expressed his concern that Scully was hindering her career by associating with "Spooky" Mulder and then asked for her assistance in a Baltimore serial killing case: three victims found with no obvious means of entry, their livers seemingly ripped out with bare hands. Mulder joined in the investigation and, despite Colton's interference, apprehended Eugene Tooms, a liver-eating mutant who awakened from hibernation every thirty years to commit murder. Colton, who angrily insinuated that Scully was a loser for sticking with Mulder, was reassigned from the Violent Crimes Unit to the white-collar crimes division in South Dakota. ("Squeeze") *Donal Logue's film credits include,* Metro *(1997),* Dear God *(1996),* Diabolique *(1996),* Jerry Maguire *(1996),* Miami Rhapsody *(1995),* Disclosure *(1994),* Little Women *(1994) and the 1993 HBO movie,* And the Band Played On.

Commodore The name of the dog belonging to Mr. Nutt, the midget proprietor of the Gulf Breeze Trailer Court in Gibsonton, Florida. Mr. Nutt was grabbed through Commodore's doggie door and killed by Lanny's detached congenital twin, Leonard. ("Humbug")

Compound X Rapid-freezing agent that MIT cryobiologist Jason Nichols had been engineering for years, but had yet to invent. An older version of Nichols came back from the future in an attempt to stop himself and others from developing the chemical compound which would make time travel possible. ("Synchrony")

Concepcion, Jorge (Mike Gomez) A terrified Puerto Rican man Mulder discovered in the lavatory of the Arecibo Ionospheric Observatory. Jabbering in Spanish, apparently about alien contact, he drew the visage of an extraterrestrial on the wall. Terrified of a sudden, piercing noise, Jorge ran into the Puerto Rican jungle where Mulder later found him dead. ("Little Green Men")

Conductor (Michael Puttonen) Mulder asked him for access to the train compartment of Dr. Shiro Zama, the Japanese scientist he was pursing. After the Red-Haired Man garroted Zama in the lavatory, Mulder "armed" the Conductor with an empty .45 pistol and ordered him not to stop the train until Mulder had captured the scientist's assassin. In the quarantined surgical car, which housed a frightened, alien-looking being, the Red-Haired Man looped a garrote around Mulder's neck, nearly killing him before the Conductor, at gunpoint, ordered him to stop. The interruption gave Mulder time to recover, while the Conductor slammed the door shut, effectively trapping both men in the bomb-laden train car. Mulder ordered the Conductor to reroute them to a place as far from a populated area as possible and uncouple the car. ("731") *Mike Puttonen also appeared in "Deep Throat" as a motel manager, in "Sleepless" as Dr. Pilsson, and as Martin Alpert, the psychiatric facility administrator in "Elegy."*

🗁 **"Conduit"** Written by Alex Gansa and Howard Gordon. Directed by Daniel Sackheim. File number 1X03. *First aired October 1, 1993. When the teenage daughter of a UFO witness in Iowa disappears from a trailer park in a flash of blinding light, Agent Mulder is forced to confront his feelings about his sister's abduction by aliens twenty-one years earlier.* **Classic Sound Bite:** *"How* *can an eight-year-old boy who can barely multiply be a threat to national security? People call* me *paranoid!"* **Background Check:** *The episode title refers to eight-year-old Kevin Morris, who was a conduit, "a means of transmitting or distributing," through which aliens were attempting to communicate. This was the first episode in which Mulder fired his gun.*

Conundrum, The (Paul Lawrence a.k.a. The Enigma) Baldheaded and heavily tattooed circus freak who lived in Gibsonton, Florida along with several other retired sideshow performers. The Conundrum was a "geek," who ate anything, including (though certainly not limited to) raw fish, live crickets, rocks, and, apparently, Lanny's murderous, but misguided congenital twin, Leonard. ("Humbug") *The Conundrum was played by real-life Jim Rose Circus performer, The Enigma, formerly known as Slug the Sword Swallower.*

Cooley, Nurse The RN on duty at the VA Medical Center in North Orange, New Jersey from which Cpl. Augustus Cole somehow escaped. She showed Dr. Pilsson the discharge papers for Cole, which he adamantly denied signing. ("Sleepless") *The actress who portrayed Nurse Cooley was uncredited.*

Cooper, Edna Local Allentown, Pennsylvania MUFON member whose name was listed on the paperwork Mulder and Scully found in Steve Zinnszer's briefcase. ("Nisei")

Coriolis effect. According to Mulder, the natural force which causes water in the Northern Hemisphere to flow down a drain clockwise. After Mulder noticed that a drinking fountain in Milford Haven, New Hampshire drained counterclockwise, the agent concluded that there was indeed something sinister going on in the small town. ("Die Hand Die Verletzt") *The Coriolis force only affects large systems like hurricanes and currents. The water in drinking fountains and toilet bowls is usually dictated by the shape of the fixture.*

Cosmo The landlord/building manager of the sleazy Desmond Arms Residence Hotel near Washington, D.C. where Tommy Philips stayed. ("Lazarus")

Covarrubias, Marita (Laurie Holden) The blonde female assistant to the U.N.'s Special Representative to the Secretary General who serves as Mulder's newest clandestine information source and facilitator. Before he died, Mr. X scrawled the initials "SRSG" in his own blood, a meager clue which led Mulder to the United Nations and to the enigmatic Covarrubias. Although she denied the existence of the Canadian colonization farm, she handed the despondent Mulder a secret U.N. file containing photographs of the apparently alien shrub nursery and a workforce of young Samantha clones. "Not everything dies," she told Mulder ("Herrenvolk"). During the investigation of several black men's disappearances/deaths in Philadelphia, Mulder once again contacted the wary but sympathetic Covarrubias, whose tip led

Mulder to Minister Diabira, a diplomatic official assigned to the Washington, D.C. embassy of the West African country of Brukina Faso ("Teliko"). Mulder contacted Covarrubias at her Upper West Side apartment in New York City late one night, requesting help in discovering the origin of a diplomatic pouch containing an alien-infested meteor fragment. She made several calls, determining the courier's flight originated in an area near Tunguska, Siberia. With credentials provided by Covarrubias, Mulder was able to travel to Russia under the guise of a UN diplomat ("Tunguska"). After two of the military's top brass were murdered by Nathaniel Teager, a seemingly invisible assassin, Mulder met with Covarrubias to determine if there was a connection between the murdered generals. During a clandestine meeting near the Lincoln Memorial in Washington, D.C., she explained that they were members of a secret three-person commission that disposed of South Vietnamese soldiers who cooperated with the U.S. government during the war. Covarrubias revealed that testimony from the generals could have been used to establish reparations, which made Mulder realize the government wanted the officers dead to maintain its policy of denial regarding POWs. Mulder believed the only way to stop Teager was to determine his next victim. Covarrubias supplied the name of the third member of the secret tribunal ("Unrequited"). After the body of a mail sorter was discovered in the rest room of an overnight delivery company, the victim of a swarm of bees, Assistant Director Skinner telephoned Covarrubias and inquired about the Canadian project involving bees. After stating that no bees or beehives had been discovered in Alberta, their conversation ended. Covarrubias appeared at the Payson, South Carolina Community Hospital after several schoolchildren were attacked and repeatedly stung by a swarm of bees. Introducing herself to Skinner, she informed the assistant director that after he telephoned her, she made some inquiries and discovered that seven overnight packages had been shipped from Canada to a post office box in Payson. Covarrubias stated that she had traveled to the small South Carolina town to see for herself what was in the parcels. Afterwards, the enigmatic Covarrubias telephoned the Cigarette-Smoking Man, who instructed her to tell Mulder whatever he wanted to hear ("Zero Sum"). *The word "Rubia" means "yellow" or "blonde" in Spanish. "Covarrubias" translates to "yellow cave" and is the name of a medieval town in Spain. Twenty-five-year-old, Toronto-reared Laurie Holden, a 1993 UCLA graduate, studied acting with the late Robert Reed (the father on the long-running Brady Bunch television series). "I think of her [Covarrubias] as a Mati Hari," Holden has said of her enigmatic character. "You can't really read what she's saying or what her intentions are."*

Cox, Dr. Clifford SEE: Franklyn, Dr. Jack

Crandall, Joe (Gordon Tipple) Wheelchair-bound prisoner at Pennsylvania's Tashmoo Federal Correctional Facility. Crandall, who befriended homicidal robber John Barnett, was the sole beneficiary of Barnett's will. He told Mulder and Scully that Barnett did not suffer from heart ailments and disclosed the reverse aging procedure he saw Dr. Joe Ridley performing on a supposedly dead Barnett in the prison infirmary. ("Young at Heart") *Gordon Tipple also played a police detective in "Eve" and artist Hepcat Helm in "Humbug."*

Crawford, Kurt (David Lovgren) Young man taken into custody by Mulder and Scully for downloading Betsy Hagopian's computer files via a phone modem. Crawford explained that he and Hagopian were members of the same Allentown MUFON group, and claimed she asked him to retrieve her files for safekeeping after her death. Mulder later encountered several other Kurt Crawfords at the Lombard Research Facility and realized they were hybrid clones. The agent found additional Crawford replicas dressed as doctors inside an incubator room housing a dozen tanks containing human forms. One of the Crawfords showed Mulder a cold storage room containing vials of human ova, harvested from women, including Scully, during their abductions and used for reproduction. Mulder realized the women were the Crawfords' birth mothers and the clones were subverting the Shadowy Syndicate's Project. ("Memento Mori")

Creutzfeldt-Jakob Extremely rare disease in which brain tissue develops spongelike holes, causing dementia and death. Twenty-seven townsfolk died of Creutzfeldt-Jakob in Dudley, Arkansas after most of the population took part in eating the body of Federal poultry inspector George Kearns. ("Our Town")

Crew-Cut Man (Lindsey Ginter) A government assassin who shot Deep Throat through the heart when the informant traded an apparently alien fetus for Mulder's life ("The Erlenmeyer Flask"). The Crew-Cut Man was later killed by Sheriff Mazeroski of Delta Glen, Wisconsin, avenging his son's murder by the shadowy government assassin. Scully's subsequent report stated that the nameless man had no identity record, and his fingerprints weren't on file with either the FBI or the National System of Records. ("Red Museum")

Crickenson, Roky (William Lucking) Blue-collar utility worker who witnessed alien abductions in Klass County, Washington while checking on a mysterious power outage. After being visited by two threatening MIBs in a black Cadillac, Crikenson handed over his handwritten "manifesto" called *The Truth About Aliens,* in which he claimed he saw two smaller, gray-skinned extraterrestrials being attacked by a large red monstrosity named Lord Kinbote, an alien from Earth's core. Mulder acknowledged that Crickenson was probably delusional but believed there was a seed of truth in his account. Crikenson eventually quit his job with the power company and relocated to El Cajon, California, to start a new life as some kind of New Age/UFO guru where he preached "to the lost and desperate." ("Jose Chung's 'From Outer Space'") *The character Roky Crickenson was a nod to the psychedelic lead singer* *for the 13th Floor Elevators. He later formed a band called Roky Crickenson and the Aliens, which supposedly reflects the singer's belief that he himself is a Martian. El Cajon, California is where Darin and Glen Morgan were born and raised.*

Crockett, Roger Vagrant whose mutilated body was discovered in the New Jersey State Park, a recent victim of a legendary man-beast. ("The Jersey Devil")

Cross, Det. Alan (James Handy) A twenty-five-year veteran of the Cleveland Police Department's homicide division, who requested Mulder and Scully's assistance in the investigation of Lauren Mackalvey's grotesquely decomposed body. Although a bit old-fashioned and initially uncomfortable treating Scully as an equal, Cross soon grew to respect and admire her intuitiveness. Unfortunately, the detective was killed by the "fat-sucking vampire" Virgil Incanto while canvassing a list of potential suspects. ("2Shy")

Crowe Medical Clinic Browning, Montanta hospital where Lyle Parker was taken by Scully after he was found nude and unconscious near his father's mutilated corpse. ("Shapes")

Crowley High School Educational institution in Milford Haven, New Hampshire, where an unintentionally summoned demon appeared in the human form of substitute teacher Phyllis Paddock. The school's PTA-like Parent Teachers Committee was comprised of members of an occult religion who worshipped "the lord of darkness." ("Die Hand Die Verletzt") *Crowley High School was named after the famous British occultist, sybarite, and author, whose theories on "magick" heavily influenced the development of modern Wicca.*

cryptomnesia Information unavailable to the conscious mind. Scully suggested that Aubrey, Missouri detective B.J. Morrow's police officer father may have discussed The Slash Killer case and the information remained in her subconscious until she dreamed. ("Aubrey")

CSICOP Committee for the Scientific Investigation of the Paranormal, referred to as "that new group" by NICAP member Max Fenig. ("Fallen Angel")

CSM-25 countermeasure filter According to the Lone Gunmen, the state-of-the-art CSM-25 countermeasure filter guaranteed secure conversations and was impervious to electronic surveillance. The Cigarette-Smoking Man, hiding in a nearby high-rise, foiled the device and, with high-tech eavesdropping equipment, listened as Frohike revealed to Mulder and Scully what he thought was the enigmatic Cigarette-Smoking Man's secret past. ("Musings of a Cigarette-Smoking Man")

Cuban Man (Gonzalo Canton) Present at a October 1962 meeting in the shadowy Fort Bragg, North Carolina office of four-star General Francis, during which members of a right-wing cabal functioning within the official government recruited a young Army captain (later to be known as the Cigarette-Smoking Man) to assassinate President John F. Kennedy in the wake of the Bay of Pigs fiasco. The incident was based on Lone Gunman Frohike's speculative dossier on the life of the Cigarette-Smoking Man. ("Musings of a Cigarette-Smoking Man")

CUFOS Center for UFO Studies, an Illinois-based organization which attempts to centralize, compare, organize and analyze thousands of reported UFO sightings and alien abductions. Mulder told Scully that Darlene Morris' name was on file with the Center for UFO Studies in Evansville, Illinois after she reported an alien spacecraft sighting at Lake Okobogee in 1967. ("Conduit") *The J. Allen Hynek Center for UFO Studies (CUFOS), a real organization whose goal is the scientific and objective study of the UFO phenomenon, maintains the world's largest repository of data about alien spacecraft sightings, second only to the United States government.*

Culver City Plasma Center Los Angeles-area blood bank investigated by Mulder in his search for the vampiric trio of serial murderers known as The Trinity Killers. ("3")

Cumberland State Correctional Facility State prison in Dinwiddie County, Virginia where drug manufacturer Pinck Pharmaceuticals and an unknown government agency conducted an experiment on the inmate population involving a newly discovered contagion that attacked the immune system. ("F. Emasculata")

Curator (Alex Diakun) An elderly man with a facial deformity who was the proprietor of the Gibsonton Museum of Curiosities, a Florida archive dedicated to circus freaks and sideshow acts from years past. The Curator gave Scully a tour, offering her a poster of Jim-Jim the Dog-faced Boy and, for an additional five dollars, promised an authentic P.T. Barnum exhibit, "The Great Unknown," which turned out to be an empty chest. ("Humbug") *Actor Alex Diakun, a personal favorite of writer Darin Morgan, also played a doomed tarot dealer in "Clyde Bruckman's Final Repose" and the hypnotist Dr. Fingers in "Jose Chung's 'From Outer Space.'"*

Curtis, Det. Joe (Jay Acovone) Providence, Rhode Island policeman whose investigation into the brutal gunshot deaths of David and Amy Cassandra led to the arrest of Mulder on suspicion of double homicide. Although Det. Curtis said he wanted to believe Mulder's claim of memory loss, which perhaps led to the agent's murderous actions during "some fit of blind insanity," the forensics evidence indicated otherwise. With Scully's assistance, though, Curtis and his investigative team pieced together enough evidence to prove Mulder's innocence. ("Demons")

Cut Bank Creek Fishing spot near Richard Watkins' Montana house where sixteen-year-old Native American Ish saw the man turn into a beastlike creature. Watkins was the subject of the very first X-File case, initiated personally by J. Edgar Hoover in 1946. ("Shapes")

Cuyahoga County Jail Detention facility in Cleveland, Ohio where an incarcerated Virgil Incanto confessed to forty-seven murders in five states. The mutant insisted he wasn't a serial killer, but was merely feeding a hunger: "I gave them what they wanted. They gave me what I needed." In Italian, Incanto added, "The dead are no longer lonely." ("2Shy")

Cuyahoga County Morgue Cleveland, Ohio temporary holding facility for Lauren Mackalvey's remains, which Scully discovered had degenerated into a skeleton and a pool of red glop. ("2Shy")

cyanogen bromide A cyanide derivative which Miracle Ministry aide Leonard Vance purchased from a Knoxville, Tennessee pesticide company. Vance poisoned some of the soft drinks at the evangelical tent revivals, which ultimately led to the deaths of Lucy Kelly, Carol Wallace, and Margaret Hohman, women who faith-healer Samuel Hartley laid hands on. After the disfigured Vance almost succeeded in incriminating Hartley in their murders and thus destroying faith in the Miracle Ministry, he committed suicide by ingesting cyanogen bromide. ("Miracle Man")

Deep Throat

Dalton, Laura (Jane MacDougall) Television reporter who covered the evacuation of Townsend, Wisconsin from Highway 38, stating that the government was vague about the "toxic cargo" forcing the removal of the town's 12,000 residents. Mulder watched the reporter on the television in his room at the Budget-Rest Motel in Townsend. ("Fallen Angel")

Daly, Dr. (Jay Brazeau) Intensive-care doctor in charge of Scully, when she was in critical condition at Northeast Georgetown Medical Center in Washington, D.C. When Mulder barged into Scully's room and demanded answers from Dr. Daly, two security guards threw Mulder out. Daly later claimed that no one knew how Scully arrived or was admitted to the hospital. ("One Breath") *Kay Brazeau also portrayed Dr. Varnes in "Lazarus."*

Daniels, Lillian (Iris Quinn Bernard) Wheelchair-bound wife of Kenwood County, Tennessee sheriff Maurice Daniels. Although Mrs. Daniels was severely arthritic, her husband believed local faith-healer, Samuel Hartley, was a fake and refused to allow the young evangelist to "lay hands" on Mrs. Daniels. ("Miracle Man")

Daniels, Officer (Russell Hamilton) Rookie cop who refused to allow Agent Jack Willis/Warren Dupre to enter the crime scene of Tommy Philips' murder at the Desmond Arms Residence Hotel without his ID badge. ("Lazarus")

Daniels, Sheriff Maurice (R.D. Call) Chief law enforcement officer for Kenwood County, Tennessee, who considered the Rev. Cal Hartley, his adopted son, Samuel, and their faith-healing Miracle Ministry a hoax. Sheriff Daniels eventually put two thugs into a jail cell with Samuel, who beat the young man to death. ("Miracle Man")

Danzinger, Leo A war vet who knew Nathaniel Teager from their tour of duty in Vietnam. Although Teager was officially reported killed in action in 1971 when his chopper was shot down over enemy territory, Danzinger was surprised to see the former Green Beret at a 1997 rededication of the Vietnam Veterans Memorial in Washington, D.C. Confronted, Teager told Danzinger that he had been abandoned by the U.S. government and left to die in an enemy prison camp. As proof, Teager handed him a tattered, handwritten list of American POWs reported as killed in action but still very much alive and imprisoned in Southeast Asia. ("Unrequited") The actor who portrayed Leo Danziger was uncredited.

Dark Man (David Palffy) Balding assassin in a dark suit, who smuggled aboard Flight 549 a composite, non-metallic handgun. Dark Man's mission was to kill passenger Max Fenig and obtain at any cost the alien energy source in his possession. But before the assassin could complete his assignment, Flight 549 was intercepted by a UFO. Scott Garrett, another assassin posing as an NTSB investigator, located Dark Man's body in the crashed jet's debris in Upstate New York and sprayed an acid-like substance on the corpse's identifiable fingertips and face. ("Tempus Fugit/Max")

dark matter Dr. Chester Banton had been experimenting with this theoretical subatomic particle at Polarity Magnetics when he was accidentally locked in a chamber, receiving a quanta bombardment equivalent to a two billion megawatt X ray. The process transformed the scientist's shadow into a black hole, reducing matter to pure energy and an instant form of death to anyone who came into contact with it. ("Soft Light")

📁 **"Darkness Falls"** Written by Chris Carter. Directed by Joe Napolitano. File number 1X19. *First aired April 15, 1994. While investigating the disappearance of thirty loggers in a Pacific Northwest forest, Agents Mulder and Scully find themselves terrorized by a swarm of deadly, green luminescent prehistoric mites when an ancient tree is cut down.* **Classic Sound Bite:** *"Come on, Scully, it'll be a nice trip to the forest."* **Background Check:** *Ninety-five percent of the mites seen in the episode were computer-generated, particularly the descending swarm. But 10,000 very temperamental real mites had to be "cast" for a few close-up shots.*

Darnell, Det. Joe (Robyn Driscoll) The assistant to Aubrey, Missouri police detective chief, Lt. Brian Tillman. ("Aubrey")

Da Silva, Dr. Nancy (Felicity Huffman) Civilian toxicologist who accompanied Mulder and Scully and other members of a scientific team investigating the unexplained deaths of Arctic Ice Core Project researchers at Icy Cape, Alaska. Although Dr. Da Silva eventually became infected with the alien ice worms, she was cured when Scully and Dr. Hodge introduced a second worm into her body through one of her ears. ("Ice")

DAT Digital audiotape of the Department of Defense files containing everything the government had compiled about UFOs and extraterrestrials since the 1940s. Lone Gunman Kenneth Soona (a.k.a. The Thinker) hacked into DOD's computer net and stole the top-secret intelligence files, which he then gave to Mulder in the form of a DAT. ("Anasazi")

Davenport, Cpl. Gary T. A member of Green Beret detachment B-11, a special forces squad also known as the "Bloody Sabers" during the Vietnam war. Davenport was reported as killed in action by the U.S. government to maintain its secret policy of denial regarding POWs. ("Unrequited")

Davenport, Renee (Lesley Ewen) Wife of Cpl. Gary Davenport. Believing her husband killed in the Vietnam war, Renee remarried and made a new life for herself. During a 1997 rededication of the Vietnam Veterans Memorial in Washington, D.C., she was approached by Nathaniel Teager, who had served with her husband in Green Beret detachment B-11. Teager, a POW for twenty-five years, informed Renee her husband remained alive in Southeast Asia, and presented his dog tags as proof. Renee was later diagnosed by an ophthalmologist at a Georgetown medical facility with a "floating blind spot," a direct physical result of Teager's ability to effectively hide himself from a person's field of vision. ("Unrequited") *Lesley Ewen played an FBI receptionist in the pilot episode, a federal agent in "Genderbender" and social worker Carina Maywald in "Revelations."*

Davey, Dr. Christopher (Kevin McNulty) Dr. Chester Banton's business partner at Polarity Magnetics. Believing Banton killed during an experiment with dark matter, Dr. Davey closed down the company. Banton, however, was not dead, but transformed into a human black hole whose deadly shadow split molecules into their atomic component. Dr. Davey witnessed Banton's reluctant murder of Richmond police detective Kelly Ryan, and locked Banton into the particle accelerator chamber where the accident first occurred, intending to deliver the "lightning in a bottle" scientist to the government. As Davey phoned his co-conspirators to alert them he had captured Banton, he was shot by Mr. X, who then disintegrated Davey's body in the particle chamber to make Mulder and Scully believe Dr. Banton was finally dead. ("Soft Light") *Actor Kevin McNulty also portrayed FBI Agent Brian Fuller in "Squeeze" and "Apocrypha."*

Davis Correctional Treatment Center Marion, Virginia psychiatric hospital where mental patient and former alien-abductee Duane Barry seized a security guard's gun and took Dr. Del Hakkie hostage. (Duane Barry")

Dawson, Sharon (Sheila Moore) Excelsis Dei convalescent home administrator. Mrs. Dawson, along with Mulder, Scully and nurse Michelle Charters, were engulfed by an aquatic surge when the door of a bathroom filled with water burst open. ("Excelsius Dei")

D.C. Correctional Complex Lorton, Virginia facility where Soviet emigrant John Mostow was incarcerated after his arrest for a series of mutilation murders. Mostow insisted that an evil spirit possessed him during the time period that he allegedly killed seven men. ("Grotesque")

D.C. General Hospital Medical facility in Washington, D.C. where Melissa Scully was taken after she was mistaken for her sister and shot by Alex Krycek and Luis Cardinal. Although Native American Albert Hosteen prayed over the comatose Melissa, she later died in the hospital. Assistant Director Skinner was ambushed and beaten in the facility's stairwell after pursuing the ominous Blue-Suited Man, who had been seen pacing outside of Melissa's room ("Paper Clip"). Dana Scully was treated at the hospital as an outpatient after experiencing a nosebleed, a sporadic manifestation of her inoperable brain tumor ("Elegy").

Dead Alien! Truth or Humbug? "Alien autopsy" video filmed by Blaine Faulkner, a science-fiction nut, and hosted by publicity-hungry TV psychic The Stupendous Yappi. Scully noted that the video was edited so as to obscure the fact that the gray-skinned extraterrestrial was in reality an Air Force officer in a costume. ("Jose Chung's 'From Outer Space'")

Dead Man's Hand Clyde Bruckman was dealt this hand of aces and eights during his poker game with Scully while she was guarding him in his room at the Le Damfino Hotel. This was the hand of cards that Sheriff "Wild Bill" Hickok was holding when he was shot in the back in Deadwood, South Dakota. Wild Bill was only holding two pair, though, whereas Clyde Bruckman had a full house of three aces and a pair of eights. ("Clyde Bruckman's Final Repose") *Interestingly, it is said that carrying a real dead man's hand will ensure a restful night's sleep.*

Death Card A playing card with a memento mori on the back, it was used by American soldiers in Vietnam to mark their kills. Nathaniel Teager, a former POW who attempted to carry out death sentences against the military brass that abandoned him in Vietnam, left the cards at the murder scenes of each of his victims. A King of Hearts with a skull and bloody sabers as crossbones was found in Lt. Gen. Peter MacDougal's limousine after he was shot in the forehead at close range. A King of Diamonds with the same image on the back was discovered in the Pentagon office where Gen. Jon Steffan was shot to death. Although Major Gen. Benjamin Bloch survived two murder attempts by Teager, the seemingly invisible assassin left a Death Card (an Ace of Clubs with the distinctive memento mori) on the podium from which the general was to deliver the keynote address for the rededication of the Vietnam Veterans Memorial in Washington, D.C. ("Unrequited")

DeBoom, Jay "Boom" (Ryan Reynolds) Comity high school quarterback who eulogized his dead friend, Bruno, allegedly the victim of a satanic cult. The next morning, Boom was found dead, dangling from a cliff in the woods, the third such death in as many months. Although Boom's death was ruled a suicide, he was actually killed by Margi Kleinjan and Terri Roberts, two blonde girls born on the same date and recently the focus of a rare astronomical alignment. At Boom's funeral, Margi and Terri clasped hands and his coffin mysteriously began to smoke. ("Syzygy")

"Deceive Inveigle Obfuscate" An alternate tag line for "The Truth Is Out There," which referred to Mulder and Scully's description of governmental response to allegations of paranormal phenomena in the mysterious disappearances/deaths of a number of African-American men in Philadelphia, Pennsylvania. ("Teliko")

Decker, Tim (Ron Sauve) Security guard at the Hall of Indigenous Peoples in Boston's Museum of Natural History, where the sacred Amaru urn was taken after it was unearthed at an archaeological dig in the Ecuadorian highlands. ("Tesodos Bichos") *The bearded Ron Sauve previously appeared as Ray, the foreman of the sewer treatment plant in "The Host."*

Deep Throat (Jerry Hardin) Mulder's influential secret government contact, an enigmatic man with a past shrouded in lies and deception. When Mulder decided to investigate unusual disappearances of military test pilots at Ellens Air Force Base in Southwest Idaho, the graying, trench-coated Deep Throat confronted the agent in a public rest room, saying he had an interest in Mulder's work and warned him "to leave this case alone" ("Deep Throat"). Named after the Watergate informant, Deep Throat was always elusive, mysterious and sometimes duplicitous, guiding Mulder and Scully into involvement with cases they might have otherwise overlooked, and occasionally diverting their attention from areas which could expose him. Deep Throat advised Mulder on the whereabouts of Eurisko Corporation founder Brad Wilczek ("Ghost in the Machine"); told him that a military operation to retrieve a downed UFO was under way near Townsend, Wisconsin, and countermanded FBI Section Chief McGrath's decision to out Mulder from the Bureau for insubordination ("Fallen Angel"); told Mulder of the top-secret Litchfield eugenics program and the location of Eve 6 at the Whiting Institute for the Criminally Insane ("Eve"); and informed the agent that the government was bargaining with homicidal robber John Barnett to obtain Dr. Ridley's age reversal research ("Young at Heart"). Although it was never clear whether Deep Throat was on the side of truth or conspiracy, he eventually demonstrated his loyalty to his protégé when he insisted on personally making the exchange of an alien fetus for Mulder's life, only to be shot in the process by the Crew-Cut Man ("The Erlenmeyer Flask"). Deep Throat, whose real name and governmental associations were never disclosed, was evidently caught squarely in the middle. While he claimed to have such a "lofty position" that he could get Mulder box seats in any baseball stadium in the country, he also admitted that he jeopardized his life every time they met. He rarely answered a question directly and, when he did, it was always on his own terms. "There are some secrets that should remain secrets," he once said. "Truths that people are just not ready to know." He obviously knew as much about Mulder's work as Mulder did, and admitted to watching him for a long time, appraising his fitness, before entrusting classified information to him. Deep Throat allegedly worked for the CIA in Vietnam and belonged to a covert organization which had been guilty of "heinous acts against man." His most remarkable revelation was that he was one of three men in the world to have not only seen, but killed, an alien, a traumatic experience that haunted him and inspired him to use Mulder as a means of penance. "Through you," he told the agent, "the truth will be known" ("E.B.E."). *In the third season episode "Apocrypha," the pre-credits sequence, set in 1953, showed the young Bill Mulder working with an equally youthful Cigarette-Smoking Man (their relationship had been commented upon as early as "Anasazi") and a third man. Although this character wasn't given a line, evidence suggests this is Deep Throat. The early '70s photos seen in "The Blessing Way/Paper Clip" substantiated that the three men worked together along with Klemper and the Well-Manicured Man. Deep Throat's motivation for assisting and protecting Fox Mulder seemed to be that Fox was the son of an old and trusted friend, and Deep Throat had chosen this as his means of atonement. In "Talitha Cumi," when the shapeshifting alien, Jeremiah Smith, challenged the Cigarette-Smoking Man with his personal demons, the forms he morphed into were Deep Throat and Bill Mulder, the implication being that the ghosts from CSM's past were his two former colleagues and friends, both of whose untimely deaths he was responsible for. Harrison R. Coe played the young Deep Throat character in the pre-credits sequence of "Apocrypha."*

📁 **"Deep Throat"** Written by Chris Carter. Directed by Daniel Sackheim. File number 1X01. *First aired September 17, 1993. Ignoring the warnings of a mysterious and powerful high-ranking government official, Agents Mulder and Scully investigate the disappearance of one of the test pilots at an Area 51-like top-secret Air Force base in southwest Idaho, which ultimately leads to the implication of possible experimentation with UFO technology by the military.* **Classic Sound Bite:** *"Let's just say this case has a distinct smell to it, a certain paranormal bouquet."* **Background Check:** *The microfiched article on Ellens Air Force Base that Scully read from in this episode was authored by a familiar name: Chris Carter.*

"Demons" Written by R.W. Goodwin. Directed by Kim Manners. File number 4X23. *First aired May 11, 1997. Scully fears for her partner's well-being after he suffers a mental blackout while investigating an alien-abductee case and becomes the prime suspect in a brutal double murder.* **Classic Sound Bite:** *"I have those people's blood on my shirt, Scully, and I was missing for two days. I have no recollection of my actions during those two days. There were two rounds discharged from my gun. I have the keys to this house, the keys to their car. Do the words 'Orenthal James Simpson' mean anything to you?"* **Background Check:** *"Demons" was the first X-Files episode written by R.W. "Bob" Goodwin, whose credits for the series included executive producer and director of each season's cliff-hanging finale.*

"Deny Everything" The tag line that replaced "The Truth Is Out There" during the opening credits of "Ascension." One of the show's most often used catch phrases, "Deny Everything" was indicative of the attitudes of Deep Throat, Mr. X, the Cigarette-Smoking Man, and the international consortium of elders known as the Shadowy Syndicate. ("Ascension")

depranil An experimental Alzheimer's drug that acts as an enzyme inhibitor and increases the amount of acetylcholine in the brain. John Grago, the doctor who provided medical attention at the Excelsis Dei convalescent home, told Mulder and Scully that he had been making progress with the facility's Alzheimer's patients using depranil. ("Excelsius Dei")

Desmond Arms Resident Hotel Run-down place of lodging near Washington, D.C. where Jack Willis/Warren Dupre, believing he had been betrayed to the FBI by his brother-in-law, shot him to death at close-range. ("Lazarus")

Diabira, Minister (Zakes Mokae) A diplomat assigned to the Washington, D.C. embassy of the West African country of Burkina Faso. Minister Diabira reluctantly met with Mulder after U.N. operative Maria Covarrubias intervened and spoke to the country's ambassador. In an attempt to protect his diplomatic position, Diabira admitted that he felt compelled to cover-up the death of a businessman whose albino-like body was discovered in the lavatory of a chartered plane from Burkina Faso. Diabira claimed that the real killer was actually one of the mythical Teliko, known in West African folklore as evil spirits of the air who came out at night to suck the life and color out of their victims. ("Teliko") *Minister Diabira was played by renowned South African theatre actor and Tony Award winner Zakes Mokae, who also has appeared in a number of films, including* Outbreak, Vampire in Brooklyn, Waterworld, Body Parts *and* The Serpent and the Rainbow, *which served as a source of inspiration for* The X-Files *episode "Fresh Bones."*

Diamond, Dr. Roger (Gregory Sierra) An expert on wildman myths and Scully's former anthropology professor at her alma mater, the University of Maryland. Dr. Diamond assisted his former student during the X-Files team's investigation of mutilation murders committed by the legendary Jersey Devil man-beast. ("The Jersey Devil") *Gregory Sierra is best remembered as Julio Fuentes on* Sanford and Son, *Det. Sgt. Chano Amenguale on* Barney Miller, *and the original vice-squad commander, Lt. Lou Rodriguez, on* Miami Vice.

Dickens, Dr. James (Dana Gladstone) The fourth of the identical physicians whose photos were E-mailed to Mulder and Scully. The doctor, who worked in Washington, D.C., leapt several stories from his apartment window in suburban Germantown, Maryland upon seeing alleged CIA agent Ambrose Chapel with Mulder and Scully. Miraculously, Dr. Dickens survived and attempted to flee from the pursing Chapel, who had morphed into his true identify of the alien Bounty Hunter. By the time the X-Files team rejoined the chase, the extraterrestrial had morphed back into Chapel, who said that Dickens had escaped to a roof. Scully, however, noticed a green ooze underneath her feet, which ate an acid-like hole through the soles of her shoes, and appeared to have been the remains of Dr. Dickens. ("Colony")

Die, Bug, Die! An insect repellent in great demand in the cockroach-infested town of Miller's Grove, Massachusetts. A panicked mob ransacked a convenience store, emptying the shelves of the bug spray. ("War of the Coprophages")

Die, Flea, Die! Pet shampoo favored by Scully when she bathed Queequeg, her little Pomeranian pooch. ("War of the Coprophages")

die hand die verletzt German for "the hand, the pain." The local Parent-Teachers Committee, an occult group, in Milford Haven, New Hampshire prayed in unison and translated the phrase to mean "His is the hand that wounds" during their ritualistic chanting to "the lord of darkness." ("Die Hand Die Verletzt")

🗁 **"Die Hand Die Verletzt"** Written by Glen Morgan and James Wong. Directed by Kim Manners. File number 2X14. *First aired January 27, 1995. Mulder and Scully travel to a small New Hampshire town to investigate a boy's murder, and find a cult of devil worshippers who have unleashed forces they can no longer control.* **Classic Sound Bite:** *"Did you really think you could summon the Devil, then ask him to behave?"* **Background Check:** *In homage to the San Diego Chargers' AFC appearance in Super Bowl XXIX (to be played two days after the original airing of this episode), writers Glen Morgan and James Wong (avid Chargers fans) changed their names in the opening credits to read: James "Chargers" Wong and Glen "Bolts, Baby" Morgan.*

digitalis A heart stimulant made from the plant of the same name, which can be used as a paralytic drug. The murderous eight-year-old clones, Cindy Reardon and Teena Simmons, used lethal doses of home-grown digitalis extract to kill their "fathers" and eugenics specialist, Dr. Sally Kendrick. The two little girls almost succeeded in murdering Mulder and Scully with the same poison by spiking their sodas. ("Eve")

Dinwiddie County Hospital Medical facility in Virginia where Elizabeth was quarantined after she was fatally infected with a plaguelike illness by the cohort of her escaped convict boyfriend, Paul. ("F. Emasculata")

Dissociative Personality Disorder Also known as Multiple Personality Disorder, an extremely rare psychological illness in which there are two or more distinct personalities or personality states (each with its own relatively enduring pattern of perceiving, relating to, and thinking about the environment and self). At least two of these identities or personality states repeatedly take control of the person's behavior. After Temple of the Seven Stars cult member Melissa Riedal Ephesian suddenly revealed a hidden personality under questioning, Scully concluded that the woman suffered from dissociative personality disorder. ("The Field Where I Died")

Dixon, Sgt. Al (James Leard) Scranton, Pennsylvania police veteran who told Mulder and Scully that he had arrested Rev. Calvin Sistrunk, a local antiabortion activist, as the suspect in the murder of Dr. Landon Price. ("Colony")

Dmitri (Raoul Ganee) Crewman aboard a Russian freighter who was violently pulled into the ship's sewage system when he tried to repair backed-up toilets. His body turned up later as a "John Doe" in the sewers of Newark, New Jersey. When Scully performed an autopsy she discovered a tattoo of Russian cyrillic letters on Dmitri's body, which aided her in identifying the body. ("The Host")

Doane, Josephine (Renae Morriseau) An administrator at the Washington, D.C. Office of the Navajo Nation, who confirmed for Scully that the encrypted Defense Department files were actually written in Navajo, the only "code" the Japanese couldn't break during WWII. Doane was only able to decipher bits and pieces of the sample Scully allowed her to examine, and assisted the agent in contacting former World War II Navajo "code-talker," Albert Hosteen. ("Anasazi") *Actress Renae Morriseau also played Gwen Goodensnake in "Shapes."*

dod kalm Norwegian for "dead calm," which referred to Captain Barclay's description of the Bermuda Triangle-like conditions his "ghost ship," the USS *Ardent,* encountered in the Norwegian Sea: "Everything stopped. Everything. Even the sea. Even the wind." ("Dod Kalm")

📁 **"Dod Kalm"** Written by Howard Gordon and Alex Gansa. Directed by Rob Bowman. File number 2X19. *First aired March 10, 1995. While investigating the disappearance of a U.S. Navy destroyer, Agents Mulder and Scully find themselves in the Norwegian equivalent of the Bermuda Triangle and experience super-accelerated aging while trapped aboard the rusty, soon-to-sink vessel.* **Classic Sound Bite:** *"As certain as I am of this life, we have nothing to fear when it's over."* **Background Check:** *Howard Gordon re-teamed with his former writing partner, Alex Gansa, to pen "Dod Kalm," which saw Mulder and Scully fall victim to the effects of rapid aging. The episode was a source of immense aggravation for Duchovny and Anderson, who spent several extra hours in the makeup chair. In fact, the second season's blooper tape featured a very annoyed Anderson announcing, "Howard Gordon is a dead man!"*

"Doesn't Somebody Want to Be Wanted?" A hit song in the early seventies by teen heartthrob David Cassidy and the first TV family of pop music, The Partridge Family. Kaye Schilling played the song louder and louder to drown out her hallucinating neighbor upstairs, Ed Jerse, who later killed her and dragged her body to the basement incinerator, as the sappy tune played on. ("Never Again")

Dole, Lisa (Sue Matthew) FBI agent specializing in graphology at the Bureau's Seattle, Washington office. She compared the scribbled numbers of retarded janitor, Roland Fuller, with complex mathematical equations on a chalkboard from the Mahan jet propulsion laboratory. ("Roland") *Sue Matthew also played Agent Caleca in "Apocrypha."*

Doll Collector A victim of the Puppet serial killer, who preyed upon fortune-tellers in St. Paul, Minnesota. Although she was a professional doll collector, the woman was also an amateur tasseographer (tea leaf reader), which eventually made her a target of the murderer. Her eyes and intestines were discovered on a table in her living room, which was filled with her doll collection. TV psychic and publicity hound, The Stupendous Yappi, claimed that the Puppet raped her before killing her; Clyde Bruckman, whose true psychic ability was limited to foretelling death, asserted that the Doll Collector initiated sex. ("Clyde Bruckman's Final Repose")

Dominion Tobacco A Raleigh-Durham, North Carolina-based tobacco company. One of the company's executives, Patrick Newirth, became nothing more than a burnt mark on a hotel room floor after Dr. Chester Banton's deadly shadow slipped beneath the door and evaporated him. ("Soft Light")

Dommann Last name of one of Mulder's apartment-house neighbors as seen on the mailbox. ("The Erlenmeyer Flask")

Door Man (Angelo Vacco) A customer of the Brothers K fast-food restaurant in Arlington, Virginia, wounded in the stomach by a deranged shooter when he tried to run out the door. He was miraculously healed by Jeremiah Smith before paramedics arrived. ("Talitha Cumi") X-Files *production assistant Angelo Vacco also played gas station attendant Angelo Garza in "F. Emasculata."*

Dorantes, Maria (Pamela Diaz) Attractive young illegal alien at a migrant workers camp in California's San Joaquin Valley. After flirting with two jealous brothers, Eladio and Soledad Buente, she pursued her escaping goats over a small hill. Suddenly, a bright light exploded out of the sky, followed by a brief but torrential yellow rain. In its aftermath, the mutilated corpses of Maria and one of her goats were discovered. The laborers at the camp were convinced she was killed by Eladio, whom they believed to be the legendary Chupacabra creature. Scully was shocked when she went to the county morgue to examine the woman's remains and found her corpse barely visible beneath mounds of greenish fungi. Mulder believed that the enzyme was alien, and arrived on Earth via space debris, such as a meteorite. ("El Mundo Gira")

Dorland, Robert (Barry Primus) Howard Graves' partner and eventual successor at military contractor HTG Industrial Technologies in Philadelphia. Dorland had his predecessor murdered (in a way that appeared to be a suicide) because he feared Graves was going to expose his illegal arms trade with a Mideast extremist group. Dorland, who attempted to have Graves' loyal secretary, Lauren Kyte, killed, was eventually indicted for Graves' murder and a significant number of federal crimes. ("Shadows")

Dougherty, Mrs. The latest nanny of eight-year-old Michelle Bishop. Mrs. Dougherty was found by the girl's mother mysteriously locked in the basement of the Bishop home after Michelle disappeared. ("Born Again")

Doyle, Sir Arthur Conan Creator of Sherlock Holmes, at whose burial site Mulder and Scotland Yard Inspector Phoebe Green shared a "certain youthful indiscretion" during Mulder's Oxford days. ("Fire")

"D.P.O." The initials of Darin Peter Oswald, the lone survivor of five lightning strikes in Connverville, Oklahoma. While investigating the death of Jack Hammond at a strip-mall video arcade, an onscreen display alerted Mulder that the record-holder on Virtua Fighter 2 was "D.P.O." ("D.P.O.")

📁 **"D.P.O."** Written by Howard Gordon. Directed by Kim Manners. File number 3X03. *First aired October 6, 1995. The X-Files agents travel to a small Oklahoma town to investigate a teenage slacker named Darin Peter Oswald, a human lightning conduit responsible for several deaths.* **Classic Sound Bite:** *"He is lightning and we've got to get to him before he strikes again."* **Background Check:** *Gillian Anderson's stand-in for scene blocking, Bonnie Hay, played the night nurse in this episode. "D.P.O." drew its inspiration from a one-line inspiration card, "Lightning Boy," which had been tacked on a bulletin board in Chris Carter's office since the first season of* The X-Files.

dragon's blood A plant named for its color. The three Romanian elders of the Calusari employed dragon's blood during the exorcism of the evil spirit from nine-year-old Charlie Holvey. ("The Calusari")

Drake, Benjamin (Tom Butler) The chief executive of the Crystal City, Virginia-based high-tech firm, Eurisko, electrocuted in his office rest room after threatening to terminate the Central Operating System (COS), Eurisko founder Brad Wilczek's pet project. ("Ghost in the Machine") *Tom Butler also played CIA Agent Ambrose Chapel in "Colony."*

Draper, Capt. Janet (Nancy Sorel) The military aide to Fort Evanston's General Thomas Callahan. After Capt. Draper informed Mulder and Scully that the general was squashing their inquiry into a "phantom soldier" at the facility's veterans' hospital, Scully threatened to have Draper's superior investigated for obstruction. Capt. Draper, swimming in the officers' gym, was later drowned by an invisible entity that yanked her under the water. The X-Files agents found bruises on her neck and shoulders consistent with a struggle. ("The Walk")

drawstring pants Fashion trend Mulder cited to vampiric serial killer John (The Son) as the reason he didn't want to live forever. ("3")

"DROP DEAD RED" Words scrawled on the fuselage of a submerged North American P-51 Mustang fighter plane discovered on the floor of the Pacific Ocean by the French salvage ship *Piper Maru*. ("Piper Maru") *The inscription "DROP DEAD RED" was an admitted tribute to Gillian Anderson, who has repeatedly been called the "Intellectually Drop Dead Gorgeous Redhead."*

Druce, Frank SEE: **Ranheim**

Druggist (Walter Marsh) Sixty-five-year-old pharmacist in Traverse City, Michigan who took the passport photos of Mary Louise LeFante only moments before she was abducted and her boyfriend murdered by paranoid-schizophrenic Gerry Schnauz. The aged druggist was later attacked when Schnauz returned to the pharmacy to steal the passport camera, all the film in the store, syringes, and a variety of drugs he used to concoct his fast-acting "Twilite Sleep" anethesia. ("Unruhe") *Actor Walter Marsh also played Judge Purdy, whose courtroom filled with locusts during "Miracle Man" Samuel Hartley's bail hearing.*

Druid Hill Sanitarium Baltimore, Maryland mental hospital where liver-eating serial killer Eugene Tooms was institutionalized until a commitment review board discharged him, despite Mulder's warning that he must remain in custody for the safety of the public. ("Tooms")

📁 **"Duane Barry (Part 1 of 2)"** Written by Chris Carter. Directed by Chris Carter. File number 2X05. *First aired October 14, 1994. Former FBI agent Duane Barry, who claims to have been a victim of multiple alien abduction and experimentation, escapes from the mental hospital where he is a patient and takes several people hostage, including Agent Scully.* **Classic Sound Bite:** *"He's bent on taking the doctor with him to an alien abduction site, only he can't quite remember where the site is so he stopped at a travel agency."* **Background Check:** X-Files *music composer Mark Snow considered this episode the hardest to score for the entire series. "It needed like forty-two minutes of music out of* *forty-four. It was almost a joke. Everyone kept saying, 'Stop the music! Enough already!' "*

Dude (Alan Buckley) A teenage drug user in the small town of Miller's Grove, Massachusetts who hacked himself to death with a razor blade after seeing cockroaches burrowing under the skin of his arm. Scully theorized that Dude was suffering from Ekbom's Syndrome, a delusional disorder associated with frequent drug use. ("War of the Coprophages")

Duff, Marcus (Carl Lumbly) A social worker employed by the U.S. Immigration and Naturalization Service (INS) office in Philadelphia. Duff, responsible for most of the casework on immigrants from Africa and the Caribbean, seemingly tried to make life easier for those from his native land. When the seed from a rare species of passion flower indigenous to certain parts of West Africa was discovered during the autopsy of Owen Sanders' body, Mulder and Scully requested Duff check the passenger manifest from a charter flight from Burkino Faso against those who had applied for a permanent resident status or work visa. Duff was later attacked and dragged to an alleyway by Samuel Aboah, a West African immigrant who was actually a Teliko. Despite acute trauma to his pituitary gland, Duff was later discharged from Philadelphia's Mt. Zion Medical Center, and was expected to testify before a grand jury against Aboah, charged with five counts of murder. ("Teliko") *Actor Carl Lumbly is best known as Dr. Miles Hawkins, the superhero star of the short-lived Fox series "M.A.N.T.I.S."*

Dukenfield, Claude The late owner of Uranus Unlimited, an investment firm which sold astrology-based marketing advice. Dukenfield, a strong believer in astrology, was a forty-three-year-old non-smoker, divorced with two kids, with an income of about $87,000 a year. He was murdered by the Puppet serial killer and his body was discovered by Mulder and Scully near a wooded area with the reluctant psychic assistance of Clyde Bruckman, who had sold Dukenfield an insurance policy a few months before his murder. ("Clyde Bruckman's Final Repose") *William Claude Dukenfield was the real name of W.C. Fields, whom Clyde Bruckman directed in numerous short films.*

Dunaway's Pub An upscale Washington, D.C. bar where Mulder told Scully that the military was stonewalling about the disappearance of Col. Robert Budahas, a test pilot assigned to Ellens Air Force Base in Southwest Idaho. The mysterious informant Deep Throat made his initial contact with Mulder when he approached the agent in the bar's rest room and calmly warned him to stay away from the case. ("Deep Throat")

Dungeons and Dragons Action/adventure role-playing game. After an MIB allegedly confiscated sci-fi fanatic Blaine Faulkner's "alien autopsy" videotape and threatened him (as did Mulder allegedly), Faulkner told author Jose Chung, "I didn't spend all those years playing Dungeons and Dragons and not learn a little something about courage." ("Jose Chung's 'From Outer Space' ")

Dunham, Pvt. Harry (Matt Hill) A Marine stationed at the Folkstone Haitian refugee camp, and a friend of Pvt. John McAlpin, a victim of zombification. A nervous Dunham told Mulder and Scully the Marines were caught in the middle of a personal war between the base commander, Col. Jacob Wharton, and a Voodoo priest, Pierre Bauvais. Pvt. Dunham was later found dead in a bloody bathtub in Mulder's room. The agents later learned that the Marine had filed a complaint against Col. Wharton for his brutal and retaliatory treatment of the Haitian refugees. ("Fresh Bones")

Dupre, Warren James (Jason Schombing) A prison guard until his affair with Lula Philips developed into a modern-day Bonnie and Clyde life of violent crime. Their string of bank robberies resulted in the death of seven civilians, including a sixty-five-year-old female teller employed at the Annapolis Savings and Loan. During the robbery of the Maryland Marine Bank, a shotgun-toting Dupre unloaded at FBI agent Jack Willis before Scully downed the homicidal robber with three shots. In the hospital emergency room, Willis survived after much defibrillation, while a dead Dupre reacted to the final two jolts. It was later discovered that Agent Willis had awakened with Dupre's consciousness in his body, an effort on the robber's part to be reunited with his wife, Lula. Dupre eventually died of diabetic complications, a condition which afflicted Willis. ("Lazarus")

Duran, Dave (Travis MacDonald) One of four Crowley High School students who unintentionally summoned a demon to the small New Hampshire town of Milford Haven. Duran borrowed the book *Witch Hunt: A History of the Occult in America* from the school library and, on a trip to the woods with classmate Jerry Stevens and their dates, read an incantation to Satan in an effort to scare the girls and get them drunk. ("Die Hand Die Verletzt")

Dwight (Peter LaCroix) The aerial tram operator at Skyland Mountain in Virginia. He told Mulder and Alex Krycek that, forty-five minutes earlier, he'd sent the fugitive Duane Barry up the back road since the tram recently had its cable refitted and was still untested. Mulder persuaded Dwight to send him up anyway, hoping to beat Barry to the top, but Krycek disposed of the tram operator moments before Mulder reached the summit. ("Ascension") *Peter LaCroix appeared in "E.B.E." as the trucker Ranheim and in "Unrequited" as phantom POW Nathaniel Teager.*

Dyer (Ken Tremblett) One in a group of frightened loggers in a remote Washington State forest who cut down an old-growth tree, freeing prehistoric mites that had been dormant. Running away, Dyer broke his ankle and was soon engulfed by the iridescent "fireflies." ("Darkness Falls") *Ken Tremblett also played an unnamed Washington, D.C. police officer in "Elegy."*

E

"Erlenmeyer Flask"

Earth 2 Short-lived sci-fi television series produced by Stephen Spielberg. The Lone Gunmen invited Mulder to join them as they hopped on the Internet to "nitpick the scientific inaccuracies" of *Earth 2*. ("One Breath")

Eastpoint State Penitentiary Leon County, Florida correctional facility where executed death-row inmate Napoleon "Neech" Manley made good on his promise to return from the dead and kill five people who had wronged him. ("The List")

E.B.E. Extraterrestrial Biological Entity, essentially any lifeform not originating on Earth. ("E.B.E.")

"E.B.E." Written by Glen Morgan and James Wong. Directed by William Graham. File number 1X16. *First aired February 18, 1994. When an Iraqi jet shoots down a UFO, it signals the beginning of an elaborate and sophisticated cover-up to conceal the spacecraft's extraterrestrial survivor in a secret U.S. government facility in Washington State, and Agent Mulder grudgingly realizes there are limits to what even Deep Throat will tell him.* **Classic Sound Bite:** *"Mulder, the truth is out there. But so are the lies."* **Background Check:** *"E.B.E." was the episode in which the Lone Gunmen, the trio of technogeeks and paranoid conspiracy theorists, made their first appearance.*

Eberhardt, Kathy A young female victim of the serial murderer The Slash Killer, who raped her and carved the word SISTER into her chest with a razor. Eberhardt, along with two other women, were murdered in Aubrey, Missouri in 1942. The Slash Killer was never caught. ("Aubrey")

Ecclesiastes 3:19 "A man has no preeminence above a beast; for all is vanity." An Old Testament passage that Mulder and Scully read on a church's marquee at the conclusion of an X-Files investigation involving the possible abduction of zoo animals by alien conservationists. ("Fearful Symmetry")

Eckerle, Dr. Jeff (Raye Birk) President and Chief Science Officer of Alt-Fuels, Inc., an experimental fuel research station in Miller's Grove, Massachusetts. Confronted by Mulder, a crazed Dr. Eckerle pulled a gun on the agent and fired at him, exploding the methane-filled facility. ("War of the Coprophages")

"Eddie the Monkey Man" SEE: **Van Blundht Sr., Edward.**

Edwards Terminal Queensgate, Ohio train station where the Red-Haired Man, a shadowy government assassin, stealthily murdered a Japanese man apparently sent to meet scientist Dr. Zama/Ishimaru. ("Nisei")

Eek the Cat The cartoon series that eight-year-old Cindy Reardon watched while Mulder and Scully questioned her mother, Ellen. ("Eve") *In appreciation, the creators of the popular children's show later depicted Mulder and Scully in cartoon form.*

Ehman, Jerry SETI astronomer at Ohio State University's radiotelescope observatory who discovered a transmission of likely extraterrestrial origin on a computer printout and called it a "Wow!" signal, which is what he scribbled in the margin of the printout. The signal fit the rise-and-fall pattern of an antenna signal perfectly, ruling out the possibility of a fragmented or bounced signal. The director of the observatory concluded that the source was beyond the distance of the moon, and no publicly known Earth satellites were near the position of the signal source. Also, the signal's frequency was near the 1420 MHz hydrogen line, where all radio transmissions are prohibited by international agreement. ("Little Green Men")

"Ei'Aaniigoo 'Ahoot'e" Navajo translation of "The Truth Is Out There," which replaced the usual opening tag line of the second-season finale. ("Anasazi")

"Einstein's Twin Paradox: A New Interpretation" Title of Dana Scully's senior thesis at the University of Maryland. When she was first assigned to the X-Files, Mulder mentioned the paper, and Scully asked somewhat testily if he had bothered to read it. Reassuring her that he had, Mulder said, "It's just that in most of my work the laws of physics rarely seem to apply" ("The X-Files: Pilot"). A few years later, Mulder quoted it to reinforce his theory that an MIT cryobiologist had come back from the future to prevent the development of the technology that made time travel possible ("Synchrony"). *Scully's research paper was referred to as her "senior" thesis in the pilot episode of the series, but in an obvious continuity error, was called her "graduate" thesis in the fourth season episode, "Synchrony."*

Eisenhower Field Air Force installation in Siquannke, Alaska where Mulder was rushed to the military hospital emergency room suffering from extreme hypothermia after being left to die by the alien Bounty Hunter in the Arctic wasteland. Scully convinced doctors at Eisenhower Field that Mulder was suffering from hyperviscosity syndrome, and needed his cold-induced hypometabolic state to live. In her report, Scully stated that blood tests confirmed Mulder's exposure to a mysterious retrovirus, but added that she couldn't accept a paranormal explanation since that would have meant abandoning science. ("Colony/End Game")

Ekbom's Syndrome A delusional disorder associated with drug abuse that causes users to hallucinate insect infestation under their skin. One of a trio of teenagers doing drugs in the small town of Miller's Grove, Massachusetts saw roaches burrowing under his skin and hacked himself to death with a razor blade in an attempt to rid himself of the bugs. Scully theorized that the boy was suffering from Ekbom's Syndrome. ("War of the Coprophages")

Eldridge, USS American Navy destroyer that became the focus of the notorious Philadelphia Experiment, a 1943 secret government project that allegedly succeeded in making the vessel invisible by manipulating wormholes on Earth. ("Dod Kalm")

📁 **"Elegy"** Written by John Shiban. Directed by Jim Charleston. File number 4X22. *First aired May 4, 1997. Mulder and Scully suspect a mentally disturbed man in the murders of several young women whose spirits were seen elsewhere at the moments of their deaths.* **Classic Soundbite:** *"I would have thought that after four years you'd know exactly what that 'look' was."* **Background Check:** *The episode's original title was "Tulpa," which, in Tibetan mystic practice, is a ghostly manifestation of a "thought-form" produced by the mind. Then the title was changed to "Revenant," which is someone who returns after death. Finally, the X-Files creative staff settled on "Elegy," a type of poem or song expressing grief for someone who is dead, or reflecting seriously on a solemn subject.*

Elizabeth (Lynda Boyd) The girlfriend of escaped Cumberland Prison convict Paul, and mother of his baby boy. She was infected with a plaguelike disease by Paul's fellow escapee, Steve. After being arrested and quarantined at Dinwiddie County Hospital, Elizabeth finally admitted to Mulder that her boyfriend had boarded a bus bound for Toronto. ("F. Emasculata") *Lynda Boyd also appeared as Miss Kotchik, the bar patron in "Fire."*

Elizabeth The single mother of a young boy named Scott, who was allegedly abused by Vernon Ephesian, the paranoid, charismatic leader of the Temple of the Seven Stars cult. Under hypnotic regression, Melissa Riedal Ephesian recalled a memory of Elizabeth and Scott, who lived near the sect's rural Tennessee compound. When the mother and her son came to visit one day, Vernon became unnaturally obsessed with the boy and took him away from Elizabeth, claiming that he was one of God's prophets. A heartbroken Elizabeth snuck into the cult's base one night to see her son, bringing Butterfinger candy bars stolen from the kitchen. Vernon caught them together and had his Mighty Men lackeys severely beat her in front of her son. The cult leader then pulled the crying boy by his hair and, after stripping off his pajamas, hit him repeatedly, all the while claiming Scott was "not a child of God," but rather "garbage who should sleep in the trash with the rats." ("The Field Where I Died")

Ellen (Tamsin Kelsey) Scully's best friend and mother of Trent, her godson. When Scully lamented the lack of men in her life, Ellen reminded her that she had previously called Mulder "cute" and asked if he was someone with whom Scully might get romantically involved. ("The Jersey Devil")

Ellens Air Force Base Located in Southwest Idaho, the military installation was a UFO-sighting mecca and allegedly one of six sites where wreckage from the 1947 Roswell UFO crash was stored. Mulder believed the government was testing top-secret aircraft at Ellens using alien flight technology, which explained why Col. Robert Budahas and five other pilots had mysteriously disappeared from the restricted facility since 1963. Ellens Air Force Base was so highly classified, it did not appear on the U.S. Geographical Survey map of Idaho. ("Deep Throat")

Ellicott, Reggie A member of the British Parliament, allegedly killed in a car explosion. Six months later, at the J. Edgar Hoover Building parking garage, Mulder and Scully found a mysterious audiotape in an FBI vehicle, informing them that a similar cassette had triggered the explosion of Ellicott's car. Mulder and Scully thought they were sitting on a bomb, but then Mulder's door opened to reveal attractive Scottland Yard Inspector Phoebe Green, a practical joker and Mulder's lover during his days at Oxford University. ("Fire")

Ellis, James A Memphis, Tennessee victim of the vampiric Trinity Killers, who called themselves The Father, The Son, and The Unholy Spirit. Ellis was the founder of Ellis & Sons clothiers. ("3")

📁 **"El Mundo Gira"** Written by John Shiban. Directed by Tucker Gates. *File number 4X11. First aired January 12, 1997. Mulder and Scully investigate California migrant workers' claims that El Chupacabra, a gray, hairless creature out of Mexican folklore, is responsible for a series of mutilation deaths.* **Classic Sound Bite:** *"Two brothers. One woman. Trouble."* **Background Check:** *El Mundo Gira is Spanish for "the world turns," a play on the title of the popular American soap opera* As the World Turns. *Scully remarked to Mulder that they had become involved in "a Mexican soap opera" during their investigation of a young woman's murder and the Cain-and-Abel blood feud between two brothers. Chris Carter rewrote almost all of John Shiban's script.*

Elvis According to Mulder, the only man ever to successfully fake his own death ("Shadows"). When Scully suggested she and Mulder venture backstage during one of the Miracle Ministry tent revivals, Mulder said, "Hang on. This is the part where they bring out Elvis" ("Miracle Man"). After Scully was kidnapped by psychotic death fetishist, Donnie Pfaster, Mulder commented, "People videotape beatings in darkened streets, they manage to see Elvis in three cities across America every day, but no one saw a pretty woman being forced off the road . . ." ("Irresistible"). As part of a "spiritual journey" to discover something about himself, Mulder toured Graceland, Elvis' estate in Memphis, Tennessee, when the Bureau forced him to use accrued vacation time in 1997 ("Never Again"). During a search of the Peacocks' dilapidated farmhouse, Mulder feigned surprise and disappointment when he found a 1977 edition of the local newspaper, which announced in bold headlines: ELVIS PRESLEY DEAD AT 42 ("Home").

"EMET" Hebrew for "truth." The single word was inscribed on the back of a golem's hand. To destroy the monstrous abomination, its creator, Ariel Luria, had to erase the "e" off the "emet" inscription, leaving the word "met," which is Hebrew for "dead." ("Kaddish")

EmGen Corporation Research facility and laboratory in Gaithersburg, Maryland where Dr. Terrence Berube worked on the Human Genome Project, the front for a secret government experiment conducted on terminal patients using extraterrestrial viruses. ("The Erlenmeyer Flask")

Emil (Seth Green) A teenage boy who secretly entered the grounds of Southwest Idaho's Ellens Air Force Base to neck with his girlfriend, Zoe, and "watch the air show" of two mysterious darting lights in the sky. The young couple helped Mulder infiltrate the base. ("Deep Throat")

Endeavor International Press According to Lone Gunman Frohike's speculative dossier on the life of the Cigarette-Smoking Man, the Pasadena, California-based publishing company sent Raul Bloodworth (CSM's *nom de plume*) a rejection letter in 1991 for another one of his Jack Colquitt action-adventure spy novels. ("Musings of a Cigarette-Smoking Man")

📁 **"End Game (Part 2 of 2)"** Written by Frank Spotnitz. Directed by Rob Bowman. File number 2X17. *First aired February 17, 1995. When the shapeshifting alien Bounty Hunter takes Scully hostage in exchange for Mulder's sister (actually a clone), the agent tracks his nemesis to a surfaced submarine at the Arctic Circle to learn the whereabouts of the real Samantha and engage the extraterrestrial in a final confrontation.* **Classic Sound Bite:** *"The key to winning the war, Mr. Mulder, is knowing which battles to fight."* **Background Check:** *The original draft of the script by Frank Spotnitz contained a few scenes that had to be cut for practical purposes. One involved a confrontation between Mulder and a U.S. Marshal, who the FBI agent believes may be the alien Bounty*

Hunter; in another sequence, Mulder picks up his sister, Samantha, by the side of the road, and then realizes that she's actually the morphing extraterrestrial.

Entertainment Weekly Magazine which Ed Jerse's ill-fated downstairs neighbor used to line the bottom of her birdcage. ("Never Again") *As an in-joke, the caption of the issue was "The Wisest Man in Hollywood" and the cover photo was of* X-Files *producer Bob Goodwin. Actually, he hardly sets foot in Tinseltown, as he is responsible for the day-to-day operations of the television series while they are filming in Vancouver for most of the year.*

Ephesian, Melissa Riedal (Kristen Cloke) One of six wives of Temple of the Seven Stars cult leader Vernon Ephesian. After a member named "Sidney" called the FBI with accusations of child abuse and illegal firearms stockpiling, FBI and BATF agents staged a raid on the cult's Apison, Tennessee compound. Ephesian and his followers were taken into custody on what Assistant Director Skinner called "B.S. charges of possession of dangerous chemicals." With only twenty-four hours to come up with a prosecutable case, Mulder and Scully were assigned to interrogate Ephesian and his wives. Although the cult leader admitted nothing, the withdrawn and openly hostile Melissa revealed a hidden personality, the mysterious Sidney, a gruff male New Yorker who had called the FBI and initiated the eighteen-month investigation into the Temple of the Seven Stars. Scully concluded that the twenty-five-year-old woman was suffering from Dissociative Personality Disorder, but Mulder thought "Sidney" (who was an adult during the Truman presidency) was actually one of Melissa's past lives. When Mulder and Scully returned her to the compound another personality manifested, a disturbed child named Lily. Outside, Melissa shifted into a grieving Civil War nurse named Sarah Kavanaugh who watched her fiancé, Sullivan Biddle, die during a battle on that same field. Even more startling was her revelation that Biddle was one of Mulder's past lives. Mulder requested she undergo regression therapy, which revealed the two had been thwarted lovers during the Civil War. Convinced he and Melissa shared a previous life together, Mulder had himself regressed, which brought to light a series of his past lives: a Jewish wife in the World War II Polish ghetto, with Melissa as his husband, and the Cigarette-Smoking Man as a Gestapo officer ("evil then, evil now"), Samantha as his son, and Scully as his friend and sergeant. Mulder said that souls were reincarnated together over and over again, such as he and his star-crossed lover and soul-mate, Melissa. Although Mulder later played her a tape of her hypnotic regression, Melissa refused to believe she and Mulder had been lovers in previous lives. After Vernon Ephesian and his followers were released from federal custody, he led the cultists in a mass suicide at the Temple of the Seven Stars compound. When Mulder discovered Melissa's body, she was clutching a photograph of Sarah Kavanaugh. ("The Field Where I Died") *Actress Kristen Cloke was formerly a cast regular on writers Glen Morgan and James Wong's short-lived Fox series,* Space: Above and Beyond *as Capt. Shane Vansen.*

Ephesian, Vernon (Michael Massee) A paranoid, charismatic sociopath, whose real name was Vernon Warren. As the leader of the apocalyptic cult, the Temple of the Seven Stars, Ephesian preached reincarnation and used his knowledge of the Bible to brainwash his followers. Mulder and Scully were assigned by FBI Assistant Director Skinner to investigate claims of Ephesian's channeling and astral projection. Fearing another Waco or Jonestown, the BATF and FBI led a joint raid on the cult's compound in Apison, Tennessee. During interrogation, the cult leader denied accusations of child abuse and weapons stockpiling, and claimed he had known of the coming raid for nine centuries. Ephesian's lawyers had him, his six wives, and his followers released within twenty-four hours after they were taken into federal custody. Believing the FBI and BATF agents were the armies of the Devil prophesied in St. John's Book of Revelation, Ephesian led his fanatical assemblage in a mass suicide, believing they would achieve "life forevermore." ("The Field Where I Died.") *The character of Vernon Ephesian was based upon Waco cult leader, David Koresh, whose real name was Vernon Howell.*

"E Pur Si Muove" Latin phrase meaning "and yet it moves," which replaced "The Truth Is Out There" at the beginning of the fourth season episode "Terma." Galileo supposedly uttered the words after being forced to renounce his ideas by the Inquisition. Scully faced her own ecclesiastic tribunal when she appeared before the Senate Select Subcommittee on Intelligence and Terrorism, which was more concerned with asking "the wrong question" because the senators didn't "want the right answer." ("Terma")

ergot A parasite that lives in rye and related grasses. An ergot alkaloid in Ed Jerse's blood caused him to experience auditory and visual hallucinations. Philadelphia tattoo artist and Russian immigrant, Comrade Svo, used rye containing ergo in his ink. Svo tattooed a Betty Page-like design on Jerse's right arm. ("Never Again") *Ergot is actually not a parasite, but a mold that grows on rye bread. Used now in medication for migraine headaches, the Salem witch trials and mass hysteria are thought by some to be the result of hallucinations caused by contaminated rye bread.*

Erikson Chief seismologist of the Cascade Volcano Research Team, whose body was discovered by the exploration robot, Firewalker. ("Firewalker")

"Erlenmeyer Flask, The" Written by Chris Carter. Directed by R.W. Goodwin. File number 1X23. *First aired May 13, 1994. The mysterious drowning of a wounded fugitive in a Maryland harbor, and a tip from Deep Throat lead Agents Mulder and Scully to the discovery of a supersecret government genetics project involving extraterrestrial DNA and terminally ill human guinea pigs. This episode, the last of the first season, marked the assassination of Deep Throat and the closing of the X-Files division.* **Classic Sound Bite:** *"The man we met yesterday kept this place looking like he was waiting for the people from*

Good Housekeeping *to show up. I would never have pegged him as one to do all this—or do a Greg Louganis out the window."* **Background Check:** *Nervous Fox executives considered the shocking season finale "unacceptable." The network told producer Glen Morgan, "We will not air it because people will believe the show's been canceled." Morgan told them, "It's your job to let them know it hasn't, and this is the best way to end the season."*

Escalante (Colin Cunningham) One of the strange-looking humanoid creatures, his skin horribly deformed, who escaped mass execution by soldiers at the seemingly abandoned Hansen's Disease Research Facility in Perkey, West Virginia. Escalante, along with a few others, were discovered by Scully hiding beneath a trapdoor. Acting as spokesperson for the group, Escalante told her they had lived at the research facility for most of their lives, among the last to contract leprosy before treatment was developed. ("731") *Colin Cunningham also played Lt. Wilmer in "End Game" and Dr. Stroman in "Wetwired."*

Estrada, Erik Spanish soap opera heartthrob and former co-star of *CHiPs* police drama on American television. When he was taken into custody at the INS Processing Center in Fresno, California, illegal alien and California migrant worker, Eladio Buente, claimed that his name was Erik Estrada. ("El Mundo Gira")

Eubanks, Walter (Ken Ryan) Special Agent in charge of the investigation surrounding the kidnapping of Amy Jacobs, a fifteen-year-old Seattle girl abducted from her bedroom. Eubanks was skeptical when Mulder suggested there was an empathic link between the girl and waitress Lucy Householder, a former kidnap victim who had the ability to feel what Amy Jacobs felt. ("Oubliette")

Eurisko The Crystal City, Virginia-based high-tech firm which developed the "learning machine," a prototype artificial intelligence (AI) program in the form of the supercomputer Central Operating System (COS). Brad Wilczek founded Eurisko at age twenty-one in his parents' garage, after having spent years following the Grateful Dead in concert. According to Wilczek, Eurisko was Greek for "I discover things." ("Ghost in the Machine") *Eurisko is the name of a famous Stanford artificial intelligence program, which has won a war game contest by beating all human opponents.*

📁 **"Eve"** Written by Kenneth Biller and Chris Brancato. Directed by Fred Gerber. File number 1X10. *First aired December 10, 1993. Thousands of miles apart, two men are killed simultaneously in the same bizarre manner by their eight-year-old daughters, who are identical copies of each other. The evidence points to a government-funded cloning project attempting to create super-intelligent children, but gone horribly awry.* **Classic Sound Bite:** *"Mulder, why would*

alien beings travel light-years to Earth in order to play 'doctor' on cattle?"
Background Check: *Although the Vancouver twins, Erika and Sabrina Krievins, were used to portray the Teena and Cindy clones, producer R.W. Goodwin originally planned to cast one young actress in the role and then film photo double and split screen. There were so many scenes in which both characters were together that the idea proved logistically impossible and too expensive. Teena and Cindy were named after the wives of X-Files producers and writers, Glen Morgan and James Wong*

Eve 6 (Harriet Harris) An extremely intelligent but criminally insane product of the Litchfield Project, a top-secret 1950s eugenics program that created identical little boys named Adam and girls named Eve. Eve 6, a dead ringer for Dr. Sally Kendrick, who was fired from a clinic for experimenting with human genetic characteristics, had been confined in a straitjacket in Cellblock Z of the Whiting Institute since 1983. Eve 6 revealed to Mulder and Scully that the only remaining, suicide-prone Eves were her and two others, Eve 7 (who escaped as a child), and Eve 8 (who escaped ten years earlier). Each Eve had extra chromosomes, according to Eve 6, giving them heightened strength and intelligence, but also psychosis. ("Eve")

Eve 8 (Harriet Harris) The last surviving child from the Litchfield eugenics experiments. Eve 8 escaped imprisonment in 1985 and assumed the identity of Alicia Hughes, a doctor with a high-level Pentagon clearance. ("Eve")

"Everything Dies" The credo which replaced the usual tag line at the beginning of the fourth season premiere episode "Herrenvolk." Also the alien Bounty Hunter's reply to Mulder after the agent begged him not to kill Jeremiah Smith and the Samantha clone. ("Herrenvolk")

Examiner, The Newspaper that reported the execution-style slaying of Kenneth J. Soona (a.k.a. The Thinker), the computer hacker who first accessed the MJ files and gave Mulder the DAT. The Lone Gunmen's Frohike showed Scully *The Examiner* article when he appeared at her apartment, having heard of Mulder's apparent death in a buried boxcar in New Mexico. ("The Blessing Way")

Excelsis Dei. A Worcester, Massachusetts convalescent home and site of bizarre deaths committed by an invisible entity. ("Excelsius Dei") *The episode title was spelled differently from that of the nursing home as shown onscreen.*

excelsius dei Latin phrase meaning "glory of God." ("Excelsius Dei")

📁 **"Excelsius Dei"** Written by Paul Brown. Directed by Stephen Surjik. File number 2X11. *First aired December 16, 1994. When a nurse is raped by an invisible entity at a nursing home, Mulder and Scully uncover a drug treatment* that awakens vegetative Alzheimer's sufferers, as well as the spirits of previous patients. **Classic Sound Bite:** *"I've got plumbing older than this building, and it don't work much better, either."* **Background Check:** *Paul Brown's script was in "really bad shape," according to producer James Wong, forcing Chris Carter to re-write it until literally the last minute, even while the episode was being filmed.*

Exorcist, The Horror movie about a young girl's possession by a demon, and two Roman Catholic priests' attempts to perform a ritual exorcism. The 70's film was one of Scully's favorites. ("E.B.E.")

F

Flukeman

"Face on Mars" A Martian geological formation resembling a human face turned skyward, revealed in photos taken by an American *Viking* orbiter in 1977. *Gemini 8* crewmember Lt. Col. Marcus Belt had flashbacks of a spacewalk where he saw the sculpted "Face on Mars" looking down on him. Years later, as head of the *Viking* space shuttle program, Belt denied that the giant sculpted face was anything more than an optical illusion created by erosion. However, he knew this not to be true: while walking in space during the *Gemini 8* mission, he was possessed by an alien entity, somehow related to the face, that controlled him ever since, forcing him to sabotage the space shuttle program. ("Space") *In later episodes, a photo of the famous "Face on Mars" can be seen on the bulletin board to the right of Mulder's "I WANT TO BELIEVE" UFO poster.*

Faciphaga emasculata A tropical insect discovered by Dr. Robert Torrence in a Costa Rican rain forest. Pinck Pharmaceuticals, which was financing research on new tropical species, was interested in the bug because it secreted a dilating enzyme, but the drug manufacturer was unaware it was the vector for a parasite which attacked the immune system, usually causing death in thirty-six hours. The disease was transmitted via erupting pustules that contained the insect larvae. An outbreak of the plaguelike infection was responsible for the deaths of eighteen people, mostly prisoners at Virginia's Cumberland State Correctional Facility, which was covered up by Pinck with the cooperation and assistance of the government. ("F. Emasculata")

Fairfax Mercy Hospital The medical facility in Virginia where Robert "Pusher" Modell obtained his refills for the prescription drug tegretol, which prevented seizures caused by epilepsy. Scully found a bottle of tegretol in Modell's medicine cabinet and traced it to the Hospital, where, during a final confrontation, Modell forced Mulder to play Russian roulette. ("Pusher")

Fairfield County Social Services Hostel Where eight-year-old Teena Simmons was temporarily housed in Greenwich, Connecticut after the bizarre murder of her father. Teena was later abducted from the hostel. ("Eve")

Fairfield Zoo An impoverished zoo in Fairfield, Idaho, known for its mysterious animal disappearances. Located near Mountain Home Air Base, a

"UFO hotspot," no inhabitant of the zoo had ever brought a pregnancy to term. Mulder theorized that the animals were being abducted by extraterrestrials and artificially inseminated, and that the embryos were harvested before they were returned to the zoo. ("Fearful Symmetry")

Fairly, Judy (Stacy Grant) An employee of Lorraine Kelleher, who operated a Washington, D.C. Georgetown escort service. After the madam's murder, Fairly helped Mulder and Scully trap the killer at the Ambassador Hotel. ("Avatar")

Faith Today The Jehovah Witness publication that Hannah left with Ed Jerse after he began ranting and raving about his neighbor downstairs. The magazine's front cover read "Are you a failure?" which spurred the taunting voice of Jerse's "Betty" tattoo to continue her litany of derogatory names for the hallucinating man. ("Never Again")

Fallen Angel Military term for a downed alien spacecraft and/or its occupant. Air Force "reclamations" expert, Col. Calvin Henderson of the U.S. Space Surveillance Center, used the code to describe a crashed UFO near Townsend, Wisconsin's Lake Michigan. ("Fallen Angel")

🗁 **"Fallen Angel"** *Written by Alex Gansa and Howard Gordon. Directed by Larry Shaw. File number 1X09. First aired November 19, 1993. The mysterious informant, Deep Throat, directs Agent Mulder to a government cover-up involving a crashed alien spacecraft near a small town in Wisconsin. Mulder risks his career to prove the existence of a top-secret UFO clean-up team and intercepts a holographic alien on the run from the U.S. military.* **Classic Sound Bite:** *"No one, no government agency, has jurisdiction over the truth."* **Background Check:** *The* Predator-*like image of a wavily semi-invisible alien was created by using a dancer in "an orange-colored, humped-back, big-headed, webbed-armed, pointy-butted outfit" on film, which special effects wizard Mat Beck later morphed and distorted in postproduction.*

Farraday, Dr. Paul (Timothy Webber) Research biologist who complained about the rapid extinction of a rare type of amphibian in Striker's Cove on Heuvelman's Lake. After a series of deaths were linked to Big Blue, a Loch Ness-like monster, Mulder theorized that depletion of the frog supply would force an aquatic dinosaur to seek an alternative food source, such as human beings. ("Quagmire") *Dr. Faraday was named for chemist and physicist Michael Faraday, who discovered the principle of electromagnetic induction, the basis for generating electric power. Actor Timothy Webber also appeared in "Tooms" as Det. Talbot and in "Our Town" as Jess Harold.*

Father, The (Gustavo Moreno) An older man, one of the vampiric trio of serial murderers known as The Trinity Killers. He was stabbed by Kristen Kilar, who then burned his body in a house fire. ("3")

Faulkner, Blaine (Allan Zinyk) A Klass County, Washington science-fiction buff in his late twenties who always dreamt of being captured by an extraterrestrial. He was interviewed by author Jose Chung while investigating the alleged abduction of two teenagers, which served as the basis for his latest book, a "nonfiction science-fiction" tome titled *From Outer Space*. Blaine found a dead alien in a field and shot footage of the autopsy, which turned out to be nothing more than an Air Force officer in a costume. ("Jose Chung's 'From Outer Space'") *Blaine Faulkner's Space: Above and Beyond T-shirt was an in-joke reference by episode writer Darin Morgan to his brother, Glen, the former* X-Files *executive producer and writer who, along with James Wong, had left the series during the previous season to create and produce the short-lived Fox space saga.*

Fazekas, Michael (Eric Breker) Admitting officer at the Providence, Rhode Island police station. Fazekas had been remanded from his "beat assignment" to a desk job a year earlier after his former partner complained on a number of occasions of his tendency toward extreme irritability and confabulation of the truth. Det. Curtis told Scully that Officer Fazekas had become something of a "joke," after acknowledging publicly that he believed in the existence of extraterrestrials and UFOs. After fatally shooting himself in the head at the police station, Scully discovered a puncture wound at the top of his frontal lobe, along the hairline, leading to the discovery that he had been treated by Dr. Charles Goldstein, a Warwick, Rhode Island psychiatrist who used an aggressive and unconventional therapy to stimulate electrical impulses in the brain and access repressed memories. ("Demons") *Eric Breker also played an ambulance driver in "Apocrypha."*

📁 **"Fearful Symmetry"** Written by Steven DeJarnatt. Directed by James Whitmore, Jr. File number 2X18. *First aired February 24, 1995. Agents Mulder and Scully investigate whether aliens have been abducting and impregnating animals from an Idaho zoo in an effort to create an extraterrestrial version of Noah's Ark.* **Classic Sound Bite:** *"In the simple words of a creature whose own future is uncertain, will man save man?"* **Background Check:** *The episode's title refers to the classic poem, "The Tyger," by William Blake: "Tyger! Tyger! Burning bright/In the forests of the night/What immortal hand or eye/Could frame thy fearful symmetry?"*

Federal Command Center Located in Chattanooga, Tennessee, the field operations command post served as the central coordinating location for the combined raid led by agents of the FBI and BATF on the Temple of the Seven Stars compound. When no evidence of "enough weapons to beat the Korean army" was found, the supervisor for the joint effort, FBI Assistant Director Walter Skinner, ordered federal agents to continue searching for a cache of illegal firearms at the cult's rural compound. ("The Field Where I Died")

Federal Correctional Facility Detention center in New York City. Terry Edward Mayhew, the leader of an extreme right-wing militia, was kept there pending trial after he and his group were arrested in Flushing, Queens for planning an explosive strike similar in size and damage to the Oklahoma City bombing. ("Tunguska/Terma")

Feejee Mermaid A legendary "humbug" that showman P.T. Barnum pulled in the nineteenth century with a mummified monkey sewn onto the tail of a salmon. The hoax that Barnum once described as "an ugly, dried-up, black-looking, and diminutive specimen," is now enduringly ensconced in the Museum of the Circus in Florida. Mulder inquired about an illustration of the Feejee Mermaid on the menu border in Phil's Diner in Gibsonton, Florida, a retirement community populated by former circus and sideshow artists. Mulder was intrigued by the description of the Feejee Mermaid because the killer in several murders across the U.S. had left simian tracks at the crime scenes. ("Humbug")

Felder, Leon (Richard Sali) Former cop and insurance salesman with Buffalo Mutual Life who conspired with police detectives Ruby Barbala and Tony Fiore in a $2 million-plus larcenous scam which resulted in the murder of another policeman. Felder was killed when his scarf became entangled in a bus' rear doors and he was dragged to his death. ("Born Again")

🗁 **"F. Emasculata"** Written by Chris Carter and Howard Gordon. Directed by Rob Bowman. File number 2X22. *First aired April 28, 1995. While pursuing two escaped convicts, Agents Mulder and Scully discover a highly contagious and deadly disease which has infected some of the prison population and, quite possibly, the escapees as well, escalating the risk of a nationwide outbreak.* **Classic Sound Bite:** *"The truth would have caused panic. Panic would have cost lives. We control the disease by controlling the information."* **Background Check:** *The numbers game continues on a grand scale in "F. Emasculata." The package mailed to convict Bobby Torrence is #DDP112148 (Chris Carter's wife, Dori Pierson, and her birthday); the house number of Elizabeth, the girlfriend of escaped prisoner, Paul, is 925 (9/25/94 is the birthdate of Gillian Anderson's daughter, Piper Maru); and the young boy buys his bus ticket at 9:25.*

Fenig, Max (Scott Bellis) Hapless UFO-conspiracy theorist who met Mulder while imprisoned in a makeshift brig by "reclamations" expert Col. Calvin Henderson during Operation Falcon. A member of NICAP (the National Investigative Committee of Aerial Phenomena), Fenig told Mulder that he had followed his career through his public-record travel expenses, saw the agent's photo in a trade magazine, and even read Mulder's UFO article on the Gulf Breeze Sightings (which he penned under the pseudonym M.F. Luder). Fenig, a sort of precursor to the Lone Gunmen, traveled the country in an Airstream camper-trailer equipped with a variety of high-tech surveillance electronics. When Fenig had an epileptic seizure, Mulder noticed a V-shaped incision scar behind his ear, the same type that Mulder had previously seen in alien-abductee photographs of two women. Pursuing Fenig to a waterfront warehouse, Mulder discovered Fenig suspended in the air like a rag doll before he was abducted once again in a burst of bright light. During a committee hearing of the Office of Professional Responsibility, Mulder was informed that Fenig's body had allegedly been discovered in a cargo container two hours after his disappearance ("Fallen Angel"). Almost four years later, a woman who identified herself as Max's sister approached Mulder and Scully stating that Fenig had died in an airliner crash in Upstate New York two hours earlier. She claimed it was Fenig's wish that the agents be sought out should any harm befall him. Mulder discovered his body, which had been exposed to extreme radiation, amongst the aircraft's debris field. Scully speculated that Fenig had been illegally transporting dangerous radioactive material after learning that Fenig (using one of his many aliases) had been employed at a Colorado environmental energy site, which handled and stored uranium 235 and weapons-grade plutonium. The agents searched his Airstream camper at a trailer park in Barnes Corners, New York, and found a videotape in which Fenig claimed that high-ranking members of the military-industrial community had recovered UFOs and were using the salvaged alien technology. Fenig also stated that he possessed irrefutable proof to back up his assertion. Mulder theorized that Fenig was carrying an alien energy source when his commercial jet was intercepted by a UFO and crashed. Fenig, a multiple alien-abductee most of his life, claimed on his videotape that all he ever wanted in life was "to be left alone." ("Tempus Fugit/Max")

Festival of the Hungry Ghosts Chinese celebration which San Francisco detective Glen Chao suspected might be associated with the death of an immigrant burned alive inside a crematorium oven. Chinese characters meaning "ghost" were discovered scratched inside the oven, and burnt paper, (identified as "hell money") used to pay off spirits during the Festival of the Hungry Ghosts, was also found at the crime scene. ("Hell Money")

Ficicello Frozen Foods Minneapolis company that hired death fetishist Donnie Pfaster as a delivery person after he was fired from the Janelli-Heller Funeral Home for cutting the locks off a young female corpse. ("Irresistible")

Fiebling, Mr. (Tim Progosh) A teacher of the night school course "Intro to Mythology and Comparative Religion" at Minneapolis' Los Cerritos Adult Education. Donnie Pfaster, described by Mulder as an escalating death fetishist, fixated on a female student in Mr. Fiebling's class. ("Irresistible")

📁 **"Field Where I Died, The"** Written by Glen Morgan and James Wong. Directed by Rob Bowman. File number 4X05. *First aired November 3, 1996.*

Fearing another Waco or Jonestown tragedy, agents of the Bureau of Alcohol, Tobacco and Firearms and the FBI lead a joint raid on the compound of a Tennessee-based doomsday cult. In the process, one of the charismatic sect-leader's six wives claims she and Mulder shared past lives together in which they were lovers. **Classic Sound Bite:** *"I wouldn't change a thing. Well, maybe that flukeman thing. I could've lived without that just fine."* **Background Check:** *The tragic love story of Civil War nurse Sarah Kavanaugh and her fiancé Sullivan Biddle was meant to recall the real life account of a soldier named Sullivan Ballou who wrote a now-famous and very poignant farewell letter to his wife, Sarah, in which he assured her that his love for her was "deathless" and he would always be with her. One week after writing the letter, Ballou was killed in the First Battle of Bull Run.*

50 Greatest Conspiracies of All Times, The A book authored by Jonathan Vankin and John Whalen and read by Kenneth Soona (a.k.a. the Thinker), a fourth member of the Lone Gunmen, shortly before he was murdered for hacking into the Defense Department's extremely sensitive MJ Files. ("Anasazi")

Findley, Rev. Patrick (R. Lee Ermey) One of eleven "false prophets" murdered by demonic industrialist Simon "Millennium Man" Gates during a three-year period. Rev. Findley used ketchup to make his palms appear as if they were spontaneously bleeding during a sermon to his Pennsylvania church congregation. ("Revelations") *R. Lee Ermey, a former Marine drill sergeant and now an acclaimed character actor, has appeared in numerous TV series and motion pictures, including* Full Metal Jacket, Mississippi Burning, Fletch Lives, Somersby, On Deadly Ground, Seven *and* Murder in the First. *He also lent his voice to the toy soldier, Sarge, in the hugely successful* Toy Story.

Fingers, Dr. (Alex Diakun) The hypnotist who induced a trance state in teenager Chrissy Giorgio in an effort to help her recall what really transpired on the night she and her date, Harold Lamb, disappeared and alleged they were abducted by aliens. ("Jose Chung's 'From Outer Space' ") *Actor Alex Diakun, a personal favorite of X-Files writer Darin Morgan, also appeared as the Curator in "Humbug" and a doomed tarot dealer in "Clyde Bruckman's Final Repose."*

Fiore, Anita (Mimi Lieber) The wife of Buffalo police detective Tony Fiore, and the widow of his partner, Charlie Morris. Anita dissuaded little Michelle Bishop, the reincarnated spirit of her murdered husband, from killing Tony with her psychokinetic powers. ("Born Again") *Mimi Lieber's film credits include* Corrina, Corrina, Wilder Napalm, *and* Night Shift.

Fiore, Tony (Brian Markinson) A Buffalo, New York police detective and former partner of Charlie Morris. Fiore, who had married Morris' widow, admitted to complicity in his partner's murder after the dead cop's reincarnated spirit, in the form of eight-year-old Michelle Bishop, attempted to kill him. Fiore later pled guilty in Federal Court to first-degree murder after the fact, grand larceny, and obstructing justice. ("Born Again")

📁 **"Fire"** Written by Chris Carter. Directed by Larry Shaw. File number 1X11. *First aired December 17, 1993. The investigation into a sadistic, pyrokinetic serial killer gets very hot indeed when Agent Mulder is asked to help an old flame, a Scotland Yard detective, protect a visiting member of the British Parliament in New England.* **Classic Sound Bite:** *"That's one of the luxuries of hunting down aliens and genetic mutants. You rarely get to press charges."* **Background Check:** *Scotland Yard Inspector Phoebe Green was originally intended by Chris Carter to be a recurring role, but the chemistry "didn't work as it might" between actress Amanda Pays and David Duchovny and the idea was dropped after the episode was filmed.*

Firewalker A robotic explorer used for descending deep into the earth's core. Invented by Daniel Trepkos, the survey device looked like a large titanium bug and was capable of transmitting video images of its fiery surroundings while working inside a volcano such as Mt. Avalon in Washington state. (Firewalker")

📁 **"Firewalker"** Written by Howard Gordon. Directed by David Nutter. File number 2X09. *First aired November 18, 1994. Reunited after Assistant Director Skinner reopened the X-Files, Agents Mulder and Scully are flown to an erupting volcano in the Pacific Northwest to investigate a scientific research team whose discovery of a silicon-based parasitic lifeform with the ability to survive the volcanic temperatures is causing a series of mysterious deaths.* **Classic Sound Bite:** *"You still believe you can petition heaven to get some penetrating answer. If you found that answer, what would you do with it?"* **Background Check:** *The episode was jokingly referred to as "Icewalker" on the set because of its obvious similarities to first season's "Ice," with both storylines centering around an ancient parasitic organism.*

First Church of the Redemption Protestant house of worship in Waynesburg, Pennsylvania, where Rev. Patrick Findley delivered a sermon on miracles and faked stigmatic bleeding from his palms. After the service, the reverend was murdered by the Millennium Man for being a "false prophet." ("Revelations")

1st Elder (Don S. Williams) A high-ranking member of the conspiratorial Shadowy Syndicate, the cabal of mysterious power-brokers representing "global interests" that convenes at a private, smoke-filled club on 46th Street in New York City. At a meeting with the Cigarette-Smoking Man to discuss the stolen MJ documents and whether "forty years of work" had been compromised, the heavyset 1st Elder inquired about "the Mulder problem" and CSM assured him that Agent Mulder was "dead and his body would not be recovered." The 1st Elder replied that "all pertinent parties should be informed, that we may continue with our work" ("The Blessing Way"). He also described the accidental shooting of Melissa Scully by the Cigarette-Smoking Man's lackeys as "a serious mistake" and cautioned him about the repercussions of an innocent woman being shot ("Paper Clip"). While investigating the seemingly deserted Hansen's Disease Research Facility in Perkey, West Virginia, Scully was met by the 1st Elder, who said that the alien-looking creatures at the facility were, in fact, human subjects that had become "victims of an inhuman project" by Dr. Zama, a.k.a. Ishimaru. He told Scully that Zama, working on his own agenda, had conducted radiation tests on lepers, the homeless, and the insane ("731"). The 1st Elder called an emergency meeting of the Shadowy Syndicate after the group received "disturbing reports" that the French salvage ship, *Piper Maru,* had limped into port in San Diego with its crew dying of radiation sickness. The 1st Elder informed the group that the ship's last given position was the site of a recovered downed UFO. Furthermore, he told his associates that the Cigarette-Smoking Man had responded in a way that none of them would have anticipated and had requested CSM to come to New York and explain this situation himself. At the subsequent meeting, the 1st Elder chastised the Cigarette-Smoking Man for acting unilaterally and moving the salvaged UFO to another location ("Apocrypha"). After setting a trap to test Mr. X's loyalty to the group, the 1st Elder and CSM identified X as Mulder's shadowy informant and ordered him ambushed and shot by the Gray-Haired Man ("Herrenvolk"). The 1st Elder questioned the Cigarette-Smoking Man several months later about the "trial run" of The Project's deadly strain of bees, which were possibly intended as an agent to introduce alien DNA to humanity at large. ("Zero Sum")

First Nations Bank of Virginia Financial institution in Desmond, Virginia whose building was adjacent to police headquarters. The bank's parking lot surveillance camera captured a blurry image of Skinner (impersonating Agent Mulder) talking to Det. Ray Thomas shortly before he was murdered execution-style. ("Zero Sum")

Flackert, Jennifer One of serial killer Virgil Incanto's forty-seven victims. ("2Shy")

Flakita (Lillian Hurst) A nosy neighbor and busybody in a migrant workers' shantytown in California's San Joaquin Valley. She discovered the mutilated corpse of Maria Dorantes, who she believed was killed by a mythical Mexican creature. Flakita later hid in her shack when she believed gray aliens, whom she called Chupacabras, descended on the camp. In reality, the "creatures" were members of a hazmat team sent to establish a perimeter around the area and contain a biological hazard of frightening proportions. ("El Mundo Gira")

Flight Attendant (Maxine Guess) Stewardess who found the pigment-depleted corpse of the Businessman in the lavatory of a charter flight from the West African country of Burkino Faso to the United States. ("Teliko")

Flight 549 A relatively new commercial airliner which hit the ground at three hundred miles per hour in an almost vertical descent in a wooded area thirty miles from Albany, New York. Of its 134 passengers and crew, there was one survivor. Although the official version of the crash was the "human error" of military air traffic controllers, which resulted in a mid-air collision or catastrophic near-miss, Mulder theorized that UFOlogist Max Fenig boarded the plane carrying physical proof of the existence of extraterrestrial life, possibly cold fusion. A government operative followed him aboard the aircraft, intending to obtain the alien energy source, but before the assassin could carry out his plan, Flight 549 was intercepted by an alien spacecraft. As the UFO began to abduct Fenig through the emergency exit door next to his seat, flight controllers ordered a military jet into 549's airspace on a mission to destroy the spacecraft. When the Air Force shot down the UFO, Flight 549, which was caught in its "tractor beam," spun out of control and crashed. ("Tempus Fugit/Max") *A mock-up of a Boeing 737 cabin was constructed from scratch and made to shake so violently that the cameramen were forced to wear protective helmets. A few of the eighty extras playing passengers even got motion sickness.*

Floyd, Ray (Charles Andre) Construction worker on a federally funded project in Fairfield, Idaho who was knocked down and trampled to death by an invisible behemoth rampaging down the road. During Mulder and Scully's investigation into his death, they discovered that Floyd's spine had been crushed and there was a circular abrasion on his chest roughly resembling an elephant's foot. ("Fearful Symmetry")

Flukeman (Darin Morgan) A quasi-vertebrate human born "in a primordial soup of radioactive sewage." The mutant was discovered in a Newark, New Jersey sewer after being flushed out to sea from a decommissioned Russian freighter hauling salvage from the Chernobyl nuclear accident. Although Mulder cut the creature in half when he dropped a sewer gate as it attempted to escape through a drain, the Flukeman floated to the surface and opened its eyes, obviously still very much alive. ("The Host") *Darin Morgan was more comfortable writing for* The X-Files *than he was suited up and swimming in the sewer with 80 pounds of makeup as the Flukeman. "For all those who had nightmares looking at it, it was much worse looking out of it." The suit kept getting wet and requiring repairs, adding to an arduous 6–7 hours in makeup. "Once it got wet, it was enormously heavy. You couldn't breathe. It was like sensory deprivation 15 hours a day."*

Fly, The Classic 1958 horror movie that was playing on Mulder's television when Eugene Tooms entered his apartment through a vent and stole one of the agent's shoes. Mulder was asleep at the time. ("Tooms")

Flying Saucer Diner, The A roadside café located near Ellens Air Force Base in Southwest Idaho. Frequented by "UFO nuts," The Flying Saucer Diner was owned and operated by a robust woman named Ladonna who sold Mulder a photo of a triangular UFO and drew him a map to the military base, which, curiously, was unlisted on official maps. ("Deep Throat")

Folkstone INS Processing Center A refugee camp in North Carolina which housed 12,000 Haitians in crude dormitories and tents. Folkstone became a battleground between Marine Col. Jacob Wharton, the base commander, and Pierre Bauvais, a self-proclaimed revolutionary and Haitian Voodoo priest. ("Fresh Bones")

Foo Fighter UFO downed in the Pacific during World War II after a dogfight with American P-51 Mustang fighters. The submarine *Zeus Faber* was sent to the area to recover what they were told was a B-52 Flying Fortress carrying the third atomic bomb (to follow the Hiroshima and Nagasaki weapons) to be dropped on Japan. Instead, the captain was attacked by an alien entity, and many of the crew died from what appeared to be radiation sickness. The Foo Fighter was eventually salvaged and stored at an abandoned missile silo in North Dakota. ("Piper Maru/Apocrypha")

Forau In religious folklore, believed to be one of the devil's disciples. Forau was the name evil industrialist Simon Gates (a.k.a. the Millennium Man) used to rent a car and kill Kevin Kryder's mother. ("Revelations")

Fornier (Mitchell Kosterman) A prison guard employed at Eastpoint State Penitentiary in Leon County, Florida. Skeptical of executed death-row inmate Napoleon "Neech" Manley's claims that he'd be reincarnated and avenge all those who mistreated him, Fornier's maggot-infested severed head was later found inside an empty paint can. The warden discovered Fornier's headless corpse in his office chair. He was the second victim on Manley's enemies list. ("The List") *Actor Mitch Kosterman played Det. Horton in "Genderbender" and reprised the role in "Sleepless."*

Forsch, Chuck (Sydney Lassick) Mentally challenged roommate of Harold Spuller at the New Horizon Psychiatric Center in Washington, D.C. Forsch's assistance in Mulder and Scully's investigation into the serial murders of several young women led to the arrest of the facility's Nurse Innes. ("Elegy") *Sydney Lassick, who played the mentally challenged Cheswick in the 1975 Academy Award-winning* One Flew Over the Cuckoo's Nest, *also appeared with David Duchovny in the 1991 film,* Don't Tell Mom the Babysitter's Dead.

Fortean event According to Mulder, a highly unusual or infrequent meteo-rological phenomenon, also known as a transient. Fortean events have been linked to alien encounters, cattle mutilations and exsanguinated animal corpses. Mulder theorized that a Fortean event had occurred at a California migrant workers' camp when witnesses described three earsplitting booms that came out of nowhere, followed by a bright flash of light thirty degrees off the horizon, then a brief but torrential downpour of yellow rain, which researchers called liquid falls. It its aftermath, the illegal aliens discovered the corpse of Maria Dorantes and one of her goats, their faces partially eaten away. Mulder later put forth the theory that the Fortean event that occurred at the migrant camp could have been an object such as a meteorite or other space debris that fell at a high rate of speed through the atmosphere into a nearby lake, superheated the water and sent it skyward, causing the sudden torrent of yellow rain from a cloudless day. ("El Mundo Gira")

Fort Evanston U.S. Army base in Maryland and site of a series of military hospital murders committed by a quadruple amputee veteran who possessed the power of astral projection ("The Walk"). In 1997, Denny Markham, leader of the Right Hand radical paramilitary group, was held in custody at the base's detention center under the terms of the new anti-terrorist law. Markham, an ex-Marine, was threatened with an assortment of conspiracy, homicide, treason, and illegal weapons possession charges, for his suspected complicity in the deaths of two high-ranking military officers. ("Unrequited")

Fort Marlene High Containment Facility Maryland location of a top-secret cryolab where the original alien tissue was kept which Scully planned to use to trade for Mulder's life. ("The Erlenmeyer Flask")

Four Past Midnight A best-selling collection of four novellas written by horror-meister Stephen King. Mulder skimmed past the book's title in the Crowley High School library's card file during his search for M.R. Kras-hewski's *Witch Hunt: A History of the Occult in America*. ("Die Hand Die Verletzt")

14th Precinct House Buffalo, New York police station where Detective Rudy Barbala mysteriously crashed backward through a window and plum-meted to his death while interrogating eight-year-old Michelle Bishop, a lost little girl found outside the station. ("Born Again")

Fowler, Dr. Jack Physician in Sioux City, Iowa who teenagers Tessa Sears and Greg Randall were scheduled to meet for an appointment to discuss Tessa's pregnancy. A handwritten note indicating the doctor's appointment was found in Randall's wallet after his body was discovered in a shallow grave. ("Conduit")

foxfire A folktale from the Ozark mountains dating back to the nineteenth century. The radiant effulgence created by disintegrating timber was believed by many settlers and modern-day Southerners to be the spirits of massacred Indians. Mulder at first suspected foxfire in the disappearance of a federal poultry inspector near Dudley, Arkansas, particularly in light of the discovery of a twelve-foot burn mark in an adjacent field and the "strange fire" seen by a woman driving along a nearby Interstate highway. ("Our Town")

Foyle, Lt. (Peter Kelamis) Military coroner at the Folkstone INS Processing Center who found a dog's corpse in the morgue's refrigerated drawer where Pvt. John "Jack" McAlpin's body was supposed to be. ("Fresh Bones")

Francis, General (Donnelly Rhodes) Four-star general stationed at the Center for Special Warfare in Fort Bragg, North Carolina in October 1962. At a meeting in his base office, General Francis and other members of a right-wing conspiracy group recruited a young Army captain (later to be known as the Cigarette-Smoking Man) to assassinate President John F. Kennedy. The incident was based on Lone Gunman Frohike's speculative dossier on the life of the Cigarette-Smoking Man. ("Musings of a Cigarette-Smoking Man") *Donnelly Rhodes also played the doomed Montana rancher Jim Parker in "Shapes."*

Franklin Community College Local educational institution in the small suburban farm town of Franklin, Pennsylvania. Prompted by subliminal messages and exposure to fear-inducing pheromones, laid-off postal worker Ed Funsch climbed to the top of the college's clock tower and began a sniper assault. ("Blood")

Franklyn, Dr. Jack (Richard Beymer) A physician at the Aesthetic Surgery Unit of Chicago's Greenwood Memorial Hospital. Franklyn, a practitioner of black magic and sorcery, compelled his cosmetic surgeon colleagues to murder patients through botched liposuctions and chemical peels in an effort to satisfy his thirst for immortality. Mulder theorized that when Dr. Franklyn reached the limits of medical miracles, the devil worshipper staged miracles of his own by killing patients and offering them as human "blood sacrifices," thus transforming his looks beyond the limits of surgery. During the course of their investigation, Mulder and Scully discovered that Dr. Franklyn had been responsible for a similar series of bizarre deaths at Greenwood Memorial Hospital in 1986 under the guise and appearance of Dr. Clifford Cox, a cosmetic surgeon who supposedly died of an overdose. In 1996, he escaped capture once again when Mulder and Scully failed to stop the final human sacrifice that completed the black magic ritual and altered Franklyn's physical features. After slicing off the face of Dr. Jack Franklyn, the sorcerer resurfaced at a Los Angeles cosmetic surgery clinic as the classically handsome and youthful Dr. Hartman. ("Sanguinarium") *Dr. Franklyn's address of 1953 Gardner Street was a reference to Gerald Gardner, the British witch who revived modern Wicca and first published his work on that religion in 1953. Richard Beymer, the actor who portrayed the surgeon/sorcerer Dr. Franklyn, is best remem-*

bered as Ben Horne, the womanizing hotel owner on the short-lived, quirky series Twin Peaks.

Fraser, Lt. (Tony Pantages) Military officer involved in Operation Falcon who led Beta Team's search-and-destroy mission for the pilot of the downed alien spacecraft near Townsend, Wisconsin. Lt. Fraser and his soldiers were severely burned when they encountered the translucent extraterrestrial. ("Fallen Angel")

Frass, Sheriff (Dion Anderson) Miller's Grove, Massachusetts sheriff who approached Mulder while the agent was investigating accounts of unidentified colored lights in the sky. Frass was quickly called away, however, when he was notified of "another roach attack." When it appeared the insects were mortally attacking people, the sheriff expressed his concern to Mulder that the government had been conducting experiments, perhaps creating "a new breed of killer cockroaches." ("War of the Coprophages")

Freddie Derogatory nickname given to Federal Forest Service officers by eco-terrorists. ("Darkness Falls")

Frederick County Morgue Where the body of a woman believed by Maryland police to be Scully's was stored while awaiting positive identification by Mulder. Although a dangerously paranoid Scully had mysteriously disappeared after becoming the victim of a mind control experiment transmitted via video signals in the town of Braddock Heights, the corpse was not her's and Scully was later found alive by Mulder at her mother's house. ("Wetwired")

Freedom of Information Act Federal law passed by Congress granting American citizens access to formerly classified documents. According to UFO-conspiracy theorist Max Fenig, he and other members of NICAP (the National Investigative Committee of Aerial Phenomena) had followed Mulder's career through his travel expense records, which had been obtained through the Freedom of Information Act. ("Fallen Angel")

Freely, Quinton "Roach" (Willie Garson) A Gulf War veteran who worked in the mail room of the Fort Evanston military hospital. The FBI found his fingerprints on mail addressed to each of the victims of a "phantom soldier," and arrested him. Under questioning, however, Roach denied killing anyone, stating that he was just the "mailman" for quadruple amputee Leonard "Rappo" Trimble. Later, Roach was discovered dead in his locked cell, a bedsheet stuffed down his throat. ("The Walk")

free radicals Highly reactive chemicals containing extra electrons that attack DNA and proteins and theoretically cause bodies to age. Scully suspected free radicals were to blame when she and Mulder experienced accelerated aging aboard the Navy destroyer USS *Ardent*. She surmised that the ship may have been drifting toward a massive metallic source, such as a meteor on the ocean's floor, which was acting like a battery terminal to electromagnetically excite the free radicals. ("Dod Kalm")

📁 **"Fresh Bones"** Written by Howard Gordon. Directed by Rob Bowman. File number 2X15. *First aired February 3, 1995. When a Marine stationed at a North Carolina resettlement camp for Haitian refugees dies after driving into a tree, Mulder and Scully investigate the widow's claim that her husband's "suicide" was the result of a voodoo curse.* **Classic Sound Bite:** *"That's a plausible diagnosis, though I'm more interested in how he came back to life."* **Background Check:** *According to R.W. Goodwin, it was the more than enthusiastic cooperation of stars Duchovny and Anderson that made the episode work so well. "We've got [Anderson] in the car at 1:00 in the morning, it's 16 degrees and she has to have blood gushing out of her mouth over and over again," he remembered. "She just thought that was great."*

Frish, Sgt. Louis (Tom O'Brien) One of two air traffic controllers who manned the tower at the Von Drehle Air Force Reserve Installation in Upstate New York on the night of the crash of commercial airliner Flight 549. During questioning by Mulder and Scully, Sgt. Frish initially claimed there was no radio contact between the Air Force and the civilian plane, but later changed his account after he discovered the body of Sgt. Armando Gonzales, the other controller in the tower on the night of the crash. Frish later told Mulder, Scully, and Mike Millar of the National Transportation Safety Board that he was the last person to communicate with Flight 549. Frish explained that his commanding officer ordered him and Gonzales to lie to investigators and not divulge that the two air traffic controllers had seen an unidentified radar blip enter 549's airspace and shadow the airliner for ten minutes. Moments later, there was an explosion. After hearing Frish's revised account of the plane crash, Scully flew the sergeant to Washington to place him in protective custody. While waiting for a federal marshal in the Headless Woman's Pub, an assassin attempted to shoot Frish, but accidentally killed FBI Agent Pendrell in the cross fire. Afterwards, Assistant Director Skinner showed up at the tavern and advised Scully that the order for Frish's protective custody had been countermanded by the office of the Joint Chiefs of Staff and that the sergeant was being placed under military arrest for suspicion of Gonzales' murder and providing false testimony in the federal investigation of Flight 549. The Air Force then issued a public announcement that the commercial airliner had collided with a military fighter jet when Frish and Gonzales made an error in judgment, effectively placing the blame on the two air traffic controllers, one of whom was already dead. ("Tempus Fugit/Max") *Actor Tom O'Brien has appeared in theatrical films such as* The Big Easy, The Accused *and* The Next Karate Kid, *in addition to the TV movies* Son of the

Morning Star, Love and Lies, *and another airline disaster,* Crash Landing: The Rescue of Flight 232.

Frohike (Tom Braidwood) The short, perpetually unshaven and combat boot-clad photographic and surveillance specialist of the Lone Gunmen. One of three editors of the conspiracy-oriented newsletters *The Lone Gunman* and *The Magic Bullet,* Frohike is basically the hands-on technical member of the group, a master of hard sciences with a special interest in military hardware. Frohike typically represents someone even more extreme than Mulder in his belief in conspiracies, a fringe personality who has taken the agent's convictions to the far edges and makes him look positively sane and staid by comparison. A bit of a lecherous hippie, Frohike originally spent most of his spare time lusting after Scully, whom he considered "hot" ("E.B.E.)" His much celebrated lust for Mulder's partner later developed into genuine respect, though, being the only person to bring her flowers when she lay in a coma in a Washington, D.C. hospital. He also stole her medical records by hiding them in his pants ("One Breath"). After hearing of Mulder's apparent death, a saddened and drunken Frohike arrived at Scully's apartment, describing his friend as "a redwood among mere sprouts" ("The Blessing Way"). The Lone Gunman was also the one who informed Scully that her sister, Melissa, had been shot and was in the hospital in critical condition ("Paper Clip"). Always attempting to assist Mulder in his pursuit of the truth, Frohike offered his expert opinion regarding LSDM, an experimental synthetic insecticide that, acting as a pheromone, had triggered a fear response in the small farming community of Franklin, Pennsylvania ("Blood"); teleconferenced with the FBI agent concerning the Fairfield, Idaho Zoo's close proximity to "UFO hotspot" Mountain Home Air Base ("Fearful Symmetry"); assisted his Lone Gunmen colleagues in identifying Japanese satellite photos of the *Talapus,* a salvage vessel out of San Diego which had supposedly been searching for a submarine sunk during World War II ("Nisei"); and after examining an amazingly sophisticated video emitting device Mulder discovered in the small town of Braddock heights, Maryland, Frohike and the other Lone Gunmen correctly ascertained that it was a mind control mechanism used to transform people's fears into dementia through their TV sets ("Wetwired"). Although the Lone Gunman strives to keep a low profile, an ice-skating Frohike joined his colleagues in a clandestine package retrieval mission for Mulder at a Washington, D.C.-area rink ("Apocrypha") and in the high-tech infiltration of a research facility via a subterranean tunnel in an attempt to secure information about the origin of Scully's cancerous tumor ("Memento Mori"). In November 1996, fittingly near the anniversary of John F. Kennedy's assassination, Frohike called Mulder and Scully to The Lone Gunmen offices and revealed to the agents his version on the Cigarette-Smoking Man's secret past. Given the dossier's incredible arch, near-satiric tone and absurd allegations, one had to wonder if Frohike's enthusiasm led him to accept parcels of disinformation. Unbeknownst to the Lone Gunman, the Cigarette-Smoking Man eavesdropped electronically on the entire conversation from inside a building across the street, his sniper's rifle trained on the front door of the office. Frohike believed the CSM was trying to kill him, much to Mulder's amusement, who replied, "No one would want to kill you, Frohike. You're just a little puppy dog." At the last minute CSM put his weapon aside, muttering to himself, "I can kill you whenever I please . . . but not today" ("Musings of a Cigarette-Smoking Man"). *Episode writer Glen Morgan's original draft of "Musings of a Cigarette-Smoking Man" called for CSM to shoot and kill Frohike with a high-powered rifle, and although Chris Carter would not allow for the Lone Gunman to be killed, director James Wong actually filmed the episode both ways. Tom Braidwood, who portrays Frohike, has been a first assistant director for* The X-Files *since the series premiered. During a casting meeting for "E.B.E.," without having found a suitable actor to play Frohike, the episode's director, William Graham said, "We need somebody slimy—somebody like Braidwood." At that very moment Braidwood walked out of the bathroom and into X-Files' history.*

From Outer Space Author Jose Chung's "nonfiction science-fiction" account of an alleged UFO abduction of two Klass County, Washington teenagers that seemed opened to a number of different interpretations. ("Jose Chung's 'From Outer Space'") *The manuscript for Jose Chung's book,* From Outer Space, *was actually a copy of the episode's script.*

fulgarite Glass formed by the heat generated when lightning strikes sandy soil. Johnston County Sheriff Teller discovered one near where three cows had been struck dead. Encased in the fulgarite, however, was a partial footprint from a size 8-1/2 standard military boot. Scully also found traces of antifreeze in the sole, leading them to human lightning rod, Darin Peter Oswald, who worked as an auto garage mechanic. ("D.P.O.")

Fuller, Agent Brian (Kevin McNulty) FBI agent who was in charge of the Violent Crimes Section's investigation into the murder of businessman George Usher and two other Baltimore, Maryland killings in which the victim's livers were ripped out with bare hands. Agent Fuller staked out Usher's office in the belief the murderer would return to the scene of the crime. Although Mulder strongly believed the killer would not make a repeat appearance, Eugene Tooms was arrested by Fuller and other agents as he slid down an air duct ("Squeeze"). Agent Fuller was assigned, along with recent Academy graduate Linda Caleca, to help protect FBI Assistant Director Skinner after he was shot at point-blank range and hospitalized ("Apocrypha"). *Kevin McNulty also portrayed Dr. Davey in "Soft Light."*

Fuller & Siegel The Philadelphia, Pennsylvania investment firm where Ed Jerse was employed as a stockbroker. After hearing a female voice call him a "loser," he verbally assaulted two female colleagues conferencing next to his cubicle, not realizing that it was his newly acquired tattoo talking to him. ("Never Again")

Fuller, Roland (Zeljko Ivanek) A mentally challenged janitor responsible for the murders of several rocket scientists at the Mahan Propulsion Laboratory. Though Scully was ready to dismiss Roland (who had a "barely 70" IQ) as a suspect after discovering highly theoretical notations at the crime scenes, Mulder was convinced that there had to be a connection. A background check showed that Roland and one of the deceased research scientists on the top-secret project, Dr. Arthur Grable, were in fact twins. Though Grable had been killed in an automobile accident, his head had been preserved and cryogenically frozen. Mulder theorized that Grable wasn't dead, but in a "rarefied state of unconsciousness" which allowed him to manipulate his retarded brother into committing murder. Although Roland was held for psychiatric evaluation, Mulder recommended his release. ("Roland") *Born in Ljubljana, Yugoslavia, Zeljko Ivanek's film credits include* Donnie Brasco, The Associate, Courage Under Fire, White Squall, School Ties, Mass Appeal, *and* The Sender. *On his* X-Files *stint as the mentally challenged Roland Fuller, Ivanek (pronounced "Ee-VAH-nek") once remarked, "It was short notice, and I didn't have time to do much research. But it came to me very easily. Once you feel it in your bones, it plays itself."*

Fulton County Airport A small-craft airport in Upstate New York near the crash site of commercial jet Flight 459. Scully and Air Force Sergeant Louis Frish flew from the airport to Washington, D.C., where the military air traffic controller was to enter protective custody as a federal witness. ("Tempus Fugit/Max")

"Funny How Time Slips Away" The Al Green song playing on the stereo when the faux-Mulder (shapeshifter Eddie Van Blundht) attempted to seduce an unsuspecting Scully in her apartment. ("Small Potatoes")

Funsch, Ed (William Sanderson) A fifty-two-year-old postal worker in the suburban farming community of Franklin, Pennsylvania who was laid off his job for budgetary reasons. Prompted by frequent digital readouts such as KILL 'EM ALL, DO IT, and BLOOD on a variety of electronic devices, Funsch (who was phobic about blood), climbed a tower at the local college and began firing indiscriminately with a rifle. Mulder, who eventually disarmed him, suspected that someone, or some thing, had subjected the town's populace to an experiment sending subliminal messages through electronic readouts, heightening the existing phobias of individuals such as Funsch, with a chemical compound known as LSDM. ("Blood") *William Sanderson is best known for his quirky role as Vermont backwoodsman Larry on* Newhart, *and as the childlike android inventor Sebastion in the 1982 sci-fi classic* Blade Runner.

fylfot SEE: **gammadion**

"Grotesque"

Gaffs According to the curator of the Gibsonton Museum of Curiosities, the name circus people and sideshow acts gave to phony freaks such as P.T. Barnum's half-man/half-fish Feejee Mermaid. ("Humbug")

Gage, Phineas Railroad worker in 1848 who survived an explosion that drove a steel rod more than three feet long through his brain. Although a portion of the rod remained in his head for the remainder of his life, Gage suffered absolutely no physical or sensory impairment. However, his personality underwent a dramatic change, transforming him into a profane, irritable and capricious man. Scully believed she found the key to escaped mental patient Duane Barry's bizarre behavior in the century-and-half-old medical case of Phineas Gage. ("Duane Barry")

Galaxy Gateway Mulder's motel (Room 756) in Atlantic City while investigating the legendary Jersey Devil man-beast. The agent exchanged his room at the Galaxy Gateway for a vagrant's cardboard box in an alley, which Mulder used as a stakeout to catch a glimpse of the creature. ("The Jersey Devil")

gammadion Also known as a fylfot, an ancient good-luck symbol in the form of a reverse swastika with four dots between its arms. Golda and the Romanian exorcists, the Calusari, used a gammadion as a protective talisman when dealing with Golda's evil-possessed grandson, Charlie Holvey. The symbol represents the four winds, four seasons, and four compass points, indicating harmony with nature. ("The Calusari")

Ganesha. Twelve-year-old Indian elephant from the Fairfield, Idaho, Zoo, whose invisible rampage sent a workman fatally flying. She was discovered later in her locked cage at the zoo, dying of apparent exhaustion. ("Fearful Symmetry") *Ganesha is the female form of Ganesh, the popular Hindu household god with an elephant-shaped head.*

Gardner, Dr. Able (Allan Lysell) Chief medical officer at the U.S. Medical Research Institute of Infectious Diseases where the body of FBI agent Barrett Weiss was quarantined. Dr. Gardner discovered a mysterious retrovirus in the corpse and told Scully that it went dormant when he lowered the temperature five degrees. ("End Game") *Allan Lysell also portrayed Chief Rivers in "E.B.E."*

Garnet Code name for a secret multinational black ops unit comprised of "School of the Americas" alumni. The Lone Gunmen claimed that they were being pursued by the covert military outfit because one of their members, The Thinker had hacked into the Department of Defense's computer system and obtained the top-secret MJ files. ("Anasazi")

Garrett, Scott (Greg Michaels) Gaunt-faced assassin with a thick mustache who infiltrated the NTSB's investigation into the disastrous downing of commercial airliner Flight 549. At the crash site in Upstate New York, Garrett sprayed an acid-like substance on one of the bodies, dissolving the identifiable fingertips and face of the man sent to kill passenger Max Fenig, a UFO enthusiast who came into possession of an alien energy source. After Scully arranged for federal protection of an Air Force traffic controller who was the last person to communicate with Flight 549, Garrett attempted to publicly execute the soldier, but accidentally killed FBI Agent Pendrell during the shoot-out in a Washington, D.C., tavern. Although Garrett escaped capture, Scully was able to wound him in the leg. When Mulder boarded a commercial jet bound for Washington, Garrett followed him and demanded the alien energy source in Fenig's knapsack, which Mulder was carrying. At gunpoint, Mulder locked Garrett into one of the jet's lavatories, but during the commotion caused by an intercepting UFO the assassin escaped from the rest room and grabbed the knapsack containing the alien technology. When the flight landed at Washington National Airport, Garrett was not onboard and Mulder told Skinner that the assassin had "caught a connecting flight." ("Tempus Fugit/Max") *Garrett's conversation with Mulder aboard the flight from Syracuse to Washington was meant to be in homage to the 1949 film* The Third Man, *in which a similar discourse took place between Joseph Cotton and Orson Wells' characters.*

Garza, Angelo (Angelo Vacco) Gas station attendant who discovered infected fugitive Steve in the rest room. Garza attempted to assist him but was knocked out by Steve's fellow Cumberland Prison escapee, Paul. Although Garza survived the attack, the terrified gas station employee became infected with the plaguelike illness and was whisked away by four contamination suit-clad persons in an ominous-looking RESCUE helicopter with no registry number. ("F. Emasculata") *Chris Carter specifically wrote the part of Angelo Garza for X-Files production assistant Angelo Vacco, who went on to play "Door Man," a fast food customer shot and healed in the third-season cliffhanger, "Talitha Cumi."*

Gates, David (Dwight McFee) Attorney representing Montana rancher Jim Parker in his lawsuit against the Trego Indian tribe over grazing rights and a boundary dispute. ("Shapes") *Dwight McFee also portrayed the commander* *of the Blue Beret UFO Retrieval Team in "Little Green Men," a suspect in "Irresistible," and Detective Havez in "Clyde Bruckman's Final Repose."*

Gates, Simon (Kenneth Welsh) Also known as the Millennium Man, Gates was the chief executive of a holding company based in Atlanta, Georgia. One of the wealthiest businessmen in the South, he was arrested in 1992 for a drunken driving accident that left a boy paralyzed. After Gates received a suspended sentence, he fled the United States for Israel. The demonic industrialist, whom Mulder believed was suffering from the psychological illness Jerusalem Syndrome, killed eleven "false prophets" (fake stigmatics) in three years in an international string of religiously motivated murders. When Gates kidnapped young Kevin Kryder, a genuine stigmatic, the devil's disciple was killed in a huge shredding machine at a recycling plant he owned in Jerusalem, Ohio. ("Revelations") *Actor Kenneth Welsh is yet another* Twin Peaks *alumnus (the mad genius Wyndham Earle) along with David Duchovny.*

Gauthier, Bernard (Ari Solomon) Deep sea diver on the French salvage ship *Piper Maru,* who, to his horror, saw what appeared to be a live human inside a sunken World War II fighter plane. He returned to the surface possessed by an alien lifeform that existed in an oil medium. By the time the *Piper Maru* limped into port in San Diego, the entire crew was horribly burned from extreme exposure to radiation, except for Gauthier, who piloted the ship into the California shipyard while the others were ailing. The alien exited Gauthier and took over his wife, Joan, when she confronted him about his odd behavior. When Mulder located Gauthier, he was completely covered in a silky black membrane and had no memory of anything after the dive in the Pacific Ocean. ("Piper Maru") *Gauthier was named in honor of* X-Files *special effects coordinator David Gauthier, who is also a certified diver.*

Gauthier, Joan (Kimberly Unger) American wife of the French diver, Bernard Gauthier. The alien that possessed her husband later used her body as a physical means to travel to Hong Kong, only to abandon her when it discovered renegade agent Alex Krycek. She was found disoriented and incoherent in the men's rest room at the Hong Kong airport. ("Piper Maru") *Kimberly Unger also appeared in "Fallen Angel" as radar operator Chief Karen Koretz, who uttered one of the series' most memorable lines: "Sir, the meteor seems to be hovering over a small town in Wisconsin."*

Gayhart, Dr. Dale (Dana Gladstone) Physician who perished in an arson fire at an abortion clinic in New York City. Mulder anonymously received Dr. Gayhart's obituary via E-mail along with two other doctors' death notices. From their accompanying photographs, they could have been triplets, except that Mulder couldn't find any record of their births or past and no bodies were recovered from any of the fires. ("Colony")

geek A circus freak that can eat anything: rocks, live insects and fish, corkscrews, etc. The Conundrum, a heavily-tattooed former sideshow performer living in Gibsonton, Florida, was a geek who apparently ate Lanny's detached and homicidal congenital twin, Leonard. ("Humbug")

Gemini 8 Off-planet exploration mission in which astronaut Marcus Belt almost died when the spacecraft made an emergency splashdown in the Pacific Ocean. ("Space") *The real Gemini 8 spacecraft, piloted by Neil Armstrong and David Scott, made an emergency landing 10 hours and 41 minutes into the flight on March 16, 1966.*

☐ **"Genderbender"** Written by Larry Barber and Paul Barber. Directed by Rob Bowman. File number 1X13. *First aired January 21, 1994. The search for a gendershifting killer takes Mulder and Scully into an Amish-style community where a black-clad group of religious recluses named the Kindred (who may or may not be aliens) hold midnight metamorphosis rituals in their Massachusetts compound's subterranean catacombs.* **Classic Sound Bite:** *"I know what I saw, Scully. I saw you about to do the wild thing with some stranger."* **Background Check:** *The large picture seen during our first glimpse of the genderbending killer was painted by Swiss surrealist H.R. Giger, the artist who designed the hideous creatures for the* Alien *movies and more recently the grotesque extraterrestrial in the sci-fi film* Species.

General Mutual Insurance Company St. Paul, Minnesota, firm that employed depressive salesman and reluctant psychic Clyde Bruckman. ("Clyde Bruckman's Final Repose")

Generoo, Michelle (Susanna Thompson) Mission Control communications commander for NASA in Houston, Texas. Generoo, who sent an anonymous letter to the FBI in Washington, D.C., later approached Mulder and Scully to report that a recent space shuttle liftoff was aborted only seconds before launch and that she feared a piece of equipment had been sabotaged. Generoo requested the agents help to solve the case before the next scheduled shuttle launch, for which her fiancé was the mission commander. The source of the sabotage was discovered to be an alien-possessed Lt. Col. Marcus Aurelius Belt, supervisor of the shuttle program. ("Space")

Georgetown Medical Center Hospital in Washington, D.C. where Assistant Director Skinner was rushed after he was shot at point-blank range by Luis Cardinal (a.k.a. the Hispanic Man). ("Apocrypha")

Georgetown University School in the Washington, D.C. area where Scully borrowed an Audio Spectrum Indentisearch from the Voice Biometrics Lab ("Ghost in the Machine"). Mulder later conducted research on gargoyles at the university's library. ("Grotesque")

George Washington Hospital Washington, D.C., medical facility where a glassblower was taken after he was attacked in the same fashion as the victims of already-captured John Mostow. ("Grotesque")

George Washington University Institution of higher learning in Washington, D.C., where an art student, John Mostow, drew a grotesque gargoyle that bore no resemblance to the male nude model. Shortly after the class ended, Mostow slashed the model to death in the parking lot with a razor blade. ("Grotesque")

Gerlach, Malcolm SEE: **Red-Haired Man**

📁 **"Gethsemane (Part 1 of 2)"** Written by Chris Carter. Directed by R.W. Goodwin. File number 4X24. *First aired May 18, 1997. Mulder and Scully's investigation into the discovery of a frozen alien corpse in the Yukon challenges his belief in extraterrestrial life and shakes her faith on several levels.* **Classic Sound Bite:** *"This is your Holy Grail, Mulder, not mine . . . It just means proving to the world the existence of alien life is not my last dying wish."* **Background Check:** *This cliff-hanger episode was the fourth-season finale and ended with Scully's revelation that "Agent Mulder died last night of an apparent self-inflicted gunshot to the head." The title, "Gethsemane," refers to the garden where Jesus Christ was betrayed by Judas Iscariot and delivered to the Romans prior to his crucifixion; in a parallel, Scully seemed to betray Mulder to the FBI review board.*

📁 **"Ghost in the Machine"** Written by Alex Gansa and Howard Gordon. Directed by Jerrold Freeman. File number IX06. *First aired October 29, 1993. Agents Mulder and Scully are asked to assist a perplexed fellow agent when all the evidence points to the electrocution of a company's CEO by his own computer, which appears to have evolved into a sentient and murderous lifeform.* **Classic Sound Bite:** *"It's a puzzle, Miss Scully, and scruffy minds like me like puzzles. We enjoy walking down unpredictable avenues of thought, turning new corners, but, as a general rule, scruffy minds don't commit murder."* **Background Check:** *The episode's title refers to a phrase coined by Descartes as a way to explain consciousness: the ghost being our soul and the machine our physical bodies. This was the first episode in which Scully fired a gun (to shut down a fan motor, however).*

Gibsonton Museum of Curiosities Museum of curiosa in Gibsonton, Florida, a community populated by former circus freaks and sideshow acts. During a guided tour through the exhibits and photos of "big top" performers from years past, Scully learned that the town sheriff had once been Jim-Jim the Dog-Faced Boy, a former sideshow attraction. For an additional five dollars, the curator promised Scully an authentic Barnum exhibit, "The

Great Unknown," which turned out to be nothing more than an empty chest. The museum's admissions policy was "Freaks free . . . Others please leave donations." ("Humbug")

Gidney, Paul One of many aliases UFOlogist and multiple alien-abductee Max Fenig used in his correspondence when he went "underground." Fenig also used the pseudonym "Paul Gidney" when he traveled aboard ill-fated commercial airliner Flight 549. ("Tempus Fugit/Max") *Paul Gidney was a reference to Gidney and Floyd, the two little alien creatures from the "Rocky and Bullwinkle" cartoon series.*

Gila Monster According to Native American Albert Hosteen, the reptile which symbolized "the healing powers of the Medicine Man." ("Paper Clip")

Gillnitz, John Next door neighbor of Helene and Victor Riddock in the small town of Braddock Heights, Maryland. Gillnitz was taking a nap with his dog in a backyard hammock when Mrs. Riddock shot him to death with a rifle. The victim of a conspiracy involving mind control through television signals, she imagined that Gillnitz was her husband and that his dog was a shapely blonde. ("Wetwired") *The actor who portrayed Gillnitz was uncredited.*

ginseng A Chinese medicinal described to Scully by San Francisco police detective Glen Chao. Ginseng has been used for centuries to stimulate the energy of the entire body. Considered by the Chinese to be a cure-all, the plant root has a stimulating effect on the gonads and central nervous system ("Hell Money"). U.N. operative Marita Covarrubias informed Mulder that The Project's secret farm in Alberta, Canada, had been abandoned and the "flowering shrub" crops, allegedly ginseng, were left to die. ("Herrenvolk")

Giorgio, Chrissy (Sarah Sawatsky) Small town teenager who became a victim of alien abduction along with her boyfriend, Harold Lamb, when their car stalled one night in Klass County, Washington. After passing out in a blinding flash of light, Chrissy was found the next morning with signs of abuse and her clothes on inside out. Although she had no memory of what happened, Mulder believed she was suffering from post-abduction syndrome and convinced her to undergo hypnosis, during which time she recalled being on an alien spacecraft. Chrissy's story became the focal point of author Jose Chung's "nonfiction science fiction" book, *From Outer Space.* ("Jose Chung's 'From Outer Space' ")

Girardi, Dr. Francis (David Adams) Harvard neurosurgery professor who worked with Dr. Saul Grissom on the sleep eradication experiments on Parris Island in 1970. Dr. Girardi, who actually performed the brain-stem surgeries the experiments required, was severely wounded by a J-7 firing squad after being taken hostage by former experimental subject Augustus "Preacher" Cole. ("Sleepless")

Glaniceanu Last name of one of Mulder's apartment-house neighbors as seen on the mailbox. ("The Erlenmeyer Flask")

Glass, Dr. William (Malcolm Stewart) Raymon County State Psychiatric Hospital doctor who treated twenty-year-old schizophrenic Ray Soames, the third victim of the mysterious killer in Bellefleur, Oregon. ("The X-Files: Pilot") *Malcolm Stewart also played Commander Carver in "3," Agent Bonnecaze in "Avatar" and Dr. Sacks in "Tunguska/Terma."*

Glazebrook, Jerald (John Payne) Reptile-skinned circus performer known as "Alligator Man," who was considered one of the best escape artists in the business. Glazebrook, who suffered from a condition known as ichthyosis, the scale-like shedding of skin, was married to the bearded-lady and had two decidedly normal sons, approximately eight and ten years old. Glazebrook was attacked and killed by an unseen creature as he played with his boys in his swimming pool. Mulder stated that his murder was similar to forty-eight other assaults over the previous twenty-eight years. ("Humbug") *John Payne also played a Fort Marlene guard in "The Erlenmeyer Flask."*

Glengarry Glen Ross David Mamet's 1992 film version of his hit play set in the seedy branch office of a metropolitan real estate firm. Scully told Ed Jerse that the last date she had been on was to see *Glengarry Glen Ross,* saying, "The characters in the movie had a much better time." ("Never Again")

Glenview Lake Minnesota body of water where Clyde Bruckman accurately predicted the Doll Collector's body would be discovered. ("Clyde Bruckman's Final Repose")

Glimpse A *Life-* or *Look-*like magazine which featured a cover story on a pre-adolescent Eddie Van Blundht and the surgical removal of his vestigial tail. ("Small Potatoes")

glossolalia An incoherent speech condition which doctors at Seattle's University Medical Center suggested that Lucy Householder was suffering from after she collapsed and began repeating, "Nobody's gonna spoil us" again and again. The words Lucy mouthed were the identical ones spoken by Carl Wade as he kidnapped fifteen-year-old Amy Jacobs at the exact same moment twenty miles away. ("Oubliette")

Godfrey, Dr. Richard W. Pediatrician for "the Perfect Harmony City" of Comity. A closet cross-dresser, Dr. Godfrey liked to wear makeup and a fluffy woman's robe inside his house. One of the doctor's old surgical bags—containing bones—was uncovered in a backyard by a hysterical group of townsfolk looking for a mass grave. Analysis proved that the skeletal remains belonged to Terri Roberts's pet Llasa Apso, Mr. Tippy ("Syzygy") *The* *cross-dressing Comity doctor was named after R.W. Goodwin, The X-Files' co-executive producer. Actor Tim Dixon also played Bob, the wounded hostage in "Duane Barry."*

Golda (Lilyan Chauvin) Highly superstitious Old World mother of Maggie Holvey and grandmother of Teddy and Charlie Holvey. Although the Romanian woman objected to her daughter marrying an American, she nevertheless came to live with them after two-year-old Teddy was killed in a freak accident at a kiddie amusement park. Golda became convinced that Charlie was possessed by an evil spirit and recruited three black suit-clad Romanian exorcists known as the Calusari to perform a Ritual of Separation. After the ghostly visage of Charlie's dead twin brother, Michael, appeared and cursed them in Romanian, Golda locked herself in the room with Charlie. As objects flew around and she was knocked to the floor, Charlie stood over her, dropping two roosters that clawed and pecked her to death. ("The Calusari") *Lilyan Chauvin's endless film credits include* Private Benjamin, Universal Soldier, *and of course,* Pumpkinhead II: Blood Wings.

Goldbaum Patient at the Bethesda Naval Hospital in whose room Jack Willis hid (and stole his clothes) while escaping from the medical facility after he took on the criminal persona of recently-deceased bank robber Warren Dupre. ("Lazarus")

Goldstein, Dr. Charles (Mike Nussbaum) Psychiatrist/psychologist in Warwick, Rhode Island, who had been in practice for over forty years with a "very good ethical and professional reputation." Dr. Goldstein was eventually arrested by Providence, Rhode Island, police after discovering that he had injected his regression therapy patients with the rapid-acting veterinary anesthetic ketamine, a powerful hallucinogen in humans, which resulted in the murder-suicide of David and Amy Cassandra, the self-inflicted death of police officer Michael Fazekas, and the violent, unpredictable behavior of Agent Mulder. ("Demons") *The psychiatrist was named in honor of Charlie Goldstein, a 20th-Century Fox executive who had known Chris Carter, Glen Morgan, and James Wong, for several years. It was Goldstein's voice exclaiming, "Watch your hands, watch your hands" when the logo for Morgan and Wong's Hard Eight production company was shown at the end of each week's episode of* Space: Above and Beyond. *Actor Mike Nussbaum appeared as Rosenberg, an alien android with a small E.T. in his head in 1997's box office hit* Men in Black.

golem A living being whom the early Kabbalists believed could be created by a righteous man from the Earth itself, fashioned from mud or clay. The creature could only be brought to life, however, by the power of certain, secret letter combinations found in *The Sefer Yezirah* ("Book of Creation"), the earliest known Hebrew text on man's mystical communion with the Divine. The ancient book instructed those who wanted to make the inanimate

animate to inscribe a single word on the golem itself: "emet," which is Hebrew for "truth." A golem is an imperfect creation, unable to speak or feel anything but the most primitive of emotions. In legend, it ran amok and had to be destroyed by its creator by erasing the "e" off "emet", leaving the word "met," which is Hebrew for "dead." Ariel Luria, a beautiful Jewish woman who lost her betrothed, Isaac Luria, in a senseless act of violence by youthful hate-mongers, returned to the cemetery after his burial and shaped a golem out of mud and in the physical likeness of her murdered lover. Although Ariel's motive was love rather than revenge, the monstrous golem immediately began strangling one by one the murderous bigots responsible for Isaac's death. Realizing that the creature was an "abomination" that had no place among the living, Ariel wiped the "e" off the inscription on the back of the golem's hand and the creature crumbled into dust. ("Kaddish")

Gonzales, Sgt. Armondo (Rick Dobran) One of two air traffic controllers who manned the tower at the Von Drehle Air Force Reserve Installation in Upstate New York on the night of the crash of commercial airliner Flight 549. After Gonzales threatened to tell Mulder and Scully the truth about the plane's crash, the sergeant's body was discovered by fellow controller Sgt. Louis Frish, allegedly the victim of a self-inflicted gunshot wound. The Air Force later publicly blamed the cause of the plane's tragic downing on Gonzales and Frish by asserting that Flight 549 collided with a military fighter jet due to the two air traffic controllers' error in judgment. ("Tempus Fugit/Max")

Gonzales, Pat Name on an airline manifest Scully examined while trying to ascertain Mulder's location when he flew to a potential extraterrestrial contact site in Puerto Rico. ("Little Green Men") *Special Agent" Pat Gonzales is a prominent online X-Phile who maintains an FAQ website about the series.*

Goodensnake, Gwen (Renae Morriseau) Sister of slain werewolf Joseph Goodensnake. She accused her tribesmen of being scared of a "stupid Indian legend" but panicked and fled when she saw a lupine yet humanoid creature slash rancher Jim Parker to death. ("Shapes") *Actress Renae Morriseau also portrayed Josephine Doane of the Navajo Nation's Washington office in "Anasazi."*

Goodensnake, Joseph Werewolf killed by Browning, Montana, rancher Jim Parker after his son, Lyle, was savaged by the beastlike creature while they were inspecting a slaughtered steer in their corral. During an inspection of the dead Trego Indian's corpse, Mulder noticed inch-long, wolflike fangs not seen on Goodensnake's dental records. Scully attributed them to calcium phosphate salts that could gather with age. Although Mulder requested an autopsy, Goodensnake's body was burned on a pyre in accordance with Trego tribal law. ("Shapes")

Good News from Outer Space, Vol I Novel by John Kessel about a tabloid reporter who comes into possession of evidence proving the existence of aliens on Earth. Mulder kept a copy of the novel on a bookshelf in his apartment.

Goodwinkle, Albert Representative of the publishing company Montgomery and Glick who sent Raul Bloodworth (the *nom de plume* for the Cigarette-Smoking Man) a scathing rejection letter in 1968 regarding his first spy thriller, *Take a Chance*. Goodwinkle complained that the characters were "unbelievable," the plot "preposterous," the ending "lame," and advised Bloodworth to "burn it!" The incident, however, was based on a rather suspicious account of the Cigarette-Smoking Man's life as pieced together by Lone Gunman Frohike. ("Musings of a Cigarette-Smoking Man")

Gordon, Mr. (David McKay) Young married man who resisted salesman Clyde Bruckman's pitch to buy a comprehensive life insurance policy ($200,000 value for $2,400 net annual cost). When Gordon stated that he would rather spend the money on a nice boat, Bruckman (who was a genuine psychic) told him how he foresaw the young man's gruesome demise two years later in a head-on collision with a drunk in a blue 1987 Mustang, leaving his wife and as-yet-unborn daughter dispossessed. A stunned and scared Mr. Gordon replied, "Mister, you really need to work on your closing technique." ("Clyde Bruckman's Final Repose")

Go-Team National Transportation Safety Board (NTSB) investigators assigned to determine why commercial airliner Flight 549 fell from the sky at three hundred miles per hour in an almost vertical descent and crashed in Upstate New York, killing 133 passengers and crew. ("Tempus Fugit/ Max")

Gouveia, Detective (Jay Donahue) Philadelphia police detective who, along with his partner, questioned Scully as to the whereabouts of Ed Jerse, the man in whose apartment she had spent the previous night. ("Never Again")

Grable, Dr. Arthur Aeronautical scientist who worked on the top-secret Icarus Project, the next generation of jet engines, at the Mahan Propulsion Laboratory. Although Dr. Grable was killed in an automobile accident in November 1993, his head had been preserved and cryogenically frozen. Mulder theorized that Grable and his mentally retarded twin brother, Roland (who worked as a janitor at the propulsion laboratory), enjoyed a psychic bond that may have been heightened by the cryogenic process. Mulder also postulated that the rocket scientist "may have reached a higher consciousness allowing him to manipulate" Roland into murdering several team members on the Icarus Project. ("Roland")

Graffia, Sharon (Chilton Crane) Young woman who claimed to be the sister of multiple alien-abductee and NICAP member Max Fenig. Before

Max's death in a commercial airliner crash, he had told her to meet with Mulder and Scully if any harm came to him. While staying at a motel close to the crash site in Upstate New York, Graffia disappeared from her room, only to be found dazed and wandering about in a wooded area, which led Mulder to speculate that she had been a victim of alien abduction. Scully's investigation revealed, however, that Graffia was not Fenig's sister, but an unemployed aeronautical systems engineer who spent time in mental hospitals, where she met Fenig. During questioning, the woman admitted she stole an object, possibly an alien energy source, from her military-contractor employer after Fenig insisted it could prove the existence of extraterrestrial life. After her release from a Georgetown mental health center, Mulder and Scully presented her with the videotapes, documents, and personal belongings Fenig's Airstream travel trailer, essentially making her the curator of his "rolling multi-media library and archives." ("Tempus Fugit/Max") *Actress Chilton Crane also appeared in "Miracle Man" as the wheelchair-bound Margaret Hohman, and as a mother at the bus station in "F. Emasculata."*

Grago, Dr. John (Jerry Wasserman) Physician who provided medical attention three days a week at the Excelsis Dei Convalescent Home in Worcester, Massachusetts. Dr. Grago boasted to Mulder and Scully that he had been successfully treating a group of the facility's Alzheimer's patients with an experimental drug for several months. ("Excelsius Dei")

Grant, Charles Name on an airline manifest Scully scrutinized while trying to determine Mulder's whereabouts when he flew to a possible alien contact site in Puerto Rico. ("Little Green Men") *Charles Grant is the author of two X-Files novels,* Goblins *and* Whirlwind.

Gravenhurst High School Connerville, Oklahoma, school attended by nineteen-year-old Darin Peter Oswald, where the barely literate teenager developed a serious romantic crush on Mrs. Sharon Kiveat, his remedial reading teacher. ("D.P.O.")

Graves, Howard Thomas Founder of the Philadelphia-based military contractor HTG Industrial Technologies. When the company began to experience devastating financial losses, Graves initially went along with his partner's plan to illegally sell technology to a Mideast extremist group. After a terrorist attack killed several American servicemen, however, Graves decided to scuttle the deal and was killed when his business partner feared he was going to expose the operation. Graves, fifty-three, was found dead in his hot tub, his wrists slit. He left no survivors. His wife divorced him in 1970 when their daughter accidentally drowned in their swimming pool. Graves' vengeful spirit lingered on, though, to protect his secretary, Lauren Kyte (who would have been about the same age as his daughter had she survived) and to reveal the truth about his death. ("Shadows")

Graves, Sarah Lynn (September 8, 1966—August 3, 1969, per gravestone) Howard Graves' daughter, who drowned at the age of three in a pool to which he'd left the gate-latch open. ("Shadows")

Gray-Haired Man (Morris Panych) Ruthless and relentless assassin for the Shadowy Syndicate. Identifying himself as someone who worked "for the Intelligence community," the Gray-Haired Man warned Skinner to leave Melissa Scully's murder investigation "inactive" and made veiled threats about the Assistant Director's "future" ("Piper Maru"). He participated in the scheme to frame Skinner in the slaying of a prostitute and the attempted murder of his wife, Sharon. Either directly or indirectly, he was actively involved in the deaths of the hooker and her madam ("Avatar"). After Mr. X was identified as a traitor by the Cigarette-Smoking Man and the 1st Elder, the Gray-Haired Man was dispatched to ambush and gun down the informant in the hallway outside Mulder's apartment ("Herrenvolk). When the Kurt Crawford hybrid clones attempted to subvert the colonization project that created them, the Gray-Haired Man used a stiletto-shaped alien weapon to kill one of the genetic replicas in the basement of Betsy Hagopian's Allentown, Pennsylvania, home. After Mulder and the Lone Gunmen infiltrated the Lombard Research Facility in search of clues pertaining to the origin of Scully's cancer, the Gray-Haired Man trapped Mulder between two security doors in a quarantine wing. The assassin opened fire, slowly cracking the bulletproof glass that separated himself and Mulder. Working frantically, Frohike broke a computer code from a remote location, allowing Mulder to open the outside door and run to safety just as the Gray-Haired Man penetrated the glass ("Memento Mori"). Upon orders from the Cigarette-Smoking Man, the assassin neutralized "a potentially compromising situation" by shooting Desmond, Virginia, police detective Ray Thomas, leaving his body to be found near the precinct. Thomas had E-mailed Mulder crime scene photos of a young mail sorter who died after being attacked by a swarm of bees in the overnight delivery company's rest room. To ensure Assistant Director Skinner's continued cooperation in the cover-up, the Gray-Haired Man shot and killed Det. Thomas with Skinner's government-issued handgun ("Zero Sum"). *Several layers of glass, as well as a special gun that fired harmless glass bullets, were used to protect David Duchovny in the "Memento Mori" scene in which the Gray-Haired Man repeatedly fired at Mulder until he'd punctured a hole in the bulletproof glass. Actor Morris Paynch also portrayed Dr. Simon Auerbach in "F. Emasculata."*

Gray, Paula (Gabrielle Miller) Lovely young line worker at the Chaco Chicken processing plant in Dudley, Arkansas, and granddaughter of founder Walter Chaco. After it was learned that federal poultry inspector George Kearns was going to recommend the closing of the processing facility for health reasons, Gray was used to lure the adulterous Kearns into the woods where he was beheaded and eaten by the cannibalistic townsfolk. Gray later began hallucinating on the assembly line, taking the floor manager hostage at knife-point before the sheriff shot her dead. An autopsy revealed that she was suffering from the same extremely rare and noncommunicable disease, Creutzfeldt-Jakob, that afflicted Kearns. Although her personnel file showed that she was born in 1948, meaning that she was forty-seven years old, she appeared to be in her early twenties the time of her death. ("Our Town") *Actress Gabrielle Miller also played Brenda Summerfield, a victim of the Ouija board in "Syzygy."*

Great Sacandaga Lake Body of water located in Upstate New York where Mulder went scuba diving in search of a UFO shot down by an Air Force fighter jet. Deep in the murky waters, the agent located the twisted wreckage and the body of a gray alien. ("Tempus Fugit/Max")

"Great Unknown, The" Allegedly an authentic P.T. Barnum exhibit, which the Curator of the Gibsonton Museum of Curiosities had recently obtained. The Curator humbugged Scully out of an additional five dollars to view "The Great Unknown," which turned out to be nothing more than an empty chest. ("Humbug")

Green, Arlan (Andre Daniels) Green, along with his wife, provided a room at their halfway house to discharged mental patient Eugene Tooms after he was released from the Druid Hill Sanitarium in Baltimore, Maryland. ("Tooms") *Andre Daniels also played postal supervisor Harry McNally in "Blood."*

Green, Phoebe (Amanda Pays) Mulder's old flame, who broke his heart while they were students at Oxford University. Ten years later, the beautiful Scotland Yard inspector requested his assistance in protecting a vacationing British lord from a pyrokinetic assassin. ("Fire") *Former model Amanda Pays' TV credits include Theora Jones on* Max Headroom *and Tina McGee on* The Flash.

Greenwood Memorial Hospital Chicago site of several bizarre and violent deaths. In 1986 and again in 1996, cosmetic surgery patients died under mysterious circumstances at the hospital's state-of-the-art Aesthetic Surgery Unit (ASU) while undergoing what should have been simple liposuction, chemical peel, and scalp reduction procedures. During each incident, the operating physicians had no memory of their psychotic actions and the patients' deaths were ruled accidental. In 1986, the hospital conspired to cover up the "deaths" in an effort to protect the very profitable ASU, which accounted for over fifty percent of the medical facility's revenue. ("Sanguinarium")

Gregor According to CIA agent Ambrose Chapel, the code-name for the identical doctors he claimed were cloned Soviet spies. During the Cold War the Gregors slowly emigrated to the United States on German passports and infiltrated government medical facilities, but were being killed under a secret agreement in 1995 in exchange for Russia ending the program and sharing the science. In actuality, the Gregors were the progeny of two alien visitors from the 1940s who were trying to establish an Earth colony by genetically merging with humans. Because the experiment wasn't sanctioned, a shape-shifting extraterrestrial Bounty Hunter had been dispatched to terminate the colonists. ("Colony/End Game")

Griffin, Lt. (Michael Rogers) Military officer involved in Operation Falcon who led Beta Team's search and destroy mission for the surviving alien lifeform from a UFO crash near Townsend, Wisconsin. ("Fallen Angel") *Michael Rogers also played a ship crewman in "Colony."*

Grissom, Dr. Saul (Claude de Martino) Prominent physician who founded the Grissom Sleep Disorder Center in Stamford, Connecticut. As a Marine, he was stationed from 1968–71 on Parris Island, South Carolina, where he participated in a secret military project to create the perfect soldier by eradicating the need for sleep. Dr. Grissom died in his sixth-floor Manhattan apartment in 1994 believing he was trapped by flames. Although firefighters discovered no sign of a fire at his residence, the autopsy showed signs of intense heat but no external burns, "as if his body believed it were burning." Mulder believed Dr. Grissom had been killed by one of his experimental subjects, Augustus Cole, whose twenty-four years without sleep had allowed the former soldier to develop the psychic ability to produce images so real they could kill. ("Sleepless") *Dr. Grissom was named in honor of astronaut Gus Grissom, who died in a launchpad fire aboard* Apollo I *in 1967.*

Grossmont Union High School District School district in El Cajon, California, where Mrs. Paddock was employed as a substitute teacher from 1992 to 1994, prior to moving to Milford Haven, New Hampshire, according to Scully's computerized background check. ("Die Hand Die Verletzt") *Co-episode writer Glen Morgan was born and raised in El Cajon, California (as was his brother, Darin).*

📁 **"Grotesque"** Written by Howard Gordon. Directed by Kim Manners. File number 3X14. *First aired February 2, 1996. When mutilation-style serial murders continue even after the killer's been apprehended, Mulder and Scully are assigned to aid Mulder's former mentor at the FBI's Behavioral Sciences Unit in tracking down the perpetrator's accomplice or copycat.* **Classic Sound Bite:** *"If you want to catch a monster, you've got to become one yourself."* **Background Check:** *Writer Howard Gordon admitted that he had a difficult time finishing the script for "Grotesque." To inspire the process, he bought a little gargoyle and put it on his desk and stared at it. For further inspiration, Gordon continuously flipped through a coffee-table book titled* Nightmares in the Sky, *a collection of gargoyle photographs with an introduction by Stephen King.*

Grover Cleveland Alexander High School Secondary educational institution in the town of Comity attended by best friends Margi Kleinjan and Terri Roberts. The two blond girls were born on the same day and were responsible for a series of deaths due to a particular alignment of the planets. ("Syzygy") *The high school's name was an in-joke about a question David Duchovny missed on* Celebrity Jeopardy! *The X-Files star later said that he thought he was still in the sports category, which is why he confused the pitcher (Alexander) with the president (Cleveland).*

Guancaste Rain Forest The Costa Rican jungle where entomogolist Dr. Robert Torrence discovered the parasite carrier *Faciphaga emasculata* while researching new insects for drug applications. ("F. Emasculata")

Guardians of the Dead Two Trego Native Americans, Bill and Tom, who guarded Joe Goodensnake's body at Sheriff Tskany's office and whose duty it was to escort the deceased spirit to the next world as part of the Indian tribe's funeral rites. ("Shapes")

Gulf Breeze Sightings, The Famous UFO sightings around the small Pensacola, Florida, suburb of Gulf Breeze from November 1987 to May 1988, primarily by real estate developer Ed Walters, who had photographs, scientific endorsement, and plausible evidence to lend credence to his story. Later on, a young man confessed that he had helped Walters promulgate the hoax. But for a long time to come, Gulf Breeze became a UFOlogist's mecca. In 1993, Mulder wrote an article concerning the Gulf Breeze Sightings (under the pseudonym M.F. Luder) for the prestigious scientific magazine *Omni*. ("Fallen Angel")

Gulf Breeze Trailer Court Mulder and Scully's place of lodging while staying in Gibsonton, Florida, a town populated by former circus freaks and sideshow acts. The trailer-court motel was managed by Mr. Nutt, the midget proprietor with a degree in hotel management. ("Humbug") *The trailer court was named after the famous 1987–88 UFO "sightings," of course.*

Gunther's disease A congenital ailment that causes lesions and blisters after exposure to sunlight, probably contributing to the creation of the vampire myth. Los Angeles police pathologist Dr. Browning suggested that Gunther's disease was responsible for the death of John, a self-confessed member of the vampiresque Trinity Killers. Assuming that John's vampire beliefs were delusional, Mulder left him in an open cell hoping fear of sunlight would scare him enough to talk, but the sun's rays burned John to death. ("3")

Gutierrez, Pvt. Manuel Second Marine at Folkstone INS Processing Center to commit suicide in two weeks. When Mulder and Scully attempted to exhume his body at the municipal cemetery, his corpse had disappeared. Further investigation revealed that Pvt. Gutierrez, along with another missing Marine, had both filed complaints against Col. Jacob Wharton, the Folkstone base commander, for his mistreatment of Haitian refugees housed at the camp. ("Fresh Bones")

Householder

hagiographic fabrications Mulder's description of the Bible during the X-Files team's investigation into a series of religiously motivated murders in which each of the victims claimed the ability to display stigmatic wounds similar to the crucified Christ. ("Revelations")

Hagopian, Betsy MUFON (Mutual UFO Network) member from Allentown, Pennsylvania. Her name was circled on a membership list found by Mulder and Scully inside a leather satchel carried by a Japanese diplomat who fled from the murder scene of MUFON member Steven Zinnszer. When Scully went to Hagopian's residence, she met several "alien-abductee" women who claimed to recognize Scully from the "unexplained event" in the previous year when she was missing. The women took Scully to the local hospital, where a tumor-filled Betsy Hagopian was dying of cancer, a result, the women contended, of repeated alien abduction and experimentation since her teenage years ("Nisei"). After Scully was diagnosed with the same type of inoperable cancer in 1997, she and Mulder returned to Hagopian's Allentown home in hopes of contacting the group of purported alien-abductees. A realtor, however, met the agents at the door and explained that Hagopian had died two weeks earlier. ("Memento Mori")

Hakkie, Dr. Del (Frank C. Turner) Psychiatrist at the Davis Correctional Treatment Center where former FBI agent Duane Barry was institutionalized. After seizing a guard's gun, Barry took the doctor hostage, demanding that Hakkie accompany him to the site of his alleged alien abduction to prove that it was real and not a figment of his imagination. ("Duane Barry") *Frank C. Turner also played Dr. Collins in "Tooms."*

Hale, George Founder of the landmark Palomar Observatory and an alias used on occasion by Mulder. When the agent traveled covertly to Puerto Rico's Arecibo Ionospheric Observatory to investigate possible alien contact, he flew on a commercial airline under the name George Hale ("Little Green Men"). After the X-Files unit had been closed, Mulder used the alias to telephone Scully at the FBI Academy where she had been reassigned. ("Sleepless")

haloperidol An anti-psychotic drug administered to Kevin Kryder's father, Michael, who had been institutionalized for believing he had to protect the young stigmatic from dark forces intent on slaying him during "the great war between good and evil." ("Revelations")

Halverson (Mar Andersons) Twenty-one-year-old Norwegian first mate aboard Henry Trondheim's trawler, the *Zeal*. Halverson's skull was fatally fractured by the pirate whaler Olafsson on the USS *Ardent*. ("Dod Kalm") *Mar Andersons also played town bully Jack Hammond in "D.P.O."*

Hamilton County Hall of Records Public archive in Tennessee where Scully researched Melissa Riedal Ephesian's claims that she and Mulder had lived and loved in a past life as Civil War nurse Sarah Kavanaugh and doomed soldier Sullivan Biddle, respectively. During her investigation of war maps and county registers, Scully found the star-crossed lovers' antique photographs. ("The Field Where I Died")

Hamilton, James (Wayne Grace) Four-term sheriff of Gibsonton, Florida, a retirement community whose residents consisted of former circus and sideshow performers. During Mulder and Scully's investigation into Jerald Glazebrook's bizarre death, a background check uncovered the fact that Sheriff Hamilton was actually once Jim-Jim the Dog-Faced Boy, a former sideshow attraction in P.T. Barnum's circus. Hamilton had run away and eventually began living a normal life outside the "big top." ("Humbug")

Hammond, Jack (Mar Andersons) Stocky youth and off-duty pizza-deliverer who bullied Darin Peter Oswald away from Virtua Fighter 2, a video-game which Oswald had left for only a minute. After knocking the scrawnier youth to the ground, Hammond left the strip-mall arcade and headed for his car, where he was killed by an Oswald-produced, lightning-like electrical surge. ("D.P.O.") *Mar Andersons also portrayed Halverson in "Dod Kalm."*

Hand, Dr. (Mina E. Mina) Baldheaded hypnotist who may or may not have been involved in an elaborate military/intelligence hoax which deliberately cultivated the alien scenario and cultural paranoia by brainwashing Klass County teenager Chrissy Giorgio with "repressed" memories of spaceships and extraterrestrial experiments in an attempt to divert suspicion from the government. ("Jose Chung's 'From Outer Space'")

Hanky Panky *Playboy*-type men's magazine enjoyed by Mulder. In his office he held up the magazine's centerfold to his X-Files partner, saying that the woman pictured claimed to have been abducted by aliens and held in an antigravity chamber. Scully, examining the woman's obvious breast implants, muttered cuttingly, "Antigravity's right." ("The Jersey Devil")

Hannah (B.J. Harrison) Jehovah's Witness who knocked on Ed Jerse's apartment door, but hurried away after the hallucinatory man began ranting and raving about his downstairs neighbor. ("Never Again") *B.J. Harrison also played a clerk in "Blood."*

Hansen's Disease Research Facility Seemingly abandoned leprosy research plant in Perkey, West Virginia, where soldiers rounded up several frightened, alien-looking creatures in concentration camp attire, brutally gunned them down, and dumped their bodies into a mass grave. With the assistance of Agent Pendrell, Scully was able to trace the Japanese manufacturer of the microchip she found implanted in her neck to a Dr. Zama at the facility, where Scully discovered several of the horribly deformed leprosy victims hiding in the darkness beneath a trapdoor. The spokesman for the group told Scully that death squads had killed hundreds of them since Dr. Zama and the medical staff abandoned the facility years earlier. Hansen's disease is the scientific name for leprosy, a progressive infectious illness of the skin, flesh, nerves, etc., characterized by ulcers, white scaly scabs and other deformities. ("731")

Hansen's Motel Lodging in Providence, Rhode Island. Mulder woke up on the floor of Room 6 of the motel after a "serious cerebral event," sweating profusely, his hands and shirt stained with blood, two rounds fired from his weapon, and no memory of how he ended up in there. ("Demons")

Harbaugh (Doug Abrahams) Agent with the Bureau of Alcohol, Tobacco and Firearms, who participated in the joint BATF and FBI raid on the Temple of the Seven Stars' rural Tennessee compound in an attempt to locate an alleged cache of illegal weapons. ("The Field Where I Died") *Doug Abrahams appeared in the pilot episode as a patrolman, as an FBI agent in "Genderbender," devil worshipper Paul Vitaris in "Die Hand Die Verletzt," and Lt. Neary in "Hell Money."*

Harbormaster (Roger Allford) Questioned by Mulder at a Naval shipyard in Newport News, Virginia, during the agent's hunt for the *Talapus,* a seagoing salvage vessel that had supposedly been searching for a Japanese submarine sunk during World War II. The Harbormaster told Mulder that U.S. Customs wouldn't allow the *Talapus* into port. ("Nisei") *Print sources listed Roger Allford in the role of the Harbormaster, although the character was never seen in this episode, only mentioned in dialogue. Evidently the scene between him and Mulder was left on the cutting room floor. Allford appeared briefly, however, as the doomed Garrett Lore in the pre-credits sequence to "3."*

Hard Eight Lounge A "crummy bar" in Philadelphia, Pennsylvania, where stockbroker Ed Jerse went to drown his sorrows immediately after leaving divorce court. A contemplative Scully, having come to a minor crisis in her life brought on by depression, asked Jerse to take her to the Hard Eight Lounge for a date instead of one of the "nice restaurants near the river." Across the street was a tattoo parlor, where Jerse and Scully separately "marked the moment." ("Never Again") *The name of the bar was an in-joke by episode writers Glen Morgan and James Wong, whose production company, "Hard Eight Pictures, Inc." and its logo could be seen after each episode of their short-lived FOX-TV series,* Space: Above and Beyond."

Hard-Faced Man (James Hong) Remorseless Chinese doctor and vicious black marketeer who operated a fixed lottery in San Francisco's Chinatown. Although the bettors drew tiles out of a vase in hopes of winning a jackpot that didn't actually exist, the losers consistently had eyes, arms, legs, livers, and an assortment of other body parts surgically removed by the Hard-Faced Man, which were then sold on the lucrative black market. After his eventual capture and interrogation, Scully accused the greedy organ thief of preying on the desperation and hopelessness of his own people, but the Hard-Faced Man maintained that hope was his gift to the Chinese immigrants who participated in the lottery. ("Hell Money") *Veteran character actor James Hong is best remembered for his role as Chew in the contemporary sci-fi classic* Blade Runner.

Harold, Jess (Timothy Webber) Floor manager at the Chaco Chicken processing plant in Dudley, Arkansas. He was taken hostage at knife-point by Paula Gray after she began hallucinating on the assembly line. Harold accused Chaco of bringing in "the outsider [federal poultry inspector George Kearns] who made us all sick." Harold was trampled to death by the panicked townsfolk after Mulder shot Sheriff Arens, who was preparing to decapitate Scully with a ceremonial axe. ("Our Town") *Actor Timothy Webber also portrayed Det. Talbot in "Tooms" and Dr. Farraday in "Quagmire."*

Harper, Lt. Richard (Dmitry Chepovetsky) Officer aboard the Navy destroyer USS *Ardent* who led a mutiny of eighteen crew members against Captain Barclay. After abandoning the ship in lifeboat 925, Harper was the last mutineer to die from the effects of a mysterious force that caused rapid aging aboard the destroyer. Before his death, however, Scully caught a brief glimpse of the lieutenant at Bethesda Navy Hospital and was stunned to note that the twenty-eight-year-old Harper appeared to be ninety. ("Dod Kalm")

Harrow Convalescent Home Nursing care facility for the elderly in Boca Raton, Florida, one of several nationwide for which prominent virologist Dr. Bonita Charne-Sayre served as the supervising physician. In an attempt to find a cure for the deadly "black cancer" of alien origin, the virologist was using elderly patients at Harrow and other convalescent facilities as human "guinea pigs." ("Terma")

Hartley, Rev. Calvin (George Gerdes) The legal guardian of young faith-healer Samuel. Although he was once a poor minister who preached from a soapbox and collected dollar bills in a coffee can, Rev. Hartley later became owner of the Kenwood, Tennessee-based evangelical Miracle Ministry. The vanity license plate on his new Cadillac read: B HEALD. ("Miracle Man")

Hartley, Samuel (Scott Bairstow) Young adopted son of Rev. Calvin Hartley, who allegedly found the boy on the banks of the muddy Mississippi River. A decade later, Samuel and the evangelical Miracle Ministry became the focus of a federal investigation when two people died shortly after the young man laid "healing" hands upon them. Although he claimed that his "gift" had been "corrupted," Samuel was arrested and placed in jail, where the youth was beaten to death by two cellmates. His body later disappeared from the county hospital morgue and a no-nonsense nurse claimed that she and others saw Samuel walk out by himself. ("Miracle Man") *Scott Baristow co-starred in the unsold ABC television pilot* Country Estates *("a parodic look at the dark underside of suburban life"), written by Howard Gordon and Alex Gansas, who specifically requested he play Samuel Hartley. After playing the fresh-faced faith healer in this episode, Bairstow went on to star as Newt Call in the syndicated* Lonesome Dove: The Outlaw Years *and co-starred in the 1997 theatrical movie,* Wild America. *Child actor Alex Doduk played Samuel Hartley in the pre-credits sequence of "Miracle Man."*

Hartman, Dr. (Martin Evans) Classically handsome and youthful-looking cosmetic surgeon hired for a staff position at a Los Angeles clinic. Dr. Hartman was actually Jack Franklyn, a sorcerer and devil worshipper who transformed his looks beyond the limits of modern surgery by killing patients and offering them as human "blood sacrifices." ("Sanguinarium") *Martin Evans also played the Shadowy Syndicate's Major Domo at their private club in New York City in "The Blessing Way/Paper Clip" and "Apocrypha."*

Harvey Mudd Medical school attended by Arthur Grable and Frank Nollette, who later became research scientists on the top-secret Icarus Project at the Mahan Propulsion Laboratory. In the 1970s, Nollette's quantum physics professor at Harvey Mudd failed him one semester because he didn't agree with one of Nollette's theories. ("Roland")

Havez, Det. (Dwight McFee) St. Paul, Minnesota, police officer who, along with partner Det. Cline, investigated a string of fortune-teller murders committed by the Puppet. While providing clairvoyant Clyde Bruckman with protective custody at the Le Damfino Hotel, Det. Havez, an incessant chain smoker, was relieved when Bruckman told him he would not die of lung cancer. Havez, however, was killed by the Puppet with a steak knife a few minutes later. ("Clyde Bruckman's Final Repose") *Detective Havez was named for Jean C. Havez, who collaborated with real-life 1920–30s Hollywood movie director Clyde Bruckman on numerous Buster Keaton screenplays. Actor Dwight McFee also portrayed Montana attorney David Gates in "Shapes," the commander of the Blue Beret UFO Retrieval Team in "Little Green Men," and a suspect in "Irresistible."*

Hawley, Elizabeth (Liz) (Lisa Vultaggio) Nineteen-year-old student at Jackson University in Raleigh, North Carolina. Hawley and her boyfriend, James (Jim) Summers, were kidnapped and tortured by Luther Jackson Henry. She was rescued when the FBI raided the hostage site at Lake Jordan. ("Beyond the Sea")

Headless Woman's Pub Upscale tavern in Washington, D.C. where Mulder surprised Scully with "Happy Birthday" singing waiters and an *Apollo 11* commemorative keychain for a present. The agents were then approached by a woman who identified herself as the sister of UFO enthusiast, and multiple alien-abductee, Max Fenig. The pub was also the site of a shoot-out between an assassin and Scully, which claimed the life of Agent Pendrell in the cross fire. ("Tempus Fugit/Max")

Hedin, Agent (Nancy Kerr) FBI Sci-Crime Lab technician at the Bureau's headquarters in Washington, D.C. Agent Hedin matched fingerprints found on a stairwell to a Michael Kritschgau, a Defense Department employee who assaulted Scully and threw her down a flight of stairs when she attempted to stop him from stealing a container of ice core samples. ("Gethsemane")

hegemony The term Jeremiah Smith used to describe "a new origin of species," supposedly a master race elevating humanity to a new plateau by way of the Shadowy Syndicate's colonization Project. ("Herrenvolk")

Heinrich Norwegian elkhound Mulder told animal control officer Eugene Tooms he needed assistance in finding. Mulder alleged that he used the dog to hunt moose. ("Tooms")

Heller, Lauren College student from Capital State University whose body was discovered in a Washington, D.C. alleyway less than an hour after she had been murdered. The fourth victim of a serial killer, she was found with her neck slit and the ring on her left hand moved to the little finger of her right. Only moments before Mulder relayed word that her body had been discovered, Scully saw the words "SHE IS ME" scrawled in blood on a bathroom mirror and an apparition of Heller standing in the room. ("Elegy") *The young actress who played the ghostly Heller was uncredited.*

hell money Specially printed paper money which is burned as a gift to the spirit world during the Chinese New Year, and on yearly anniversaries of a relative's death. It is also traditional to burn paper images or facsimiles of houses, cars, food, or other offerings to the ancestors. With San Francisco police detective Glen Chao's assistance, Mulder and Scully were able to use "hell money" found at a crime scene to identify the cremated body of a recent Chinese immigrant. ("Hell Money")

📁 **"Hell Money"** Written by Jeffrey Vlaming. Directed by Tucker Gates. File number 3X19. *First aired March 29, 1996. When a young Chinese immigrant is found burned to death, Agents Mulder and Scully are assigned to the investigation of a series of murders in San Francisco's Chinatown where a potentially lucrative lottery can* literally *cost participants an arm and a leg.* **Classic Sound Bite:** *"What good is an interpreter when everyone speaks the language of silence?"* **Background Check:** *Episode writer Jeffrey Vlaming originally had two different story ideas. One dealt with a lottery in a small undetermined town and the other was about the goings-on in Chinatown where a "corporate being assembled the destitute." Chris Carter simply combined the two ideas.*

Helm, Hepcat (Gordon Tipple). Artist living in "Circus Performer Haven" Gibsonton, Florida, who drew the Feejee Mermaid illustration on the menu at Phil's Diner. Helm was also a mechanic, carnival operator, and owner of the Tabernacle of Terror funhouse. He was killed in his artist's studio by Lanny's congenital twin, Leonard. ("Humbug") *Gordon Tipple also played a police detective in "Eve" and wheelchair-bound prisoner Joe Crandall in "Young at Heart."*

hemorrhagic fever A deadly, highly infectious, leprosy-like ailment. The Cigarette-Smoking Man stated that there was an outbreak of hemorrhagic fever in Sacramento, California in 1988, which was covered up. "The truth would have caused panic," he said. "Panic would have cost lives. We controlled the disease by controlling the information" ("F. Emasculata"). Scully told Mulder that the alien-looking creature imprisoned in the quarantined railway car was a test subject with hemorrhagic fever and if the bomb-laden train exploded thousands would die. According to the Shadowy Syndicate's 1st Elder, the international consortium was attempting to develop a hardier, germ-warfare-resistant strain of humanity. ("731")

Henderson, Col. Calvin (Marshall Bell) Air Force "reclamations" expert in command of Operation Falcon. After Henderson was advised at the U.S. Space Surveillance Center that an unidentified object had crashed west of Lake Michigan, he ordered the radar observer to report the sighting as a meteor and the radar findings as "instrument malfunction." Henderson then mobilized Operation Falcon, the top-secret military mission with the objective of retrieving a crashed UFO and any surviving members of the alien crew. Henderson placed Mulder in the brig at the Townsend, Wisconsin, site of the downed UFO and advised the FBI agent to forget what he saw—or what he *thought* he saw. ("Fallen Angel")

Henderson, Heather (Christine Estabrook) Attractive and brilliant FBI lab technician in her thirties whose analysis showed a ninety-five percent probability that John Barnett's old handwriting and the new notes addressed to Mulder were a match. Agent Henderson appeared to have a romantic interest in Mulder. ("Young at Heart")

Hendrix, Jimi 1960s musician whose soul Mulder asked alleged psychic Luther Lee Boggs to channel. ("Beyond the Sea")

Henry (Jacques LaLonde) Resident of Bright Angel Halfway House who befriended Lucy Householder. At the exact moment that fifteen-year-old kidnap victim Amy Jacobs was quivering in a cold, dark, basement cell with scratches on her face, Lucy, too, shivered uncontrollably as scratches appeared on her face, and she moaned to Henry, "It's dark. I can't see." ("Oubliette")

Henry, Lucas Jackson (Lawrence King) Small, thin criminal in his late twenties, with a history of sexual assault and narcotics charges. Durham, North Carolina, law enforcement officials believed that Henry was death row inmate Luther Lee Boggs' partner in Boggs' last five serial murders. He kidnapped and tortured Jackson University students Elizabeth Hawley and James Summers in a psychotic attempt to work out his mental problems associated with the death of his girlfriend and decapitation of his mother in an automobile accident seven years earlier. Scully believed that Henry and the imprisoned Boggs orchestrated the kidnapping in an attempt to kill Mulder, who was shot when he rescued the Hawley girl. Henry fell to his death while fleeing Scully at the Blue Devil Brewery. ("Beyond the Sea")

Heritage Halfway House The Colson, Washington, residence of retarded janitor Roland Fuller. ("Roland")

Herman, Dr. Doug SEE: **Odin, Richard**

herrenvolk Emotionally-charged German word meaning "master race," which Adolph Hitler attempted to create by having Germans breed "appropriately" and by the systematic elimination of anyone who wasn't sufficiently Aryan. The word aptly described the Shadowy Syndicate's Project, an attempt to create a new species (or "hegemony"), thus raising humanity to a new level. ("Herrenvolk")

📁 **"Herrenvolk"** Written by Chris Carter. Directed by R.W. Goodwin. File number 4X01. *First aired October 4, 1996. In the conclusion to the third season's cliff-hanger, Agent Mulder and shapeshifting alien clone Jeremiah Smith are pursued by the icepick-wielding alien Bounty Hunter to a Canadian farm, where Mulder glimpses "The Project," and Scully discovers the real purpose of Smith's work at the Social Security Administration.* **Classic Sound Bite:** *"Nothing happens in contradiction to what we know of it. And that's a place to start. That's where the hope is."* **Background Check:** The X-Files *crew* *originally tried to use several thousand stingless bee drones in the episode, but after David Duchovny, the director of photography and a little girl got stung, the series' new fourth season special effects wizards, Area 51, scrapped the real insects and went with "photo-real and undetectable" computer-generated bees.*

"HE/SHE IS ONE." Words scrawled on the backs of kidnapped teenagers from the town of Delta Glen, Wisconsin, who were later found wandering aimlessly, clad only in their underwear. ("Red Museum")

Heuvelman's Lake Rigdon, Georgia, body of water with forty-eight miles of coastline located in the Blue Ridge Mountains. The lake was reportedly the home of Big Blue, the Southern Serpent, an American version of the Loch Ness monster. ("Quagmire") *Heuvelman's Lake was named in honor of one of the most famous water monster researchers, Van Heuvels, a Dutch cryptozoologist who wrote* In the Wake of the Sea Serpents. *Heuvelman's Lake was located in Millikan County, named after Rick Millikan, a casting director for* The X-Files.

High Containment Facility Quarantine unit located in Winthrop, Washington, where Mulder, Scully and Federal Forest Service ranger Larry Moore were immediately transported after their cocoon-filled Jeep was discovered in a remote Pacific Northwest forest. ("Darkness Falls")

Highland Park Cemetery Graveyard in San Francisco where Mulder and Scully discovered the recently buried remains of a Chinese immigrant whose body was missing a heart and several other body parts. ("Hell Money")

Hill, Agent Cameron (Ryan Michael) One of several FBI agents assigned to an anti-terrorist unit responsible for the protection of dozens of high-ranking military officials in Washington, D.C., for the rededication of the Vietnam Veterans Memorial. Although Agent Hill escorted Gen. Jon Steffan to his Pentagon office, he was unable to stop Nathaniel Teager, a phantom POW with the ability to hide himself from a person's field of vision, from slipping past him and murdering the general. The agent redeemed himself, however, when he shot and killed Teager as the seemingly invisible assassin tried to make a getaway from the site of his murder attempt on the life of Major Gen. Benjamin Bloch. ("Unrequited") *Ryan Michael also played the Overcoat Man in "One Breath."*

Hindt, Sheriff Lance (Chris Ellis) Millikan County law enforcement official who refused Mulder's request to close Heuvelman's Lake, insisting that he didn't have the manpower to patrol its forty-eight miles of shoreline. The sheriff believed that several disappearances and deaths were ordinary accidents rather than the work of Big Blue, a legendary aquatic serpent supposedly residing in the lake. But when Sheriff Hindt fell into the water and felt "something big" brush past him, he yelled "Close the lake!" as he quickly climbed out. ("Quagmire")

Hirsh, Judge One of two magistrates who flanked Judge Kann during Eugene Tooms' psychiatric hearing and commitment review. ("Tooms") *The actor who portrayed Judge Hirsh was uncredited.*

Hispanic Man SEE: **Cardinal, Luis**

Hodge, Dr. Lawrence (Xander Berkeley) Physician who accompanied Mulder and Scully and the scientific unit sent to investigate the unexplained deaths of the Arctic Ice Core Project research team on assignment at Icy Cape, Alaska. Egotistical and dubious, Hodge mistakenly believed that the two federal agents knew more about the situation at the research station than they were letting on. He thought that Mulder had slit Dr. Murphy's throat until it was discovered that Dr. Da Silva was infected with the parasitic ice worm. ("Ice") *Xander Berkeley is familiar to moviegoers for his roles in such films as* Mommie Dearest, Terminator 2: Judgment Day, *and* Leaving Las Vegas.

Hohman, Margaret (Chilton Crane) Wheelchair-bound victim who died after young faith-healer Samuel Hartley laid hands on her at a Miracle Ministry tent revival. Scully's autopsy revealed lesions on the lungs and throughout the cardiovascular and pulmonary systems. Scully theorized cellular hypoxia caused by arsenic or by sodium or potassium cyanide (the poison actually proved to be cyanogen bromide, a cyanide derivative). ("Miracle Man") *Actress Chilton Crane also appeared as a mother at the bus station in "F. Emasculata," and Max Fenig's accomplice Sharon Graffia in "Tempus Fugit/Max."*

Holloway, Lottie (Corrine Koslo) MUFON (Mutual UFO Network) member living in the Allentown, Pennsylvania, area. When she met Scully at Betsy Hagopian's house, she seemed to recognize the agent, claiming her as a fellow alien-abductee. ("Nisei")

Holly (Julia Arkos) Research librarian in the FBI's Computer Records Office in Washington, D.C. Robert Modell used his psychokinetic powers to persuade her to access Mulder's FBI file. A recent mugging victim, Holly was manipulated by Modell to believe that Assistant Director Skinner, who challenged Modell's presence in the building, was the man who had assaulted her. Modell escaped after Holly sprayed Skinner with mace and repeatedly kicked him with her size 7 shoes while he lay on the floor. ("Pusher")

Hollywood Blood Bank Los Angeles-area plasma storage facility investigated by Mulder in his search for the vampiric serial murderers known as The Trinity Killers. Phoning blood banks to check on recent hirings, Mulder learned that the Hollywood Blood Bank had a new night watchman, "Frank," which was the alias for John, one of the members of The Trinity Killers. Mulder caught him slurping blood when he arrived at the scene. ("3")

Holtzman, Victor (Don Thompson) Agent of the National Security Agency who demanded to know the origin of "the documents" (eight-year-old Kevin Morris' binary number scribblings) which Mulder had faxed to Washington for analysis. Agent Holtzman threatened Mulder with obstruction of justice charges, explaining that the pages were a highly classified fragment of a Defense Department satellite transmission. Holtzman and other MIBs ransacked the Morris residence looking for evidence and then spirited away young Kevin and his mother, Darlene. ("Conduit") *Don Thompson also played war veterans Henry Willig in "Sleepless" and Lt. Col. Victor Stans in "The Walk."*

Holvey, Charlie (Joel Palmer) Eight-year-old son of Maggie and Steve Holvey and grandson of Golda, an Old World Romanian who tried to protect the boy from the evil spirit that took the form of his stillborn twin, Michael. Romanian holy men, known as the Calusari, were recruited by Mulder to perform a ritual exorcism that separated the souls of the two boys. ("The Calusari") *Child actor Joel Palmer also portrayed Charlie Holvey's evil-possessed dead brother, Michael, and Kevin Morris, a boy whose sister was abducted by aliens in "Conduit."*

Holvey, Maggie (Helene Clarkson) Romanian woman who wed Steve Holvey, a State Department diplomat, in 1984, although her highly superstitious mother, Golda, objected to the marriage and her daughter's relocation to America. They had three children: Charlie, Michael (his stillborn twin), and Teddy (who was killed by a demonic force that possessed the physical likeness of Michael). Although Maggie questioned Golda's Old World belief in omens and the supernatural, the mysterious deaths of her mother, husband and son, Teddy, forced her to reconsider the legitimacy of Romanian folklore and spiritual phenomena. ("The Calusari")

Holvey, Michael (Joel Palmer) The stillborn son of Maggie and Steve Holvey and twin brother of Charlie. His evil spirit followed Charlie and was responsible for the death of his brother, father, and grandmother before Mulder and the Calusari effectively divided the souls of the twin boys through the Ritual of Separation. The holy men hinted, however, that the demonic spirit was not Michael's, but a much more malevolent entity that took his form and didn't care if it killed "one boy or a million men." The Calusari's white-bearded elder warned Mulder, "You must be careful. It knows you." ("The Calusari")

Holvey, Steve (Ric Reid) American State Department official who met his wife, Maggie, in Romania in 1984. His two-year-old son's unusual death at a Virginia amusement park led to an FBI investigation because of Holvey's position in the U.S. government. As he prepared to take his son Charlie to a social worker, an unseen evil presence grabbed Holvey's tie and caught it in the garage door-opener mechanism, strangling him to death while his son cried in horror. ("The Calusari") *Actor Ric Reid appeared in the pilot episode as an astronomer.*

Holvey, Teddy (Oliver and Jeremy Isaac Wildsmith) Two-year-old son of Maggie and Steve Holvey and brother of Charlie. An invisible entity unhooked Teddy from a restraining device at a Murray, Virginia, amusement park and using a helium balloon as bait, lured the small boy across a kiddie railroad track, where he was killed by an oncoming train. Three months later, Mulder analyzed a photo of Teddy taken only seconds before the tragedy, which with digital-imaging software, raised an image of electromagnetic concentration pulling the balloon's string, prompting Mulder's suspicion of "some kind of poltergeist activity." ("The Calusari")

Holy Cross Memorial Hospital The medical facility in Washington, D.C. where Scully was diagnosed with inoperable brain cancer. Mulder met Scully at the hospital's oncology unit, where she showed him an MRI X ray indicating she had a cancerous mass on the wall between her sinus and cerebrum. ("Memento Mori")

"Holy Grail, The" Mulder's description of the stolen MJ documents, which detailed the international conspiracy that had kept the existence of extraterrestrials secret since the 1940s. ("Anasazi")

Holy Spirit, The A Portland, Oregon, New Age bookstore whose owner was drained of blood when he became one of several victims of the vampiric serial murderers, The Trinity Killers. ("3")

📁 **"Home"** Written by Glen Morgan and James Wong. Directed by Kim Manners. File number 4X03. *First aired October 11, 1996. In the bucolic small town of Home, Pennsylvania, agents Mulder and Scully discover evidence of infanticide committed by the reclusive Peacock family: inbred hillbillies and genetic mutants determined to perpetuate their line.* **Classic Sound Bite:** *"Well, aside from the need for corrective lenses and the tendency to be abducted by extraterrestrials involved in an international governmental conspiracy, the Mulder family passes genetic muster."* **Background Check:** *A parental warning at the beginning of this gratuitously violent and gross episode was an X-Files first. "Home" also marked the return of writers Glen Morgan and James Wong, who left after the airing of the second season's "Die Hand Die Verletzt" to concentrate on the short-lived Fox science-fiction series* Space: Above and Beyond.

Hoover, J. Edgar (David Fredericks) Legendary and long-term director of the Federal Bureau of Investigation. According to Lone Gunman Frohike's questionable version of the Cigarette-Smoking Man's life, by 1968 the shadowy government operative (who worked hard to keep any president from knowing he even existed) was giving Director Hoover orders. ("Musings of a Cigarette-Smoking Man")

Horning, Craig Researcher at the Boston Museum of Natural History whose death was linked to a jaguar-spirit curse after the remains of an ancient Ecuadorian artifact were unearthed and shipped to America. ("Teso dos Bichos")

Horton, Det. (Mitch Kosterman) Germantown, Maryland, police detective who sought answers to a bizarre murder committed by a genderbending killer ("Genderbender"). After transferring to the NYPD, Det. Horton investigated the mysterious death of Dr. Saul Grissom, "a pioneer in sleep disorders" ("Sleepless"). *Actor Mitch Kosterman also played prison guard Fornier in "The List."*

📁 **"Host, The"** Written by Chris Carter. Directed by Daniel Sackheim. File number 2X02. *First aired September 23, 1994. Angry at being given meaningless assignments by his Bureau superiors, Agent Mulder considers leaving the FBI until his "routine murder case" opens up a brand-new can of (fluke) worms and leads to the discovery of a genetically-mutated parasitical creature living deep in Newark's sewers.* **Classic Sound Bite:** *"It looks like I'm going to have to tell Skinner that the suspect is a giant bloodsucking worm after all."* **Background Check:** *Chris Carter has acknowledged that he got the "disgusting" idea for "The Host" from a close examination of his dog's worms.*

Hosteen (Bryon Chief Moon) Eric Hosteen's father, first name unknown. Albert told him that "the Earth has a secret it needs to tell" after an earthquake shook the Navajo Reservation. He also took part in the Navajo Blessing Way ceremony that saved Mulder's life. ("Anasazi/The Blessing Way")

Hosteen, Albert (Floyd "Red Crow" Westerman) World War II Navajo code-talker who helped Mulder and Scully translate the encrypted MJ files. He told Scully that while most of the documents were in jargon, they did refer to an international conspiracy dating to the 1940s ("Anasazi"). Albert and his family were brutalized in their home by the Cigarette-Smoking Man and camouflaged soldiers who demanded Mulder and the MJ documents. After Mulder's unconscious body was found at a quarry in the New Mexico desert, Albert performed the healing, days-long Blessing Way Chant ("The Blessing Way"). To insure Mulder and Scully's safety and reinstatement to the Bureau, Assistant Director Skinner had Albert memorize the MJ files' contents and relate it to twenty other men according to his tribe's narrative tradition. "So unless you kill every Navajo in four states," Skinner told the Cigarette-Smoking Man, "that information is available with a simple phone call." ("Paper Clip") *Floyd "Red Crow" Westerman played Uncle Ray Fire-walker in the CBS-Chuck Norris series,* Walker, Texas Ranger. *He made two appearances on* Northern Exposure *as the spirit guide One Who Waits.*

Hosteen, Eric (Dakota House) Albert Hosteen's grandson, a Navajo teen-ager who collected rattlesnake skins. After a 5.6 earthquake hit the Navajo Reservation in Two Grey Hills, New Mexico, a motorcycling Eric discovered a buried railway refrigeration car and brought the desiccated corpse of some alien-looking creature into town. When Mulder came to the reservation, Eric drove him to the quarry site of the unearthed railroad car on his motorcross bike ("Anasazi"). He also participated in Mulder's Blessing Way healing ceremony ("The Blessing Way").

Hotel Catherine Washington, D.C., hotel where Mulder and Scully tracked the gendershifting killer known as Marty. After a struggle, he/she was caught, but members of the reclusive Kindred sect spirited him away. ("Gender-bender")

Hotel George Mason Hotel in Richmond, Virginia, where Morley Tobacco company executive Patrick Newirth was vaporized by Dr. Chester Banton's shadow. A smudge on the carpet consisting mostly of carbon, with some potassium and trace minerals, was all that remained of Newirth. ("Soft Light")

Hotel Hartley Worcester, Massachusetts, place of lodging where Mulder and Scully stayed (rooms 206 and 210) while investigating the paranormal phenomena surrounding nurse Michelle Charters' rape allegations at the Excelsis Dei convalescent home. ("Excelsius Dei")

Hotel James Monroe Place of lodging in the Boston/Cambridge area where Dr. Yonechi, a Japanese researcher, was met by a futuristic version of MIT cryobiologist Jason Nichols. After Yonechi checked into his room, the elderly Nichols murdered the noted scientist with a rapid freezing compound in his attempt to alter the course of history. ("Synchrony")

Hotel Niagra An old hotel in Raleigh, North Carolina, with a neon sign of a waterfall and an "angel of stone" statue across the street. The two landmarks fit death row inmate Luther Lee Boggs' alleged psychic vision and led Scully to a nearby condemned warehouse where Lucas Jackson Henry had hidden his two kidnap victims before moving them to a Lake Jordan lakehouse. ("Beyond the Sea")

Householder, Lucy (Tracy Ellis) Thirty-year-old Seattle, Washington, res-taurant worker who inexplicably began to bleed from the nose and collapsed to the floor, repeating "Nobody's gonna spoil us" again and again. Lucy's watch said 10:05, the exact same time fifteen-year-old Amy Jacobs was being abducted twenty miles across town by Carl Wade. When Lucy was eight, she, too, was kidnapped by an unidentified man (actually Carl Wade) and spent five years locked in a dark basement before escaping. Whatever trauma Amy experienced, Lucy underwent the same feelings, prompting Mulder to suggest that "some kind of empathic transference" was involved. An arrest warrant for complicity in Amy's kidnapping was issued for Lucy (who had a criminal record of prostitution and narcotics) when the blood on her clothes proved to be a DNA match with Amy's blood, but Lucy had already fled. She was later discovered trembling in the basement of Wade's cabin, fueling the suspicions of Scully and other federal agents that Lucy was the kidnapper's accomplice. Although Amy was resuscitated after Wade nearly drowned her, Lucy died on dry land at the same moment. A Washington state pathologist found five liters of water in her lungs. ("Oubliette")

Houston Space Center Mission Control site for NASA's *Viking* Orbiter project. Mulder and Scully investigated claims of a mysterious force sabotaging the space shuttle program from the Texas-based control center. ("Space")

How AIDS Was Created by the Jews Title of an anti-Semitic pamphlet left at the apartment door of Jacob Weiss, a Hasidic Jew grieving over the brutal murder of Isaac Luria, his daughter's soon-to-be husband. Curt Brunjes, an outspoken neo-Nazi who owned a copy shop across the street from Luria's market, printed and distributed the racist propaganda. Brunjes' rabid hate-mongering incited three teenagers to brutally murder Luria in his store. ("Kaddish")

"howlers" Paranoid-schizophrenic Gerry Schnauz kidnapped and lobotomized several young women in an attempt to "save" them from the "howlers" that he believed were tormenting them. Schnauz described the "howlers" as living inside his head. "They make you do things and say things that you don't mean. All your good thoughts won't wish them away. You need help . . . to kill them." ("Unruhe")

Hsin, Kim (Lucy Liu) Young Chinese-American woman stricken with leukemia. Gambling that he would hit the jackpot and be able to pay for his daughter's medical care, Kim's desperate father continued to play a mysterious Chinatown lottery where bettors risked losing their body parts to menacing black marketeers. ("Hell Money")

Hsin, Shuyang (Michael Yama) Chinese-American carpet layer who lost an eye playing a dangerous Chinatown lottery in hopes of paying for his daughter's needed surgery. Hsin was rescued by San Francisco police detective Glen Chao just before the Hard-Faced Man operated on him and removed his heart. ("Hell Money")

HTG Industrial Technologies Small Philadelphia-based military contractor founded by Howard Graves. After it became apparent that the company was on the brink of financial ruin, Graves' partner, Robert Dorland, began illegally selling technology to a Mideast extremist group, which eventually cost Graves his life. ("Shadows")

Hudak, Det. (Daniel Kamin) Plain clothes police officer in charge of the investigation into a series of young women's murders in Washington, D.C. Detective Hudak told Mulder and Scully that an anonymous caller phoned 911 with a message regarding Penny Timmons, one of the serial killer's victims. The caller claimed that her last words were "She is me." But Hudak noted that Timmons' larynx was severed, making it impossible for her to utter any dying words. Hudak was exceptionally relentless during his interrogation of the suspect, an autistic man named Harold Spuller. ("Elegy")

"Huggs" Online handle for lonely and overweight Ellen Kaminsky, which she used in the Internet chatroom "Big and Beautiful." ("2Shy")

Hughes, Dr. Alicia Eve 8's assumed identity after she escaped imprisonment in 1985. Dr. Hughes had high-level military security clearance which granted her access to visit Teena Simmons and Cindy Reardon at the Whiting Institute for the Criminally Insane. ("Eve")

Human Genome Project According to Mulder, "the most ambitious scientific endeavor in the history of mankind" involving thousands of scientists who were attempting to map all human genes. Dr. Terence Berube was supposedly working on the Human Genome Project at EmGen Corporation's molecular research laboratory in Gaithersburg, Maryland. In reality, Dr. Berube was conducting experiments on terminally-ill human beings by injecting them with extraterrestrial DNA. ("The Erlenmeyer Flask")

humbug A deception or a hoax. The Feejee Mermaid, a legendary P.T. Barnum act that was just a dead monkey with a fish's tail sewn on, was a classic humbug. Hepcat Helm, a local artist in Gibsonton, Florida (a town populated by former circus performers) once said, "You never know where the truth ends and the humbug begins." ("Humbug")

"Humbug" Written by Darin Morgan. Directed by Kim Manners. File number 2X20. *First aired March 31, 1995 (the day before April Fool's Day). Agents Mulder and Scully's investigation into a series of horrific killings leads them to a small Florida town populated by a variety of former carnival sideshow artistes.* **Classic Sound Bite:** *"If people knew the true price of spirituality, there'd be more atheists."* **Background Check:** *After filming the episode for five days in March in Vancouver, the X-Files crew returned to work to find their entire set covered under four inches of snow. Considering that the episode was* *supposed to take place at a retirement community in sunny Florida, the FX team was immediately forced to use water trucks with fire hoses to blow the snow away.*

Humphreys, Steve (Tom O'Rourke) Security chief for Schiff-Immergut Lumber Company who accompanied Mulder, Scully, and U.S. Forest Service ranger Larry Moore to the logging camp in the remote Olympia National Forest of Northwest Washington. Humphreys was cocooned inside his vehicle at night and killed by a swarm of prehistoric green mites that entered through the air vents. ("Darkness Falls")

Hunsaker, George His son received an anonymous call from someone who said he knew where a mass grave was located in "the Perfect Harmony City" of Comity. All the panic-stricken townsfolk unearthed, however, was an old medical bag belonging to the local pediatrician with the bones of a Llasa Apso inside. ("Syzygy")

Hunt, Mr. According to Lone Gunman Frohike's speculative dossier on the Cigarette-Smoking Man, Mr. Hunt was the name JFK assassination patsy Lee Harvey Oswald called the CSM. ("Musings of a Cigarette-Smoking Man") *A number of conspiratorialists have promoted the theory that Watergate conspirator and former CIA operative E. Howard Hunt may have been present— and in fact briefly detained—at the Kennedy assassination scene in Dealy Plaza. Their "evidence" is a press photo of the Dallas police with three unidentified "tramps" in tow. The shortest of the three looked something like Hunt.*

Hyneck, Sgt. (Michael Dobson) Air Force officer who claimed the body of alien-costumed Major Robert Vallee from a hospital in Klass County, Washington. ("Jose Chung's 'From Outer Space'") *In an episode loaded with in-jokes, Sgt. Hyneck's character was named for J. Allen Hyneck, a UFO investigator and author, leading member of the Project Bluebook team, and a creative consultant for the Stephen Spielberg movie* Close Encounters of the Third Kind.

hypokalemia An electrolyte imbalance of high sodium and low potassium. Medical records from Community Hospital in Felton, Oklahoma, where Darin Peter Oswald was treated after being struck by lightning, showed that he suffered from acute hypokalemia. Mulder theorized that the medical condition explained Oswald's ability to generate electricity. ("D.P.O.")

hypovolemia Official cause of death of Joel Simmons and Doug Reardon after each man had over seventy-five percent of his blood exsanguinated. ("Eve")

Ivanov

Ianelli, Lisa (Susan Hoffman) Massachusetts Institute of Technology (MIT) cryobiolgist and girlfriend of fellow scientist Jason Nichols, who covered for her when another researcher threatened to go public with claims of falsified data. A time-traveling, elderly version of Nichols explained to her that in the future, she would develop a rapid freezing compound so remarkable that it would change the course of history. The futuristic Nichols then pricked Ianelli with a metallic stylus that injected the rapid freezing agent. Scully and a team of medical personnel successfully resuscitated Ianelli and she later attempted to reconstruct the history-altering chemical compound on the cryolab's computers after the futuristic Nichols erased all of the present-time Nichols' files from the facility's mainframes. ("Synchrony")

Icarus Project Official name for a top-secret jet propulsion experiment conducted at the Mahan Propulsion Laboratory of the Washington Institute of Technology. The Icarus Project's goal was to develop the next generation of jet engines that could achieve Mach 15 (fifteen times the speed of sound). ("Roland")

"Ice" Written by Glen Morgan and James Wong. Directed by David Nutter. File number 1X07. *First aired November 5, 1993. Mulder and Scully's latest X-File investigation leads them to an isolated Arctic research station where they discover extraterrestrial parasitic worms have been unearthed by the deep underground drilling and are burrowing their way into host bodies.* **Classic Sound Bite:** *"We are not who we are."* **Background Check:** *Rather than mock up a fake human body for the space worms to slither around in, makeup effects wizard Toby Lindala (in his first major assignment for the series) actually created a false skin for the neck, complete with a channel for the creepy-crawly parasite to burrow in.*

ice worm Alien parasitic lifeform brought to Earth by a meteor 250,000 years ago. The wormlike organism remained dormant until researchers with the Arctic Ice Core Project brought the extraterrestrial to the surface when they set a depth record for ice-sheet drilling at Icy Cape, Alaska. In its quiescent state, the ice worm appeared to be an ammonia-based microorganism, but after it entered the bloodstream, the single-celled creature (possibly the larval stage of a larger organism) developed into a worm approximately one foot long that penetrated the hypothalamus gland in the brain and increased the production of acetylcholine, causing aggressive behavior in its host. After examining a blood sample, Scully discovered that when larva from two different ice worms invaded the same host they would kill each other, releasing the victim from the control of the first alien lifeform. Surgical removal of the ice worm would have proved fatal to the host body. ("Ice")

ichthyosis Medical condition characterized by the scale-like shedding of the skin. Circus performer Jerald Glazebrook suffered from ichthyosis, which gave him the appearance of reptile epidermis and earned him the stage name of "Alligator Man." ("Humbug")

Idaho Mutual Insurance Trust Downtown Fairfield, Idaho, insurance company whose windows were shattered when an invisible behemoth rampaged down the street. ("Fearful Symmetry")

Ilaqua, Dr. Eric (Paul Raskin) Goateed cosmetic surgeon at the Aesthetic Surgery Unit of Chicago's Greenwood Memorial Hospital, who claimed he had no memory or knowledge of going into a psychotic rage and using a laser to burn through the flesh of a patient's face. ("Sanguinarium") *Paul Raskin played Florida State medical examiner Dr. Jim Ullrich in "The List."*

Incanto, Virgil (Timothy Carhart) Serial killer who preyed on lonely, overweight women via the Internet. After a skin sample from under one victim's fingernails showed a lack of oils or essential fatty acids, Mulder theorized that Incanto wasn't psychotic but rather a genetic mutant ("fat-sucking vampire") seeking to replenish those chemicals. It was later discovered that Incanto's body produced a digestive mucous, like stomach acid, which allowed him to rob his victims' corpses of all their adipose tissue. An academic and translator of obscure sixteenth-century Italian poetry, the suave and charming serial killer first used the romantic literature to seduce women through personal columns and then moved onto the Internet with the online handle of "2Shy." One of his intended victims, Ellen Kaminsky, wounded him with Scully's revolver. A week later, a jailed Incanto, his skin mottled and curdling, confessed to forty-seven murders in five states. Unrepentant, he declared, "I gave them what they wanted. They gave me what I needed." His name was an alias drawn from the Italian poet he translated, Dante Alighieri (1265–1321): In *The Divine Comedy* Virgil was the guide through Dante's seven circles of hell; and the rhyme scheme Dante invented, the terza rima verses, are divided into long sections called "cantos." ("2Shy") *Timothy Carhart played Geena Davis' would-be rapist in* Thelma and Louise, *and the villain in Eddie Murphy's widely panned* Beverly Hills Cop III.

Indigo Echo Delta Niner The military code used by Air Force "reclamations" expert Commander Calvin Henderson to confirm a downed alien spacecraft and immediately mobilize Operation Falcon. ("Fallen Angel")

Innes, Nurse (Nancy Fish) Registered nurse on staff at the New Horizon Psychiatric Center in Washington, D.C. In less than a month, she murdered four young, blonde women, all approximately the same age, height, and weight, their bodies found within six blocks of each other. Scully noted that each victim's ring had been switched from their left hand to their right. The main suspect was Harold Spuller, a mentally-challenged patient at the psychiatric hospital, where Spuller's roommate and best friend, Chuck Forsch, told Scully that Spuller had quit taking his medication because Innes was trying to poison him. When Scully realized that Innes, whose husband left her for a younger woman, was actually the serial killer, she confronted the nurse in a hospital washroom and was attacked with a scalpel. Scully drew her weapon and fired, striking Innes in the shoulder. Afterward, Scully told Mulder that the nurse had been ingesting Spuller's medication, the unregulated effect of which was violent and unpredictable behavior. ("Elegy") *Nancy Fish, whose lengthy film credits include* The Mask, Sleeping with the Enemy, Dr. Giggles, Beethoven *(along with David Duchovny) and* Death Becomes Her, *also played a nurse in* The Exorcist III.

INS Service Processing Center The district office of the Immigration and Naturalization Service in Fresno, California, where Conrad Lozano worked as an agent. Migrant worker Eladio Buente was held in custody at the processing center, segregated from other fearful Mexican immigrants who believed he was the mythical Chupacabra creature. ("El Mundo Gira")

Investigative Support Unit (ISU) The behavioral science unit of the FBI's Violent Crimes Section. The Quantico-based ISU was supervised by legendary Special Agent Bill Patterson, who practically "wrote the book" on the science of profiling serial killers. ("Grotesque")

Ionesco (Stephen Dimopoulos) Crew member aboard the Canadian fishing trawler *Lisette* who threw a line to the lifeboat containing the rapidly-aged survivors of the USS *Ardent.* ("Dod Kalm") *Stephen Dimopoulos also played a detective in the third season finale "Talitha Cumi."*

"Iron Maiden, The" Less-than-flattering nickname given to FBI Academy forensic instructor Nancy Spiller by her students. ("Ghost in the Machine")

🗁 **"Irresistible"** Written by Chris Carter. Directed by David Nutter. File number 2X13. *First aired January 13, 1995. Scully experiences disturbing flashbacks to her abduction when the X-Files unit investigates a Minneapolis agent's suspicion that a number of mutilated female corpses may have been ravaged by paranormal phenomenon.* **Classic Sound Bite:** *"You know, people videotape police beatings on darkened streets. They manage to spot Elvis in three cities across America every day. But no one saw a pretty woman being forced off the road in* *her rental car."* **Background Check:** *The original title of this episode was "Fascination."*

Isfahan Exiled, Philadelphia-based Mideast extremist group. Military contractor HTG Industrial Technologies was guilty of illegally selling technology to the terrorist organization. ("Shadows")

Ish (Jimmy Herman) An old Native American tribal leader with one blind eye and shoulder-length gray hair who told Mulder of the legend of the Manitou, the Algonquin name for an evil spirit capable of turning men into beastlike creatures. Ish predicted that Mulder would return in another eight years when the curse continued its cycle and the murders would resume. ("Shapes")

Ishimaru, Dr. Takeo (Robert Ito) Member of a World War II Japanese medical corps code-named 731, which performed heinous experimentation on living human beings. Although Dr. Ishimaru reportedly died in 1965, Scully seemed to recognize him from a photograph Mulder obtained of four slain Japanese scientists he believed were killed by the U.S. government because of their attempt to create an alien-human hybrid. After reviewing the alleged alien autopsy video, Scully recalled one of the Japanese doctors, Ishimaru, looming over her during her own abduction. Ishimaru (who adopted the alias Dr. Shiro Zama) was later garroted in the lavatory of a train compartment by the hawk-like assassin, the Red-Haired Man. ("Nisei/731")

Iskendarian Construction Northern Michigan building construction company which employed kidnapper/killer Gerry Schnauz as a site foreman. Scully noted that two crime scenes were near Iskendarian Construction company job sites. ("Unruhe")

Iskendarian, Mr. Owner of Iskendarian Construction, the northern Michigan company that employed Gerry Schnauz. Wary of IRS problems, Mr. Iskendarian told Scully and investigative police officers that he didn't hire "workers off the books," but said that any of his seven foremen might have hired cash-only day laborers without his knowledge. Scully asked Mr. Iskendarian to generate a list of the men who worked on both job sites near the crime scenes, which led her to question site foreman Schnauz. ("Unruhe") *The actor who portrayed Mr. Iskendarian was uncredited.*

Ivanov, Dr. Alexander (Ken Kramer) Wheelchair-bound scientist who specialized in the design and creation of insect-like robots. Dr. Ivanov strongly believed that extraterrestrial visitors to Earth would be robots and that anyone who envisioned the stereotypical small, gray-skinned, bug-eyed alien beings had been "brainwashed by too much science fiction." The scientist apparently bonded with stunning entomologist Dr. Bambi Berenbaum, a USDA researcher studying roaches in the small Massachusetts town of Miller's Grove. ("War of the Coprophages") *Dr. Ivanov's name is a nod to author Isaac Asimov, who wrote numerous science-fiction books dealing with the "laws of robotics." Actor Ken Kramer also portrayed Dr. Berube in "The Erlenmeyer Flask" and Dr. Browning in "3."*

"Jose Chung's 'From Outer Space'"

J-7 Marine special forces and recon squad that was subjected to a secret Vietnam-era project to create the perfect soldier by eradicating the need for sleep. The military lost control of J-7 after the squad went AWOL and began murdering and massacring civilians at random. ("Sleepless")

Jack (Hrothgar Matthews) Vagrant in his thirties who gave Mulder information about the legendary Jersey Devil and the Atlantic City police department's cover-up. Mulder traded his motel room at the Galaxy Gateway for Jack's alleyway cardboard box, which the agent used on his unofficial stakeout. ("The Jersey Devil") *Hrothgar Matthews also played mental patient Creighton Jones in "Our Town" and Galen Muntz, the restaurant shooter in "Talitha Cumi."*

Jackson A member of Operation Falcon's Beta Team, the search-and-destroy mission for the pilot of the downed alien spacecraft near Townsend, Wisconsin. Jackson and other soldiers were severely burned when they encountered the translucent extraterrestrial. ("Fallen Angel")

Jackson Assistant to the military coroner, Lt. Foyle, at the Folkstone INS Processing Center. ("Fresh Bones") *The actor who portrayed Jackson was never shown, but was heard from off-camera.*

Jackson University School of higher learning in Raleigh, North Carolina, where students Elizabeth (Liz) Hawley and James (Jim) Summers were kidnapped by Lucas Jackson Henry disguised as a police officer. ("Beyond the Sea")

Jacobs, Amy (Jewel Staite) Fifteen-year-old student at Seattle's Valley Woods High School. At 10:05 p.m. Carl Wade, a school photographer who had fixated on the girl, kidnapped her from her home. Wade kept her in a cold, dark basement cell of his remote cabin where he repeatedly subjected her to the blinding flash of his camera. At one point she pried a board loose and escaped into the woods, but Wade pursued and captured her once again. She was eventually rescued by Mulder and other agents when Wade attempted to drown her in a river. ("Oubliette")

Jacobs, Dr. (John Tierney) Los Angeles Police Department forensic dentist who discovered human bite marks from three different people on a victim of the vampiresque Trinity Killers. ("3")

Jacobs, Myra (Sidonie Boll) Mother of Seattle kidnap victim Amy Jacobs. Mulder comforted Mrs. Jacobs at the crime scene, saying he truly knew how she felt. ("Oubliette")

Jacobs, Sadie (Alexa Mardon) Five-year-old sister of Amy Jacobs. She shared a bedroom with Amy and called out for their mother when she saw the back of a man (Carl Wade) as he carried her sister out the open window. ("Oubliette")

Jale New Guinea headhunting tribe "whose cannibalism practices have been long suspected but never proven," according to Scully. Walter Chaco, founder of the Chaco Chicken processing plant in the flesh-eating rural community of Dudley, Arkansas, spent six months with the Jale tribe when his transport plane was shot down near their Pacific island during World War II. ("Our Town")

Janadi, Sadoun Iraqi jet fighter pilot who encountered and shot down a UFO after he feared he was under attack. The alien spacecraft crashed near a U.S. installation along the Iraq/Turkey border. ("E.B.E.") *The actor who played the fighter pilot was uncredited.*

Janelli-Heller Funeral Home Minneapolis mortuary where Donnie Pfaster was employed until he was fired by the director for mutilating the corpse of a young woman. ("Irresistible")

Janet, Auntie Elderly woman whose attempted mercy killing by a Kervorkian-type doctor went horribly wrong at the Harrow Convalescent Home in Boca Raton, Florida. ("Terma") *The actress who played Auntie Janet was uncredited.*

Janie Taylor Memorial Recital Hall Washington, D.C., concert auditorium where John Barnett stalked Scully after he learned through messages left on her answering machine that she planned to attend a friend's cello recital. After Barnett shot Scully (who was wearing a bulletproof vest) and took a female hostage, Mulder killed him with a single shot. ("Young at Heart")

Janus, Agent (Prince Maryland) A trained medic and FBI agent who accompanied Mulder into the Travel Time Travel Agency after escaped mental patient Duane Barry inadvertently wounded a hostage. ("Duane Barry")

Jarvis, Owen Lee (Michael Berryman) A strange-looking man hired by Kevin Kryder's mother to do yard work after her husband was institutionalized for believing he had to protect his young son from evil forces. Although described by Mulder as looking like "Homer Simpson's evil twin," Jarvis insisted that he was the young stigmatic's guardian angel, claiming that he was asked by God to protect Kevin against the "Forces of Darkness." When Jarvis was accused of abducting Kevin from a shelter, he leapt from a second-story window and escaped. He successfully intervened when the Millennium Man found the boy but was strangled to death in the process. When his body didn't decompose normally, the Catholic-reared Scully remembered what she was taught in Cathechism about "incorruptibles" whose bodies would not decay. ("Revelations") *Michael Berryman's distinct facial features and his appearances in such films as* The Hills Have Eyes *have made him a cult-favorite among horror movie fans.*

J.A.S.D. Beef Company The Delta Glen, Wisconsin, meat packing plant that slaughtered and processed cows injected with antibodies derived from alien DNA. ("Red Museum")

Jason Twelve-year-old boy who gave escaped Cumberland Prison convict Paul the correct time (9:40) on a bus bound for Toronto. When Paul noticed Mulder he took the boy hostage, while one of his highly-infectious boils bulged near Jason's face. ("F. Emasculata"). *The young actor who played Jason was uncredited*

J. Edgar Hoover Building Washington, D.C., headquarters of the Federal Bureau of Investigation, which was named after the law enforcement agency's long-serving original director. The X-Files unit's cluttered office was located in the basement of the Hoover Building. *Although Washington, D.C. stock shots were often used during* The X-Files' *first season for what are called "establishing exteriors," Simon Fraser University, which is about four miles east of downtown Vancouver, has since been used as a stand-in for FBI Headquarters. For interior shots of the X-Files' basement office, set designers were prohibited from using the real FBI logo. So they created their own "Bureau of Investigations" seal which hangs on the wall next to Mulder's NASA moon-walk photo.*

Jeffers, Dr. Peter Listed as one of the doctors on call at the Lombard Research Facility when Mulder and the Lone Gunmen covertly infiltrated the building. ("Memento Mori")

Jefferson Memorial Hospital Medical facility in Richmond, Virginia, where escaped mental patient Duane Barry was taken after he was wounded by an FBI marksman. At the hospital, Barry was jolted into consciousness by a white light and the images of aliens. After clubbing a police officer posted outside his door with a fire extinguisher, Barry escaped once again. ("Duane Barry")

Jerse, Ed (Rodney Rowland) Handsome Philadelphia stockbroker and father of two, who was so devastated by the terms of his divorce settlement that he went on a drinking binge and "marked the moment" with the tattoo of a Betty Page-like character on his right arm. Within hours, he began to hear the tattoo's female voice in his head, taunting and mocking him, repeatedly calling him a "loser." "Betty" was an extremely jealous control freak who hated women and urged Jerse to kill his downstairs neighbor and viciously attack Scully, his date for an intimate evening ("Kiss her . . . and she's dead"). Just before he stuffed the unconscious agent into the basement furnace of his apartment building, he gathered enough control over his own actions to thrust his arm inside the incinerator and burned off the murderous tattoo. It was later discovered that Comrade Svo, the Russian tattoo artist that etched "Betty" on Jerse's arm, used a rye in his ink that contained a hallucinatory-producing and psychotic-inducing alkaloid ergot. After recovering at Philadelphia's St. John's Burn Center, Jerse was scheduled to undergo a psychiatric evaluation. ("Never Again") *Rodney Rowland portrayed Cooper Hawkes on Glen Morgan and James Wong's short-lived sci-fi series,* Space: Above and Beyond.

Jersey Devil, The (Claire Stansfield) Legendary Bigfoot-like creature believed to be responsible for a series of grisly murders in Atlantic City. Although Park Ranger Peter Boulle told Mulder that a few months earlier he had found the body of a hairy humanoid-like creature in the woods and turned it over to the authorities, Mulder theorized that the man-beast's mate had moved to the city to forage for food. Police later killed a female Jersey Devil after cornering her in the woods. An examination of the woman-beast's uterus indicated, however, that she had given birth. ("The Jersey Devil") *The Jersey Devil, sometimes referred to as the Leeds Devil, is an actual folkloric creature and has been the state's "official demon" since the 1930s, serving as the title inspiration for the New Jersey Devils professional ice hockey team. Claire Stansfield, the 6'1" actress who portrayed the beast-woman in this episode, has also appeared on* Twin Peaks *and "The Bounty Hunter" episode of David Duchovny's Showtime original anthology series,* Red Shoe Diaries.

🗀 **"Jersey Devil, The"** Written by Chris Carter. Directed by Joe Napolitano. File number 1X04. *First aired October 8, 1993. The discovery of a vagrant's partially eaten corpse leads Agents Mulder and Scully to a murderous Bigfoot-type creature which lurks in the back alleys of Atlantic City and could very well be the missing link in human evolution.* **Classic Sound Bite:** *"This thing chewed somebody's arm off! That's not exactly a DEFENSIVE posture!"* **Background Check:** *The inspiration for Chris Carter's tale of an evolutionary mutation, one that was almost a throwback to the Neanderthal, was a scholarly essay written by noted biologist E.O. Wilson.*

Jerusalem Syndrome Abnormality characterized by religious delusions and irrational fanaticism instigated by a visit to the Holy Land. Industrialist Simon Gates, who committed an international string of religiously motivated murders, was suspected of suffering from Jerusalem Syndrome. ("Revelations")

Jessamin, Clyde Unscrupulous business associate of Pvt. Harry Dunham's father in his hometown of New Orleans. Dunham was set to marry Jessamin's daughter but the elder Jessamin's shady business dealings enraged a voodoo practitioner, and the young woman died of some mysterious ailment. Snakes were discovered in her belly during the autopsy. ("Fresh Bones")

Jesus Christ Superstar Acclaimed musical that the demon-worshipping Parents-Teacher Committee (PTC) forbade the students of Crowley High School to perform. ("Die Hand Die Verletzt")

"JFK" According to Lone Gunman Frohike's speculative dossier on the Cigarette-Smoking Man, "JFK" was the first word to come out of one-year-old Fox Mulder's mouth. A young Bill Mulder gleefully shared the information with his bunkmate, the unnamed CSM, while they were stationed at the Center for Special Warfare in Fort Bragg, North Carolina. The word was prophetically conspiracy related: while at the military facility, the Cigarette-Smoking Man was recruited to assassinate President Kennedy. ("Musings of a Cigarette-Smoking Man")

J.F.K. Elementary School Payson, South Carolina, site of a playground attack by a swarm of bees engineered by the Shadowy Syndicate as a "trial run" for spreading a specially virulent strain of the smallpox contagion. ("Zero Sum") *The bee attack on the schoolchildren was in homage to legendary film director Alfred Hitchcock and a nearly identical scene in his modern horror classic,* The Birds.

J. Hartling Records Producer of a music video titled "Mary Beth Clark I Love You," by The Rosemarys. The video appeared on the television screen after Darin Peter Oswald changed the channel from across the room without using the remote control. ("D.P.O.") *J. Hartling is a prominent AOL X-Phile.*

Jim-Jim the Dog-Faced Boy Orphan discovered in an Albanian forest who became a young sideshow attraction in a 1930s circus. After running away, Jim-Jim grew up to eventually become James Hamilton, the four-term sheriff of Gibsonton, Florida. ("Humbug")

Jimmy Doolittle Airfield Small airstrip in Nome, Alaska, where Mulder and Scully picked up Dr. Denny Murphy, professor of geology at the University of California at San Diego; toxicologist Dr. Nancy Da Silva; physician Dr. Hodge; and bush pilot Bear, who flew the small party to Icy Cape to investigate the unexplained deaths of the Arctic Ice Core Project research team. ("Ice")

Johansen, Maj. Christopher (Robert Clothier) World War II–era executive officer aboard the submarine *Zeus Faber* who led a mutiny against the alien-possessed Capt. Kyle Sanford and locked him below decks with the crewmen dying of radiation sickness. Later in his career he became close friends with Capt. William Scully, Dana's father, and relayed the true story of what transpired aboard the submarine when she visited him at Miramar Navy Air Base. ("Piper Maru") *Actor Tom Scholte portrayed the young Johansen during the flashback scenes. Robert Clothier briefly appeared in the second season episode, "Red Museum," as an old man in a truck who led Mulder and Scully to a field of cows injected with what they believed were genetically engineered growth hormones.*

John SEE: **Son, The**

John 52:54 "Bible" passage (which doesn't actually exist in the New Testament) written in blood on the wall next to the body of Garrett Lorre, a victim of The Trinity Killers. The verse read: "He who eats my flesh and drinks my blood has eternal life, and I will raise him up on the last day." ("3)

Johnson, Det. (James Bell) Baltimore policeman present at the murder scene of a man named Werner, another victim of the mutant serial killer Eugene Tooms. Det. Johnson later informed Mulder that Tooms was missing from his job as an animal control officer. ("Squeeze")

Jo Jo's Copy Shop Speedy print shop in Fairfield, Idaho, where Mulder teleconferenced with the Lone Gunmen, who said that the Fairfield Zoo was near a major UFO hotspot and that no animal there had ever brought a pregnancy to term. ("Fearful Symmetry")

Jones, Creighton (Hrothgar Matthews) Traveler along Interstate 10 near Dudley, Arkansas, who stopped to take a nap and was found three days later by State Police. Traumatized from what he had evidently witnessed in the rural community, the deranged man was committed to an insane asylum. A film of the institutionalized Jones ranting and raving about fire demons hungry for flesh gave Mulder nightmares while in college. He played Scully a videotape of Jones' tirades while discussing the disappearance of a federal poultry inspector in the town of Dudley. ("Our Town") *Hrothgar Matthews also played Jack, an Atlantic City vagrant, in "The Jersey Devil" and Galen Muntz, the fast-food restaurant shooter in "Talitha Cumi."*

📁 **"Jose Chung's 'From Outer Space'"** Written by Darin Morgan. Directed by Rob Bowman. File number 3X20. *First aired April 12, 1996. Flattered by the attention of one of her favorite authors, "nonfiction science-fiction" novelist Jose Chung, Agent Scully discusses a recent case in the Pacific*

Northwest in which two teenagers mysteriously vanished, only to reappear with conflicting stories of alien abduction. **Classic Sound Bite:** *"Although we may not be alone in the universe, in our own separate ways, on this planet, we are all . . . alone."* **Background Check:** *Darin Morgan, who said that his stint writing for* The X-Files *constituted his first "real" job, finished his run with the critically-acclaimed and fan favorite "Jose Chung's 'From Outer Space,'"* an *episode that producer Paul Rabwin claimed would one day be as revered as* The Twilight Zone'*s "Eye of the Beholder" or the original* Star Trek'*s "The Trouble with Tribbles." Busy working on the* Millenium *pilot at the time, Chris Carter was unable to screen "Jose Chung" before it aired.*

Josephs, Dr. (Paul McLean) Physician in Browning, Montana, who released Lyle Parker from the hospital and into Scully's care. Dr. Josephs told Mulder that traces of his father's blood were found in Lyle's stomach, which could only have gotten there through ingestion. ("Shapes") *Paul McLean also portrayed FBI ballistics expert, Agent Kautz, in "Anazazi" and the Coast Guard Officer in "Nisei."*

Josh Crowley High School student and lab partner of Shannon Ausbury during a classroom pig embryo dissection. ("Die Hand Die Verletzt") *The young actor who portrayed Josh went uncredited.*

Journey to the Center of the Earth Classic 1959 science-fiction movie (starring James Mason) that was showing on Mulder's TV when Deep Throat telephoned and told him to watch the WDF Newscan telecast of Ardis Police Captain Roy Lacerio discussing a fugitive manhunt. ("The Erlenmeyer Flask")

J & P Scotch Brand of alcohol favored by both insurance salesman/psychic Clyde Bruckman and FBI Assistant Director Skinner. ("Clyde Bruckman's Final Repose" and "Avatar")

JTT0331613 Special Agent Dana Scully's FBI badge number, which she gave to a 911 operator in Philadelphia after requesting emergency medical services for a wounded Mulder and Samuel Aboah. ("Teliko") *The fact that Scully's badge number has two fewer digits than Mulder's has never been addressed.*

JTT047101111 Special Agent Fox Mulder's FBI badge number, which he gave to a telephone company operator in order to obtain pay phone call records ("F. Emasculata"). Mulder also used the number to verify his identity as an FBI agent in order to secure a removal order for federal prisoner John Lee Roche. He attempted to use the badge number to obtain a passenger manifest from Seaboard Air, but was cut-off by an airline employee who stated that an Agent Mulder (in actuality escaped prisoner Roche) had already requested the list. ("Paper Hearts")

Judaica Archives Institution on the Upper East Side of Manhattan, where Mulder and Scully consulted Hebrew scholar Kenneth Ungar in regards to the ancient Hebrew text, *The Sefer Yezirah*, and the golem of Jewish lore. ("Kaddish")

K

Krycek

Kaddish Hebrew "prayer for the dead" which is recited at the gravesite by close relatives daily in synagogue services for the period of mourning, and thereafter on the anniversary of the death. ("Kaddish")

"Kaddish" Written by Howard Gordon. Directed by Kim Manners. File number 4X12. *First aired February 16, 1997. Mulder suspects that a golem, a man-made creature of clay and mud described in mystical Hebrew text, may be responsible for the deaths of several neo-Nazis who murdered a Jewish shopkeeper.* **Classic Sound Bite:** *"Spectral figures are not often known to leave fingerprints. Casper never did."* **Background Check:** *As originally penned the victim was to have died at the hands of black teenagers; they were changed to white racist youths after Fox's race-sensitive Standards and Practices department rejected the initial script as "unacceptable for broadcast standards." The episode was dedicated to the "loving memory of Lillian Katz," writer/executive producer Howard Gordon's grandmother.*

Kallenchuk, Jeraldine (Jo Bates) San Francisco salvage broker who flew to Hong Kong to purchase classified government secrets from Alex Krycek. While handcuffed to Mulder, she was shot and killed by operatives working for the Cigarette-Smoking Man. ("Piper Maru")

Kallenchuk Salvage Brokers San Francisco-based salvage company owned and operated by Jeraldine Kallenchuk, who pretended to be Mr. Kallenchuk's uncooperative (and heavily armed) "secretary" when Mulder attempted to question her. ("Piper Maru")

Kaminsky, Ellen (Catherine Paolone) Intended victim of Virgil Incanto, a "fat-sucking vampire" who used the Internet to meet and kill forlorn, overweight women. Kaminsky, whose computer-handle was "Huggs," first encountered the serial killer in the "Big and Beautiful" chatroom. After Mulder and Scully put out a localized online warning, a friend of Kaminsky dissuaded her from actually meeting Incanto in person for a restaurant date. The outwardly charming serial murderer eventually talked his way into Kaminsky's apartment, which turned out to be an almost fatal mistake. An injured but alive and angry Kaminsky shot him with Scully's gun as he tried to kill the FBI agent. ("2Shy")

Kane, Beth (Gillian Barber) Single mother of young Steve and sixteen-year-old Gary. The forty-year-old woman was employed at the J.A.S.D. meat processing plant in Delta Glen, Wisconsin, and for many years was the target of her landlord Gerd Thomas' voyeurism, especially when she took a shower. ("Red Museum") *Gillian Barber also portrayed Agent Nancy Spiller in "Ghost in the Machine," and doomed alien-abductee Penny Northern in "Nisei" and "Memento Mori."*

Kane, Gary (Bob Fraser) Teenage son of Beth who disappeared, then was found by two sheriff's deputies twelve hours later wandering in the road, wearing only his underwear and with the words "HE IS ONE" scrawled with a red-marker on his back. He recalled very little of what happened, but thought that maybe an animal spirit had entered him. Gary was first string on the varsity football team and a member of the 4-H club. ("Red Museum")

Kane, Jay Beth's late husband, who was killed seven years earlier in an accident with a meat processing machine at the J.A.S.D. packing plant. ("Red Museum")

Kane, Steve Nine-year-old son of single mother Beth Kane. ("Red Museum") *The young actor who portrayed Steve Kane was uncredited.*

Kann, Judge (Jan D'Arcy) Maryland state magistrate who presided over the psychiatric hearing and institutional commitment review of serial killer Eugene Tooms. Mulder grew agitated as Judge Kann dismissed the testifying agent's genetic mutation theory, despite Mulder's showing that Tooms' fingerprints were at seven of nineteen crime scenes committed since 1903. Believing that Mulder might be the one who belonged in a mental hospital, Judge Kann and her judicial panel decided to discharge Tooms from the sanitarium despite the agent's warning that he was a danger to public safety. ("Tooms")

Karetzky, Dr. Pamela (Mikal Dughi) Therapist who testified at Eugene Victor Tooms' psychiatric hearing and commitment review that the serial killer had no psychological dysfunction. ("Tooms").

Katie (Elisabeth Rosen) Teenage girlfriend of Rick Mazeroski, the son of the Delta Glen, Wisconsin sheriff. She was discovered clad only in her underwear wandering through the woods, hallucinating, with the words SHE IS ONE written on her back. Tests showed that she had a strange opiate derivative in her blood. ("Red Museum")

Katz, Dr. (George Touliatos) Director of the Luther Stapes Center for Reproductive Medicine in San Francisco. Dr. Katz explained in vitro fertilization to Mulder and Scully and revealed that the Simmons family had tried the procedure nine years earlier under the care of Dr. Sally Kendrick, who was later fired for allegedly conducting eugenics experiments. ("Eve") *George Touliatos also portrayed county supervisor Larry Winter in the second season episode "Blood."*

Kautz, Agent (Paul McLean) Ballistics expert with the FBI Firearms Unit. After William Mulder was shot and killed, Scully asked Kautz to compare Fox Mulder's gun with the bullet removed from the dead body. ("Anasazi") *Paul McLean also portrayed Dr. Josephs, in "Shapes," and the Coast Guard Officer in "Nisei."*

Kavanaugh, Sarah SEE: **Ephesian, Melissa Riedal**

Kazanjian, Dan (William MacDonald) Young federal agent who worked in one of the FBI's regional office's computer crime section. Kazanjian gradually restored serial killer Virgil Incanto's erased computer files on his hard drive and broke the password and encryption to retrieve a list of Incanto's chatroom victims. ("2Shy") *William MacDonald also played Dr. Oppenheim in "Fallen Angel," Officer Trott in "Unruhe," and a federal marshal in "The Host."*

Kazdin, Lucy (CCH Pounder) FBI special agent in charge of hostage negotiations with escaped mental patient and alleged former alien-abductee Duane Barry. After Barry was wounded and hospitalized, Agent Kazdin showed Mulder his X rays, which displayed strange metal objects in the gums, sinus cavity, and abdomen, and tiny drill holes in his left and right rear molars. ("Duane Barry") *CCH (Carol Christine Hilaria) Pounder, who was nominated for an Emmy Award for her portrayal of Agent Kazdin, is best known for the role of no-nonsense surgeon Dr. Angela Hicks on the acclaimed television hospital drama E.R.*

Kearns, Doris (Caroline Kava) Widow of federal poultry inspector George Kearns. Although her philandering husband was reported as missing, Mrs. Kearns knew that he had been killed and eaten by the cannibalistic townsfolk in Dudley, Arkansas. Promised protection by the founder of the small town's chicken processing plant, Mrs. Kearns was murdered by a figure in a carved tribal mask. ("Our Town") *Carolina Kava played NYPD Detective Jean Harp in three of the Richard Crenna "Janek" television movies.*

Kearns, George (John MacLaren) Middle-aged poultry inspector with the U.S. Department of Agriculture murdered by the residents of Dudley, Arkansas, after recommending that the small town's Chaco Chicken processing plant be closed for health violations. Assigned to investigate his disappearance, Mulder and Scully discovered Kearns' decapitated skeleton after the local river was dragged, his polished bones suggesting that he had been the victim of cannibalism. Kearns, however, had been suffering from the rare Creutzfeldt-Jakob disease and twenty-seven residents had contracted the fatal illness after eating him. ("Our Town")

Keats, Dr. (Garry Davey) Abrasive research scientist who worked at the Mahan Propulsion Laboratory. Retarded janitor Roland Fuller forced Dr. Keats' head into liquid nitrogen and then shattered it like glass when he dropped it on the floor. ("Roland") *Garry Davey also played Hunter in "Eve," a ship's captain in "End Game," and Bob Spitz in "Syzygy."*

Keep-It Storage Pennsylvania self-storage facility where Leonard Betts went to ingest the cancerous left lung of the Bearded Man and regenerate his body. After Mulder and Scully found a Keep-It Storage receipt at Elaine Tanner's house, they attempted to open the locker door (#112), but were almost run down by Betts, who was driving the Bearded Man's early model Camaro. The agents dove for cover and opened fire, igniting the car's fuel tank and incinerating Betts. ("Leonard Betts")

Kelleher, Lorraine (Janie Woods-Morris) A madam in her sixties who operated a Washington, D.C., escort service. She told Mulder and Scully that she took Assistant Director Skinner's credit card number the night he was suspected of killing call girl Carina Sayles. Kelleher either fell or was pushed from the roof just moments before the agents arrived to question her about who might have been framing Skinner. ("Avatar") *Janie Woods-Morris also portrayed Ms. Lane in "Shadows."*

Kelly, Laura (Tasha Simms) Married daughter of strangely youthful Stan Phillips, resident of the Excelsis Dei convalescent home. She told Mulder and Scully that her father had needed twenty-four-hour attention when arriving at the nursing facility three years earlier. Kelly's father protested when she attempted to take him home to live with her. ("Excelsius Dei") *Tasha Simms also portrayed Ellen Reardon in "Eve," and Assistant Director Skinner's divorce attorney, Jane Cassal, in "Avatar."*

Kelly, Lucy Woman with an inoperable tumor who died twenty minutes after Samuel Hartley attempted to heal her by the laying on of hands. ("Miracle Man") *The actress who portrayed Lucy Kelly (who had no lines but appeared in the FBI videotape) was uncredited.*

keloid scar The surgical cicatrix found on the neck of Henry Willig and other human subjects involved in Dr. Grissom's top secret sleep eradication experiments. The neurological procedure to induce a permanent waking state included brain-stem surgery, which explained the scar. ("Sleepless")

Kemper, Mrs. (Theresa Puskar) Teacher at J.F.K. Elementary School in Payson, South Carolina, killed during a playground attack by a swarm of bees engineered by the Shadowy Syndicate as a "trial run" for spreading a virulent strain of smallpox. ("Zero Sum")

Kendrick, Dr. Sally (Harriet Harris) Biogenetics specialist at the Luther Stapes Center for Reproductive Medicine in San Francisco who was fired from the fertility clinic for conducting eugenics experiments. A product of the top-secret 1950s Litchfield program that created identical little boys named Adam and girls named Eve, Dr. Kendrick implanted her own clones in patients at the Stapes Center. Her genetic replicas, eight-year-olds Cindy Reardon and Teena Simmons, murdered her by slipping four ounces of digitalis extract into her soda. Dr. Kendrick was Eve 7. ("Eve") *Theater heavyweight Harriet Harris (also known as Harriet Sansom Harris) is best known for her recurring role as Bebe Glaser on* Frasier.

Kennedy, Agent (Gary Hetherington) FBI agent and member of a surveillance team assigned to maintain a constant vigil outside Eugene Tooms' apartment on Baltimore's Exeter Street. After Agent Tom Colton angrily called Kennedy off the stakeout duty, the mutant serial killer was able to stalk Scully to her residence, which almost resulted in her death. ("Squeeze") *Gary Hetherington also played FBI Agent Lewin in "Little Green Men."*

Kennedy Center Landmark performing arts complex located in Washington, D.C., named in honor of the former president of the United States. Mulder interrupted Mr. X while he was enjoying a performance of Wagner's "Ring" cycle in an attempt to find the alien Bounty Hunter. X reluctantly told Mulder that the extraterrestrial's spacecraft was found in the Arctic and that an attack fleet had been dispatched to prevent him from leaving. ("End Game")

Kenwood County Jail Sheriff Maurice Daniels' Tennessee lock-up where Samuel Hartley was incarcerated and beaten to death, allegedly after he picked a fight with two rowdies booked on DUI. ("Miracle Man")

Kerber, Scott (D. Neil Mark) Loudoun County, Virginia, deputy sheriff who was killed when Robert "Pusher" Modell used his psychokinetic powers of persuasion to "talk" Kerber into pulling his car into the path of a truck. ("Pusher")

ketamine Rapid-acting anesthetic typically used by veterinarians, which causes hallucinations in humans. Dr. Charles Goldstein, a Warwick, Rhode Island, psychiatrist, used the powerful drug in conjunction with an aggressive and unconventional form of therapy to stimulate electrical impulses in the brain and access buried and repressed memories. ("Demons")

Keyser, Dr. Benjamin (Allan Franz) Forensics specialist at the Army Central Identification Lab who examined the alleged physical remains of Nathaniel Teager, recovered after the Green Beret's helicopter was shot down in enemy territory during the Vietnam War. Dr. Keyser showed Mulder the extent of Teager's remains: two teeth, which had been stored at the Army Forensics Lab since they were retrieved from the chopper crash site in 1971. Keyser noted that there was "pronounced scoring" on each tooth, which strongly suggested extraction and possibly a faked death. ("Unrequited")

Keystone Kops Slapstick performers dressed as police officers who entertained movie audiences in a series of films during the silent comedy era. Every channel on Mulder and Scully's TV set in their motel rooms in Comity, Caryl County, showed a Keystone Kops movie. ("Syzygy") *The script for "Syzygy" called for Stanley Kubrick's modern classic* A Clockwork Orange, *but the film footage proved too expensive and Chris Carter had to settle for his second choice.*

Kilar, Kristen (Perrey Reeves) Mysterious woman whom Mulder met at Club Tepes during his investigation of a series of vampiresque murders in Hollywood. She poked her finger with a syringe and offered him the opportunity to taste her blood. When Mulder refused, she left with another man. Mulder eventually tracked Kristen to her residence where he found veterinary hypos, and a piece of a snakebite kit that was used to extract blood. He also discovered blood-baked bread in an oven which, according to European legends, was used as vampire protection. After she told him that she was running from The Trinity Killers (who had pursued her from city to city), Kristen and Mulder had an off-screen sexual close encounter. She sacrificed her own life when she destroyed the trio of vampire-like murderers in a house fire. ("3") *In response to fan criticism that Mulder engaged in spontaneous sex with a woman who practiced blood sports, episode co-writer Glen Morgan posted on AOL that Mulder wore a condom. Actress Perrey Reeves was David Duchovny's long-time love interest at the time this episode was filmed. Episode co-writer James Wong believed that because the two actors had a relationship off-screen, there was absent the kind of sexual tension that exists between two people who have not previously "messed around."*

Kindred Mysterious and reclusive Amish-like religious sect that had lived near Steveston, Massachusetts, for decades and was known for its distinctive white clay pottery. The genderbending killer Marty (formerly known as the Kindred's Brother Martin) ventured into the outside world to pursue sex with "human men and women" but before he was apprehended by Mulder and Scully, other sect members spirited him away. The entire Kindred community disappeared from their compound in Massachusetts, leaving behind a large crop circle in a hayfield. ("Genderbender")

Kip (Don Gibb) Longhaired, burly biker who was tending bar at the Pennsylvania Pub in Sioux City, Iowa, when Mulder and Scully came looking for Greg Randall. After Mulder commented on the flying saucer tattoo on Kip's right arm, the biker pulled back his hair to show them a mutilated ear, supposedly the result of intense heat from a flying saucer during a nighttime motorcycle excursion around local UFO hotspot Lake Okobogee. ("Conduit")

Kirtland Air Force Base Space shuttle landing site located in Albuquerque, New Mexico. ("Space")

Kissell, Col. Blain (Vince Metcalfe) Ellens Air Force Base's evasive director of communications. He refused to be questioned by Mulder and Scully after the two agents traveled to Southwest Idaho to investigate the unusual disappearances (and inexplicable re-appearances) of several military test pilots. ("Deep Throat")

KISS/KILL Words tattooed on the knuckles of death row convict Luther Lee Boggs. ("Beyond the Sea") *Although the KISS/KILL tattoos evoked the famous LOVE/HATE tattoos on Robert Mitchum's hands in the 1955 movie* Night of the Hunter, *episode co-writer Glen Morgan attributed KISS/KILL to lyrics in a song by the band X.*

Kittel, Alfred (Dexter Bell) Seventeen-year-old African-American youth who became a victim of Samuel Aboah. Kittel was immobilized with a paralyzing dart fired from Aboah's blowgun while pacing at a city bus stop in Philadelphia. Kittel's mother reported him missing when he didn't come home from his job at a fast-food restaurant. ("Teliko")

Kittel, Private (Roger Cross) Military aide to Marine Col. Wharton, the base commander at the Folkstone INS Processing Center in North Carolina. Pvt. Kittel detained Mulder and Scully when they were discovered rifling through Col. Wharton's office. After Mulder revealed that privates Dunham and Guiterrez had both filed complaints against the colonel for his treatment of the Haitian refugees at Folkstone, Kittel confessed to the agents that self-proclaimed Haitian revolutionary Pierre Bauvais had been buried in a municipal cemetery. ("Fresh Bones") *Roger Cross also portrayed a SWAT lieutenant in the third season episode, "Pusher."*

Kiveat Auto Body Darin Peter Oswald's place of employment in Connerville, Oklahoma. The auto body repair shop was owned and operated by Frank Kiveat. ("D.P.O.")

Kiveat, Frank (Steve Makaj) Darin Peter Oswald's employer and husband of Sharon Kiveat. Oswald, who had a crush on Sharon, used his remarkable electrical powers to cause Frank to have a heart attack. When paramedics found their portable defibrillator somehow wasn't charged, Oswald attempted to impress Sharon by using his own hands to jolt Frank's chest and get his heart beating again. ("D.P.O.") *Steve Makaj also played a patrolman in "Ascension" and the assassin Ostelhoff in "Gethsemane."*

Kiveat, Sharon (Karen Witter) Frank Kiveat's attractive wife and Darin Peter Oswald's remedial reading teacher at Gravenhurst High School. Oswald, who was infatuated with Sharon, kept a picture of her hidden in a skin magazine in his room. Frightened by his "dangerous powers," Sharon nevertheless placed herself in harm's way in order to protect her hospitalized husband from the teenage lightning boy. ("D.P.O.") *Finding Sharon Kiveat's*

*yearbook photo between the pages of an adult magazine was an in-joke reference
to actress Karen Witter, who once appeared in* Playboy *magazine. The yearbook
page from which Oswald had cut Sharon's picture also contained photos of* X-
Files *director Kim Manners and prop master Ken Hawryliw.*

Klebanow, Congressman Member of the Department of Corrections Subcommittee and one of Deep Throat's Capitol Hill sources. After Eurisko
founder and AI (artificial intelligence) creator Brad Wilczek "disappeared,"
Deep Throat told Mulder that he had checked with both the attorney general
and Congressman Klebanow as to Wilczek's whereabouts. ("Ghost in the
Machine")

Kleinjan, Margi (Wendy Benson) Pretty blonde cheerleader and senior at
Comity's Grover Cleveland Alexander High School who, along with her best
friend, Terri Roberts, possessed strange telekinetic powers due to "a rare
planetary alignment of Mars, Uranus, and Mercury." An astrologer, Madame
Zirinka, told Mulder that two people born at the same time on January 12,
1979 (as Margi and Terri) would be under the influence of "a grand square,"
when "all the energy of the cosmos would be focused" on them. After a
series of murders, the two girls finally turned on each other in a telekinetic
rage. Mulder locked the girls in the same small room until 12:01 a.m., when
they were no longer the focal point of unseen galactic forces beyond their
grasp. ("Syzygy")

Klemper, Victor (Walter Gotell) Nazi scientist who conducted inhuman
experiments on Jews and was granted immunity in the U.S. after World War
II under a secret alliance code-named Operation Paper Clip. The Lone
Gunmen recognized Klemper from a 1970s photograph taken of Mulder's
father and other associates (including Deep Throat, the Cigarette-Smoking
Man, and the Well-Manicured Man). Mulder and Scully tracked down
Klemper, who said that the photograph was taken at the Strughold Mining
Company in West Virginia, and then asked them cryptically if they knew
the formula of Napier's Constant, which was a clue to the numeric code
sequence needed to open the abandoned mine's security doors. After the
agents departed, Klemper telephoned the Well-Manicured Man and taunted
him by saying he had been visited by "the son of one of our old colleagues."
Mulder and Scully later returned to Klemper's orchid greenhouse but were
met by the Well-Manicured Man, who told them the old Nazi was dead.
("Paper Clip") *The late Walter Gotell is familiar to millions of James Bond
fans as KBG chief General Anatol Gogol, in six 007 movies from* The Spy Who
Loved Me *to* The Living Daylights. *He also had a bit part as a heavy in the
first Bond movie,* Dr. No.

Koretz, Crew Chief Karen (Kimberly Unger) Radar observer at the U.S.
Space Surveillance Center who detected an unidentified object that broke
into the radar grid off the Connecticut coast going north-by-northwest, "went

crazy" in unearthly trajectories, and impacted west of Lake Michigan at over 800 miles per hour. She was ordered by Commander Calvin Henderson to report the sighting as a meteor and the radar findings as "instrument malfunction." Chief Koretz later identified "flash traffic" from a new "meteor," which was much larger than the first one, and was detected "hovering" over Townsend, Wisconsin. ("Fallen Angel") *Kimberly Unger also played Joan Gauthier in "Piper Maru."*

Kosseff, Karen (Christine Willes) Psychiatric social worker assigned to the FBI's Employee Assistance Program Office at the Bureau's headquarters in Washington, D.C. During the Donnie Pfaster investigation, Scully discussed her fears with the professional counselor. Though she said she would trust Mulder with her life, Scully admitted, "I don't want him to know how much this is bothering me. I don't want him to think he has to protect me" ("Irresistible"). State Department diplomat Steven Holvey agreed to allow his eight-year-old son, Charlie, to be interviewed by Scully and Kosseff. As Holvey prepared to leave with the boy, however, the garage door mechanism caught his tie, choking him to death in front of his son. Kosseff, who was later assigned to file a court report, arrived at the Holvey home slightly before Mulder and Scully and witnessed a ritual being conducted by Romanian exorcists known as the Calusari. During an interview with Kosseff afterwards, Charlie blamed his grandmother's death on his stillborn twin ("The Calusari"). After encountering the ghost of a young murdered woman moments before Mulder relayed news that her body had been found nearby, Scully once again visited Kosseff in her Bureau office. Scully, stricken with inoperable cancer, was visibly disturbed by the apparition and was confused as to whether she witnessed the spirit because the "stress" of her terminal illness had somehow "suggested" the image or whether she saw the ghost because of her fear of failing Mulder. ("Elegy")

Kotchik, Miss (Lynda Boyd) Patron of Boston's Provincetown Pub who was amused when pyrokinetic Cecil L'ively used his finger to light her cigarette. She wasn't as jolly, though, after he ignited his arm and torched the bar. At Boston Mercy Hospital, Kotchik described the events to Mulder and Scully and helped a police artist create a composite of L'ively. ("Fire") *Lynda Boyd also portrayed the girlfriend of Paul, the escaped convict, in "F. Emasculata."*

Kramer, Agent (Rob Morton) FBI agent involved in the initial arrest of Eugene Tooms after he was captured slithering through an air vent at the crime scene. Along with Agent Kennedy, he was assigned to surveillance duty outside Tooms' apartment in Baltimore. ("Squeeze")

Kramer, Dr. According to Cleveland, Ohio, police Detective Cross, he was the Cuyahoga County coroner. ("2Shy")

Kreski (David Lewis) Young FBI agent who participated in the search for kidnapper Carl Wade and his fifteen-year-old victim, Amy Jacobs. Lucy Householder gasped and began vomiting water in Kreski's car when Wade tried to drown the Jacobs girl in a nearby river. ("Oubliette") *David Lewis also played a police officer in "The Jersey Devil" and Vosberg in "Firewalker."*

Kreutzer, Leo (Ernie Prentice) Resident at the Excelsis Dei Convalescent Home in Worcester, Massachusetts. Kreutzer, who had worked as an artist for the WPA in the 1930s, drew a sketch of a woman with shadowy, almost invisible figures hovering around her. ("Excelsius Dei")

Kritschgau, Michael (John Finn) Department of Defense operative who assaulted Scully and threw her down a flight of stairs when she attempted to stop him from stealing a cannister of core samples retrieved from a block of ice entombing an alleged alien corpse. Fingerprints found on the stairwell matched Kritschgau's, which were on record in the federal employee database. After viewing his computerized personnel file, Scully positively identified him as her attacker and noted his place of employment: the Pentagon's Research Division in Sethsburg, Virginia. Later, she confronted Kritschgau inside a parking garage and placed him under arrest. But he warned Scully that if he was taken into custody, the same people who gave her cancer would also kill him. Kritschgau detailed point-by-point the systematic way that Mulder had been deceived and manipulated over the years and how Scully, his partner, had been led down the same path, ending with her contraction of terminal cancer. Scully contacted her partner and convinced him to meet her and Kritschgau in person so that Mulder could hear the conspirator's story firsthand. Kritschgau claimed to have run the Department of Defense's agitprop arm for a decade, telling the agents that the government had been orchestrating an elaborate hoax to make Mulder believe in the existence of extraterrestrial lifeforms and that the government had been in contact with the alien beings. "They invented you," Kritschgau continued to elucidate, "and your regression hypnosis, the story of your sister's abduction, and the lies they fed your father. You wanted to believe so badly, who could have blamed you?" When Scully told her partner that Kritschgau had revealed that the conspirators had given her cancer in an effort to make him a believer in their lies, Mulder was visibly stunned. Later that evening, supposedly unable to face the fact that his quest for the truth had been all for naught, Mulder apparently died from a self-inflicted gunshot wound to the head. ("Gethsemane")

Krycek, Alex (Nicholas Lea) FBI special agent who moved into the role of Mulder's partner after the X-Files unit was shut down and Scully was reassigned to a teaching position at Quantico Academy. Handsome, charming, and well-spoken, he gained Mulder's trust and even adopted some of the agent's dry wit in an attempt to get closer to him during their investigation of a secret Vietnam-era experiment on sleep eradication. But Krycek's hidden agenda was exposed when it was revealed that he was a lackey of the Cigarette-

Smoking Man sent to spy on Mulder and hinder his attempt to re-open the X-Files section ("Sleepless"). The darker side of the traitor emerged more clearly during the Duane Barry incident. Krycek may have provided the escaped mental patient with Scully's home address, and acting upon orders from CSM, he thwarted Mulder's rescue of his former partner by stalling the Skyland Mountain tram and killing its operator. Mulder also suspected Krycek of poisoning Barry and attempting to frame Mulder for the man's death. With his treachery exposed and the reopening of the X-Files unit, the operative disappeared ("Duane Barry/Ascension"). Ostensibly on orders from the Cigarette-Smoking Man, Krycek reappeared briefly to murder Mulder's father, William, after the top-secret MJ files were stolen and the elder Mulder summoned his son to reveal the true nature of his former work with the State Department. After framing Mulder for the murder, he almost killed Krycek, but Scully shot her partner in the shoulder to keep him from committing murder ("Anasazi"). Assigned to kill Scully by the Cigarette-Smoking Man, Krycek and another operative, Luis Cardinal, accidentally murdered her sister, Melissa, in a tragic case of mistaken identity ("The Blessing Way"). After ambushing Assistant Director Skinner and recovering the digital tape copy of the MJ documents, Krycek was rewarded by the Cigarette-Smoking Man by almost being eliminated in a car bomb explosion. Krycek narrowly escaped and vowed revenge on CSM, while fleeing the country with the DAT that revealed the extent of U.S. government involvement with extraterrestrials since the 1940s ("Paper Clip"). In Hong Kong Krycek managed to break the encryption code of the digital tape and began a lucrative career selling classified government secrets. He sold the French the location of where a UFO had been recovered from the Pacific, and was in the process of hawking more information on covert operations to salvage broker Jeraldine Kallenchuk when he was abruptly recaptured by Mulder. Before leaving Hong Kong for the U.S. he became possessed by the very alien whose secrets he had been selling on the black market ("Piper Maru"). The extraterrestrial, in the body of Krycek, made a deal with the Cigarette-Smoking Man to turn over the digital tape in return for being taken to his spacecraft. The double-crossing CSM locked the terrified Krycek in the abandoned missile silo in North Dakota where the UFO was stored ("Apocrypha"). After anonymously feeding tips to Mulder about an extreme right-wing militia organization, Krycek resurfaced once again to join Mulder in his search for a meteor of extraterrestrial origin and to help bring the Cigarette-Smoking Man to justice. This led them both to Tunguska, where they discovered a Siberian gulag, its hard-working prisoners sentenced to mine the alien rocks. Mulder was captured, beaten and jailed, but Krycek (whose parents were allegedly Russian Cold War refugees) was freed by their captors, who seemed to know him rather well ("Tunguska"). Mulder escaped the gulag and forced Krycek to accompany him, but Krycek escaped once again. While running through the woods he encountered a group of men, all of whom were missing their left arm. Krycek told them he was an American fleeing from the gulag, and the one-armed men, who believed he was an enemy of their enemy, took him to their home. That night while Krycek slept, the men grabbed him and cut off his arm in order to save him from being poisoned by the "black cancer," a biotoxin injected in his arm. Krycek was last seen with a prosthetic limb in the company of a former KGB assassin who had been dispatched to America by a Comrade Arntzen to dispose of those involved in experiments with the alien-infected meteor fragment. Krycek, who proved to be "Comrade Arntzen," commended the Russian on a successful mission abroad ("Terma"). *Canadian-born actor Nicholas Lea earned his first real exposure with a recurring role in ABC's* The Commish, *where he also met his former girlfriend, Melinda McGraw, who played Melissa Scully on* The X-Files. *Lea's TV credits include* John Woo's Once a Thief, Highlander, *and* Sliders. *He also played Baines in the sci-fi film* Xtro II: The Second Encounter.

Kryder, Kevin (Kevin Zegers) Ten-year-old genuine stigmatic from Loveland, Ohio, who began to bleed from his palms while writing on the chalkboard at Ridgeway Elementary School. Kevin, who had previously bled from his hands and feet, was temporarily removed from his mother's custody and placed in a shelter, where he was abducted by Owen Jarvis, a self-described guardian angel who offered his own life to protect his young charge from the Millennium Man. ("Revelations")

Kryder, Michael (Sam Bottoms) Father of Kevin Kryder, who had been institutionalized after a standoff with police in which he claimed Kevin was the son of God. During an interview with Mulder and Scully, Kryder stated flatly that his son had been chosen and that dark forces would come to slay him in the form of a powerful man as part of "the great war between good and evil." Kryder also told the Catholic-raised Scully that she must "come full circle to find the truth," but she didn't understand what he was saying. "You will," he replied vaguely. ("Revelations")

Kryder, Susan (Hayley Tyson) Mother of Kevin Kryder, who was given sole custody of the boy after her husband was arrested and institutionalized. Susan was angry at the suggestion that her son should be placed in a shelter after he began bleeding from his hands in class. After she was killed in an automobile wreck in an attempt to safeguard her son from demonic industrialist Simon "Millennium Man" Gates, Scully vowed she would protect the boy. ("Revelations")

Kyte, Lauren (Lisa Waltz) Howard Graves' secretary at Philadelphia-based military contractor HTG Industrial Technologies. Graves treated Lauren like his daughter after his own child died in a drowning accident. After Graves allegedly committed suicide, his spirit protected her from his treacherous successor at HTG, Robert Dorlund, and the same murderous forces within the company that had killed Graves when he threatened to expose Dorlund's illegal involvement with a Mideast terrorist cell. Lauren later relocated to Omaha, Nebraska, where she went to work for Monroe Mutual Insurance Company. ("Shadows")

L

Lord Kinbote

Laberge, Dr. (John MacLaran) The physician who treated Mrs. Mulder at a hospital in Rhode Island. She had suffered a debilitating stroke after arguing heatedly with the Cigarette-Smoking Man at her family's deserted summer home. ("Talitha Cumi") *John MacLaran also portrayed federal poultry inspector George Kearns in "Our Town."*

Lacerio, Capt. Roy (Jim Leard) Ardis, Maryland, police captain in charge of the search for Dr. William Secare, who had fled from officers by leaping into the bay, leaving behind a trail of green blood. ("The Erlenmeyer Flask")

Ladonna (Monica Parker) The owner and operator of the Flying Saucer Diner near Ellens Air Force Base in Southwest Idaho where "UFO nuts" gathered. For twenty dollars, Ladonna sold Mulder a grainy photo of a triangular-shaped UFO that looked uncannily like one supposedly taken in Roswell, New Mexico in 1947. Curiously, Ellens Air Force Base did not appear on official maps and Ladonna drew a map to the military installation on one of the café's napkins. ("Deep Throat")

Lake Betty A campsite/recreation area in Newark, New Jersey. After killing a U.S. Marshal, the sewer-dwelling Flukeman hid in one of the campground's portable toilets. ("The Host")

Lake Jordan North Carolina hostage site of kidnapped youth Elizabeth (Liz) Hawley. Acting on information from alleged psychic and death row inmate Luther Lee Boggs, the FBI and local police rescued the Hawley teenager from Lucas Jackson Henry. Mulder, however, was downed by a single gunshot when he approached a suspicious-looking boat and Henry escaped with his other hostage, Jim Summers. ("Beyond the Sea")

Lake Okobogee National Park A "UFO hotspot" located near Sioux City, Iowa. Mulder told Scully that Lake Okobogee was the site of four UFO sightings in August 1967, one by a Girl Scout troop of which Darlene Morris was a member. Her teenage daughter, Ruby, was later abducted by aliens from a campsite near the lake in 1993. ("Conduit")

Lakeview Cabins Lodging where Mulder and Scully stayed while investigating a series of deaths that may have been linked to Big Blue, a prehistoric aquatic creature that supposedly resided in Heuvelman's Lake in the Blue Ridge Mountains of Georgia. ("Quagmire")

Lamana, Jerry (Wayne Duvall) Mulder's former partner in the FBI's Violent Crimes unit who derailed his career by losing critical evidence while working hate crimes in Atlanta. After turning to Mulder for assistance in the electrocution death of Eurisko chief executive Benjamin Drake, Lamana stole Mulder's killer-profile notes and presented them as his own. Voice analysis showed that Brad Wilczek, founder of Eurisko, was the last person to speak to Drake, but when Lamana went to arrest him the agent was killed in a mysterious elevator "malfunction." ("Ghost in the Machine")

Lambert, Gail Anne Engineer at Polarity Magnetics, Inc. who was the first unintentional victim of Dr. Chester Banton, a human black hole. Lambert was evaporated when the scientist simply stood in her doorway. ("Soft Light")

Lamb, Harold (Jason Gaffne) Washington state teenager abducted, along with his date, Chrissy Giorgio, by extraterrestrials. When Chrissy was found disoriented, bruised, and her clothes on inside out, police suspected date rape. Arresting authorities scoffed when Harold told them that the teenage couple had been experimented on by aliens. ("Jose Chung's 'From Outer Space'")

Landis, Jesse (Aloka McLean) The blind, twelve-year-old daughter of Monica Landis, the landlady of suave serial murderer Virgil Incanto. Jesse went to Incanto's apartment looking for her mother, and dialed 911 after smelling her perfume inside, which led Mulder and Scully to the killer's residence. ("2Shy")

Landis, Monica (Glynis Davies) Virgil Incanto's landlady, who, thinking him a novelist or editor, asked him to critique her poetry. Although the slender Landis was obviously attracted to him, Incanto was a "fat-sucking vampire" who preyed on overweight women to satisfy his physical need for fatty tissue. Incanto murdered her only after she discovered the decomposing corpse of police Det. Cross in his bathtub. ("2Shy") *Glynis Davies also portrayed housewife Ellen Brumfield in "Irresistible" and Eugene Tooms' sanity hearing attorney in "Tooms."*

Lange, Ms (Janie Woods-Morris) Lauren Kyte's new boss at the Monroe Mutual Insurance Company in Omaha, Nebraska, where the ghost of Howard Graves, Kyte's deceased former employer, may have followed, still protecting her. ("Shadows") *Janie Woods-Morris also played Lorraine Kelleher in "Avatar."*

Lang, Kyle (Lance Guest) Spokesperson for the Wild Again Organization (W.A.O.), an anticaptivity group dedicated to liberating circus and zoo animals. Kyle was crushed to death by a crate when he attempted to meet with Willa Ambrose, a naturalist hired by the Fairfield, Idaho Zoo. ("Fearful Symmetry")

Langly (Dean Haglund) Sporting black-rimmed glasses, long blond hair, and T-shirts from a dozen hard-rock bands, the wiry Langly is the communications expert of the Lone Gunmen. One of three operatives who formed the editorial staff of the conspiracy-oriented newsletters known as *The Lone Gunman* and *The Magic Bullet,* Langly once bragged that he had breakfast with the "guy who shot John Kennedy," saying he was dressed as a police officer on the grassy knoll. Although the paranoid conspiracy theorist has a lot of respect for Mulder, he is also quite prepared to lie and didn't trust him enough to turn off a recording device after Mulder asked him to. In exchange for a photo of an actual E.B.E. (Extraterrestrial Biological Entity), Langly supplied Mulder and Scully with computer-hacked IDs to gain access to a secret government facility. ("E.B.E.") When Mulder teleconferenced with the Lone Gunmen from Fairfield, Idaho, while investigating the disappearances of several zoo animals, Langly didn't participate due to his philosophical aversion to having his image bounced off a satellite. ("Fearful Symmetry") After the newest Lone Gunman, an anarchist and computer hacker called The Thinker, requested a clandestine meeting with Mulder, Langly told the agent that the radical's real name might be Kenneth Soona. ("Anasazi") Langly and his colleague Byers identified Nazi scientist and war criminal Victor Klemper in a 1970s photograph of Mulder's father and others. ("Paper Clip") The Lone Gunmen also assisted in identifying Japanese satellite photos of the *Talapus,* a salvage vessel out of San Diego which had supposedly been searching for a gold-carrying submarine sunk in the Pacific during World War II. ("Nisei") After examining an amazingly sophisticated video emitting device Mulder discovered in the small town of Braddock Heights, Maryland, Byers and the other Lone Gunmen correctly surmised that it was a mind control mechanism used to transform people's fears into dementia through their TV sets. ("Wetwired") Although the Lone Gunmen strove to keep a low profile, an ice-skating Langly joined his colleagues in a clandestine package retrieval mission for Mulder at a Washington, D.C.-area rink ("Apocrypha") and in the high-tech infiltration of a research facility via a subterranean tunnel ("Memento Mori"). *The character's name is of course a reference to the Virginia site of CIA headquarters. Dean Haglund is a stand up comedian and member of the improvisational group Vancouver TheaterSports, whose stage works include such spoofs as "Star Trick: The Next Improvisation" and "Free Willy Shakespeare." His TV credits include guest appearances on* The Commish, Sliders, Street Justice *and HBO's* Mask of Death.

Lanny (Vincent Schiavelli) A former circus headline performer living in the retirement community of Gibsonton, Florida, a town filled with circus freaks and sideshow acts. Unbeknownst to everyone, Lanny's congenital twin, Leonard, was able to extract himself and committ several murders while seeking to conjoin with a new brother. After Lanny died of cirrhosis of the liver, his autopsy showed some offshoots of his esophagus and trachea that seemed umbilical. ("Humbug") *Character actor Vincent Schiavelli's unique facial features have been a frequent and well-loved sight in movies and television for decades. From* One Flew Over the Cuckoo's Nest, Amadeus *and* Batman Returns *to the subway spirit in* Ghost, *Schiavelli has played a variety of eccentrics and charlatans.*

Laramie Tobacco The company that employed Margaret Wysnecki as a production-line worker until she retired after approximately thirty-six years. The similarity between her disappearance and that of Dominion Tobacco executive Patrick Newirth, led Mulder to briefly theorize that there was a connection based on their professions. ("Soft Light")

La Ranchera Market Grocery store located in downtown Fresno, California where Eladio Buente, the carrier of a highly contagious and fatal fungus, ate a handful of nuts from an aisle container before being confronted by a clerk and running away. After examining one of the nuts that fell to the floor, the clerk rapidly succumbed to the lethal lichen. Mulder, Scully, and INS agent Conrad Lazano arrested Eladio's vengeance-seeking brother, Soledad, after they followed him to the store. ("El Mundo Gira")

Lariat Rent-A-Car Mulder and Scully's car rental agency of choice when on assignment in other cities and states.

Larken (David Fredericks) Owner and operator of the Seattle-based Larken Scholastic photography company who fired his assistant, Carl Wade, after he became abnormally obsessed with fifteen-year-old Amy Jacobs during a class picture assignment at Valley Woods High School. ("Oubliette") *David Fredericks also appeared in "Blood" as a security guard and as a 1968-era J. Edgar Hoover in "Musings of a Cigarette-Smoking Man."*

Larken Scholastic Seattle, Washington photography company that took the student pictures at Valley Woods High School. ("Oubliette")

Larson, Dr. Jerrold Delta Glen, Wisconsin, physician who was killed when his small plane crashed. It was later discovered that Larson had been treating several local teenagers with "vitamin shots" since childhood and then tracking them over the years. An empty chemical vial found at the crash site contained a residue of synthetic corticosteroids containing unidentified amino acids, believed to be antibodies derived from alien DNA. Larson was also carrying a briefcase full of hundred-dollar bills when he died. ("Red Museum") *The actor portraying Dr. Larson was uncredited.*

Lazard, Det. Sharon (Maggie Wheeler) A twenty-eight-year-old police detective assigned to Buffalo, New York's 14th Precinct. She found eight-year-old Michelle Bishop wandering around outside the station and brought her inside for questioning, which resulted in the mysterious death of another detective. ("Born Again") *Maggie Wheeler (billed as Maggie Jakobson) appeared in the movie* New Year's Day *with a nude David Duchovny. Reportedly the two were dating at the time. In addition to her TV appearances on* Friends *(as Chandler's girlfriend, Janice) and* Everybody Loves Raymond *(as Linda, the jet ski store owner), Wheeler also co-starred in* These Friends of Mine, *the first version of the Ellen DeGeneres' sitcom* Ellen.

📁 **"Lazarus"** Written by Alex Gansa and Howard Gordon. Directed by David Nutter. File number 1X14. *First aired February 4, 1994. Scully's former lover, FBI agent Jack Willis, is either suffering from trauma or is possessed by the spirit of a dead bank robber after a fatal shoot-out supposedly kills them both.* **Classic Sound Bite:** *"My name is Warren James Dupre, and I was born in Clamett Falls, Oregon, in the year of the rat!"* **Background Check:** *The title of this episode is a reference to the Biblical character of Lazarus, who was resurrected by his good friend Jesus Christ (which is paralleled by the "resurrection" of Willis on the operating table).*

Le Damfino Hotel St. Paul, Minnesota, hotel where psychic Clyde Bruckman was guarded to protect him from the Puppet, a serial killer who murdered fortune-tellers. The Puppet, disguised as a bellhop, was fatally shot by Scully in the hotel's kitchen. ("Clyde Bruckman's Final Repose") *The name of the hotel was a nod to Buster Keaton's boat* Damfino *in* The Boat. *The real-life Clyde Bruckman, who was a writer and director of comedies of the silent film era, wrote many screenplays for Keaton.*

Ledbetter, Tim The murdered partner of legendary FBI agent Sam Chaney. The two federal officers were in Aubrey, Missouri in 1942 investigating The Slash Killer, a serial murderer whose three female victims were raped and had SISTER razored onto their chests. Ledbetter's skeletal remains were discovered by Mulder in 1995, underneath the floorboards of a house rented by rapist and murderer Harry Cokely fifty years earlier. ("Aubrey")

Lee, Mr. The manager of the apartment house where Eugene Tooms claimed to have resided in 1993. A follow-up investigation by Mulder and Scully proved that the address was merely a cover; the genetic mutant preferred to make his hibernation nest at 66 Exeter Street, Baltimore, his home for sixty years. ("Squeeze")

LeFante, Mary Louise (Sharon Alexander) A young Northern Michigan woman who was abducted and her boyfriend murdered outside of a Traverse City drugstore where just moments earlier she had passport photos taken. Rather than displaying the expected smiling portraits, the pictures showed LeFante in screaming terror, surrounded by a host of nightmarish images. Mulder theorized that the kidnapper had psychically influenced the camera film, leaving behind "thoughtprints" that revealed the criminal's darkest fantasies. Mulder and Scully later discovered that LeFante, an employee of the U.S. postal service, was being investigated for the theft of several credit cards from the branch post office where she worked as a sorter. Although she was originally believed to have faked her own death, the young woman was found alive, but practically brain-dead, having suffered a botched transorbital lobotomy at the hands of her abductor, Gerry Schnauz, a previously institutionalized paranoid schizophrenic. ("Unruhe")

Leikin, Skye (Norma Wick) Television news reporter who covered widespread panic caused by cockroach attacks in Miller's Grove, Massachusetts. ("War of the Coprophages") *Skye Leikin was a reference to Leikin Skye, an online X-Phile who won an AOL trivia contest and the prize of being named onscreen during an episode. Actress Norma Wick also played a news reporter in the first season episode, "Space."*

Lemenchik, L. Crowley High School student who had previously checked out M.R. Krashewski's *Witch Hunt: A History of the Occult in America* from the library. ("Die Hand Die Verletzt")

Leonard. The name Lanny, a slow-witted former circus performer, gave to his congenital twin. Leonard, a tiny, bald, ape-like creature, somehow disjoined himself from Lanny and inadvertently committed several murders. "I don't think he knows he is harming anyone," Lanny sadly admitted. "He's merely seeking . . . another brother." Apparently, the Conundrum, a circus "geek" who would eat anything, consumed Leonard as a snack. ("Humbug")

📁 **"Leonard Betts"** Written by Frank Spotnitz, John Shiban, and Vince Gilligan. Directed by Kim Manners. File number 4X14. *First aired January 26, 1997. After a decapitated corpse walks out of a hospital morgue under its own power, Mulder and Scully begin searching for a mutant humanoid lifeform that possesses the ability to regenerate body parts.* **Classic Sound Bite:** *"Do you think Mom knows that her dead son is still tooling around in her car?"* **Background Check:** *The episode was selected by the network to air after Fox's inaugural Super Bowl game in the hopes of garnering even more viewers for their most popular show. The strategy worked as* The X-Files *enjoyed its largest audience ever with an overnight Nielsen rating of 17.2 (a rating point represents 970,000 households). Long-time X-Philes were treated to a subtle tie-in to the second season episode "One Breath" (File Number 2X08) in which Scully was* *mysteriously returned from her abduction. In "Leonard Betts" the number 208 showed up as the number of the ambulance to which Betts was assigned, and the time digitally displayed on Scully's bedside clock after she was awakened with a nosebleed.*

Lesky, Diana "Nonfiction science-fiction" author Jose Chung's thinly-disguised alias for Dana Scully in his book *From Outer Space,* which documented the alien abduction of two teenagers in Klass County, Washington. ("Jose Chung's 'From Outer Space'")

Les Trois Etoiles A French restaurant in Cleveland, Ohio where serial killer Virgil Incanto was stood up by Ellen Kaminsky, an overweight and lonely woman he had been communicating with on the Internet. Les Trois Etoiles means "The Three Stars" in French. ("2Shy")

Lewin (Gary Hetherington) A federal agent who staked-out Mulder's apartment when he secretly journeyed to a possible extraterrestrial contact site in Arecibo, Puerto Rico. Lewin and his partner, Agent Rand, confronted Scully at Mulder's residence when she also sought clues to his disappearance. ("Little Green Men") *Gary Hetherington also played FBI Agent Kennedy in "Squeeze."*

Lewton, Dr. Jerrold (Tom McBeath) Curator of Boston's Museum of Natural History, where a sacred Amaru urn was taken after it was unearthed during an archaeological dig in the Ecuadorian highlands. Dr. Lewton was devoured by the jaguar spirit of the female shaman whose remains he housed in the museum's Hall of Indigenous Peoples. ("Teso dos Bichos") *Episode writer John Shiban acknowledged that Dr. Lewton's name was in homage to Val Lewton, who directed the original* Cat People *horror classic. Actor Tom McBeath also played a scientist in "Space" and L.A. police Det. Munson in "3."*

Liberty Bell Revolutionary War landmark that Mulder wanted to see while he and Scully were in Philadelphia investigating unusual murders committed by an unseen force protecting Lauren Kyte. ("Shadows")

Liberty Plaza. An asbestos-laden demolition site in Philadelphia, which served as Samuel Aboah's hideaway and the dumping ground for his victims. During a final confrontation, the metamorphic ghost creature was shot and captured by Scully. ("Teliko")

lifeboat 925 The small rescue boat commandeered by Lt. Richard Harper and seventeen other crew members of the USS *Ardent* when they defied Capt. Phillip Barclay's orders and abandoned the Navy destroyer in the Norwegian Sea. Eighteen hours later, lifeboat 925 and its shriveled and rapidly aged occupants were rescued by the Canadian fishing vessel *Lisette.*

("Dod Kalm"). *Lifeboat 925 received its numerical significance in honor of the birthdate (9/25) of Gillian Anderson's infant daughter, Piper Maru.*

Lighthouse Bungalows Motel Lodging north of San Francisco where Dr. Sally Kendrick took her eight-year-old clones Cindy Reardon and Teena Simmons while on the run from the authorities. The motel manager alerted the FBI about a woman fitting the doctor's description, but not soon enough to keep the two homicidal girls from poisoning Kendrick. ("Eve")

Lighthouse Resident Motel Sleazy motel in the Cambridge, Massachusetts, area where an older version of MIT cryobiologist Jason Nichols stayed after he came back from the future to stop himself and others from developing the technology that made time travel possible. During their search of Nichols' room, Mulder and Scully discovered a faded color photograph of Nichols and two other scientists taken five years in the future. ("Synchrony")

Lily SEE: **Ephesian, Melissa Riedal**

Limo Driver (Bob Wilde) After picking up diplomat Kazuo Sakurai on Embassy Row in Washington, D.C., he remained impassive while the shadowy assassin, the Red-Haired Man, killed Sakurai in the back of the limousine. ("Nisei") *Actor Bob Wilde also portrayed Agent Rand in "Little Green Men."*

Lincoln Park Amusement park in Murray, Virginia where two-year-old Teddy Holvey mysteriously escaped his baby harness, followed a helium balloon out of a public rest room, and was killed while crossing a miniature railroad track. ("The Calusari")

line hypnosis A medical condition caused by high-speed, repetitive activities. George Kearns, a USDA poultry inspector stationed in Dudley, Arkansas, claimed to be suffering from line hypnosis in his workers' compensation complaint filed against the federal government. Unfortunately for the cannibalistic townsfolk of Dudley, Kearns' headaches and irritability were not symptoms of line hypnosis, but the rare and extremely fatal Creutzfeldt-Jakob disease, which was passed along to the citizens when they ingested his brain tissue. ("Our Town")

Linhart, Harry (Peter Lapres) FBI composite artist who sketched a profile of deceased policeman Charlie Morris based upon eight-year-old Michelle Bishop's description. ("Born Again")

Linley Home for Children Loveland, Ohio, shelter where social services temporarily placed Kevin Kryder after his palms began bleeding in an elementary school classroom. Kevin was abducted from the Linley Home by guardian angel Owen Jarvis, who was attempting to protect the stigmatic boy from evil industrialist Simon "Millennium Man" Gates. ("Revelations")

Linzer, Dr. Emile (Barry Greene) Emergency room physician at the Payson, South Carolina, Community Hospital who oversaw the medical treatment of several schoolchildren repeatedly stung by a swarm of bees on the playground. Skinner told Dr. Linzer that the children should not be treated for bee stings, but for smallpox, and urged the physician to vaccinate every child in the town. ("Zero Sum") *Barry Greene also played Perkins, one of the loggers in "Darkness Falls."*

liquid falls SEE: **Fortean event**

Liquori, Bart "Zero" (Jack Black) Connerville, Oklahoma, video arcade clerk and the only friend of human lightning conduit Darin Peter Oswald. Believing that Zero had betrayed him to Mulder and Scully, Oswald zapped his friend to death with a powerful bolt of electrical energy. ("D.P.O.")

Lisette The Canadian fishing vessel (registry #CV233) that rescued the eighteen mutineers from the abandoned Navy destroyer USS *Ardent* in the Norwegian Sea. ("Dod Kalm")

📁 **"List, The"** Written by Chris Carter. Directed by Chris Carter. File number 3X05. *First aired October 20, 1995. An executed convict's enemies list and his promise to come back from the grave to wreak revenge become the focal points of Mulder and Scully's investigation into the grisly murders at a southern prison.* **Classic Sound Bite:** *"A woman gets lonely, sometimes she can't wait around for her man to be reincarnated."* **Background Check:** *As an "inside" joke, death row executioner Perry Simon bore the same name as an NBC executive Chris Carter knew during his years with the Peacock network. The prison chaplain was played by X-Files line producer Joseph Patrick Finn.*

Litchfield Project Top-secret eugenics program that created identical little boys named Adam and girls named Eve. In the 1950s, the United States government heard that the Soviet Union was using crude genetic transmission in an attempt to develop a super-soldier and the U.S. naturally followed suit at a compound in Litchfield, Connecticut. The Adams and Eves had fifty-six pairs of chromosomes (rather than the normal forty-six), which gave them heightened strength and intelligence, but also caused them to become extremely psychotic. ("Eve")

lithium carbonate Medication taken by volcanologist and expedition leader Dr. Daniel Trepkos, which he took to control manic episodes. His girlfriend told Scully that Trepkos had become paranoid and stopped taking the drug. ("Firewalker")

Little Buddha, The One of Scully's favorite novels, which was written by *From Outer Space* author Jose Chung. ("Jose Chung's 'From Outer Space'")

📁 **"Little Green Men"** Written by Glen Morgan and James Wong. Directed by David Nutter. File number 2X01. *First aired September 16, 1994. With the Bureau's X-Files section closed, Agent Mulder covertly searches for recorded evidence of alien contact at an abandoned SETI research site in Puerto Rico while Scully is reassigned to a teaching post at Quantico.* **Classic Sound Bite:** *"Deep Throat said, 'Trust no one.' It's hard, Scully. Suspecting everyone, everything, it wears you down. You even begin to doubt what you know is the truth. Before, I could only trust myself. Now, I can only trust you. And they've taken you away from me."* **Background Check:** *"Little Green Men" was actually written as a non-*X-Files *motion picture script, but writers Morgan and Wong decided to adapt the alien encounter screenplay for the series. The term "little green men," which is widely used to refer to extraterrestrials, is believed to have originated in a series of science fiction installments in the magazine* Amazing Stories *in the late 1940s.*

L'ively, Cecil (Mark Sheppard) British assassin who possessed the powers of pyrokinesis, the ability to control and conduct fire. He was employed on the estates of several members of Parliament who died after L'ively set each of them ablaze. One MP, Sir Malcolm Marsden, escaped, but anticipating the British lord's arrival in Cape Cod, Massachusetts, for a vacation, L'ively murdered the estate's caretaker and took his place. L'ively earned the Marsden family's trust after "saving" the MP's two children from a hotel fire that he actually started. Before he could kill again, Scotland Yard inspector Phoebe Green doused him with fire accelerator at the Marsdens' vacation house and he sustained fifth- and sixth-degree burns over his entire body. Specialists at Boston Mercy hospital found phenomenally rapid regeneration of his fundamental, basal cell tissue, leaving authorities uncertain how to incarcerate him after he was completely recovered. The name Cecil L'ively was probably an alias after an Interpol check revealed that a solid British citizen of the same name died in a London tenement fire in 1971 *and* a child named L'ively was murdered during a British Satanic-cult sacrifice in Tottingham Woods near London in 1963. ("Fire")

Lloyd, Dr. Harrison (John Juliani) A cosmetic surgeon at the Aesthetic Surgery Unit of Chicago's Greenwood Memorial Hospital, who claimed he was a victim of demonic possession after he went into an uncontrollable frenzy and literally sucked the life blood out of a patient during a liposuction operation. When Dr. Lloyd maintained he had no memory or knowledge of the botched surgery, Scully theorized that the physician's sleeping pill addiction caused his psychotic outbreak. Mulder, however, correctly assumed that black magic was somehow involved after discovering evidence of a pentagram, an occult protective symbol, on the floor of the operating room. ("Sanguinarium")

Lloyd P. Wharton County Building The administration building of Johnston County, Oklahoma, where Scully performed the autopsy on lightning victim Jack Hammond in the coroner's postmortem facilities. ("D.P.O.")

Lofoten Basin Ships were prohibited from navigating beyond this area of the Norwegian Sea unless they were ice-class vessels. Trawler captain Henry Trondheim's fifty-ton vessel easily maneuvered through the Lofoten Basin until it crashed into the USS *Ardent*. ("Dod Kalm")

Lo, Johnny (Derek Lowe) A recent Chinese immigrant who was burned alive in a Chinatown funeral home's crematory oven. Mulder, Scully, and San Francisco Detective Glen Chao discovered the Chinese characters meaning "ghost" scratched inside the oven, along with burnt paper, "hell money" used to pay off spirits during the Festival of the Hungry Ghosts. ("Hell Money")

Lombard Research Facility The location of one of the Shadowy Syndicate's human/alien hybrid laboratories. After the Lone Gunmen hacked into Lombard's dedicated computer mainframe, they downloaded Scully's secret medical file, which revealed branched and mutating DNA. Convinced that a cure to Scully's inoperable cancer could be found in the research facility, Mulder and the Lone Gunmen infiltrated the complex. ("Memento Mori")

Lone Gunman, The A conspiracy-oriented magazine named after the Warren Commission's official ruling that Lee Harvey Oswald acted alone in the assassination of President John F. Kennedy in 1963. *The Lone Gunman* was published by the earnest and eccentric trio of Byers, Langly, and Frohike, who collectively functioned as a kind of alternative think tank for Mulder.

Lone Gunmen, The The paranoid, truth-seeking editors of *The Lone Gunman* and *Magic Bullet* underground newsletters, whom Mulder once described as "an extreme government watchdog group" ("E.B.E."). Byers, Langly, and Frohike have contacts and inside knowledge in a diversity of fields and supply Mulder with often unreliable but sometimes first-rate information regarding political conspiracies, UFO sightings, and government agencies—particularly the CIA—and their covert operations. They have also displayed their wide-ranging expertise on various fly species and experimental insecticides ("Blood"), human DNA ("One Breath"), the mating habits of zoo animals ("Fearful Symmetry"), Nazi war criminals ("Paper Clip"), Japanese shipping routes ("Nisei"), clandestine package retrieval and the technology used to heighten the impression left by writing on paper ("Apocrypha"), sophisticated television emitting signals used for mind control ("Wetwired"), and the covert infiltration of a research facility via subterranean tunnels ("Memento Mori"). A fourth member of the Lone Gunmen, a radical anarchist computer hacker known as The Thinker, a.k.a. Kenneth Soona, was captured and killed by a multinational black ops unit after he penetrated the top-secret MJ files detailing government involvement with aliens ("Anasazi/Blessing Way"). *The Lone Gunmen were originally intended to appear in only one episode ("E.B.E."), but fan reaction was so enthusiastic that* The X-Files *producers decided to make them mainstays of the series' mythology.*

Longstreet Motel Washington, D.C. location of Mulder's electronic surveillance of white-collar criminals after the X-Files unit was disbanded and he was reassigned. ("Little Green Men")

Looker, Dr. Kingsley (Robin Mossley) Scientist who examined the comatose exobiologist Dr. Sacks inside a biohazard lab at the NASA Goddard Space Flight Center and discovered a black vermiform organism attached to the pineal gland of Sacks' brain. The exobiologist had remained in some sort of biostastis after being attacked by small, leech-like worms that emerged from an alien-infected meteor fragment. ("Terma") *Robin Mossley also played Dr. Ridley in "Young at Heart" and Dr. Randolph in "Our Town."*

Lord Kinbote A large, growling, red-skinned alien who abducted Klass County, Washington, teenagers Chrissy Giorgio and Harold Lamb, as well as two military officers disguised as smaller, gray-colored extraterrestrials (Lt. Jack Shaeffer and Maj. Robert Vallee). The alien's name was derived from a "manifesto" written by Roky Crikenson, entitled *The Truth About Aliens.* Roky claimed that Lord Kinbote had originated from the Earth's core. ("Jose Chung's 'From Outer Space'") *Episode writer Darin Morgan named the alien Lord Kinbote in honor of the crazily unreliable narrator of Vladimir Nabokov's nonlinear novel,* Pale Fire.

Lord's Prayer, The The example of how to pray as established by Jesus Christ in the New Testament. Scully awoke during the night to see her father sitting across the room, his lips silently mouthing the Lord's Prayer. A few seconds later, Scully received a phone call from her sobbing mother who stated that Dana's father had suffered a coronary an hour earlier and died. ("Beyond the Sea")

Lorenz, Dr. (Crystal Verge) Staff physician at the Northeast Georgetown Medical Facility where Scully was hospitalized after suffering effects from the dementia-inducing mind control experiments conducted on the populace of Braddock Heights, Maryland through television signals. Dr. Lorenz told Mulder that Scully's spinal tap revealed high levels of seratonin in her body, which had been associated with accounts of mania in the past. ("Wetwired") *Crystal Verge had a bit part in the episode "Red Museum."*

Lorraine Motel The Memphis, Tennessee, lodging where civil rights activist Dr. Martin Luther King, Jr., was gunned down by the Cigarette-Smoking Man in 1968. The allegation that CSM was the actual assassin was made in Lone Gunman Frohike's account of the shadowy operative's life. ("Musings of a Cigarette-Smoking Man")

Lorre, Garrett (Roger Allford) A businessman who was killed during sex with a mysterious woman he met at a party. This was the seventh vampiric murder committed by the notorious Trinity Killers. ("3") *Actor Roger Allford was listed in print sources as portraying the Harbormaster in the third season episode, "Nisei," although the character was only mentioned in dialogue and never actually shown. Evidently the scene between him and Mulder was left on the cutting room floor.*

Los Cerritos Adult Education Night school in Minneapolis, Minnesota, where psychotic death fetishist Donnie Pfaster studied comparative religions. ("Irresistible")

"LOVE FOREVER SHARON" Inscription engraved on the inside of Walter Skinner's gold wedding band. ("Avatar")

Lowe, Mrs. (Doris Rands) The senile apartment-house neighbor of insurance salesman and genuine psychic Clyde Bruckman. When he took out her trash, he had a momentary vision of her pet Pomeranian eating her entrails after she died. After committing suicide, Bruckman left Scully a note, asking if she would see to the remains of Mrs. Lowe, who had passed away the night before, and perhaps adopt her dog. ("Clyde Bruckman's Final Repose")

Lozano, Conrad (Ruben Blades) Immigration agent assigned to the INS District Office in Fresno, California. The good-natured but cynical Lozano helped Mulder track Eladio Buente, the carrier of a powerfully fatal fungus who was also suspected of killing his brother Soledad's girlfriend. Believing that there would be a curse on the man who came between two feuding brothers, Lozano brought Eladio together with Soledad, and demanded that Eladio face his brother "like a man." Believing that his hideously disfigured brother was the legendary Chupacabra creature, Soledad refused to shoot him. He and Lozano struggled briefly over the gun, and the INS agent took a bullet in the chest. When Lozano's body was later discovered, it showed signs of the deadly pathogen. ("El Mundo Gira") *Panamanian Ruben Blades is a noted poet, musician, politician, humanist, and actor. His most recent film appearance was in* The Devil's Own *as Harrison Ford's trigger-happy police partner.*

LSDM Lysergic dimethrin, a toxic synthetic botanical insecticide that evoked a fear response in bugs. The chemical compound was found in the bodies of several Franklin, Pennsylvania, residents who had suddenly turned violently homicidal before being killed by police. Mulder discovered that the experimental insecticide, which reacted with adrenaline to produce a substance similar to the hallucinogen LSD, had been sprayed on surrounding field crops by a "stealth" helicopter. ("Blood")

Lucilia cuprina Also known as the green bottle fly. Executed prisoner Napoleon "Neech" Manley's victims were found covered with the fly maggots, eating away at the rapidly decomposing flesh. The medical examiner told Scully that a murdered prison guard's lungs were filled with the larvae of the fly, which could lay eggs within a minute after death occurred, and that hot, humid environments promoted rapid growth. ("The List")

Luder, M.F. Pseudonym used by Mulder for an *Omni* magazine article he authored on the famous 1987–88 Gulf Breeze UFO "sightings." NICAP member Max Fenig told the agent that he was familiar with his work in the area of UFOs and had no problem unscrambling the anagram "M.F. Luder." ("Fallen Angel")

Ludwig, Jason (Leland Orser) Robotics engineer for the active volcano research team assigned to Mt. Avalon in Washington State. Ludwig was killed by expedition leader and visionary volcanologist Daniel Trepkos. ("Firewalker")

Luria, Ariel (Justine Miceli) Beautiful Jewish woman who lost her betrothed, Isaac Luria, in a senseless act of violence by youthful hate-mongers. After Isaac's burial in Brooklyn's Ben Zion Cemetery, Ariel returned after nightfall and created a golem in the physical likeness of her murdered lover. Although Ariel's motive for its creation was love rather than revenge, the monstrous golem immediately began strangling one by one the murderous bigots responsible for Isaac's death. Realizing that the creature had no place among the living, Ariel destroyed the golem after tearfully expressing her love for Isaac during their secret wedding ceremony in a synagogue. ("Kaddish") *Justine Miceli is best remembered as the tough, no-nonsense cop and ardent feminist, Det. Adrienne Lesniak, on the ABC-TV series* NYPD Blue.

Luria, Isaac (Harrison Coe) Young Hasidic Jew who was severely beaten and shot five times at point blank range by three teenage racists in the market he owned in the Williamsburg section of Brooklyn, New York. After Luria's fingerprints were discovered on the corpse of one of the killers, Mulder and Scully were called in to investigate. Although Mulder theorized that Luria had somehow been resurrected and was intent on murderous retribution, the vengeful killer was later discovered to be a golem. ("Kaddish") *The character of Isaac Luria was named in honor of the sixteenth-century rabbinical mystic of Safed. Actor Harrison Coe played a young Deep Throat in the pre-credits sequence of "Apocrypha."*

Luther Stapes Center for Reproductive Medicine San Francisco fertility clinic where Dr. Sally Kendrick, a resident who earned a Yale medical degree after completing her doctorate in biogenetics, treated the Simmons and Reardon families. The center, however, believed Dr. Kendrick was experimenting with eugenics—the science of improving human hereditary characteristics, usually through breeding—and fired her. ("Eve")

Lynch, Thomas SEE: **Teager, Nathaniel**

Lynn Acres Retirement Home Dilapidated convalescent residence where former Baltimore police detective Frank Briggs lived. Briggs, who originally investigated the Powhatten Mill murders committed by shapeshifting serial killer Eugene Tooms, was visited by Scully at the retirement home. ("Tooms")

"Musings of a Cigarette-Smoking Man"

MacDougall-Kessler Conglomerate whose subsidiary Warden White, Incorp., owned the company that published author Jose Chung's books. ("Jose Chung's 'From Outer Space'") *As an in-joke MacDougall-Kessler was named in honor of Heather MacDougall, who edited this episode, and Sue Kessler, an* X-Files *assistant editor.*

MacDougal, Lt. Gen. Peter (Bill Agnew) High-ranking military officer gunned down in the back of his limousine by former POW Nathaniel Teager. Gen. MacDougal was one of the officials who had signed Teager's death certificate after he was declared killed in action during the Vietnam War. ("Unrequited") *General McDougal was named for series editor Heather Mac-Dougall.*

Macguire, Clinton (Jabin Litwiniec) One of three anti-Semitic youths who brutally murdered Isaac Luria inside his Brooklyn market. After one of the teenagers was strangled and police discovered Luria's fingerprints on the boy's body, Macguire and the other killer Derek Banks, dug up Luria's coffin to see with their own eyes if he had risen from the grave to avenge his murder. When Macguire walked to the car to retrieve some tools, he was strangled to death by a monstrous creature whose facial features matched those of Isaac Luria. ("Kaddish")

Mackalvey, Lauren (Randi Lynne) Overweight "lonely heart" whose grotesquely decomposed body was found in a parked car after being killed by her date, Virgil Incanto, a genetic mutant she had met online three months earlier. When Scully prepared to perform an autopsy, she discovered that the corpse had totally liquefied in a matter of hours, leaving nothing but a skeleton and a pool of red glop. ("2Shy")

Magic Bullet, The Conspiracy-oriented newsletter published by the eccentric and paranoid Lone Gunmen. It was named after the Warren Commission's theory that a single bullet struck President Kennedy in the upper back, exited from his throat, tore through Governor John Connally's torso and right wrist, burrowed into his left thigh, and later fell out in pristine condition onto a hospital stretcher. ("Musings of a Cigarette-Smoking Man")

Magician, The Mulder's favorite TV series as a boy. He was about to watch the show when his sister was abducted from their house in Chilmark, Massachusetts, at nine P.M. on November 27, 1973. ("Little Green Men")

Mahan Propulsion Laboratory Rocket research facility located at the Washington Institute of Technology in Colson, Washington, where retarded janitor Roland Fuller was responsible for a series of scientists' murders. ("Roland")

Maier, L. Robbie Prisoner jailed in the cell adjoining Eugene Tooms'. ("Tooms") *L. Robbie Maier is the name of the construction coordinator for* The X-Files. *Maier also had a credited bit role in "Piper Maru" as a World War II pilot.*

Majestic Project Subject of a top-secret report that Deep Throat gave Mulder during a clandestine meeting at the Jefferson Memorial in Washington, D.C. The document contained an intercepted Iraqi transmission regarding a downed UFO. ("E.B.E.")

Major Domo (Martin Evans) Goateed man in charge of removing coats, answering the phone, making drinks, and otherwise attending to the Elders, members of the international Shadowy Syndicate, when they met at their luxurious private club on 46th Street in New York City. ("The Blessing Way/ Paper Clip" and "Apocrypha") *Martin Evans also played Dr. Hartman in the closing scenes of "Sanguinarium."*

Malawi The African country whose government sued naturalist Willa Ambrose over possession of Sophie the gorilla, an ape she had rescued there ten years earlier and raised as a child. ("Fearful Symmetry")

Manchurian Candidate, The According to Lone Gunman Frohike's speculative dossier on the Cigarette-Smoking Man, the 1959 Cold War thriller by author Richard Condon was one of the young Army captain's favorite books while he was stationed at the Center for Special Warfare in 1962. The novel detailed the story of Sgt. Raymond Shaw, an ex-POW (and winner of the Congressional Medal of Honor) who, brainwashed by a Chinese psychological expert during his captivity in North Korea, had come home programmed to kill. Sgt. Shaw's primary target was a U.S. Presidential nominee. Ironically, while stationed at the Fort Bragg, North Carolina, military facility, the Cigarette-Smoking Man was recruited to assassinate President Kennedy. ("Musings of a Cigarette-Smoking Man")

Mandas, Marilyn (Denalda Williams) Employee of Ficicello Frozen Foods who interviewed Donnie Pfaster for a delivery person job after he was fired from a funeral home for cutting locks of hair off a corpse. ("Irresistible") *Denalda Williams also appeared as Madame Zirinka in "Syzygy."*

mandroid A male android with a "blank and expressionless" face, which was what young sci-fi fanatic Blaine Faulkner believed Mulder was, according to Jose Chung. ("Jose Chung's 'From Outer Space'")

Man in Black #1 (Jesse "The Body" Ventura) Nefarious MIB who along with his partner, visited utility worker Roky Crikenson in an attempt to convince him that what he saw was Venus, not a UFO. The MIB and his equally dark-suited cohort met with Mulder at a hotel and strongly suggested that some close encounters with extraterrestrials were actually deceptions executed by the government. ("Jose Chung's 'From Outer Space'") *Man in Black #1 was portrayed by professional wrestler Jesse "The Body" Ventura, whom episode writer Darin Morgan considers one of his boyhood idols with the "potential to be a real star."*

Man in Black #2 (Alex Trebek) MIB of few words who accompanied Man in Black #1 in his efforts to persuade witnesses associated with the alien abduction case in Klass County, Washington, to remain silent about their close encounters. Mulder noted that Man in Black #2 "looked like Alex Trebek." ("Jose Chung's 'From Outer Space'") *Alex Trebek is the host of the popular television trivia game show* Jeopardy! *and his appearance in this episode of* The X-Files *was in part a joking reference to David Duchovny's surprising loss on Celebrity* Jeopardy! *Trebek, however, was approached only after attempts to cast country singer Johnny Cash failed.*

Manitou According to the Algonquian Indians, an evil spirit capable of transforming a man into a beast. A Trego tribal elder named Ish told Mulder of the legend of Richard Watkins, who was attacked by a Manitou and passed the curse down to his son and, eventually, to Joe Goodensnake. ("Shapes")

Manley, Danielle (April Grace) Wife of executed death row inmate Napoleon "Neech" Manley, who promised he would return from the grave and avenge those who had mistreated him. As he was about to be put to death in the electric chair, Danielle swore she'd never love another man again. Believing that her husband's soul had passed into the host body of her lover, prison guard Vincent Parmelly, Danielle killed him with two gunshots as Mulder and Scully burst into her house. ("The List")

Manley, Napoleon "Neech" (Badja Djola) Inmate executed in the electric chair at Florida's Eastpoint State Penitentiary. Manley was convicted in 1984 for double homicide even though he only drove the getaway car during a liquor store robbery in which two people were murdered. Strapped in the electric chair, Manley swore, "I will return to avenge all the petty tyranny and the cruelty I have suffered," announcing that five people would die. Manley made good on his promise to be reincarnated and kill those who had wronged him, including the executioner, the warden, and his court-appointed lawyer. ("The List") *Badja Djola's film credits include* A Rage in

Harlem, *written by John Toles-Bay, who played fellow inmate John Speranza in this episode.*

Manners, Det. (Larry Musser) Foul-mouthed Klass County, Washington, police detective who interviewed alleged alien-abductee Harold Lamb. Det. Manners didn't believe his story and instead suspected the young man was guilty of raping his date, Chrissy Giorgio. After Mulder requested that the teenage girl undergo hypnosis, during which she recalled being on an alien ship, Detective Manners told Mulder that he'd "really bleeped up this case." ("Jose Chung's 'From Outer Space'") *Det. Manners spoke in sentences that would have been laced with four-letter words, except that he actually said "bleeped" and "blankety-blank." The original script's dialogue read more like, "that's an f-ing dead alien body," but that form of faux-profanity wasn't approved by Fox's Standards and Practices department. Episode writer Darin Morgan named the continuously swearing police detective after Kim Manners, a frequent X-Files director who helmed both "Humbug" and another of Morgan's episodes, "War of the Coprophages." Manners, who is well-known for his colorful dialogue in real-life, considered playing the detective himself, but was too exhausted from directing an earlier episode. Larry Musser, the actor who portrayed Det. Manners, also appeared in "Die Hand Die Verletzt" as Sheriff Oakes and in "Unrequited" as Denny Markham.*

Marcus Scully's prom date in high school and "twelfth grade love of my life." ("Small Potatoes")

Markham, Denny (Larry Musser) Ex-Marine and leader of the Right Hand, a radical paramilitary group. Markham and his extreme right-wing movement were initially suspected of the execution-style murder of Lt. Gen. Peter MacDougal after the officer's driver was discovered to have been one of two thousand on the Right Hand's mailing list. Under the provisions of the new anti-terrorist law, Mulder and Scully arrested Markham at the Right Hand's compound in Demeter, Virginia, where federal agents discovered "more weapons and ammo than most third world armies." Markham gave Mulder a 1995 photo of a man named Nathaniel Teager, a Green Beret officially reported as killed in action in 1971. In reality, Teager was captured by Viet Cong and imprisoned for almost twenty-five years. In December 1995, Markham and the Right Hand liberated Teager from a Vietnamese POW camp. U.S. military commandos boarded the Right Hand's plane in California in an attempt to kidnap Teager, but the former Green Beret had already fled from his hiding place in the aircraft's cargo hold. Scully scoffed at Markham's story and called him "a one man threat to national security." He was held in custody at the Ft. Evanston, Maryland, detention center where he was threatened with an assortment of conspiracy, homicide, treason, and illegal weapons possession charges. ("Unrequited") *Actor Larry Musser portrayed Sheriff John Oakes in "Die Hand Die Verletzt" and, of course, the bleeping Det. Manners in "Jose Chung's 'From Outer Space.'"*

Marriette Field Airport where Mulder and Scully's plane landed when they traveled to Southwest Idaho to investigate unusual disappearances of military test pilots. ("Deep Throat")

Marsden, Jimmie (Christopher Gray) Young son of Lord and Lady Marsden. He was "saved" by pyrokinetic assassin Cecil L'ively during a fire at Boston's Venable Plaza Hotel.("Fire")

Marsden, Lady (Laurie Paton) The wife of British Lord Malcolm Marsden, she became the object of Cecil L'ively's affections. ("Fire")

Marsden, Michael (Keegan Macintosh) Young son of vacationing British Lord and Lady Marsden. Pyrokinetic Cecil L'ively set fire to the upper floor of a Boston hotel where Michael and his brother, Jimmie, were staying and then "saved" them in an attempt to earn the family's trust. ("Fire")

Marsden, Sir Malcolm (Dan Lett) A member of the British Parliament and pyrokinetic Cecil L'ively's intended victim. After Lord Marsden barely escaped a garage fire, he brought his wife and two young sons to Cape Cod, Massachusetts, for safety. Although Marsden escaped the fiery fate of several other members of Parliament, the married lord could not escape the charms of beguiling Scotland Yard inspector Phoebe Green. ("Fire") *Malcolm Marsden was named after the series' chief hairdresser.*

martingale A tie-down chain used by some insensitive animal handlers to force an elephant to its knees by pulling its tusk to the ground. ("Fearful Symmetry")

Marty (Peter Stebbings as "Male" Marty and Kate Twa as "Female" Marty) Formerly Brother Martin of the reclusive and Amish-like Kindred religious sect. After he found some discarded men's magazines, Brother Martin got a taste of the outside world and left the Kindred to pursue sex with what he referred to as "human men and women." Marty had the ability to change gender at will, but sexual relations with the "walking aphrodisiac" proved fatal to both men and women due to Marty's possession of incredibly high amounts of pheromones, chemicals secreted by animals as sexual attractants. After Mulder and Scully tracked Marty to a hotel, the Kindred spirited him away before he could be apprehended. ("Genderbender") *Actress Kate Twa, who portrayed the "female" Marty, also appeared in "Soft Light" as Det. Ryan.*

"Mary Beth Clark, I Love You" Song by the fictitious Rosemarys whose music video appeared on the television screen after Darin Peter Oswald changed the channel from across the room without using the remote control. ("D.P.O.") *Mary Beth Clark is a prominent AOL X-Phile.*

Mary Ellen One of two pregnant women living in the small town of Home, Pennsylvania. Sheriff Taylor checked to make sure she hadn't miscarried her baby after a deformed stillborn was discovered in a shallow grave. ("Home")

Maryland Marine Bank Financial institution where Scully and fellow agent Jack Willis engaged in a shoot-out with Warren James Dupre and Lula Phillips. The site of the murderous robbers' last heist, the FBI was staking out the bank due to an anonymous tip from Lula, who escaped capture. ("Lazarus")

Maryland Women's Correctional Facility Prison where career criminal Lula Philips served time for manslaughter. While there she became involved in a clandestine affair with guard Warren James Dupre. ("Lazarus")

Massachusetts Institute of Robotics Research facility operated by Dr. Alexander Ivanov, a wheelchair-bound scientist who created insect-like robots. ("War of the Coprophages")

Massachusetts Institute of Technology (MIT) An independent, coeducational university located in Cambridge. Considered one of the world's outstanding schools of higher education, MIT is noted for research that has spawned a host of scientific breakthroughs and technological advances. MIT cryobiologist Jason Nichols engineered a rapid-freezing compound at the university's Bio-Medical Research Facility while studying the effects of freezing temperatures on biological systems. After he was killed in the computer mainframe room at the cryogenic lab by a time-traveling version of himself, Nichols' girlfriend, MIT researcher Lisa Ianelli, continued the development of the deep freeze agent. ("Synchrony")

Matheson, Sen. Richard (Raymond J. Barry) Influential and visionary United States senator and one of Agent Mulder's "connections in Congress." Sen. Matheson summoned Mulder to his Capitol Hill office and urged the agent to covertly investigate the Arecibo Ionospheric Observatory in Puerto Rico, the most recent site of alien visitation. With strains of Bach's *Second Brandenburg Concerto* playing loudly on the senator's stereo system in an attempt to circumvent possible eavesdropping equipment, Matheson informed Mulder that he could hold off the secret Blue Beret UFO Retrieval Team for only twenty-four hours. Matheson also warned the agent that the soldiers were authorized to use terminal force and would certainly kill him if they found him with evidence. "What am I looking for?" Mulder asked. "Contact," the senator replied ("Little Green Men"). Although it appeared that Matheson was a powerful force to be reckoned with, when Mulder went to his office to seek his assistance after Scully's disappearance, Mr. X informed him that the senator couldn't help him anymore or he would be committing political suicide ("Ascension"). Mulder sought out his former benefactor once again after a Japanese murder suspect was found dead and

Mulder's apartment was ransacked by someone trying to locate a leather satchel containing satellite photos, which the agent had withheld instead of logging in as evidence. Sen. Matheson urged Mulder to return the photos, while seeking to earn the agent's trust by providing him with the names of the four Japanese scientists who were murdered during an alleged alien autopsy aboard a railroad car in Knoxville, Tennessee. "What am I onto here?" Mulder asked. "Monsters begetting monsters," the senator answered ("Nisei"). After escaping from a bomb-laden quarantine train car that was carrying what might have been an alien cargo, Mulder attempted to telephone Matheson, but the senator was ostensibly out of the country and not returning any calls ("731"). *Sen. Matheson was named for sci-fi and horror writer Richard Matheson. Chris Carter, a longtime fan of* The Night Stalker *and its star, Darren McGavin, originally sought out that actor to play the part of Sen. Matheson. Raymond J. Barry, a member of Willem Dafoe's celebrated Wooster Group theater ensemble group, had major roles in* The Chamber, Dead Man Walking, *and* Born on the Fourth of July. *Barry also appeared in Gillian Anderson's pre-X-Files film* The Turning.

Matola, Salvatore (Jonathan Gries) A previously unknown survivor of Special Forces and Recon Squad J-7, who had been reported as killed in action. Located working at a greasy-spoon café in Roslyn, Long Island, Salvatore told Mulder and Krycek that J-7 had gone AWOL, making up their own missions, killing civilians, and finally massacring a school full of Vietnamese children. Salvatore provided the agents with the name of Dr. Francis Girardi, the physician who actually performed the brain-stem surgeries Dr. Grissom's sleep eradication experiments required. ("Sleepless")

📁 **"Max (Part 2 of 2)"** Written by Chris Carter and Frank Spotnitz. Directed by Kim Manners. File number 4X18. *First aired March 23, 1997. The military issues an official explanation of "human error" in the downing of a commercial airliner, which Mulder believes is a cover-up after discovering that one of the plane's passengers, multiple alien-abductee Max Fenig, was carrying irrefutable proof of the existence of extraterrestrial life.* **Classic Sound Bite:** *"Mulder, what are these people dying for? Is it for the truth or for the lies?"* **Background Check:** *After Mulder's plane landed in Washington, D.C., the time according to Skinner's watch was 10:56, an in-joke reference to Chris Carter's birthday (month and year). The episode also showcased another track from* The X-Files *music CD,* Songs in the Key of X: *"Unmarked Helicopters" by Soul Coughing.*

Mayhew, Terry Edward (Bret Stait) Leader of an extreme right-wing militia organization, which an anonymous tipster warned Mulder was planning an explosive strike similar in size and damage to the Oklahoma City bombing. During a raid in Flushing, Queens, Mayhew and his soldiers were arrested and a bomb recovered; the informant turned out to be Mulder's nemeis,

Alex Krycek, who claimed he had been freed from an abandoned missile silo in North Dakota by Mayhew and his group during a salvage operation. Seeking clues to Krycek's true motives, Mulder and Scully interviewed Mayhew at a federal correctional facility in New York City. The militia leader denied ever salvaging material from a missile silo and said that Krycek had approached his organization, bragging that he had two bombs and telling them that his name was "Arntzen." Mayhew also stated "off-the-record" that Krycek/Arntzen had talked about the U.S. government's role in covering-up evidence that Soviet-developed "black cancer" had been deployed by Saddam Hussein during the Gulf War. Although Mayhew at first refused to provide the location of Krycek/Arntzen's second bomb, with a little physical persuasion from Mulder, he revealed the other hiding place: Terma, North Dakota. ("Tunguska/Terma") *Bret Stait also played Cpl. Taylor in "Fallen Angel."*

Maywald, Carina (Leslie Ewen) A social services worker who summoned Mulder and Scully to Ridgeway Elementary School in Loveland, Ohio, after Kevin Kryders palms began bleeding. Maywald explained that ten-year-old Kevin had exhibited stigmata before and that his father was institutionalized for believing he had to protect Kevin from evil forces. ("Revelations") *Leslie Ewen also played an FBI receptionist in the pilot episode, a federal agent in "Genderbender" and grieving widow Renee Davenport in "Unrequited."*

Mazeroski, Rick (Cameron Labine) The sixteen-year-old son of the Delta Glen, Wisconsin, sheriff. The teenager was abducted and found dead from a bullet to the head, with the words HE IS ONE scrawled on his back. ("Red Museum")

Mazeroski, Sheriff (Steve Eastin) Chief law enforcement officer in the Wisconsin town of Delta Glen, Mazeroski suspected a possible connection between a local religious cult, the Church of the Red Museum, and the disappearance of several teenagers. After Crew-Cut Man (the assassin who executed Deep Throat) arrived on the scene, he murdered Mazeroski's son in an effort to cover-up the truth about the town's unwitting involvement in alien DNA experimentation. The sheriff, still mourning his loss, emptied his gun into his son's killer. ("Red Museum")

McAlpin, John "Jack" (Kevin Conway) A twenty-three-year-old Marine private stationed at the INS Processing Center for Haitian refugees in Folkstone, North Carolina. After committing suicide by slamming his car into a tree adorned with Voodoo symbols, a dazed and unresponsive McAlpin was later discovered walking in the middle of a road, the victim of zombification. ("Fresh Bones")

McAlpin, Luke. The infant son of Private John "Jack" McAlpin and his wife, Robin. ("Fresh Bones") *The child or children who played eighteen-month old Luke were uncredited.*

McAlpin, Robin (Katya Gardner) Wife of Marine private John McAlpin. After the military ruled her husband's automobile death a suicide, she told Mulder and Scully that she suspected he had been the victim of a Haitian voodoo curse. ("Fresh Bones") *Katya Gardner also portrayed Peggy O'Dell in the pilot episode.*

McCall, Dorothy (Frances Bay) An elderly, wheelchair-bound resident at the Excelsis Dei convalescent home in Worcester, Massachusetts. Although she was able to see disembodied spirits, the nursing home's director attributed her visions to senile dementia. ("Excelsius Dei") *Frances Bay played the eerie Mrs. Tremond on* Twin Peaks, *a quirky series that also featured a cross-dressing David Duchovny.*

McCallister, Doreen Member of a Girl Scout group that witnessed and photographed a UFO near Lake Okobogee, Iowa in 1967. ("Conduit")

McCallister Penitentiary Correctional facility where Harry Cokely served his prison sentence from 1945 to 1993 for the rape and attempted murder of Linda Thibedeaux. ("Aubrey")

McClain, Holly (Beverly Elliot) Slightly overweight Cleveland, Ohio, prostitute attacked and killed by mutant serial killer Virgil Incanto after Ellen Kaminsky stood him up for a date. The "$20 hooker" savagely scratched him on the hand before she died, leading to an important break in the case. A skin sample removed from under her fingernails showed a lack of oils or essential fatty acids, prompting Mulder to theorize that the killer was acting on a physical need, seeking to replenish those chemicals. ("2Shy")

McClennen, Jim (Doc Harris) A test pilot at Ellens Air Force Base in Southwest Idaho. McClennen disappeared and then mysteriously returned home disoriented and prone to compulsive, repetitive behavior like picking at his hair. Scully theorized that McClennen suffered from a stress-related syndrome called stereotypy. ("Deep Throat")

McClennen, Verla (Sheila Moore) The long-suffering wife of former test pilot Jim McClennen. She resented her friend Anita Budahas bringing Mulder and Scully to her house to witness first-hand her husband's strange behavior. ("Deep Throat")

McCue, Father (Arnie Walters) Roman Catholic priest and friend of the Scully family. Mrs. Scully invited Father McCue to a dinner party for the purpose of discussing with Dana the importance of returning to her faith at "a time of personal crisis." Dana made it clear that she wasn't going to "come running back" to the Church just because she had been diagnosed with an inoperable brain tumor. "It's just not who I am," she told him. "I would be lying to myself and to you." ("Gethsemane")

McGrath, Joseph (Frederick Coffin) FBI section chief who wanted to shut down the X-Files unit and fire Mulder for insubordination and misconduct. His decision was countermanded by Deep Throat. ("Fallen Angel")

McNally, Harry (Andre Daniels) Ed Funsch's supervisor at the Franklin, Pennsylvania, postal center. McNally was forced to lay Funsch off for budget reasons. ("Blood") *Andre Daniels also played Arlan Green in "Tooms."*

McRoberts, Bonnie (Kimberly Ashlyn Gere) Young, attractive resident of the small suburban farming community of Franklin, Pennsylvania, who was told by a garage mechanic that repairs to her Volvo would be very expensive. She saw the word LIAR on the diagnostic computer's digital readout, then HE'S A LIAR and HE'LL RAPE YOU, followed by HE'LL KILL YOU and finally, KILL HIM FIRST. Mrs. McRoberts hit the auto repairman with a wrench and then stabbed him to death with an oil-can spout. When Mulder and the local sheriff went to her house to investigate, her microwave oven readout instructed her to KILL 'EM BOTH. Going berserk, she tried to stab Mulder but was shot and killed by the sheriff. An examination of her body revealed adrenaline levels two hundred times normal, adrenal glands showing signs of wear, and the presence of an unknown chemical compound similar to the hallucinogen LSD. ("Blood") *Kimberly Ashlyn Gere is better known as porn star Ashlyn Gere and, as Kimberly Patton, played the recurring role of Feliciti OH 519 on the short-lived Morgan-Wong sci-fi series* Space: Above and Beyond.

Meadowview Estates Affluent California housing development where illegal alien Gabrielle Buente worked as a maid. Her cousin, Eladio, whom she believed to be El Chupacabra of Mexican folklore, asked her for money to return to his native Mexico. ("El Mundo Gira")

Meecham, Ed (Jack Rader) Operations chief of the impoverished Fairfield Zoo in Idaho, which was the site of several animal abductions. The Wild Again Organization (W.A.O.), an anticaptivity activist group, believed Meecham had been needlessly torturing inhabitants of the zoo. After he killed an escaped tigress, the facility was permanently closed and the animals shipped to other zoos. Meecham and naturalist Willa Ambrose were charged with manslaughter in the death of W.A.O. spokesperson Kyle Lang. ("Fearful Symmetry")

Megadeath Heavy Metal band whose albums Mulder sarcastically recommended should be hidden since the sheriff of Milford Haven, New Hampshire, believed that such music had probably influenced the local youths' involvement in devil worship. ("Die Hand Die Verletzt")

memento mori A reminder of mortality, such as the classic emblem of a skull and crossbones; in Latin, "remember that you must die." Medieval and

Renaissance artists routinely used memento mori in their works, a particularly famous example being Holbein the Younger's painting "The Ambassadors," which featured an elongated and distorted skull in the foreground. Scully's terminal cancer was considered a memento mori that served as an effective reminder of her impending death. ("Memento Mori")

🗀 **"Memento Mori"** Written by Chris Carter, Frank Spotnitz, John Shiban, and Vince Gilligan. Directed by Rob Bowman. File number 4X15. *First aired February 9, 1997. After Scully learns that she has an inoperable brain tumor, she contacts a MUFON group of alleged female alien-abductees who are dying of the same type of cancerous mass after having implants removed from the base of their necks.* **Classic Sound Bite:** *"The truth is in me, and that's where I need to pursue it."* **Background Check:** *An improvised kiss on the mouth between Duchovny and Anderson during the episode's denouement was cut and replaced with a hug by the couple and a kiss by Duchovny on his co-star's forehead.*

Menand, Lucas (Jed Rees) A bright and promising post-doctoral fellow at the Massachusetts Institute of Technology, Menand threatened to go public with his claim that his academic advisor, cryobiologist Jason Nichols, had falsified data on a research paper. Menand and Nichols were embroiled in a heated argument as they walked down a city street, when suddenly they were approached by an elderly man (actually an older version of Nichols from the future) who warned Menand that he would be run over by a bus at exactly 11:46 P.M. At precisely the predestined time, Menand stepped into the path of an oncoming bus and was killed. ("Synchrony")

"Merchandise, The" Cryptic reference to the desiccated corpses Mulder discovered buried in a train refrigeration car in a New Mexico quarry. William Mulder used this term, which also appeared in the Defense Department's top secret MJ files, referring to the human subjects of Axis power scientists granted amnesty after the war. Although Mulder noticed what appeared to be a smallpox vaccination scar on one of the bodies, it remained unclear whether the corpses were human, alien or some type of hybrid. ("Anasazi")

Mercy Mission Atlantic City soup kitchen where Mulder asked the homeless about cannibalized vagrant Roger Crockett. In exchange for a few bucks, an itinerant man named Jack showed Mulder a drawing of a beast-person, possibly the Jersey Devil. The agent also exchanged his motel room for Jack's alleyway cardboard box, which he used as an unofficial stakeout. ("The Jersey Devil")

MIB Short for the singular "Man in Black" or the plural "Men in Black," who typically visit people and warn them to remain silent about their close encounters with extraterrestrials or alien spacecraft. One such MIB visited Roky Crikenson, insisted that it was Venus he saw, not a UFO, and threatened to kill him if he told anyone. Mulder later met the same MIB, who strongly suggested that some alien encounters were hoaxes perpetrated by the government ("Jose Chung's 'From Outer Space'"). MIBs were also nefarious government agents dressed in dark suits who used any means necessary to effectively silence witnesses to clandestine government activities. MIBs were present during former FBI agent Duane Barry's 1985 alien abduction ("Duane Barry") and appeared briefly with double-agent Alex Krycek after Barry's capture high atop Virginia's Skyland Mountain ("Ascension"). Mysterious dark-suited men who said they worked "for the intelligence community" warned Assistant Director Skinner not to reopen Melissa Scully's murder investigation ("Piper Maru").

Michael (Nicholas Lea) A potential victim of the genderbending Marty. After meeting at a club, the two went to a car where they were interrupted by a police officer who believed the female Marty was a prostitute. Suddenly "she" transformed into a man, decked the cop and escaped. Later at the hospital, Michael told Mulder and Scully what he had witnessed, lamenting, "The club scene used to be so simple." Scully theorized that Marty was a transvestite killer. ("Genderbender") *Nicholas Lea's one shot performance as Michael particularly impressed director Rob Bowman, who kept the actor in mind for a return and immediately thought of him for the recurring role of Alex Krycek when the character was introduced in the second season episode "Sleepless."*

Middlesex County Psychiatric Hospital Facility in Sayreville, New Jersey where the Flukeman was held for a mental evaluation at the request of the U.S. Justice Department, which prompted Mulder to argue that the mutant was not a man but a monster. ("The Host")

Midnight Inquisitor *National Enquirer*-like supermarket tabloid read by psychic Clyde Bruckman at the checkout counter of a St. Paul, Minnesota, liquor store only moments before his first encounter with the Puppet serial killer. In addition to the attention-grabbing banner headline HOW TO STAY YOUNG FOREVER, the cover featured THE STUPENDOUS YAPPI'S FORESEEABLE FUTURES, including the romance of Madonna and Kato Kaelin. ("Clyde Bruckman's Final Repose")

Mighty Man (Douglas Roy Dack) Bearded aide-de-camp to Vernon Ephesian, the dangerously charismatic leader of the Temple of the Seven Stars doomsday religious cult in Apison, Tennessee. Mighty Man called the sect's members to a final worship service, where they committed mass suicide by drinking poison-laced cocktails. ("The Field Where I Died")

Mighty Men The foot-soldiers of the Temple of the Seven Stars, used by the apocalyptic cult's paranoid leader, Vernon Ephesian, to dominate his followers through physical intimidation. While Ephesian convinced his proselytes to commit mass suicide, the armed men held off approaching federal agents. ("The Field Where I Died")

Mihai The Romanian form of the name Michael, used by Golda during the performance of an unsuccessful ritual of soul separation. ("The Calusari")

Miles, Billy (Zachary Ansley) A friend of the victims of the mysterious youth murders in Bellefleur, Oregon, who were all members of the graduating high school class of 1989. Billy, the son of Detective Miles of the county sheriff's department, was a live-in patient at the Raymon County State Psychiatric Hospital after being seriously injured in an auto accident with classmate Peggy O'Dell. Billy was in a vegetative "walking coma," except during those times when he was roused and controlled by an alien force that guided him into the woods. During an armed confrontation in the woods between Mulder, Scully, and Det. Miles, an eerie light appeared and the teenage boy was suddenly returned to normal health. ("The X-Files: Pilot")

Miles, Det. (Leon Russom) A detective with the country sheriff's office and father of Billy Miles. When Mulder and Scully searched the Oregon forest where the four victims of the mysterious youth murders had been found, a rifle-brandishing Det. Miles told the agents that they were on private property and ordered them to leave immediately. When Mulder and Scully later returned to the forest for further investigation, Det. Miles knocked Scully down and was about to shoot Mulder when they heard a woman scream. Finding his son, Billy, poised to offer Theresa Nemman as a sacrifice to aliens, the detective raised his rifle to shoot him, but was tackled to the ground by Mulder. ("The X-Files: Pilot")

Millar, Mike (Joe Spano) Head of the National Transportation Safety Board (NTSB) crash investigation Go-Team assigned to determine the cause of Flight 549's downing in Upstate New York, which claimed the lives of 133 passengers and crew. Intense but compassionate, Millar complained to Mulder that his theory of a UFO's involvement in the commercial airliner's crash "trivialized" the tragedy. Later, however, Millar encountered an alien spacecraft hovering above the crash site. The NTSB investigator also showed Mulder and Scully evidence of fatigue cracks caused by stress on the new plane's fuselage, which radiated from a central point as if an emergency exit door had been shaken and blown straight off the frame. ("Tempus Fugit/ Max") *Actor Joe Spano is best-remembered for his long-running role on* Hill Street Blues *and as an LA cop turned security specialist from the first season of* Murder One.

Millennium Man SEE: **Gates, Simon**

Miller, Kathy One of serial killer Virgil Incanto's forty-seven victims in five states. ("2Shy")

Miller's Grove Motor Lodge Mulder's place of lodging while investigating a number of deaths linked to cockroaches in the Massachusetts town of Miller's Grove. Another guest of the motel was attacked and killed by the insects while watching the local news. ("War of the Coprophages")

mindscan According to Mulder, the telepathic ability of some alien races to "read" their human abductees' minds. ("Duane Barry")

Minette, Ethan A romantic interest with whom Scully had planned to spend a long weekend until she was ordered to accompany Mulder to Northwest Oregon to investigate their first X-File together. ("The X-Files: Pilot")

📁 **"Miracle Man"** Written by Howard Gordon and Chris Carter. Directed by Michael Lange. File number 1X17. *First aired March 18, 1994. Agent Mulder sees visions of his missing sister when he and Scully investigate several deaths related to a young faith healer's tent-show crusade in Tennessee.* **Classic Sound Bite:** *"God never lets the Devil steal the show."* **Background Check:** *A scene of the dying Samuel Hartley silhouetted against the jail cell wall in a crucifix pose was ordered cut by the network censors. Director Michael Lange said that he was attempting to "create the image of the son of Jesus."*

Miracle Ministry A Kenwood, Tennessee, evangelical ministry operated by Rev. Calvin Hartley and his faith-healing adopted son, Samuel. The marquee slogan above the tent read: "Come As You Are . . . Leave As You Always Wanted To Be." ("Miracle Man")

Miramar Navy Air Base Military installation north of San Diego, California, where Scully went to visit Major Christopher Johansen, an old friend of her father's who served as an officer aboard the World War II submarine *Zeus Faber*. ("Piper Maru")

Miriskovic, Lladoslav Bosnian war criminal who personally ordered the rape and murder of thousands of innocent civilians in war-torn regions of the former Yugoslavia. Braddock Heights, Maryland, resident Joseph Patnick murdered five people, including his wife, in the belief he was slaying Miriskovic over and over again. ("Wetwired") *The actor who portrayed Miriskovic during the televised news report was uncredited.*

missing time A period of time ranging from minutes to days missing from one's memory after a UFO sighting. Mulder experienced missing time in "The X-Files: Pilot" (nine minutes), "Deep Throat" (undetermined), "E.B.E." (undetermined), "Little Green Men" (undetermined), and "Max" (nine minutes). Scully lost time in the pilot episode (nine minutes), "E.B.E." (undetermined), and "Ascension" and "One Breath" (approximately three months).

MJ documents The top-secret Department of Defense UFO intelligence files documenting everything the government had compiled about extraterrestrial existence for the past fifty years. After the fourth member of the Lone Gunmen, a computer hacking genius known as The Thinker, penetrated DOD's system, he secretly met with Mulder and gave the agent a digital audiotape (DAT) of the Navajo-encrypted files. WW II code-talker Albert Hosteen told Scully that while most of the files were in jargon, they did refer to an international conspiracy dating back to the 1940s and that her name and Duane Barry's were among the most recent entries, "having something to do with a test." ("Anasazi") *The real-life Majestic-12 Documents have divided opinion in the UFO community almost as severely as the alleged Roswell autopsy film footage, ever since they were made public in 1987. The documents include a one-page memo, apparently from President Harry Truman to Defense Secretary James Forrestal, dated September 24, 1947, authorizing the establishment of a top-secret Majestic-12 group to investigate crashed alien spacecraft and the bodies of extraterrestrials. Noted UFO debunker Philip Klass, however, has claimed that the documents are a hoax and the president's signature a forgery.*

MKULTRA (Pronounced M-K-Ultra). CIA mind-control experiments conducted in the 1950s in a covert effort to plant unwitting spies in enemy territory. ("Jose Chung's 'From Outer Space'")

Mob Man (Peter Mele) Mysterious figure present at an October 1962 meeting in the Fort Bragg, North Carolina, office of four-star General Francis, in which a young Army captain (later to be known as the Cigarette-Smoking Man) was recruited to assassinate President John F. Kennedy in the wake of the Bay of Pigs fiasco. The incident was based on Lone Gunman Frohike's speculative dossier on the life of the Cigarette-Smoking Man. ("Musings of a Cigarette-Smoking Man")

Moby Dick Novel by Herman Melville. Scully called her Navy officer father "Ahab," after the despotic captain who sought the White Whale, and he called her "Starbuck," after the loyal and capable lieutenant who served him ("Beyond the Sea" and "One Breath"). Scully also named her pet Pomeranian "Queequeg," in homage to a cannibalistic sailor from the classic tale. When they wrongly believed they were stranded on a rock in the middle of Lake Heuvelman, Scully compared the obsessive Mulder to Ahab (Quagmire").

Modell, Robert Patrick (Robert Wisden) Also known as "Pusher," a cold-blooded but charismatic assassin who possessed unique psychic powers that allowed him to induce his "hits" to commit suicide or otherwise bring about their own deaths. Mulder and Scully discovered that Modell had been a military supply clerk who tried to become a Navy SEAL and then a Special Forces Green Beret, but promptly failed at both attempts. He had also applied to the FBI (but was turned down after failing the Bureau's psych test) and claimed to have studied under ninjas in Japan, describing himself as a "masterless samurai." Scully contended that most of Modell's claims were lies or exaggerations and that he was simply "a little man who wanted to feel big." Calling Mulder a "worthy opponent," Modell forced the agent to participate in a deadly game of Russian roulette until Scully cleverly broke Modell's concentration long enough for Mulder to be freed from his psychic grip and shoot him. Modell's psychokinesis was apparently the result of an operable brain tumor, but he refused treatment in order to retain the powers that made him feel superior to other people for the first time in his life. "It was like you said," Mulder told Scully. "He was always such a little man. This was finally something that made him feel big." ("Pusher")

Molitch, Harvey A resident of "the perfect harmony city" of Comity, whose backyard was dug up by Bob Spitz and other panicked townsfolk after George Hunsaker's son received an anonymous call from someone who said he knew where a mass grave was located. ("Syzygy")

monkey wrenchers Radical eco-activists who spike trees, sabotage logging equipment, and chain trees. Monkey wrenchers were originally suspected of being responsible for the disappearances of over thirty loggers in the remote Olympic National Forest in northwest Washington State. ("Darkness Falls")

Monogahela Medical Center The hospital in Pittsburgh, Pennsylvania, where Leonard Betts was employed as an Emergency Medical Technician (EMT). After he was killed in an automobile accident, the decapitated corpse kicked its way out of a freezer drawer, knocked an attendant unconscious, and then walked out of the medical center's morgue under its own power. ("Leonard Betts")

Monroe Insurance Company Omaha, Nebraska, employer of former HTG Industrial Technologies secretary Lauren Kyte. The ghost of her former boss, Howard Graves, may have followed her to the company after she relocated from Philadelphia. ("Shadows")

Monroe, Kimberly (Sarah Strange) An employee of the Travel Time Travel Agency who was taken hostage by escaped mental patient Duane Barry. Allegedly a former alien-abductee, Barry wanted safe passage for himself and hospital psychiatrist Dr. Del Hakkie to the site of his abduction. Unfortunately, he couldn't remember its location, so Barry stopped at the travel agency. Monroe told him that she believed his claims. ("Duane Barry")

Montagu, Dr. Ashley Noted Princeton University anthropologist who participated in a NASA symposium at Boston University on November 20, 1972, to discuss the possible existence of extraterrestrial life. Mulder was watching a videotape of the conference when he allegedly killed himself with a gunshot to the head. ("Gethsemane")

Monte, Dr. Aaron (Paul Ben Victor) The Druid Hill Sanitarium psychiatrist who supervised Eugene Victor Tooms' institutionalization. Although Tooms was a cannibalistic serial killer, a commitment review board decided to release him with the stipulation that he remain under Dr. Monte's care. Tooms later killed the psychiatrist and ate his liver. ("Tooms")

Montgomery and Glick Publishing Book publishing company that sent Raul Bloodworth (the *nom de plume* of the Cigarette-Smoking Man) a caustic rejection letter in 1968 regarding his first spy thriller, *Take a Chance,* in which the company's representative, Albert Goodwinkle, advised Bloodworth to "burn it!" The incident, however, was based on a rather dubious account of the Cigarette-Smoking Man's life as pieced together by Lone Gunman Frohike. ("Musings of a Cigarette-Smoking Man") *Those words in the Cigarette-Smoking Man's first rejection letter were his last words in the second season finale, "Anasazi"—"Burn it!"*

Montifiore Cemetery Graveyard in Minneapolis, Minnesota, where Catherine Ann Terle's body was desecrated by death fetishist Donnie Pfaster. ("Irresistible")

Moore, Larry (Jason Beghe) U.S. Forest Service ranger who assisted Mulder and Scully in their investigation of several loggers who had mysteriously disappeared in the Pacific Northwest's remote Olympia National Forest. Mulder, Scully, and Moore were later quarantined after they were found inside the huge cocoon of prehistoric mites. ("Darkness Falls") *Jason Beghe has been David Duchovny's best friend since they were in the ninth grade and was instrumental in Duchovny's decision to take up acting. Beghe recently co-starred in the movie thriller G.I. Jane with Demi Moore.*

Morgan, Wayne (Stephen E. Miller) A U.S. Navy investigator who accompanied Mulder and Scully aboard the French salvage ship, the *Piper Maru,* after it limped into port in San Diego. ("Piper Maru")

Morleys Brand of cigarettes puffed incessantly by the enigmatic Cigarette-Smoking Man. ("One Breath")

Morley Tobacco Cigarette manufacturing company in Raleigh-Durham, North Carolina. One of Morley's executives, Patrick Newirth, heard a distraught man knocking on another door in the hallway of his Richmond, Virginia, hotel. Newirth watched the commotion through his peephole until a shadow slipped beneath the door and evaporated him, leaving behind a mysterious scorch mark on the carpet. ("Soft Light")

Morris, Agent (Deryl Hayes) Dressed as a tourist, he was assigned to follow Scully when she boarded a plane at the Miami International Airport. Scully, who suspected she was being tailed, cleverly eluded Morris and his partner. ("Little Green Men") *Deryl Hayes also played mysterious CIA operative Webster in "Shadows" and an army doctor in "The Walk."*

Morris, Charlie Buffalo, New York, police officer who worked narcotics out of the 27th Precinct until his gangland style murder in Chinatown. Nine years later his reincarnated spirit possessed eight-year-old Michelle Bishop in an attempt to seek revenge against the police officers who conspired to have him murdered. ("Born Again")

Morris, Darlene (Carrie Snodgrass) Member of a Girl Scout troop who witnessed and photographed a UFO near Lake Okobogee, Iowa, in 1967. Twenty-five years later, her teenage daughter Ruby was abducted by aliens at a campsite near the same lake. At first cooperative, Darlene refused to assist Mulder and Scully in their investigation after black-suited NSA agents ransacked her home. After Ruby was returned unconscious but alive, Darlene told Mulder and Scully that she didn't want her daughter to be ridiculed for discussing what happened, bitterly declaring, "the truth has brought me nothing but a heartache," and said that she'd claim Ruby fell off the back of a Harley-Davidson motorcycle. ("Conduit") *Carrie Snodgrass was nominated for an Academy Award and won a Golden Globe for her title role in 1970's* Diary of a Mad Housewife. *After retiring from the entertainment business, she returned to movie theaters in the very X-Filish thriller* The Fury.

Morris, Gwen (Barbara Pollard) An employee of the Travel Time Travel Agency who was one of four people taken hostage by escaped mental patient and former alien-abductee Duane Barry. Mulder convinced Barry to release Morris and Kimberly Monroe only moments before he was wounded by an FBI marksman. ("Duane Barry")

Morris, Jane (Nora McLellan) A secretary at the Philadelphia-based HTG Industrial Technologies, who comforted Lauren Kyte after her boss, Howard Graves, allegedly committed suicide. ("Shadows")

Morris, Kevin (Joel Palmer) The eight-year-old son of Darlene Morris. Kevin screamed for his mother when his teenage sister vanished from their campsite. The young boy began acting strangely afterwards, writing down a binary number sequence that Mulder sent to Washington. NSA agents spirited Kevin and his mother away, claiming that the code was a classified fragment of a Defense department satellite transmission. From a second-floor vantage point at the Morris' house, Mulder and Scully saw that the spread-out pages of Kevin's binary code eerily formed a mural-sized picture of the little boy's missing sister. ("Conduit") *Child actor Joel Palmer also* *portrayed Charlie Holvey and his evil-possessed stillborn twin, Michael, in "The Calusari."*

Morris, Ruby (Taunya Dee) The sixteen-year-old daughter of Darlene Morris. While sleeping near her little brother, Kevin, she disappeared at a campsite near Iowa's Lake Okobogee, which Mulder described as a "UFO hotspot." A month later she was discovered comatose and showing signs of someone subjected to prolonged weightlessness. When the agents asked her what happened, she merely replied, "They told me not to say." ("Conduit")

Morrison, Dr. Philip Noted Cornell professor and nuclear physicist who took part in the design and building of the atom bomb at Los Alamos Laboratory. Dr. Morrison, who faced a Congressional anticommunist investigative committee in 1952, participated in a NASA symposium at Boston University on November 20, 1972, to discuss the possible existence of extraterrestrial life. Mulder was watching a videotape of the conference when he allegedly killed himself with a gunshot to the head. ("Gethsemane")

Morrow, Det. B.J (Deborah Strang) A second generation police officer in Aubrey, Missouri, she was having an affair with her married boss, detective chief Lt. Brian Tillman, and became pregnant with his child. One evening a painful vision led her to a vacant field, where she dug up the skeletal remains of an FBI agent who had been missing since 1942. Before his disappearance, legendary G-man Sam Chaney had been investigating a serial killer who razored SISTER into his victims' chests. Harry Cokely was convicted and sentenced to prison in 1945 for the rape and attempted murder of Linda Thibodeaux and carving SISTER on her before she escaped. After similar murders began again in the mid-1990s, Mulder and Scully discovered that Thibodeaux had given birth to Cokely's baby after the assault and put it up for adoption. B.J. was actually Cokely's granddaughter and was responsible for the new wave of mutilation murders, the killer's genetic memory having been passed on after skipping a generation. Scully theorized that B.J.'s pregnancy may have been "a catalyst for her transformation." She was later incarcerated at the Shamrock Women's Prison Psychiatric Ward on suicide watch after attempting to abort her unborn child, a boy, which Lt. Tillman petitioned to adopt. ("Aubrey")

Morrow, Raymond An Aubrey, Missouri, police officer and father of detective B.J. Morrow. He was the son of suspected Slash Killer Harry Cokely as a result of his 1945 rape of Linda Thibedeaux. ("Aubrey")

Mosier, Gary The name of a man the tow-truck driver was looking for when he stopped to offer help to child kidnapper Carl Wade, whose car was disabled on the side of the road. ("Oubliette")

Mossinger, Paul (Michael Bryan French) A military security agent (codenamed Redbird) who masqueraded as a local newspaper reporter in an attempt to divert Mulder and Scully from investigating the unusual disappearances of test pilots at Southwest Idaho's Ellens Air Force Base. Mossinger directed the agents to The Flying Saucer Diner where "UFO nuts" gathered, not realizing that Mulder would make contacts at the café that would bolster his theory that the government was testing planes built using UFO technology. When Scully returned to their motel she found Mossinger coming out of her room. Hearing a walkie-talkie in his car, she leapt inside to find his handgun and Airbase Security ID. At gunpoint, she forced Mossinger to drive her to the base, where a drug-injected and disoriented Mulder stumbled out, unable to remember recent events. ("Deep Throat")

Mostow, John (Levani Outchaneichvili) An art student and divorced, unemployed house painter, Mostow emigrated to the United States from Uzbekistan, where he'd spent the better half of his twenties in an insane asylum. He was arrested by the FBI in connection with the mutilation death of an artist's model and was a suspect in the serial murders of at least seven men (ages seventeen to twenty-five) who all died from massive blood loss due to facial mutilations. Mostow insisted that a spirit possessed him during the three year period in which he committed the killings. Investigating Mostow's artist's studio, Mulder found a secret room full of sculpted gargoyles with human corpses inside them. ("Grotesque")

Motel Black Where Aubrey, Missouri, police detective B.J. Morrow went to meet her married boss, Lt. Brian Tillman, to discuss her pregnancy. ("Aubrey")

Mount Avalon Active volcano in Washington State where Mulder and Scully encountered a deadly, silicon-based lifeform while investigating the death of one of the Cascade Volcano Research Project's scientists. ("Firewalker")

Mount Foodmore Supermarket Grocery store in Loudoun County, Virginia, where Robert Modell was initially apprehended by a small company of FBI agents and local law enforcement officers led by Frank Burst. ("Pusher")

Mountain Home Air Base A major UFO hotspot near Fairfield, Idaho, according to the Lone Gunmen. Mulder theorized that alien conservationists may have been responsible for animal abductions from the nearby zoo. ("Fearful Symmetry")

Mr.X SEE: **X**

Mt. Zion Medical Center Hospital in Philadelphia, Pennsylvania, where West African immigrant Samuel Aboah, a suspected carrier of a deadly disease, was quarantined pending a battery of examinations by Scully and Dr. Bruin of the Centers for Disease Control. Aboah escaped from the medical center after hiding in the drawer of a hospital food cart. INS social worker Marcus Duff was hospitalized at Mt. Zion after being attacked by Aboah and undergoing acute trauma to his pituitary gland. ("Teliko")

MUFON Acronym for the Mutual UFO Network, Inc., the world's largest civilian UFO research group. When Scully investigated a MUFON membership list in Allentown, Pennsylvania, she interrupted a meeting of women who claimed to recognize her from the previous year's abduction or, as they termed it, "unexplained event." All the MUFON women had the same marks on their necks as Scully ("Nisei"). In 1997, Scully returned to Allentown in hopes of finding clues to the origin of her inoperable brain tumor, but discovered that almost all of the women in the MUFON group had died of the same type of cancer. Penny Northern passed away shortly after Scully's arrival, the last of eleven women who were allegedly alien-abductees with similar recollections regarding the experience and subsequent identical brain tumors ("Memento Mori"). *The Mutual UFO Network actually exist and was founded in 1969 as a multi-disciplinary, grassroots approach to resolving the UFO mystery. The organization has more than 5,000 members, field investigators and consultants worldwide.*

mugwort Herb used by the Calusari, a group of Romanian exorcists, during the ceremonial Ritual of Separation. Mugwort has been recognized since medieval times in Europe as a talisman against evil. ("The Calusari")

Mulder, Fox William (David Duchovny) FBI badge number JTT047101111. Current address: 2630 Hegal Place, Apt. #42, Alexandria, Virginia. Born on October 13, 1961. Mulder is an Oxford-educated behavioral psychologist with a life-long, at times obsessive, interest in the paranormal ("The X-Files: Pilot"). He developed an intense fear of fire in his youth when his best friend's house burnt down and Mulder spent the night in the rubble to keep away looters. Following the traumatic experience, he suffered years of nightmares about being trapped in burning buildings ("Fire"). Possessing a photographic memory, Mulder was once one of the most promising young agents in the FBI's Violent Crimes Section and was considered the Behavioral Science Unit's finest analyst during his three-year tenure in the division under the supervision of ASAC Reggie Purdue. On his first case, Mulder distinguished himself in the pursuit of homicidal bank robber John Barnett ("Young at Heart"). His celebrated ability to create perceptive psychological profiles for some of the Bureau's most difficult criminal cases (his 1988 monograph *On Serial Killers and the Occult* aided in the capture of Monte Propps) insured him a lengthy and fruitful career ("The X-Files: Pilot). But a buried memory from Mulder's past would take him away from the Violent Crimes Section and propel him into some of the most bizarre and unconventional cases in the bureau's history: the X-Files.

Mulder's penchant for theories based in the realm of extreme possibility earned him the nickname "Spooky" at the FBI's Quantico Academy ("The X-Files: Pilot" and "Young at Heart"). But his fascination with unexplained phenomena escalated into full-blown obsession after Dr. Heitz Werber's hypnotic regression therapy revealed that, as a young boy, Mulder had witnessed the abduction of his eight-year-old sister Samantha (X-File #X-42053), while he was paralyzed by some unknown power, and his memories of the tragic event altered. Convinced that his sister was taken away by extraterrestrial forces, perhaps assisted by shadowy government organizations, Mulder set himself the task of uncovering the truth about Samantha's abduction ("Conduit").

Using his success as the Bureau's best crime investigator and his influential "connections in Congress" ("The X-Files: Pilot") such as SETI proponent Senator Richard Matheson ("Little Green Men"), Mulder persuaded his superiors to transfer him to the X-Files section, the FBI's special designation for unassigned cases outside the Bureau's mainstream that could not be explained by conventional science. Fearing that Mulder might expose their secret agenda, a conspiracy inside the government (represented by the enigmatic Cigarette-Smoking Man) arranged for him to be assigned a partner, Special Agent Dr. Dana Scully, who would file field reports on Mulder's X-Files investigations ("The X-Files: Pilot"). Scully's assistance continues to prove invaluable to Mulder, her natural skepticism and painstakingly scientific approach to the cases balancing his own proclivity to favor the most extreme explanation for the unusual phenomena they encounter.

Mulder is single-mindedly devoted to his work ("The Jersey Devil"). He has never been married, lives alone, and does not appear to own a bed, sleeping instead on the sofa in his small Alexandria, Virginia, apartment ("Small Potatoes"). Among the few recreational pursuits he enjoys are the New York Knicks ("Beyond the Sea," "Little Green Men," and "Clyde Bruckman's Final Repose"), Washington Redskins ("Irresistible"), pornography ("Jersey Devil," "Beyond the Sea," "Blood," "3," and "Small Potatoes"), classic rock music ("Beyond the Sea" and "Genderbender"), old sci-fi movies ("Tooms" and "The Erlenmeyer Flask"), basketball ("Paper Hearts" and "Small Potatoes"), running ("The X-Files: Pilot," "Deep Throat," and "Humbug"), swimming ("Duane Barry"), and eating shelled sunflower seeds, a habit he picked up from his father ("Aubrey"). When he was forced to use his accrued vacation time in 1997, he chose to tour Elvis Presley's Graceland estate in Memphis, Tennessee ("Never Again").

A few individuals sympathetic to Mulder's quest for the truth have come forward to provide him with information and other assistance. Byers, Langly and Frohike, the three eccentric operatives that form the editorial staff of the conspiracy-oriented magazine known as *The Lone Gunman,* have on several occasions used their contacts and inside knowledge in a diversity of fields to function as a quasi-think tank for Mulder ("E.B.E.," etc.). Additionally, two highly placed yet unnamed informants, Deep Throat ("Deep Throat," etc.) and Mr. X ("The Host," etc.), alternately helped/hindered Mulder's investigations by providing mostly valuable but sometimes misleading information. After Mr. X's death, Marita Covarrubias, the assistant to the U.N.'s Special Representative to the Secretary General, took his place as Mulder's clandestine information source ("Herrenvolk," etc.).

Mulder's inquiry into the government conspiracy would reveal a personal connection. In the midst of investigating the arson murders of identical doctors around the country, he was summoned home on a "family emergency" to Martha's Vineyard, where a woman arrived claiming to be Samantha, his sister who'd been missing for twenty-two years. Convinced by the woman's recollection of events and intimate details from his childhood, Mulder tried to protect her from an alien bounty hunter—only to discover that she was not his sister at all, but an alien-human hybrid ("Colony/End Game").

Mulder perceived the woman's explicit knowledge of Samantha's life to mean that his sister was still alive. Committing himself to his quest for the truth with renewed enthusiasm, Mulder's attempt to decode the encrypted top-secret Defense Department files on UFO activity since the 1940s led to another shocking disclosure about his family. His father revealed that he had been a key player in the Shadowy Syndicate and hinted that it was the U.S. government, not extraterrestrials, that took Samantha away. But before he could tell his son what he knew about Samantha's ultimate fate, Mulder's father was fatally shot by the nefarious double-agent Alex Krycek. His final words to his son: "Forgive me" ("Anasazi").

Mulder now sought more than just the truth about his sister—he wanted vengeance for what the conspirators had done to his family. Seeking more detailed information on his father's State Department connection to the conspiracy, Mulder found a circa-1973 photograph of his father in the company of several other men, among them Mulder's former informant Deep Throat, the sinister Cigarette-Smoking Man, who seemed to coordinate much of the Shadowy Syndicate's conspiratorial activities, and the even more mysterious Well-Manicured Man (whom Mulder had not yet met). Mulder asked his mother about the photograph, but she claimed not to have known anything about her husband's professional life ("The Blessing Way"). Later, she painfully revealed that she and Mulder's father had been forced by the conspiracy to make a choice of which of their two children would be taken from them and that Mulder's father had chosen Samantha, who was then abducted by the government, apparently to ensure his silence. ("Paper Clip"). Later, Deep Throat's successor, the informant known only as Mr. X, brought Mulder recent photographs of his mother arguing heatedly with the Cigarette-Smoking Man at the Mulders' deserted summer home, indicating that she knew more about the conspiracy than she initially disclosed ("Talitha Cumi").

Mulder soon found the first conclusive evidence that his sister was abducted by the conspiracy when he was led by the mysterious Jeremiah Smith to an eerie, isolated farming community in Canada, where he was stunned to see identical clones of the eight-year-old Samantha ("Herrenvolk"). This discovery gave Mulder new faith and resolution in his search for the truth, however implausible and inconceivable it appeared to Scully and others. He even went so far as to subject himself to aggressive drug-induced regression therapy in order to access buried or suppressed memories of his sister's abduction, which ultimately led to disastrous and life-threatening results ("Demons"). And although he has been beaten up, buried alive in a boxcar, brainwashed, and alien-infested over the years, Mulder's idealistic agenda has remained unchanged. He knows that the truth is *still* out there.

In mid-1997, however, Mulder met Michael Kritschgau, who claimed to have run the Department of Defense's agitprop arm for a decade, telling Mulder that the government had been orchestrating an elaborate hoax to make him believe in the existence of extraterrestrials. "They invented you," Kritschgau alleged, "and your regression hypnosis, the story of your sister's abduction, the lies they fed your father. You wanted to believe so badly, who could have blamed you?" When Scully told Mulder that the shadowy conspirators within the government had planted an inoperable cancer in her in an effort to ensure his belief in their campaign of propaganda about aliens and UFOs, the agent appeared stunned. Shortly thereafter, as either the unwitting or witting participant in an elaborate hoax, Scully appeared before a group of FBI officials led by Section Chief Scott Blevins and stated that the purpose of the current meeting was to report on the illegitimacy of Agent Mulder's work in the X-Files unit. Struggling to maintain her composure, she revealed to the officials present that her partner had died of an apparent self-inflicted gunshot wound to the head ("Gethsemane"). *David Duchovny's acting resume includes appearances on the TV shows* Twin Peaks, Space: Above & Beyond, Fraiser, Duckman, The Larry Sanders Show, Red Shoe Diaries, *and* Saturday Night Live. *In addition to his first starring role as disgraced physician Eugene Sands in the movie* Playing God, *Duchovny has appeared in* Beethoven, Ruby, Don't Tell Mom the Babysitter's Dead, The Rapture, New Year's Day, Working Girl, Bad Influence, Julia Has Two Lovers, Venice/Venice, Chaplin, Kalifornia, *and* Denial. *Marcus Turner and Alex Haythorne portrayed twelve-year-old Fox Mulder in the Samantha-abduction flashback episodes.* X-Files *producers and frequent episode writers Glen Morgan and James Wong at one point early on in the series considered creating a brother for Fox. The actor they had in mind was Geoff Nauffs, a cast member on* The Commish *with Nicholas Lea and Melinda McGraw, who later played Alex Krycek and Melissa Scully on* The X-Files. *Kevin Sorbo, star of the* Hercules *TV series, reportedly auditioned for the role of Fox Mulder.*

Mulder, Marty The alias used by Fox Mulder when he phoned Los Angeles blood banks to check on the hiring of new employees ("3"). A 1-900 phone sex operator named Chantal called and left a message for "Marty" on Mulder's answering machine, advising him of new "lower rates" ("Small Potatoes").

Mulder, Mrs. (Rebecaa Toolan) The mother of Fox and Samantha Mulder. A warm, gentle woman, her marriage to William disintegrated after the disappearance of eight-year-old Samantha in November 1973. Mrs. Mulder was skeptical when an adult version of her daughter reappeared twenty-two years later (it was discovered later that the young woman was a clone of

Samantha) ("Colony"). When Fox confronted her with a 1970s–era photo-graph of his father with Deep Throat, the Cigarette-Smoking Man, and other, more sinister associates, she refused to deal with the memories it awoke. In complete denial about her family's tragic past, she unconvincingly swore she didn't recognize any of the men ("The Blessing Way"). After the Shadowy Syndicate's Well-Manicured Man told Fox that his father had threatened to expose their elaborate eugenics program and Samantha was abducted to ensure his silence, Fox once again challenged Mrs. Mulder about the family's past, demanding to know if his father had asked her to decide between him and his sister. "No, I couldn't choose," she admitted, weeping. "It was your father's choice, and I hated him for it. Even in his grave, I still hate him" ("Paper Clip"). Several months later, Mrs. Mulder went to the family's deserted summer house at Quonochontaug, Rhode Island, where she met the Cigarette-Smoking Man, who reminisced about the good times of years past. He noted that he was a better water-skier than her husband, "but that could be said about so many things . . . couldn't it?" Mrs. Mulder shot back that she had "repressed it all," but CSM needed her to remember something, and they argued heatedly. Mrs. Mulder, violently angry, suffered a severe and debilitating stroke after he left. Only because Mr. X had been covertly observing her and made an anonymous 911 call did she receive immediate paramedic assistance. Although the stroke left her unable to speak, when she saw her son at the hospital she scribbled the word "PALM" on a notepad. Later that night, Fox returned to the family's summer home to conduct a search of the premises. After toying with the word "PALM" and writing down the anagram "LAMP," he found hidden inside a lamp a stiletto-like weapon, the kind used to kill alien clones. After learning that his mother might not recover, Fox discovered the Cigarette-Smoking Man lighting up a Morley in a hospital hallway. "Are you going to smoke that, or do you want to smoke this?" Mulder demanded, grabbing him and sticking a gun in his face. CSM noted that he had known Mulder's mother since "before you were born, Fox" ("Talitha Cumi"). Fearing that Mulder could become a fierce enemy with "nothing left to lose" if his mother died, the Cigarette-Smoking Man directed the alien Bounty Hunter to heal her with his paranor-mal powers ("Herrenvolk"). After undergoing a drug-induced radical type of regression therapy, Fox apparently recalled suppressed memories from his childhood that included seeing a young Cigarette-Smoking Man pulling Mrs. Mulder close to him, as if to kiss her, and his mother and father reacting as if some terrible tragedy had entered their home. Mulder and Scully drove to his mother's Greenwich home, where he accused her of lying to him about Samantha and of being unfaithful to his father. Mrs. Mulder slapped Fox hard across the face and angrily denied his allegations: "I am your mother and I will not tolerate any more of your questions" ("Demons"). *Although Mrs. Mulder has never received a first name in the series' episode credits, Chris Carter has stated in interviews that her name is "Tena." Actress Rebecaa Toolan, who plays Mrs. Mulder, has said that her hospital wristband in "Talitha Cumi/ Herrenvolk" read "Elizabeth Mulder." Toolan is a local Vancouver actor whose film credits include* Hideaway *(1995)*, Little Women *(1994) and* Exquisite Tenderness *(1994). She also played Mrs. Whelan in "The Choice" episode of* The Outer Limits. *Shelley Adam played the young Mrs. Mulder in the flashback scenes in "Demons."*

Mulder, Samantha Ann (Vanessa Morely) Fox Mulder's sister, she was abducted on November 27, 1973, when she was eight and her brother was twelve. The traumatic experience tore the Mulder family apart ("No one would talk about it," Fox later told Scully), leading to the separation and eventual divorce of the elder Mulders. Although Fox himself repressed the incident, he underwent hypnotic regression therapy with Dr. Heitz Werber on June 16, 1989 and was finally able to recall a bright light, a presence in the room where they were asleep, his own helpless paralysis by an unknown power, and a voice reassuring him that all would be well and his sister would be returned ("Conduit"). This revelation convinced him that Samantha had been abducted by aliens, perhaps aided by rogue government organizations; he now dedicated his life to the recovery of his sister and the uncovering of the conspiracies concealing the aliens' existence. Fox's memories of Samantha's abduction permanently changed several months later. In a new flashback, he recalled the Mulder home in Chilmark, Massachusetts (their parents were out for the evening), when over TV news of Rose Mary Woods' partial Nixon-tape erasure, the young Fox played the game Stratego with his kid sister, Samantha, while he waited for *The Magician* starring Bill Bixby to come on television. Suddenly, the house shook violently, and amid eerie lights, a thin figure appeared silhouetted in the doorway. Fox broke open a locked gun box, but then became paralyzed as his sister floated away. Due to the fact that Fox's memories were derived from regression therapy, the images were vague, explaining why he recalled the incident differently at a later time ("Little Green Men"). Although young faith healer Samuel Hartley hinted that Samantha might still be alive ("Miracle Man") and self-proclaimed alien abductee Duan Barry warned Mulder that children were often seen in alien ships, undergoing painful "tests" ("Duane Barry"), Mulder was visibly shaken when in early 1995 a woman claiming to be Samantha suddenly turned up. She knew a great deal about him and his sister, right down to their fondness for the game Stratego, and claimed to have been returned to Earth and raised by aliens passing for human beings. According to her, the identical aliens were the progeny of two visitors who had arrived in the 1940s, and were trying to establish an Earth colony by genetically merging with humans. Because their duplicate appearances made it necessary to disperse across the world, the clones were experimenting with the melding of alien and human DNA in order to diversify their physical appearance and increase their number. Mulder was later shocked to discover that his "sister" was in fact one of a number of clones, who claimed to know the fate of the real Samantha ("Colony/End Game"). Mulder later was told by the Shadowy Syndicate's Well-Manicured Man that during the cold war, men like Mulder's father, William, collected genetic material from millions of people through smallpox vaccinations ostensibly for use in disaster management after a nuclear war. William objected to the use of the data in selecting citizens to be abducted and mutated as part of an experiment to create an alien/human hybrid immune to biological warfare and threatened to expose the eugenics program, but was kept silent via the abduction of his daughter, Samantha. Mulder confronted his mother with the revelation, who painfully revealed that his father was told to make a choice between their two children ("Paper Clip"). Approximately a year later, Jeremiah Smith, an extraterrestrial shapeshifter, escorted Mulder to the Shadowy Syndicate's isolated Canadian farming community, whose agrarian workforce consisted of several clones of Samantha at the age she was abducted. Smith told Mulder that the children had been bred as worker drones, but before the shapeshifter could reveal more about the "colonization" conspiracy, he was killed by an alien Bounty Hunter dispatched by the Cigarette-Smoking Man ("Herrenvolk"). Mulder was led to question what really happened to Samantha after he uncovered evidence that a serial killer he helped capture years earlier, John Lee Roche, had left three victims unfound. Roche manipulated Mulder into believing that Samantha was one such victim, and then escaped imprisonment. Mulder was forced to kill Roche when he abducted another young girl and held her at gunpoint. After identifying two of the victims, Mulder was left wondering if the final victim was really Samantha ("Paper Hearts"). *Samantha's medical record, uncovered by Mulder and Scully in the Strughold Mining Company, stated that her middle name was Ann and her birthdate was November 21, 1965. In the pilot episode her middle initial was "T" and her birthdate January 22, 1964. Actress Megan Leitch played the adult "Samantha" in "Colony/End Game."*

Mulder, William (Peter Donat) Fox Mulder's father, a cold and distant man, formerly of the U.S. State Department. He telephoned his son at the FBI when a woman claiming to be his daughter, Samantha, returned to their Massachusetts home twenty-two years after her disappearance. After the alien Bounty Hunter forced Fox to trade his sister for Scully's life, a distraught Fox had to face his unforgiving father once again ("Colony/End Game"). (Note: This was before Fox learned that "Samantha" was actually an alien clone of his sister.) The Cigarette-Smoking Man met with William at his home on Martha's Vineyard on "pressing business" after the top-secret MJ files were breached by The Thinker and a digital tape copy given to Fox. The elder Mulder appeared equally concerned that his involvement in a covert government experiment not be revealed, and that his son not be harmed. "I've protected him this long, haven't I?" the Cigarette-Smoking Man reassured him, not entirely convincingly. After the CSM left, William summoned Fox to his home, where the seemingly repentant father tried to tell his son about "the choice that needed to be made." He warned Fox that the meaning of words like "the merchandise" would become horribly clear. William excused himself to use the bathroom, where he was fatally shot by the Cigarette-Smoking Man's lackey, Alex Krycek, who was hiding in the shower. ("Anasazi"). Fox later learned from the Well-Manicured Man that after the 1947 Roswell crash, Nazi scientists were brought to the U.S. under Operation Paper Clip to conduct experiments in creating an alien/human hybrid. When William Mulder threatened to expose the eugenics project, his daughter, Samantha, was abducted to guarantee his silence and cooperation ("Paper Clip"). *Peter Donat's recurring role on* The X-Files *led to a Showtime* Outer Limits *portrayal of an evil prep school principal who controlled his students by inserting neural implants. Donat, the nephew of the late Oscar-winning actor Robert Donat* (Goodbye, Mr. Chips), *also played the nefarious Dr. Mordecai Sahmbi in the sci-fi series* Time Trax. *Dmitry Chepovetsky portrayed the young William Mulder in the pre-credits sequence of "Apocrypha" and Dean Aylesworth played him in the flashback scenes in "Musings of a Cigarette-Smoking Man" and "Demons."*

Muldrake, Reynard "Nonfiction science-fiction" author Jose Chung's thinly-disguised alias for Fox Mulder in his alien abduction book *From Outer Space.* Chung described the Muldrake character as "a ticking time bomb of insanity. His quest into the unknown has so warped his psyche one wonders how he can elicit any pleasure from life." ("Jose Chung's 'From Outer Space'") *The word "reynard" is French for "fox."*

Multrevich Reward-minded landlord in Boyle Heights, Maryland, who called the FBI hotline to turn in Lula Philips for $10,000. Multrevich was the manager of the apartment building where Philips moved after the death of her bank robber husband/accomplice, Warren Dupre. ("Lazarus")

Munchausen syndrome by proxy Psychological illness in which a parent or caretaker induces illness in a child. Scully found documentation of young Teddy Holvey's recurrent hospitalization (ten times in two years) and suggested that the boy's grandmother, Golda, was committing Munchausen syndrome by proxy. ("The Calusari")

Munson, Det. (Tom McBeath) Plain-clothed Los Angeles police detective who assisted Mulder in the investigation of the vampiresque murders in Hollywood. During a search of Kristen Kilar's Malibu home, Det. Munson found veterinary hypos and a piece of a snakebite kit that was used to extract blood. ("3") *Actor Tom McBeath also played a scientist in "Space" and Dr. Lewton, victim of a jaguar-spirit curse, in "Teso dos Bichos."*

Muntz, Galen (Hrothgar Matthews) Disturbed man who opened fire on the customers inside a Brothers K fast-food restaurant in Arlington, Virginia, before being shot himself by a police marksman. Jeremiah Smith stepped from the crowd and miraculously closed the gunman's wound with just the touch of his hands. ("Talitha Cumi") *Hrothgar Matthews also played Jack, an Atlantic City vagrant in "The Jersey Devil," and mental patient Creighton Jones in "Our Town."*

Murphy, Dr. Denny (Steve Hynter) Professor of geology at the University of California at San Diego and an avid San Diego Chargers football fan who listened to audiotapes of old playoff games. He accompanied Mulder and Scully to investigate the unexplained deaths of a research team at Icy Cape, Alaska. Mulder later discovered the murdered Dr. Murphy stuffed in one of the ice station's lockers, a victim of Dr. Nancy Da Silva, who had become the human host of an alien ice worm. ("Ice") *Steve Hytner was a member of the series cast of* Disney Presents the 100 Lives of Black Jack Savage, *which starred the future Mr. X, Steven Williams.*

📁 **"Musings of a Cigarette-Smoking Man"** Written by Glen Morgan. Directed by James Wong. File number 4X07. *First aired November 17, 1996. Lone Gunman Frohike delivers to Mulder and Scully a secret dossier on the sinister chain-smoker whom Mulder calls "Cancer Man," while the target of the fascinating dissertation eavesdrops from a nearby high-rise with a sniper's rifle at the ready.* **Classic Sound Bite:** *"I can kill you whenever I please. But not today."* **Background Check:** *Other than a few flashback scenes and voice-overs, Mulder and Scully did not even appear in this episode. William Davis, who plays the enigmatic Cigarette-Smoking Man, asked Chris Carter if the episode was the actual backstory of his character, to which* The X-Files *creator firmly replied, "No."*

Nisei, the "children" of Dr. Zama

Nabokov, Vladimir One of several Russian immigrants to Philadelphia whom Mulder suspected of possessing valuable UFO information. While he was on a forced vacation, the agent requested that Scully confirm Nabokov's identity by conducting an immigration and criminal background check and conducting an eye-to-eye surveillance of Nabokov and his compatriots' activities while in Philadelphia. ("Never Again") *The real Vladimir Nabokov was the author of* Lolita *and* Pale Fire, *whose crazily unreliable narrator is named Kinbote (as is the alien monstrosity in "Jose Chung's 'From Outer Space' ").*

Nagata, Misty (Nicolle Nattrass) Mail sorter at the Transcontinental Express Routing Center in Desmond, Virginia. Nagata discovered the body of her co-worker and best friend, Jane Brody, in the rest room, the victim of a smallpox-carrying swarm of bees which had escaped from a damaged overnight package in the adjoining room. Assistant FBI director Skinner later questioned Nagata, who revealed that the parcel had been confiscated by men claiming to be other investigators working on the case. ("Zero Sum")

Nancy One of two pregnant women living in the small town of Home, Pennsylvania. Sheriff Taylor checked to make sure she hadn't miscarried her baby after a deformed stillborn was discovered in a shallow grave. ("Home")

Napier's Constant The five-digit numerical basis for all natural logarithms, which served as the entry key to an incongruous set of security doors inside the abandoned Strughold Mining Company facility in West Virginia. ("Paper Clip")

NASA Goddard Space Flight Center Research facility in Greenbelt, Maryland, dedicated to excellence in scientific investigation, in the development and operation of space systems, and in the advancement of essential technologies. Dr. Sacks, a government exobiologist assigned to the center, attempted to examine a rock fragment of possible extraterrestrial origin but was attacked and paralyzed by black, alien worms. ("Tunguska")

National Comet Tabloid newspaper in which Mulder learned of the UFO abduction of Ruby Morris, a teenage girl from Sioux City, Iowa ("Conduit"). Someone (possibly Mr. X) wanted Scully to see an article about an alleged monster on a Russian ship and slipped a copy of the supermarket tabloid under the door of the X-Files basement office, which ultimately led to the agent's identification of a "John Doe" body discovered in the Newark, New Jersey, sewer system. ("The Host")

Nature Scientific journal in which, jet propulsion researcher Dr. Frank Nollette boasted, he had been published. ("Roland")

Navajo code-talkers Native American servicemen used by the U.S. military in World War II to encrypt sensitive messages in the Navajo language, which was the only code the Japanese couldn't break. The top-secret MJ files stolen by The Thinker and passed on to Mulder in digitized form were encoded in Navajo and later deciphered by Native American Albert Hosteen, a WW II code-talker. ("Anasazi/The Blessing Way/Paper Clip")

Neary, Lt. (Doug Abrahams) San Francisco homicide detective assigned to investigate the premature cremation of several Chinese immigrants who were missing internal organs. ("Hell Money") *Doug Abrahams appeared as a patrolman in "The X-Files: Pilot," an FBI agent in "Genderbender," demon-worshipper Paul Vitaris in "Die Hand Die Verletzt" and ATF Agent Harbaugh in "The Field Where I Died."*

necrotizing fascitis A virulent bacterial infection (a.k.a. the "flesh-eating disease") suffered by a Crowley High School teacher, necessitating a substitute, Mrs. Phyllis H. Paddock. Necrotizing fascitis is believed to affect only one person in a million and can be horribly disfiguring in as few as twelve hours, and fatal in less than two days. ("Die Hand Die Verletzt")

Neil, Marty A classmate of Scully and Agent Tom Colton at the FBI Academy at Quantico. Nicknamed "J. Edgar Junior" because of his gung-ho, over-enthusiastic attitude, Agent Neil went on to work the World Trade Center bombings and become supervisor in the Foreign Counterintelligence Office of the FBI's New York City bureau. ("Squeeze")

Neiman, Fred (Paul McGillion) Martinsburg, West Virginia, man whose wife became impregnated by fertility clinic janitor Eddie Van Blundht after the shapeshifter metamorphosed into his image and likeness. Van Blundht was forced to impersonate Neiman once again when he hid in the neighborhood from a pursuing Mulder and Scully. The real Fred Neiman arrived home, however, and Van Blundht was compelled to exit the bathroom as a duplicate of Agent Mulder. ("Small Potatoes")

Nelligan, Amanda (Christine Cavanaugh) The fifth woman in three months to give birth to a baby with a four-inch vestigial tail in Martinsburg, West Virginia. The *Star Wars* groupie (who had seen the sci-fi classic 368 times) told Mulder and Scully that the baby's father was Luke Skywalker, who had "dropped by" her apartment one day and romanced her. In reality, Nelligan was unknowingly impregnated by shapeshifter Eddie Van Blundht, a *Star Wars* fan and "loser" whom she had dated in high school. ("Small Potatoes") *Actress Christine Cavanaugh is best known as the voice of the gallant pig in the Oscar-nominated motion picture,* Babe, *and for the cartoon* Rugrats.

Nelson (Glynis Davies) Eugene Tooms' attorney who represented the mutant serial killer at his psychiatric commitment review. ("Tooms") *Glynis Davies also appeared briefly as housewife Ellen Brumfield in "Irresistible" and as Monica Landis in "2Shy."*

Nemhauser, Greg (Greg Thirloway) One of the FBI agents who accompanied senior agent Bill Patterson during the apprehension of serial killer John Mostow. Nemhauser, who was bitten by the murderer during his arrest, was later killed by an evil spirit-possessed Agent Patterson. ("Grotesque") *Agent Nemhauser was named in honor of Post Production Supervisor Lori Jo Nemhauser. Actor Greg Thriloway also portrayed a doctor in "Sanguinarium."*

Nemman, Dr. Jay (Cliff DeYoung) The county medical examiner in Bellefleur, Oregon. He demanded to know why Mulder and Scully were exhuming the body of self-confessed murderer Ray Soames. Nemman's bluster was cut short, however, by his frightened daughter, who had accompanied him to the cemetery and convinced him to leave. ("The X-Files: Pilot")

Nemman, Theresa (Sarah Koskoff) The daughter of the county medical examiner in Bellefleur, Orgeon, and classmate of four high schoolers who had been found dead near the woods, each with two peculiar marks on the back. Fearing for her life, she asked Mulder and Scully for protection. At a diner, she told them that ever since graduation, she had been finding herself mysteriously in the woods, with the same tell-tale marks and nosebleeds. ("The X-Files: Pilot")

Nettles, Det. (Frank Ferrucci) Bespectacled plain-clothes cop who investigated the Hollywood Hills vampiresque killing of businessman Garrett Lorre. ("3")

"NEVER AGAIN" The two words emblazoned underneath the tattoo on Ed Jerse's right arm. ("Never Again") *"Never Again" was Glen Morgan and James Wong's final script contribution before leaving to create and write the unsold series pilot episode for* The Notorious Seven *during* The X-Files' *fourth season. The two previously left the series during the second year to concentrate on producing and writing for their short-lived sci-fi endeavor,* Space: Above and Beyond. *"Never Again" reportedly indicated the likelihood that they would return to* The X-Files *for a third time. Morgan and Wong were named the co-executive producers of Chris Carter's other Fox series,* Millenium, *in the fall of 1997.*

📁 **"Never Again"** Written by Glen Morgan and James Wong. Directed by Rob Bowman. File number 4X13. *First aired February 2, 1997. While Mulder is on a forced vacation, Scully accepts a date with a handsome divorcee, unaware that the man has murdered his neighbor, motivated by a taunting and mocking voice that he believes is emanating from his Betty Page-like tattoo.* **Classic Sound Bite:** *"It doesn't always have to do with you, Mulder. It's my life."* **Background Check:** *"Never Again" was written specifically for planned guest-director Quentin Tarantino, but the Directors Guild of America forbade it because of his non-membership in the union organization. Two years earlier, the powerful DGA had bent the rules to allow Tarantino to direct the critically-acclaimed "Mother's Day" episode of* ER, *but decided not to give the director a second chance.*

Newark County Sewage Processing Plant New Jersey sewage treatment facility where the Flukeman was captured and later killed ("The Host")

New Friends Daycare Child care facility in Swampscott, Massachusetts, where escaped prisoner John Lee Roche, posing as Agent Fox Mulder, kidnapped Caitlin Ross, a little girl he spotted on a flight from Washington, D.C. to Boston. ("Paper Hearts")

New Horizon Psychiatric Hospital Mental health facility in Washington, D.C., where Harold Spuller resided as a voluntary patient and serial killer Nurse Innes was employed. ("Elegy")

Newirth, Patrick Fifty-two-year-old executive of the Morley Tobacco company who heard a distraught man knocking on another door in the hallway of his Richmond, Virginia, hotel. Newirth watched the commotion through his peephole until a shadow slipped beneath the door and evaporated him, leaving behind a mysterious scorch mark on the carpet. ("Soft Light") *The actor who portrayed Patrick Newirth was uncredited.*

Newton, Dr. Rick (Bill Dow) The panic-stricken medical examiner in the roach-infested town of Miller Grove, Massachusetts, who asked Mulder if he or his family were in danger. He was later found dead in the bathroom next to a toilet covered with cockroaches. ("War of the Coprophages") *Bill Dow also portrayed digital-imaging expert Dr. Charles Burks in "The Calusari" and reprised the role in "Leonard Betts." The actor also appeared briefly as a father in "The Jersey Devil."*

"nexus" The word Mulder used to describe the psychic connection between convicted serial child killer John Lee Roche and himself. Mulder theorized that because he had profiled Roche, a metaphysical bond had been formed that allowed the murderer to somehow manipulate his subconscious and emotions. ("Paper Hearts")

NICAP National Investigative Committee of Aerial Phenomena, a UFO fringe organization primarily obsessed with Roswellian-type cover-ups. Mulder and NICAP member Max Fenig were detained by the military when they investigated the crash-landing of an alien spacecraft near Townsend, Wisconsin. Fenig's NICAP hat was later seen on a stand in the X-Files basement office in Washington. ("Fallen Angel")

Nichols, Jason (Joseph Fuqua) A Massachusetts Institute of Technology (MIT) associate professor and cryobiologist researching the effects of freezing temperatures on biological systems. An older version of Nichols traveled back in time to thwart his younger self from successfully synthesizing a rapid freezing compound that would someday make time travel possible and in the process create a world in which there was no history or hope. During a confrontation in the computer mainframe room at the MIT cryolab, the futuristic Nichols wrapped his arms around his younger self, creating a spontaneous combustion that consumed both the present and future versions in flames. Although the younger Nichols' corpse was found in the aftermath of the fire, the elderly version from the future was never discovered. ("Synchrony") *Well-known character actor Michael Fairman portrayed the time-traveling older Jason Nichols.*

"Night Chicago Died, The" Popular song by Paper Lace, which Mulder sarcastically described as "devil music" after the local sheriff of Milford Haven, New Hampshire, commented that such music had probably influenced local youths' involvement in satanic cults. ("Die Hand Die Verletzt")

NIH The National Institutes of Health in Bethesda, Maryland, where in the 1970s Dr. Joe Ridley performed secret, unauthorized human experimentation on children suffering from progeria, a disease that causes rapid aging. In 1979, Ridley was dismissed from the NIH and had his medical license revoked for research malpractice and misuse of a government grant. ("Young at Heart")

Nisei A Japanese word meaning "second generation," commonly used for Japanese-Americans during the World War II-era, but more accurately for the North American-born children of Japanese parents. The word was also applied to the human-alien hybrids that were the "children" of the Japanese scientists, such as Dr. Zama, who worked in the U.S after the war. ("Nisei")

📁 **"Nisei (Part 1 of 2)"** Written by Chris Carter, Howard Gordon and Frank Spotnitz. Directed by David Nutter. File number 3X09. *First aired November 24, 1995. After receiving a mail order videotape of a suspiciously realistic alien autopsy, the agents' follow-up investigation leads Scully to a group of women who claim to recognize her from their alleged abduction experience the previous year, while Mulder pursues a train car which possibly carries a living* *and breathing captured extraterrestrial.* **Classic Sound Bite:** *"Whatever you stepped in on this case is being tracked into my office and I don't like the smell of it."* **Background Check:** *Co-episode writer Frank Spotnitz, whose favorite movies were set on trains, originally planned for "Nisei" to be a single-part installment, but filming in the train car that was to be the show's centerpiece proved too expensive to justify for a single hour. "The Walk" and "Oubliette" episodes' air dates were moved back and "Nisei" was expanded into an important two-part mythology installment.*

Nishigaba, Daisuke One of four Japanese doctors assassinated by black-clad soldiers during a purported alien autopsy aboard a secret government train car in Knoxville, Tennessee. ("Nisei") *The actor who portrayed Nishigaba went uncredited.*

Nollette, Dr. Frank (James Sloyan) A research scientist involved in the top-secret Icarus Project, the development of the next generation of jet engines, at the Mahan Propulsion Laboratory. Dr. Nollette attended Harvey Mudd medical school with former project team-member Dr. Arthur Grable, who had died in an automobile accident a few months earlier. Nollette eventually confessed to stealing his deceased colleague's research material. ("Roland")

Norman, Det. (Freddy Andreiuci) New Jersey policeman who was Mulder's contact when the agent arrived to investigate the mutilated body of a John Doe discovered in the Newark sewers. Det. Norman presented Mulder with a pair of yellow boots to put on before descending to the crime scene. ("The Host")

Northeast Georgetown Medical Center Hospital in Washington, D.C., where Scully mysteriously turned up after her lengthy disappearance. Although Mulder heatedly demanded answers from the medical staff, no one knew how she arrived or who admitted her to the facility's intensive care unit ("One Breath"). Over a year later, Scully was once again hospitalized at Northeast Georgetown Medical Center to recover from the dementia-inducing effects of a mind control experiment. ("Wetwired")

Northeast Georgetown Mental Health Center Psychiatric facility in the Washington, D.C., area where Sharon Graffia was temporarily institutional-ized after she was found disoriented at the crash site of commercial airline Flight 549 in Upstate New York. ("Max")

Northern, Penny (Gillian Barber) Mutual UFO Network (MUFON) member in Allentown, Pennsylvania, who claimed that Scully was an alien-abductee and pointed out that there was a distinguishable scar on the back of her neck from where a computer chip implant was extracted, which Scully hadn't been aware of ("Nisei"). A year later, Northern was confined to a hospital bed at the Allentown-Bethlehem Medical Center and died of the same type of inoperable brain cancer that had killed the other female MUFON members who claimed they had been alien-abductees. Scully, afflicted with a similar tumor, sat at Northern's bedside and consoled her during the final moments of her life. Ironically, Northern had told Scully earlier that she had held and comforted the agent after she was subjected to "tests" during her alien abduction ("Memento Mori"). *Actress Gillian Barber portrayed Agent Nancy Spiller in "Ghost in the Machine," and Beth Kane in "Red Museum," in which the catch phrase was "He is one." In "Nisei," Barber's character said of fellow abductee, Dana Scully, "She is one."*

Nutt, Mr. (Michael Anderson) Midget proprietor of the Gulf Breeze Trailer Court in the "circus performer haven" of Gibsonton, Florida, a town populated by former sideshow acts. Mr. Nutt took exception to Mulder's innocent question as to whether he'd performed in a circus, lecturing the agent about his degree in hotel management. Mr. Nutt was grabbed through his doggie door and killed by Lanny's detached congenital twin, Leonard. ("Humbug") *Michael Anderson appeared in the quirky, short-lived series* Twin Peaks, *as did David Duchovny.*

O

"One Breath"

Oakes, Sheriff John (Larry Musser) Chief law enforcement officer in the New Hampshire town of Milford Haven. Sheriff Oakes and his deputies were in charge of the investigation into the mutilation death of teenager Jerry Stevens, whose body was found with the eyes and heart cut out. Oakes told Mulder and Scully that there were rumors of Satan worship in the town, which Scully typically dismissed as folklore. ("Die Hand Die Verletzt") *Actor Larry Musser also portrayed Det. Manners in "Jose Chung's 'From Outer Space'" and Denny Markham in "Unrequited."*

Oakley, Brother (David Thomson) The Kindred member who demanded that Mulder and Scully surrender their weapons when they arrived at the abstruse sect's Massachusetts settlement. ("Genderbender")

O'Dell, Peggy (Katya Gardener) A friend of the victims of the mysterious killings in Bellefleur, Oregon, who were all high school classmates. A car accident with Billy Miles left her wheelchair-bound and a permanent resident of the Raymon County State Psychiatric Hospital. Mulder and Scully noted that she had the same peculiar, tell-tale marks on her back as the murder victims. O'Dell died after disappearing from the hospital one night and running out onto the highway and into the path of a truck. ("The X-Files: Pilot") *Actress Katya Gardener also portrayed Robin McAlpin in "Fresh Bones."*

Odin, Richard (Mark Rolston) Leader of the Wisconsin-based Church of the Red Museum, a cult that believed in soul transference and abstention from eating meat. Odin's true identity was Dr. Doug Herman, a physician who was banished from the American Medical Association in 1986 over an ethics issue. ("Red Museum")

Office of the Navajo Nation Washington, D.C., administration office of the Native American tribe. Scully consulted Josephine Doane at the agency to confirm that the encrypted Defense Department files in her possession were actually written in Navajo. ("Anasazi")

Oklahoma State Psychiatric Hospital State institution where human lightning rod Darin Peter Oswald was restrained. Inside his cell, the teenager stared continuously at a television screen, changing channels from across the room without a remote control. ("D.P.O.")

Olafssen (Vladimir Kulich) Norwegian pirate whaler and black marketeer who was rescued by the USS *Ardent* when his ship sank. Olafssen eluded the Navy destroyer's rapid aging disease when he discovered that the vessel's sewage processing system contained the only source of uncontaminated water. After revealing his secret to trawler captain Henry Trondheim, Olafssen allegedly escaped from the *Ardent*, although Mulder and Scully suspected that Trondheim murdered him. ("Dod Kalm")

Old Memorial Bridge Location in Bethesda, Maryland where the alien Bounty Hunter requested Mulder meet him to exchange "Samantha" for the captured Scully. Assistant Director Skinner arranged for an FBI sniper to shoot the alien during the hostage swap, but the plan failed and both "Samantha" and the assassin plummeted into the river below the bridge. ("End Game")

Oliver, Tony (Timur Karabilgin) One of three anti-Semitic youths who brutally murdered Isaac Luria in his Brooklyn market. Police ruled out robbery as a motive as nothing was stolen but the store surveillance tape, which was later found in the VCR of sixteen-year-old Oliver. The teenager had been strangled by a golem whose physical features matched those of Isaac Luria. ("Kaddish")

Olympia National Forest Remote Washington State wooded area and site of several loggers' disappearances. ("Darkness Falls")

"One Breath" Written by Glen Morgan and James Wong. Directed by R.W. Goodwin. File number 2X08. *First aired November 11, 1994. Agent Scully is discovered comatose in a Washington, D.C. hospital suffering from the aftereffects of genetic experimentation, while Mulder confronts the Cigarette-Smoking Man.* **Classic Sound Bite:** *"We all know the field we play and we all know what can happen in the course of the game. If you're unprepared for all the potentials, then you shouldn't step on the field."* **Background Check:** *The episode title refers to Captain Scully's soliloquy to his daughter, Dana, in which he compared the length of a lifetime to "one breath, one heartbeat."*

O'Neil, Jesse (Shawnee Smith) University student and member of the Cascade Volcano Research Team. Realizing she was infected with the silicon-based lifeform, Scully locked O'Neil in a Plexiglas chamber just before a snakelike spike burst out of her throat and splattered the window with numerous spores. Expedition leader Daniel Trepkos, who had been O'Neil's lover, carried her body deep into the volcano's caverns. ("Firewalker")

"One To-day is Worth Two To-morrows" Benjamin Franklin quote displayed on a desk plaque in Howard Graves' Philadelphia office. ("Shadows")

Operation Falcon Top-secret military mission with the objective of "sanitizing" the crash area of an alien spacecraft. Usually the cover story of a toxic chemical spill and subsequent government quarantine was used to evacuate nearby civilians and deter inquisitive news-gathering organizations. Mulder, who was investigating the possible downing of a UFO, was detained by the military when he infiltrated an Operation Falcon near Townsend, Wisconsin. ("Fallen Angel")

Operation Paper Clip According to Mulder, the U.S. government's "deal with the devil," a secret program in which several Nazi scientists were granted immunity in the United States after World War II in exchange for their research knowledge. For example, after the 1947 Roswell UFO crash, Victor Klemper was allegedly protected by the American government from the Nuremburg trials in order to exploit his "expertise" in the search to create an alien/human hybrid immune to genetic warfare. ("Paper Clip")

Operation Zapata According to Lone Gunman Frohike's speculative dossier on the Cigarette-Smoking Man, the code-name for the abortive April 1961 invasion of Cuba at the Bay of Pigs, involving Cuban nationals trained by the young operative. The blame for the failure of the operation fell directly into the lap of President Kennedy and the subsequent fallout caused a rise in tensions between the U.S. and the Soviets, which ultimately led to the Cuban Missile Crisis and, indirectly, the assassination of the young American president. ("Musings of a Cigarette-Smoking Man")

Oppenheim, Dr. Carl Listed as one of the doctors on call at the Lombard Research Facility when Mulder and the Lone Gunmen infiltrated the building in hopes of discovering the origin of Scully's inoperable cancer. ("Memento Mori")

Oppenheim, Dr. Jeffrey (William MacDonald) Emergency room physician on duty at County Hospital in Townsend, Wisconsin, when deputy sheriff Jason Wright and three firefighters arrived DOA after being horribly burned by a translucent alien being. Although the government whisked the bodies away before autopsies could be conducted, Oppenheim solicited Scully's assistance when later some severely burned soldiers were admitted to the hospital. ("Fallen Angel") *William MacDonald also played Agent Kazanjian in "2Shy," Officer Trott in "Unruhe," and a federal marshal in "The Host."*

origami The art of Japanese paper folding, an unusual hobby shared by Charlie Morris and eight-year-old Michelle Bishop, who was the murdered policeman's reincarnated spirit. Morris learned origami in Japan, where he was born to a military father. ("Born Again")

Osborne, Dr. (Charles Martin Smith) One of the doctors involved in Pinck Pharmaceuticals' outbreak of a contagion at the Cumberland State Correctional Facility during an apparent experiment to test possible treatments for the parasite carried by the *F. emasculata* insect. Dr. Osborne initially told Scully that he was with the CDC and that fourteen inmates had been infected with a "flulike illness," ten of whom died. However, after Osborne became fatally infected himself, he admitted to Scully that the prison had been quarantined not by the CDC, but by his real employer, Pinck Pharmaceuticals, one of the largest drug manufacturers in the United States. His body was later cremated in the prison incinerator. ("F. Emasculata")

Ostelhoff (Steve Makaj) Conspiracy assassin who executed members of a Canadian survey team that discovered the frozen corpse of a gray alien in a Yukon Territory ice cave. As part of a clean-up operation, he also murdered his co-conspirator, Babcock, and Smithsonian forensics anthropologist Arlinsky, after the two men transported the alleged extraterrestrial to Washington, D.C. for authentication. ("Gethsemane") *Steve Makaj also played a patrolman in "Ascension" and Frank Kiveat in "D.P.O."*

Oswald, Darin Peter (Giovanni Ribisi) Nineteen-year-old resident of Connerville, Oklahoma, who had the ability to channel powerful electrical currents. During Mulder and Scully's investigation into a fatal series of apparent lightning strikes, they discovered that Oswald had been admitted to a hospital five months earlier in cardiac arrest after he had been struck by lightning. Oswald also suffered from acute hypokalemia, an electrolyte imbalance of high sodium and low potassium, and Mulder theorized that the chemical disparity somehow explained Oswald's ability to generate electricity levels much higher than normal. Several people who annoyed him (not to mention several head of cattle) eventually died of electrocution before his capture, including the town bully, his best friend, and the county sheriff. After Oswald attempted to kidnap Sharon Kiveat, the high school teacher on whom he harbored a crush, he was held at the Oklahoma State Psychiatric Hospital. ("D.P.O.") *Darin Peter Oswald was named in honor of frequent* X-Files *writer Darin Morgan. Actor Giovanni Ribisi's film credits include* Lost Highway, The Grave, That Thing You Do!, *and the HBO movie* The Positively True Adventures of the Alleged Texas Cheerleader-Murdering Mom. *Ribisi has also appeared on TV's* NYPD Blue, Chicago Hope, Walker: Texas Ranger, *and as Phoebe's long-lost brother on* Friends.

Oswald, Lee Harvey (Morgan Weisser) Alleged assassin of President John F. Kennedy. According to Lone Gunman Frohike's dossier on the life of the Cigarette-Smoking Man, the shadowy operative assassinated JFK from a sewer in Dallas' Dealey Plaza and set the gullible Oswald up to be the "patsy" for his history-altering crime. ("Musings of a Cigarette-Smoking Man"). *Actor Morgan Weisser formerly appeared on Glen Morgan and James Wong's short-lived sci-fi adventure series,* Space: Above and Beyond.

Oswald, Mrs. (Kate Robbins) Darin Peter Oswald's couch-potato mother, who constantly belittled her teenage son. She was neither shocked nor surprised when he changed the TV channels from across the room without the remote control. ("D.P.O.")

oubliette French word for a dungeon of total darkness, consisting of a deep hole opened from the top; from the verb "oublier," which means "to forget." Carl Wade's unlit basement, which held his young kidnap victims, was an "oubliette." But the word also applied to the unforgettable emotional prison of Lucy Householder, who was abducted at age eight and held by Wade for five years before she escaped. ("Oubliette")

📁 **"Oubliette"** Written by Charles Grant Craig. Directed by Kim Manners. File number 3X08. *First aired November 17, 1995. While Agent Mulder protects a suspect in a kidnapping case who simultaneously manifests the experiences of the abductor's latest victim, Scully insists that the psychic bond may actually point to the woman's role in the crime.* **Classic Sound Bite:** *"I've probably experienced everything once or twice. It's all been pretty temporary."* **Background Check:** *Bonnie Hay, Gillian Anderson's stand-in for scene blocking and lighting appears again (previously the night nurse in "D.P.O.") as a therapist. Kyrie Eleison, commonly a dirge for the dead and part of most requiem masses, can be briefly heard during the closing scenes of this episode. Fox's Standards and Practices department felt that the original script for "Oubliette" offered some uncomfortable parallels to the widely-publicized Polly Klaas abduction case.*

ouroboros The mythical serpent that eats its own tail, symbolizing death and rebirth and the unending cycle of the universe. The circle formed by the snake has come to represent both constancy and change. After dinner and a few drinks at a sleazy Philadelphia bar, Scully and her handsome date, Ed Jerse, went across the street to a tattoo parlor, where Scully had an ouroboros design tattooed on her lower back. The symbol of a snake eating its own tail was appropriate for Scully, who had complained to Jerse that she had "always gone around in this circle," one of loyalty and rebellion. ("Never Again") *Alternate spellings include: oroborus, uroboros, and oureboros. As an obvious tie-in to Chris Carter's other series on the Fox network, Scully's tattoo was almost identical to the ouroboros used as the logo for* Millennium, *which caused David Duchovny to get "kinda pissed off."*

"Our Town" Written by Frank Spotnitz. Directed by Rob Bowman. File number 2X24. *Mulder and Scully's search for a missing federal poultry inspector in a small Arkansas town leads to the discovery of the rural community's cannibalistic rituals that keep the locals from aging.* **Classic Sound Bite:** *"She claims that she saw some kind of a foxfire spirit. I'm surprised she didn't call Oprah as soon as she got off the phone with the police."* **Background Check:** *The* *network's Standards and Practices department was dubious, but Chris Carter felt* The X-Files *installment was "tastefully done."*

Ovaltine Diner Café in Klass County, Washington, where Mulder allegedly met with Air Force officer Jack Schaeffer, who claimed that he and his partner were flying a UFO as part of a covert government operation when they were abducted themselves by a real alien monstrosity, Lord Kinbote. ("Jose Chung's 'From Outer Space'") *The Ovaltine Diner is actually one of Vancouver's oldest cafés.*

Overcoat Man (Ryan Michael) An overcoat-wearing operative for the Shadowy Syndicate who stole a sample of Scully's blood while she was in intensive care at Northeast Georgetown Medical Center. After Mulder pursued him to an underground parking garage, Mr. X ruthlessly killed the Overcoat Man, execution-style, to show Mulder what it took "to find the truth." ("One Breath") *Ryan Michael also played Agent Cameron Hill in "Unrequited."*

Owens, G. (Nicola Cavendish) An intensive care nurse who ministered to Scully while she was in critical condition at Northeast Georgetown Medical Center. When Scully awakened from her coma she learned that Nurse Owens, who had spoken to her and encouraged her during her unconscious state, had never worked at the hospital. ("One Breath") *Episode co-writer Glen Morgan named Nurse Owens after his grandmother.*

Oxford University Prestigious school of higher learning in England where Mulder earned a bachelor's degree in psychology in the early '80s ("The X-Files: Pilot"). Mulder "shared a certain youthful indiscretion" with Phoebe Green while attending the university. ("Fire")

P

Peacock

Paddock, Mrs. Phyllis H. (Susan Blommaert) A substitute teacher at Crowley High School in Milford Haven, New Hampshire, whom no one remembered hiring. Mrs. Paddock was the human form of a demon accidentally summoned by teenager Jerry Stevens when he read a Satanic prayer. She kept the boy's eyes and heart in a desk drawer and bewitched another teenager, Shannon Ausbury, into fatally slashing her wrists. After Mrs. Paddock mysteriously disappeared from the town, Mulder and Scully found a note on her classroom chalkboard: "Goodbye. It's been nice working with you." Paddock is an old English word for "toad." ("Die Hand Die Verletzt") *Actress Susan Blommaert has appeared in the films* Crossing Delancey, Pet Semetary, *and* Edward Scissorhands, *and as one of* Murphy Brown's *hapless secretaries.*

"PALM" The word Mrs. Mulder scribbled on a notepad after suffering a debilitating stroke. Upon leaving her hospital room, her son Fox returned to the family's deserted summer home in Quonochontaug, Rhode Island, to conduct a search of the premises. After playing with the word "PALM" and coming up with the anagram "LAMP," he found hidden inside a lamp a stiletto-like weapon, the kind used to kill alien clones. ("Talitha Cumi")

Palomar Observatory Landmark astronomical observation post located a few miles north of San Diego, California. Mulder claimed founder George E. Hale got the idea for the observatory from an "elf" that climbed in his window. ("Little Green Men")

Pao/Hu The name of one of Mulder's apartment-house neighbors as seen on the mailbox. ("The Erlenmeyer Flask")

📁 **"Paper Clip (Part 3 of 3)"** Written by Chris Carter. Directed by Rob Bowman. File number 3X02. *First aired September 29, 1995. Mulder and Scully seek evidence of human-alien hybrid experimentation by Nazi war criminals pardoned through Operation Paper Clip, while Assistant Director Skinner, now in possession of the missing DAT tape, tries to bargain with the Cigarette-Smoking Man for the lives of the two X-Files agents.* **Classic Sound Bite:** *"I've heard the truth, Mulder. Now what I want are the answers."* **Background Check:** *This episode was dedicated to the memory of Mario Mark Kennedy (1966–1995),* *a major* X-File *fan who organized online chat sessions on the Internet. Kennedy died as a result of injuries he sustained from an automobile accident.*

📁 **"Paper Hearts"** Written by Vince Gilligan. Directed by Rob Bowman. File number 4X08. *First aired December 15, 1996. A series of vivid dreams lead Mulder back to imprisoned serial child killer John Lee Roche, who hints he may have been Samantha Mulder's abductor and murderer.* **Classic Sound Bite:** *"Dreams are the answers to questions we haven't learned to ask."* **Background Check:** *Episode writer Vince Gilligan has said that "Paper Hearts" demonstrates that none of the series' complex conspiracy mythology is decided in advance at the beginning of the season: "I had this idea I thought would be fun to tell, which sort of turned the whole mythos on its ear—was Mulder's sister abducted by aliens or was it something much more mundane and horrifying, with no chance of her still being alive? I went in and pitched it to Chris [Carter], and he said, 'Go ahead.' If you have a good enough story to tell, Chris will try to figure out a way to work it into the mythology."*

"Paracelsus" A poem by Robert Browning, quoted by Mulder while standing in the middle of the field where he believed he had died in a past life. ("The Field Where I Died")

Paradise Motel Place of lodging in Northville, New York, where Sharon Graffia was abducted from her room by extraterrestrials. ("Tempus Fugit")

Parker, Eric (David Kaye) Local TV reporter/science editor who interviewed visionary volcanologist Daniel Trepkos in regards to the Firewalker exploration robot. ("Firewalker") *David Kaye also appeared briefly as a doctor in "Apocrypha."*

Parker, Jim (Donnelly Rhodes) Owner of the Two Medicine Ranch in Browning, Montana. Parker had sued the neighboring Trego Indian reservation over grazing rights and a border dispute. One night he shot and killed a werewolf that had slaughtered a steer in his corral and savagely attacked his son, Lyle. Shortly afterward, Parker was ripped to pieces on his porch by another humanoid wolf creature. ("Shapes"). *Donnelly Rhodes also played General Francis in "Musings of a Cigarette-Smoking Man." Winnipeg-born Rhodes had a prominent stint on* Soap *before starring in the Canadian hit series* Danger Bay. *He also played the recurring role of Tony Danza's father on the long-running* Taxi.

Parker, Lyle (Ty Miller) Grown son of Jim Parker, who was wounded by a werewolf before it was shot and killed by the elder Parker. After becoming one of the legendary man-beasts himself, Lyle slashed his father to death. The local sheriff later killed a fierce-looking beast at the Parker ranch, which turned out to be Lyle. ("Shapes") *Ty Miller co-starred on the ABC television Western series* The Young Riders.

Park Street Synagogue House of worship for a sect of Hasidic Jews in Brooklyn, New York. The synagogue had been vandalized by racists thirteen times in one year. A golem killed a teenage hate-monger in an upstairs section of the synagogue and later attacked Jacob Weiss when he attempted to stop his daughter from marrying the monstrous "abomination." ("Kaddish")

Parkway Cemetery Boston burial site where William Mulder was interred in the Garden of Reflection. At the funeral service, Scully was approached by the Well-Manicured Man, who warned her that she was in real danger of being killed, perhaps by someone she knew. ("The Blessing Way")

Parmelly, Vincent (Ken Force) An Eastpoint State Penitentiary guard present at the electric-chair execution of death row inmate Napoleon "Neech" Manley. Parmelly pulled Scully aside at the prison and told her that a convict named Roque possessed a list of people Manley intended to kill after he returned from the dead. Parmelly, who became romantically involved with Manley's widow, Danielle, was shot and killed by his lover when she became convinced that he was actually her dead husband reincarnated. ("The List") *Ken Foree has appeared in numerous horror movies, including* Leatherface: Texas Chainsaw Massacre III *and* Dawn of the Dead.

Paster, Deputy Barney (Sebastion Spence) Sheriff Andy Taylor's young gung-ho deputy in the Mayberry-like town of Home, Pennsylvania. After Taylor and his wife were massacred by the inbred Peacock clan, the well-armed deputy participated in the raid on the Peacocks' farmhouse outside of town. Although Paster wore a bulletproof vest and carried a high-caliber handgun during the assault, he was decapitated by a swinging ax when he attempted to enter the Peacocks' booby trap-laden house. ("Home")

Patnik, Joseph (Linden Banks) Braddock Heights, Maryland, resident who murdered five people, including his wife, when the small town's populace was subjected to a mass experiment involving mind control through television signals. After Patnik was taken to the Frederick County Psychiatric Hospital, he saw a TV news segment on Bosnian war criminal Lladoslav Miriskovic, prompting an hysterical outburst. The secret video signal had taken Patnik's fears and turned them into dementia, provoking him into murdering five people while hallucinating that he was slaying Miriskovic over and over again. ("Wetwired") *Linden Banks played the Rev. Calvin Sistrunk, the antiabortion activist suspected of murdering Dr. Prince in "Colony."*

Patricia Rae Heuvelman's Lake boat that Mulder and Scully rented with a $500 deposit. In search of the legendary aquatic monster, Big Blue, Mulder and Scully went out onto the lake at night, but the boat sank after something large crashed into it. ("Quagmire") *The* Patricia Rae *was named in honor of episode writer Kim Newton's mother.*

Patterson, Bill (Kurtwood Smith) The mean-spirited head of the FBI's Investigative Support Unit (ISU) and Mulder's former mentor, who literally wrote the book on the field of behavioral science. Patterson's unit spent three years working the case of serial mutilation killer John Mostow and Patterson led the FBI raid that apprehended the former insane asylum patient. After an apparent copycat murder occurred, Patterson, who actually admired his former protégé, secretly arranged for Mulder's involvement in the investigation, for he had become possessed by the same murderous evil spirit that had lived previously in Mostow and hoped that Mulder would stop him from killing. After Scully shot and wounded Patterson during a violent confrontation with Mulder, the former FBI agent was incarcerated pending trial on murder charges. Like Mostow before him, Patterson cried out from his jail cell that he was innocent, the victim of a demonic force. In the pursuit of a monster, Patterson had become one himself. ("Grotesque") *Agent Bill Patterson was loosely modeled on John Douglas, the former FBI agent who actually started modern psychological criminal profiling. Actor Kurtwood Smith has made a name for himself playing the bad guy in a host of TV movies and theatrical films, most notably as the villainous Clarence in 1987's* RoboCop *and more recently as a KKK leader in* A Time to Kill.

Paul (John Pyper-Ferguson) One of two convicts from Virginia's Cumberland State Correctional Facility who escaped from the prison in a laundry cart during the confusion surrounding the death of inmate Bobby Torrence. After taking refuge at his girlfriend's house, Paul attempted to flee on a bus to Toronto, but was shot and killed by government forces attempting to cover up the *F. emasculata* contagion. ("F. Emasculata")

Payson Community Hospital Medical facility in Payson, South Carolina, where emergency room physician Dr. Emile Linzer oversaw the medical treatment of several schoolchildren attacked and repeatedly stung by a swarm of bees on the playground. Skinner told Dr. Linzer that the children should not be treated for bee stings, but for smallpox, and urged the physician to vaccinate every child in the town. Mulder's mysterious U.N. informant, Marita Covarrubias, showed up during the crisis at the hospital and introduced herself to Skinner. She informed the assistant director that after he telephoned her, she made some inquiries and discovered that seven overnight packages had been shipped from Canada to a post office box in Payson. Covarrubias stated that she had traveled to the small South Carolina town to see for herself what was contained in the parcels. ("Zero Sum")

Peacock, Edmund Creighton (John Trottier) Forty-two-year-old brother of George and Sherman Peacock, a reclusive and deformed family living in a shabby farmhouse on the outskirts of Home, Pennsylvania. After all three brothers mated with their mother, she gave birth to a horribly disfigured baby that was afflicted with every birth defect known to science. The three dim-witted Peacock men then buried the newborn alive in a vacant lot adjacent to their farmhouse but the shallow grave was discovered by a group of young boys during an afternoon game of sandlot baseball. After Sheriff Taylor issued arrest warrants for the Peacocks, they retaliated by bludgeoning the sheriff and his wife. In turn, Mulder and Scully stormed the Peacocks' booby-trapped farmhouse, which ultimately led to the deaths of Edmund's two brothers. During the confusion surrounding the raid, Edmund escaped with his mother. ("Home")

Peacock, George Raymond (Chris Nelson Norris) Approximately thirty-year-old brother of Edmund Peacock. George was killed during a violent showdown between the Peacock family and Mulder and Scully. ("Home")

Peacock, Mrs. (Karin Konoval) Fiercely protective matriarch of the reclusive and deformed Peacock family, she was believed to have died along with her husband in a tragic automobile accident in 1986. When Sheriff Taylor and others tried to administer medical attention to Mr. and Mrs. Peacock, the mutant sons spirited their bodies away to their dilapidated farmhouse and neither parent was seen again for the following decade. For years, the clan had lived on the outskirts of the small rural town of Home, Pennsylvania, in a house that still had no electricity, running water, or heat. The Peacocks grew their own food, raised their own pigs, bred their own cows and, as Sheriff Taylor said, "raised and bred their own stock." After generations of inbreeding the family had seemingly dwindled down to the three deformed brothers. Mulder and Scully became convinced that the grown men had forced a kidnapped woman into involuntary pregnancy as part of a grotesque scheme to continue the propagation of their family. After the brothers murdered the local sheriff and his wife, Mulder and Scully stormed the rundown house and discovered Mrs. Peacock, a multiple amputee horribly disfigured through interbreeding and the results of the car crash, tied to a wooden board on wheels under a bed. Mulder and Scully finally comprehended the appalling truth that Mrs. Peacock had given birth to the murdered baby. Although the agents were able to kill two of the rampaging Peacock brothers during a bloody confrontation inside the booby-trapped house, the oldest son was able to escape with Mrs. Peacock in their ancient white Cadillac. ("Home") *Not that she was easily recognizable in this episode, but Mrs. Peacock was played by Canadian actress Karin Konoval, who also played the fake gypsy psychic and palm reader, Madame Zelma, in "Clyde Bruckman's Final Repose."*

Peacock, Sherman Nathaniel (Adrian Hughes) Approximately twenty-six–year-old youngest brother of Edmund Creighton Peacock. The murderous Sherman was killed along with his brother George during a raid on their booby trap-laden farmhouse on the outskirts of Home, Pennsylvania.

("Home") *The Peacocks were named after the family who lived next door to episode co-writer Glen Morgan's parents.*

Pendrell, Agent (Brendan Beiser) FBI Sci-Crime Lab technician at the Bureau's headquarters in Washington, D.C., whose assistance proved to be an invaluable asset to Mulder and Scully on numerous occasions. The red-haired, white-coated, and frequently scarlet-cheeked Pendrell also was known to have an endearing romantic crush on Agent Scully and frequently put in long hours in the lab to assist her in any way he could. After examining the implant removed from her neck, Pendrell told Scully that the mysterious computer chip had state-of-the-art microlithography and appeared capable of storing biological information traveling to and from a person's nervous system and mimicking memory formation, so that it could, theoretically, reproduce a person's mental processes. Examining the chip effectively destroyed it, but the manufacturer's name was printed on the silicon matrix. Pendrell's search through U.S. and Japanese records traced a courier mailing label to a Dr. Zama at a disease research facility in West Virginia ("Nisei/731"). Pendrell's DNA testing of saliva taken from Assistant Director Skinner's shirt and the chromosome-staining of hair fibers resulted in irrefutable proof that the man who shot Skinner and murdered Scully's sister were one and the same ("Apocrypha"). After Skinner was framed for the attempted murder of his wife, Pendrell analyzed the airbag in the Assistant Director's car and found residue personalizing the face of the actual person driving the vehicle, thus eliminating Skinner as a suspect ("Avatar"). While examining the hair, skin, and fiber forensic evidence belonging to the pigment-depleted corpse of a nineteen-year-old Philadelphia youth, Agent Pendrell discovered the seed of a species of passion flower, a rare night-blooming plant native to certain parts of West Africa ("Teliko"). Pendrell downloaded the data from each Jeremiah Smith clone's computer workstation at regional Social Security Administration offices and in each case discovered password-protected files, containing approximately a billion entries. Combining their efforts, Pendrell and Scully deciphered the files, which contained Smallpox Eradication Project (SEP) numbers and an inventory of protein tags used for "cataloguing" purposes ("Herrenvolk"). After a government exobiologist drilled into a meteor fragment and was attacked by leech-like black worms, Pendrell and Scully, appropriately protected in contamination-suits, investigated the deadly enigma ("Tunguska"). Pendrell was shot in the chest and later died from his injuries after being caught in the cross fire between an assassin and Scully ("Tempus Fugit/Max"). *Although a sentimental Scully sadly commented at the end of "Max" that she had never known Agent Pendrell's first name, several fans have stated that they clearly heard Mulder call him Danny in the episode "Avatar." Agent Pendrell's first name is also listed as Danny on the official X-Files collectable card game. The character was named after Pendrell Street in Vancouver, where the series is produced and filmed. Pendrell was played by Boston-born but Vancouver-based Brendan Beiser, a Shakespearean stage actor, whose credits include the 1996 TV movie* Harvey *and a guest appearance* *on* The Sentinel. *In 1997 he appeared briefly in the Alicia Silverstone movie,* Excess Baggage.

Pennsylvania Pub A biker bar in Sioux City, Iowa, where Mulder and Scully went looking for Ruby Morris' alleged boyfriend, who worked at the tavern. Instead the agents met the bartender, a longhaired, burly biker with a flying saucer tattoo on his arm and an ear that was horribly burned during a close encounter. ("Conduit")

Penology Review A criminology magazine dealing with prison management and the treatment of offenders. In her spare-time and in between X-File cases, Scully was writing a monograph on the topic of "Diminished Acetylcholine Production for Recidivist Offenders" for publication in the periodical. ("Small Potatoes")

pentagram A five-pointed star used as a magical symbol of protection and to positively control the elemental forces. Chicago hospital nurse Rebecca Waite, a practicing witch, used pentagrams in an effort to protect patients from becoming the human blood sacrifices of cosmetic surgeon/sorcerer Dr. Jack Franklyn. Mulder discovered a pentagram scorched into the floor of the operating room, on the stomach of a dead patient, and above the door of Nurse Waite's house. Mulder and Scully also found an inverted pentagram on the floor of the foyer in Dr. Franklyn's house, with the names of each of his victims inscribed at the points. ("Sanguinarium")

Perkins, Bob (Barry Greene) Leader of a group of frightened loggers in the Olympic National Forest in Northwest Washington State, who were pursued and cocooned by a swarm of prehistoric mites after they cut into an ancient tree. ("Darkness Falls") *Barry Greene also played emergency room physician Dr. Emile Linzer in "Zero Sum."*

Perry, Simon (Bruce Pinard) The executioner of Eastpoint State Penitentiary death row inmate Napoleon "Neech" Manley. After the warden reluctantly provided his name, Mulder and Scully found Perry dead in his home, his face and neck decomposed and covered with maggots like the other victims on Manley's revenge list. ("The List")

Peskow, Vassily (Jan Rubes) Former KGB assassin living in St. Petersburg, who was asked to come out of retirement via a message from Comrade Arntzen requesting his assistance and informing him that the Cold War wasn't over. During the course of his North American mission, Peskow killed Dr. Bonita Charne-Sayre, a prominent virologist and the Well-Manicured Man's personal physician; Dr. Sacks, a government exobiologist whose examination of a meteor fragment infected him with an alien biotoxin ("black cancer"); and several elderly nursing home patients, human "guinea pigs" in Dr. Charne-Sayre and the Shadowy Syndicate's program to find an "inoculation" against the "black cancer." Always one step ahead of Mulder and Scully, Peskow drove a stolen truck containing a fertilizer bomb and the remaining alien-inhabited meteor fragment to a Canadian oil refinery. The agents arrived too late to prevent Peskow from igniting a fiery explosion which engulfed their last piece of evidence. Escaping from North America, Peskow returned home to St. Petersburg to find former KGB agent Alex Krycek (a.k.a. Comrade Arntzen), who commended him on a successful mission abroad. ("Terma")

Peter (Zoran Vukelic) Nude artist's model slashed to death with a razor by John Mostow, a Soviet emigré possessed by an evil spirit. ("Grotesque")

Peterson, Claude (Blu Mankuma) Undercover government spy with the Defense Department who infiltrated the high-tech Eurisko firm in the position of building engineer. His mission was to access Brad Wilczek's Central Operating System (COS), a computer with artificial intelligence. ("Ghost in the Machine")

Pfaster, Donnie Addie (Nick Chinlund) Minneapolis funeral home employee who was fired for cutting off locks of hair from a young female corpse. Twenty-eight-year-old Pfaster, whom Mulder described as an escalating death fetishist, later resorted to murder to procure more dead bodies and satisfy his growing compulsion. Mulder led a raid on Pfaster's deceased mother's residence and rescued Scully only moments before she was to become his next victim. In his final report, Mulder described the idea of such a human monster "as frightening as any X-File." ("Irresistible") *Fox's network program standards department forced Chris Carter to change the Pfaster character from a necrophiliac to a death fetishist, diminishing any overt sexual overtones. Actor Nick Chinlund, who was a last-minute find, made his movie debut in 1992's* Lethal Weapon 3. *He has also appeared in Showtime's erotic anthology series* Red Shoe Diaries, *which is hosted by David Duchovny, and as Billy "Bedlam" Bedform in the 1997 box-office blockbuster* Conair.

P-51 Mustang World War II single-seat fighter plane, also known as "the ultimate warbird." A North American P-51 Mustang was downed in the Pacific Ocean during the war after attacking a "Foo Fighter" alien spacecraft. Decades later, a diver from the French salvage ship *Piper Maru* located the submerged plane on the ocean floor. An alien possessing the P-51's dead pilot ascended to the surface inside the host body of the diver. ("Piper Maru/Apocrypha")

pheromones Chemical substance secreted by animals as sexual attractants. Mulder and Scully investigated a bizarre series of deaths involving three women and two men who suffered massive coronaries during the throes of passion. All the victims exhibited one hundred times the natural level of pheromones, prompting Mulder to describe the killer as "the ultimate sex machine." ("Genderbender")

Philadelphia Experiment A top-secret U.S. military project in which the brand-new naval destroyer USS *Eldridge* was the focus of a 1943 experiment to render it invisible with a force field based on the principles of Nobel Prize-winning physicist Albert Einstein's Unified Field Theory. Allegedly, the military experiment was a complete success as the *Eldridge* vanished from its Philadelphia port—only to reappear in Norfolk, Virginia more than two hundred miles away, all in a matter of a few minutes. Mulder suspected that the "Philadelphia Experiment" involved wormholes on Earth, and initially believed that the USS *Ardent's* disappearance had been caused by something similar in the 65th-parallel area in the Norwegian Sea. ("Dod Kalm")

Philips, Lula (Cec Verrell) A career criminal who served time at the Maryland Women's Correctional Facility for manslaughter. While in the penitentiary she became romantically involved with a guard, Warren James Dupre, who was fired after prison officials discovered their clandestine affair. After Lula was released the two married and the latter-day Bonnie and Clyde embarked on a short-lived but violent criminal career that took the lives of seven people in a string of bank robberies. She eventually set up her husband by anonymously tipping off the FBI to their final bank heist, which led to his death in a shoot-out with Scully. But FBI agent Jack Willis seemed to become inhabited by Dupre's spirit. After they kidnapped Scully, Lula refused to give the diabetic Willis his insulin so that she could keep the $1 million ransom for herself. After wresting a gun from her, Willis/Dupre killed her shortly before federal agents raided their hideout. ("Lazarus")

Philips, Tommy (Callum Keith Rennie) Lula Philips' brother, who was shot to death by Willis/Dupre in his room at the sleazy Desmond Arms Residence Hotel. After hearing a TV news report that an anonymous tip had brought the FBI to the scene of Dupre's final bank robbery, Willis/Dupre was convinced that his brother-in-law had betrayed him. ("Lazarus") *Actor Callum Keith Rennie also appeared as the Folkstone cemetery groundskeeper in "Fresh Bones."*

Phillips, Dr. The physician at the University of Pennsylvania Hospital tissue bank who told Mulder and Scully that shortly after Howard Graves' death, his kidney was transplanted in Boston, his liver in Dallas, and his corneas in Portland, which Scully accepted as proof that Graves didn't fake his own death. ("Shadows") *The actor who portrayed Dr. Phillips was uncredited.*

Phillips, Stan (Eric Christmas) An Alzheimer's patient at the Excelsis Dei convalescent home in Worcester, Massachusetts. The surprisingly frisky oldster had been a resident of the facility for three years and protested when his daughter prepared to take him home. After Excelsis Dei orderly Gung

Bituen was remanded to the INS for illegal-medication activity, Phillips and the other patients suffered debilitating relapses of Alzheimer's. ("Excelsius Dei") *Eric Christmas is better remembered as Sam Malone's parish priest, Father Barry, on the long-running NBC comedy series* Cheers, *and played a hapless government scientist with a proclivity for opening time warps in the theatrical movie* The Philadelphia Experiment.

Pierce, Dr. Adam (Tuck Milligan) A scientific member of the Cascade Volcano Research Team who accompanied Mulder and Scully to Washington State's Mount Avalon. Shortly after arriving, Dr. Pierce was garroted to death by soot-covered volcanologist Daniel Trepkos. ("Firewalker")

"Pierre Paris & Sons" Building sign located at 66 Exeter Street in Baltimore, Maryland, a condemned building where Eugene Tooms made his hibernation nest. ("Squeeze")

Pilot SEE: **Bounty Hunter**

Pilsson, Dr. Erik (Michael Puttonen) Physician who monitored Augustus Cole's sleep-deprived condition for several years at the V.A. Medical Center in North Orange, New Jersey. Dr. Pilsson kept Cole isolated from other patients at the military hospital because he disrupted their natural sleep cycles. ("Sleepless") *Michael Puttonen also appeared as a motel manager in "Deep Throat," the conductor in "731," and as Martin Alpert, the psychiatric facility administrator in "Elegy."*

Pinck Pharmaceuticals One of the largest drug manufacturers in America, based in Wichita, Kansas. The company conspired with an unknown government agency to conduct a controlled experiment involving a highly contagious illness on unsuspecting inmates at the Cumberland State Correctional Facility in Virginia. The illness was introduced through a misaddressed package, so that it could be blamed on "postal error" if the experiment were ever discovered. ("F. Emasculata")

Pintero, Angelo (Alex Bruhanski) Working-class owner and operator of Angie's Midnight Bowl in Washington, D.C. Before closing down for the evening, Pintero encountered the disembodied soul of a young woman who had just been murdered across the street from the bowling alley. Pintero later "just keeled over," the victim of congestive heart failure. ("Elegy") *Alex Bruhanski also played the doomed exterminator, Dr. Bugger, in "War of the Coprophages."*

Piper Maru A French salvage vessel whose crew suffered severe radiation burns after they located "the needle in the haystack," the wreckage of a sunken World War II fighter plane that contained an alien lifeform. Visiting the docked vessel, Mulder and Scully found no traces of radiation, but they did discover the ship's videotape, which revealed the submerged aircraft. ("Piper Maru") *The* Piper Maru *was named after Gillian Anderson's daughter, whose middle name means "calm and gentle" in Polynesian. Curiously, the term also loosely translates to the Japanese word for "ship."*

📁 **"Piper Maru (Part 1 of 2)"** Written by Frank Spotnitz and Chris Carter. Directed by Rob Bowman. File number 3X15. *First aired February 9, 1996. When the crew of the French salvage ship* Piper Maru *begin to die from severe radiation burns after discovering an extraterrestrial lifeform trapped in a sunken World War II aircraft on the floor of the Pacific, Mulder and Scully become entangled in a deadly conspiracy dating back to the Hiroshima atomic bombing.* **Classic Sound Bite:** *"You're in the basement because they're afraid of you, of your relentlessness—and because they know that they could drop you in the middle of the desert and tell you the truth is out there and you'd ask them for a shovel."* **Background Check:** *The episode's underwater scenes were shot in two different locales: some of them were actually filmed in the ocean and others in a testing tank for the Vancouver-made limited edition Newt-suit, which has been used for all kinds of salvage operations.*

Pitcher (Douglas Smith) One of several boys who discovered a hideously deformed baby buried in a shallow grave. ("Home")

Pivotal Publications The New York publishing company that purchased the Cigarette-Smoking Man's novel *Second Chance* for serialization in one of its weekly magazines, *Roman à Clef.* The incident was based on Lone Gunman Frohike's rather dubious dossier on the life of the Cigarette-Smoking Man. ("Musings of a Cigarette-Smoking Man")

Plain-Clothed Man (Tim Henry) A source who gave Mulder a newspaper article about Joseph Patnik and the five people he murdered in Braddock Heights, Maryland. The Plain-Clothed Man refused to admit who sent him, but warned Mulder that "more people will die" if he didn't pursue the case. Mulder later accused Mr. X of using the Plain-Clothed Man as a third-party intermediary. ("Wetwired") *The development of the Plain-Clothed Man came about because Steven Williams (Mr. X) had a production conflict with his other TV series,* L.A. Heat. *Three of his scenes in "Wetwired" were re-worked to utilize X's new mysterious messenger.*

Planet of the Apes Classic science-fiction movie revered by wheelchair-bound scientist Dr. Alexander Ivanov, and by shapely USDA researcher Dr. Bambi Berenbaum. Mulder also made references to the Charleston Heston film during a conversation with Scully while investigating the cockroach attacks in the small town of Miller's Grove, Massachusetts. ("War of the Coprophages")

Plith, Dr. (Jerry Wasserman) A professor at the Smithsonian Institution's Forensic Anthropology Lab, he examined the skeletal remains found at Powhattan Mill's Ruxton Chemical Plant. Dr. Plith discovered that the skull matched the photo of a missing person suspected of being a 1933 victim of mutant serial killer Eugene Tooms. ("Tooms")

Poeti Italiani Del Novecento A book of obscure sixteenth-century Italian poems which scholar and mutant serial killer, Virgil Incanto, received from Strautcher Publishing via Transcontinental Express. ("2Shy")

Polarity Magnetics The company owned by Dr. Chester Banton and his business partner, Dr. Christopher Davey, whose main product was electric people movers. The firm was closed after Banton was believed to have died during an experiment with dark matter. In fact, when he was accidentally locked inside a particle accelerator chamber he received a quanta bombardment equal to a two billion megawatt X-ray which didn't kill him but turned his shadow into an instant form of death. Mulder learned the company's name from a logo patch on Banton's jacket caught on a train terminal's security camera videotape. ("Soft Light")

polycythemia A medical condition characterized by the excessive production of red blood cells. Scully suspected polycythemia after discovering during an autopsy that deceased Syracuse FBI Agent Barrett Weiss' blood had curdled. ("Colony")

Pomerantz, Dr. Mark (Alf Humphreys) A psychotherapist and regression-hypnosis specialist who helped Scully hazily recall her "lost" abduction time. After she began to panic, though, the agent cut the session short before anything substantial could be recalled. ("The Blessing Way") *Alf Humphreys appeared in "Space" as a mission controller.*

Post-abduction syndrome The affliction Mulder believed Chrissy Giorgio was suffering from, although Scully suspected sexual trauma brought on by date rape. ("Jose Chung's 'From Outer Space'")

povidone-iodine A topical antiseptic that is often used by lab researchers on reptiles and amphibians to aid regeneration. Leonard Betts soaked in tubs filled with the fluid in order to accelerate his own regenerative powers. ("Leonard Betts")

Powertech The government's "Northwest Facility" in Mattawa, Washington, where an E.B.E. (Extraterrestrial Biological Entity) was being held. Mulder and Scully entered Powertech with phony security passes courtesy of the Lone Gunmen. Mulder offered Langly an E.B.E. photograph in exchange for the computer-hacked IDs. ("E.B.E.")

Powhattan Mill Killings The 1933 Baltimore-area serial murder spree during which genetic mutant Eugene Tooms killed five people and ripped out their livers with his bare hands. Although only four of the five victims were initially found, the skeletal remains of the fifth victim were discovered at Powhattan Mill's Ruxton Chemical Plant in 1994. ("Squeeze" and "Tooms")

"Preacher" SEE: **Cole, Cpl. Augustus D.**

Priest (Fulvio Cecere) Catholic clergy who received Scully's confession (her first in six years) after she saved the life of young stigmatic Kevin Kryder. She asked the priest if he believed in miracles and asserted her own doubts, since only she and not Mulder had witnessed them during the case. "Maybe they weren't meant for him to see," the priest replied, telling her that we must sometimes "come full circle to find the truth." ("Revelations") *A new vocal track was added in postproduction using a different performer after the producers felt dissatisfied with the actor's voice. Cecere also made a brief appearance in "Little Green Men" as an aide to Senator Matheson.*

Prince, Dr. Landon (Dana Gladstone) An abortion doctor who perished in an arson fire at the Woman's Care Family Services and Clinic in Scranton, Pennsylvania. Mulder was anonymously sent Landon's obituary along with those of two other abortion clinic physicians who looked exactly like him and similarly lacked birth records. A Scranton police officer confirmed that Landon's body was not found at the site of the fire, just as in the other two cases. ("Colony")

Prisoner, The (Stefan Arngrim) A fellow captive and "test subject" jailed in the cell next to Mulder's at the Siberian gulag in Tunguska. He explained that all men in the camp were injected with the "black cancer that lived in the rock" until the biotoxin finally killed them. A former geologist quite well-known and respected in his profession, The Prisoner had been present during the first retrieval of extraterrestrial rocks from the Tunguska crash site. Over the years, he explained, "hundreds of men, perhaps more" had died during the experiments with the "black cancer." Impressed with Mulder's will to survive, The Prisoner gave the agent his home-made knife, which he had originally constructed for the purpose of committing suicide. ("Tunguska/ Terma")

progeria A rare debilitating disease first discovered in 1886 that causes children to age seven times faster than the normal rate. Life spans range from seven to twenty-seven years; the average victim dies by the age of thirteen. Death is generally due to congestive heart failure or loss of circulation to the brain. While at the National Institute of Health, Dr. Joe Ridley conducted secret, unauthorized experimentation on children suffering from progeria, believing that a cure for the disease possibly held the ultimate key to aging in general. ("Young at Heart")

Project, The The Shadowy Syndicate's elaborate colonization joint venture with extraterrestrials. Seeking "hegemony . . . a new origin of species," the Shadowy Syndicate aims to recreate humanity (a new master race) utilizing the genetic data of millions of Americans retrieved through Operation Paper Clip. Under the guise of providing smallpox vaccinations, they injected everyone born since the mid 1950s with a DNA identification tag. Each "donor" received a Smallpox Eradication Project (SEP) number, the details of which were then stored in the Social Security Administration computer system. Thousands of individuals were abducted for invasive experiments and then later returned with implants, Japanese-designed subcutaneous mechanisms that functioned both as tracking devices and memory retrieval units. Using techniques perfected by Axis scientists during World War II, human and extraterrestrial DNA were fused and cloned, possibly to create an army immune to biological warfare. The Shadowy Syndicate maintained a farm in Alberta, Canada, populated by an agrarian workforce of such clones, including those of a young Samantha Mulder. The genetic replicas (or "ovo-types") harvested an alien shrub, creating pollen for a deadly strain of bees, intended as an agent to introduce alien DNA to humanity at large. A "trial run" involving a swarm of the contagion-carrying insects was initiated in Payson, South Carolina at an elementary school. Jeremiah Smith, an alien shapeshifter, threatened The Project by exposing it to Mulder and Scully. One of many duplicate aliens working in the Social Security system, his task was to track the Paper Clip test subjects using their SEP numbers. When he went rogue, the Cigarette-Smoking Man sent the alien Bounty Hunter to kill him. The date for colonization presumably is set and CSM made it clear to Smith before he was terminated that he wanted to be a "commandant," ruling over his own people when that day comes. ("Anasazi/The Blessing Way/Paper Clip," "Nisei/731," "Talitha Cumi/Herrenvolk," and "Zero Sum")

Props, Monte Notorious serial killer whose 1988 capture was credited to Mulder's monograph "On Serial Killers and the Occult" during his early years with the FBI's Behavioral Sciences Unit. ("The X-Files: Pilot")

Provincetown Pub A Boston bar where Cecil L'ively/Bob used his finger to light a cigarette for a Miss Kotchik. The woman thought it was just a clever little magic trick, until he set his arm on fire and burned down the pub. ("Fire")

psychic photography The paranormal ability to project the images in one's mind onto photographic film. Mulder suspected Gerry Schnauz, a formerly institutionalized paranoid schizophrenic with a history of violence, of possessing the ability to bring his paranoid delusions to life through a series of pictures taken of his victims. ("Unruhe")

Pudovkin, Vsevlod (Igor Morozov) Russian immigrant with a doctorate in astronautical engineering who allegedly smuggled out of a former Soviet military spacecenter reports of two UFOs that crashed in the Bering Sea. When Mulder was forced to use accrued vacation time, he reluctantly left Scully in charge of running an immigration and criminal background check on Pudovkin, and administering eye-to-eye surveillance on the Russian and his contacts in Philadelphia. After determining that Pudovkin was simply a con artist and swindler specializing in extortion, credit card fraud, and other criminal activities, Scully turned the case over to the Philadelphia office of the FBI. ("Never Again") *The character of Vsevlod Pudovkin was named in honor of the 1920s Russian filmmaker.*

Puett, Inspector (Ron Chartier) U.S. postal inspector who told Mulder and Scully that Mary Louise LeFante, an employee of the U.S. postal service, was the subject of a mail fraud investigation along with her recently murdered boyfriend, for the theft of several credit cards from the branch post office where she worked as a sorter. Inspector Puett believed that the missing North Michigan woman had faked her own death. ("Unruhe")

Puget Presbyterian Hospital where twins Arthur and Roland Grable were born to Mr. and Mrs. Lewis Grable, with Arthur being the oldest by four minutes. ("Roland")

Pugh, Dr. Alton (Robert Rozen) A gynecologist specializing in obstetrics in the small West Virginia town of Martinsburg. Dr. Pugh was originally suspected of being the genetic father of four newborns whose mothers he had treated for infertility. ("Small Potatoes")

Pupperdog The name of the small, mixed-breed dog belonging to Katie, a Delta Glen, Wisconsin, teenager who was found stumbling through the woods, hallucinating, with the words SHE IS ONE scrawled on her back. ("Red Museum")

Puppet (Stu Charno) A serial killer who committed a string of murders involving professional psychics in St. Paul, Minnesota. He felt like a puppet because he would see psychic images of his crimes before he committed them, yet he couldn't understand why he had no control over his horrible actions. "Because you're a homicidal maniac," reluctant psychic Clyde Bruckman explained matter-of-factly. Puppet was killed by Scully with a single gunshot as he was about to knife Mulder. ("Clyde Bruckman's Final Repose") *Stu Charno is the husband of former X-Files episode writer Sara Charno ("Aubrey" and "The Calusari").*

Purdue, Reggie (Dick Anthony Williams) FBI agent in his fifties who was Mulder's supervisor during his tenure in the Bureau's Violent Crimes Unit. It was Purdue who requested Mulder take on the "Paper Hearts" case because he thought Mulder "could get into the killer's head." Mulder's profile of the child killer ultimately led to the capture and imprisonment of door-to-door vacuum salesman John Lee Roche ("Paper Hearts"). Agent Purdue later called his old friend when evidence indicated that homicidal robber John Barnett, whom Mulder helped convict and who supposedly died in prison, was somehow responsible for a recent jewelry store heist. Purdue was strangled by Barnett, who left a note for Mulder on the body. ("Young at Heart")

Purdy, Judge Hamish (Walter Marsh) The Kenwood, Tennessee, magistrate whose courtroom filled with locusts when he set a $100,000 bail at young faith-healer Samuel Hartley's pre-trial hearing for murder. ("Miracle Man") *Actor Walter Marsh also played the druggist in "Unruhe."*

Purity Control The secret government project involving human experiments with extraterrestrial DNA to create alien-human hybrids. In Dr. Terrence Berube's lab, Mulder discovered a liquid-filled Erlenmeyer flask labeled "Purity Control" ("The Erlenmeyer Flask"). Agents Mulder and Scully later suspected that teenagers from the town of Delta Glen, Wisconsin, had been injected with antibodies derived from alien DNA as part of a Purity Control experiment ("Red Museum").

Purple Rain According to Mulder, a "great album" by the artist formerly known as Prince, but "a deeply flawed movie." ("El Mundo Gira")

"Pusher" SEE: **Modell, Robert Patrick**

⌐ **"Pusher"** Written by Vince Gilligan. Directed by Rob Bowman. File number 3X17. *First aired February 23, 1996. Mulder and Scully become involved in a case in which the apprehended suspect, a rejected candidate for the FBI Academy, has apparently murdered more than a dozen people with the unique ability to control their minds. Deeply sunk in his fantasy of being a masterless Japanese samurai, the killer escapes and leaves clues for Mulder, whom he considers a "worthy opponent."* **Classic Sound Bite:** *"Made you look."* **Background Check:** *David Grohl, former drummer of Nirvana and lead singer of the Foo Fighters, and his wife, Jennifer, appeared as extras in the scene in which Modell infiltrated FBI headquarters. Gillian Anderson invited the musician and his wife to appear.*

Queequeg

📁 **"Quagmire"** Written by Kim Newton. Directed by Kim Manners. File number 3X22. *First aired May 3, 1996. When a series of mysterious deaths and disappearances occur near a small town lake in Georgia's Blue Ridge Mountains, Agents Mulder and Scully investigate reports of a legendary prehistoric aquatic serpent in the mode of the Loch Ness Monster.* **Classic Sound Bite:** *"We eat fish and fish eat us."* **Background Check:** *The episode's title refers to land with a soft, yielding surface, or a difficult or irksome situation. After initial efforts to create the waterfaring monster as a big "rubber thing" proved to be rather unconvincing on film, the visual effects department was drafted to generate the scene in which the serpentine creature knifed through the moonlit lake. Fan favorite, Darin Morgan, penned the "rock talk" between Mulder and Scully.*

Quantico Virginia location of the FBI Training Academy, which is often referred to simply as "Quantico" by federal officials, instructors and students. After joining the FBI directly from medical school, Scully became an instructor at Quantico from 1990–1992, during which time she become romantically involved with Agent Jack Willis. Scully was reassigned to Quantico for a short period when the X-Files unit was temporarily closed. Mulder earned the nickname "Spooky" while attending Quantico as a student because of his belief in paranormal phenomena. However, Mulder was considered one of the Bureau's most respected serial killer profilers during his tenure (1989–1992) at Quantico's Violent Crimes Section, Behavioral Sciences Unit. When a frustrated Mulder threatened to quit the FBI after the X-Files unit was officially disbanded, Scully suggested he request a transfer back to the Behavioral Sciences Unit. ("X-Files: The Pilot," "Lazarus," "Little Green Men," "The Host," and "Grotesque")

quarantine car Train boxcar #82517 which operated as part of the government's "secret railroad." Mulder believed it was transporting an alien-human hybrid, although the Shadowy Syndicate's 1st Elder told Scully that the deformed creature was a human experimental subject from a leper colony. Mr. X rescued Mulder before the quarantine car and its contents were destroyed in a bomb explosion rigged by the Red-Haired Man. ("Nisei/731")

Queequeg Scully's pet Pomeranian, given to her by doomed psychic Clyde Bruckman. When his senile apartment-house neighbor Mrs. Lowe died, the dog apparently had no food and ate the entrails of his deceased mistress to remain alive. Bruckman left Scully a note after he killed himself, asking her to adopt the Pomeranian ("Clyde Bruckman's Final Repose"). Scully aptly named the pet "Queequeg," after the cannibal sailor in her father's favorite book, Herman Melville's classic *Moby Dick*. The dog disappeared in the wooded shoreline of Heuvelman's Lake, either the victim of an enormous alligator or the Southern Serpent, Big Blue ("Quagmire"). *Darin Morgan originally planned to pen a scene or two for Queequeg in "Jose Chung's 'From Outer Space,'" but the final script draft came in too long and there wasn't enough time for the Pomeranian to make an appearance. However, since the writing staff had been conspiring to kill off the little mutt, Queequeg's demise was written into the "Quagmire" episode. Morgan has said in interviews that he doesn't know why he gave Scully a dog, "I just thought it was funny to see this dog that had eaten this woman living with Scully."*

"Revelations"

Ra Closed Los Angeles restaurant (named for the Egyptian sun god) where Mulder followed Kristen Kilar and David Yung, the man she picked up at Club Tepes. Yung knocked Mulder unconscious, but then shortly afterwards was attacked and killed by The Father and The Unholy Spirit, two of the vampiresque Trinty Killers. ("3")

Radio Shack An international franchise chain of electronic stores. Mulder purchased a laser pointer for $49.95 at one of their outlets in Richmond, Virginia. ("Soft Light")

Rana spenocephala According to biologist Dr. Paul Farraday, a rare type of frog species whose population had dwindled to less than 200 in Georgia's Heuvelman's Lake. Mulder theorized that the frog species' depletion and rapid extinction was forcing Big Blue, the lake's legendary aquatic dinosaur, to seek out humans as an alternative food source. ("Quagmire")

Rand (Bob Wilde) One of the federal agents who had Mulder's apartment under surveillance after he secretly journeyed to a possible alien contact site in Puerto Rico. Rand and his partner, Agent Lewin, confronted Scully when she went to Mulder's apartment seeking clues to his whereabouts. She told them that she was there to feed Mulder's fish during his absence. ("Little Green Men") *Bob Wilde also played the limo driver in "Nisei."*

Randall, Greg Bartender at the Pennsylvania Pub, in Sioux City, Iowa, who disappeared at approximately the same time as Ruby Morris. His body was discovered by Mulder and Scully in a shallow grave near Lake Okobogee, a victim of jealous lover Tessa Sears, who was pregnant with his child. ("Conduit")

Randolph, Dr. Vance (Robin Mossley) The staff physician at the Chaco Chicken processing plant in Dudley, Arkansas. Dr. Randolph complained that Chaco had refused to address his medical concern that several of the workers had exhibited signs of the extremely rare and fatal Creutzfeldt-Jakob disease. ("Our Town") *Robin Mossley also portrayed Dr. Joe Ridley in "Young at Heart" and Dr. Kingsley Looker in "Terma."*

Ranford, Christine (Gillian Carfa) The wife of Frank Ranford, a business-man whom genetic mutant Eugene Tooms stalked after he was released from a mental institution. Mrs. Ranford discovered that her toilet was blocked and was unaware that the serial killer was using the sewer pipe to gain entrance to her house. Mulder thwarted her possible murder, with Tooms fleeing after wriggling through a barred window. ("Tooms")

Ranford, Frank (Pat Bermel) A bald businessman in his thirties who was pursued by Eugene Tooms in his Baltimore animal regulation van. ("Tooms")

Ranheim (Peter LaCroix) Tractor-trailer driver whose rig lost power in Reagan, Tennessee, after he heard three CBers report UFOs in the area. Ranheim saw his cargo doors fling open by themselves, fired his gun at something in the bushes and witnessed an apparent spacecraft overhead. Ranheim, who was held in jail on a weapons-firing charge, kept changing his story about what he saw. When Mulder tried to question him, the police chief released him, saying he wouldn't cooperate. Scully discovered that the tractor-trailer's cargo and the identity of its driver were both bogus. The manifest gave 108 auto-parts cartons totaling 3,100 pounds, but three weigh stations each recorded the cargo's weight as 5,100 pounds. Scully also learned that Ranheim (whose real name was Frank Druce) had been in the Persian Gulf War as a Special Operations Black Beret and was in Mosul, northern Iraq, four days earlier when the Iraqis shot down a UFO. The U.S. Army recovered wreckage from the spacecraft and possibly alien bodies, which were being transported via Druce's unmarked tractor-trailer west toward Colorado. ("E.B.E.") *Actor Peter LaCroix appeared in "Ascension" as Dwight, the doomed Skyland tram operator, and in "Unrequited" as phantom POW Nathaniel Teager.*

Rat Tail Productions Videotape production and distribution company owned by Steven Zinnszer and based in Allentown, Pennsylvania. Mulder had ordered the "guaranteed authentic alien autopsy" video from Rat Tail Productions through the mail. ("Nisei")

Ray (Ron Sauve) Foreman at the Newark County Sewage Processing Plant who explained how the system worked to Mulder: "Fifty thousand people a day call my office on the porcelain telephone." When Ray investigated an ancient storm-overflow part of the plant, he fell into the water and was pulled under by the Flukeman, but Mulder rescued him and pinned the monster beneath a sewer gate. ("The Host") *Ron Sauve also portrayed Tim Decker, a security guard at the Boston Museum of Natural History in the third season episode, "Teso dos Bichos."*

Ray, James Earl (Paul Jarrett) The convicted and imprisoned assassin of civil rights leader Martin Luther King, Jr. According to Lone Gunman

Frohike's speculative case file on the life of the enigmatic Cigarette-Smoking Man, the shadowy operative, who by 1968 was giving orders to FBI Director J. Edgar Hoover, personally took charge of the operation against King and assassinated him while he stood on the balcony of his motel room in Memphis, Tennessee. James Earl Ray was nothing more than an operational "patsy" duped into a gun-running scheme by the Cigarette-Smoking Man and set up to take the fall for the assassination. ("Musings of a Cigarette-Smoking Man")

Raymon County State Psychiatric Hospital Northwest Oregon mental institution where vegetative Billy Miles and wheelchair-bound Peggy O'Dell, friends of the victims of the mysterious youth killings in the town of Bellefleur, were hospitalized. ("The X-Files: Pilot")

Reardon, Cindy (Erika Krievins) Eight-year-old clone of Dr. Sally Kendricks. Through an apparent psychic connection, she plotted with her genetic replica, Teena Simmons, to simultaneously murder their fathers on different coasts. The two girls poisoned Dr. Kendrick with four ounces of home-grown digitalis extract and attempted to murder Mulder and Scully using the same method when the two agents grew suspicious. The two homicidal girls were later incarcerated at the Whiting Institute for the Criminally Insane. ("Eve")

Reardon, Doug The father of Cindy Reardon, he was killed in Marin County, California, at the exact same time as Joel Simmons, a resident of Greenwich, Connecticut, and in the same fashion: Both men died of hypovolemia after having over seventy-five percent of the blood drained from their bodies. ("Eve")

Reardon, Ellen (Tasha Simms) Wife of Doug and mother of Cindy Reardon. She told Mulder that her daughter was conceived by in vitro fertilization at the Luther Stapes Center for Reproductive Medicine in San Francisco after she and her husband had tried unsuccessfully for six years to get pregnant. Ellen disowned Cindy after she learned that her daughter was actually a result of cloning experiments conducted by Dr. Sally Kendrick. ("Eve") *Actress Tasha Simms also portrayed Stan Phillips' daughter, Laura Kelly, in "Excelsius Dei," and Skinner's divorce attorney, Jane Cassal, in "Avatar."*

Rebhun, Larold (Jerry Schram) Scotch-drinking passenger aboard commercial airliner Flight 549, who sat in the aisle seat next to Max Fenig. Rebhun, who used to be deathly afraid of flying, explained to his seat-mate statistically how safe it was to travel aboard planes. Ironically, Rebhun was the only one of 134 passengers and crew to survive Flight 549's crash in Upstate New York. ("Tempus Fugit/Max"). *Crash survivor Larold Rebhun shared his name (but not its pronunciation) with* The X-Files' *sound mixer.*

Redbird SEE: **Mossinger, Paul**

Red Crescent Designation of the NATO base near the border in Hakkari, Turkey. ("E.B.E.")

Red-Haired Man (Stephen McHattie) Well-dressed professional assassin who garroted Kazuo Sakurai in the back of a limousine to cover up the Japanese diplomat's sloppy handling of the Steven Zinnszer murder. After killing Dr. Shiro Zama (a.k.a. Dr. Takeo Ishimaru) in the lavatory of a train compartment, the Red-Haired Man nearly garroted Mulder to death before the conductor, at gunpoint, ordered the hawk-like assassin to stop. The interruption gave Mulder time to recover, pulling his own gun. The Red-Haired Man claimed to be an agent for the National Security Agency, although Mulder didn't believe him. The assassin (whose real name was Malcolm Gerlach) was executed at point-blank range by Mr. X, who rescued Mulder from the bomb-laden train car. ("Nisei/731") *Although print sources referred to the character as the "Red-Haired Man," actor Stephen McHattie obviously does not have red hair. Compare his brown locks with Scully's or Agent Pendrell's. McHattie, a Nova Scotia native, is best known as crime lord Gabriel from the final season of CBS's* Beauty and the Beast, *and as psychiatrist Dr. Reston in episodes of the comedy series* Seinfeld.

Red Head Kid (Garvin Cross) Member of the anticaptivity activist group Wild Again Organization (W.A.O.). Scully, who believed the animal liberators were behind the mysterious disappearances of several inhabitants of the Fairfield Zoo, tracked the Red Head Kid (who was in actuality a young adult) to the closed zoo one night, where, with a flash of light, a tigress was suddenly transported outside of her cage and the kid was mauled to death by an invisible attacker. ("Fearful Symmetry"). *It seems that Agent Mulder is not the only one on* The X-Files *who is color blind. Garvin Cross, the actor who portrayed the Red Head Kid, has short-cropped blond hair. Cross also appeared as the telephone company line repairman who fell to his death after being swarmed by bees in "Herrenvolk."*

📁 **"Red Museum"** Written by Chris Carter. Directed by Win Phelps. File number 2X10. *First aired December 9, 1994. When several missing teenagers are found wandering through the woods in their underwear with the words "HE IS ONE" scrawled on their backs, Wisconsin cattle ranchers believe the series of abductions to be the work of a bizarre local religious cult. An investigating Mulder, however, suspects the youths may be unwilling test subjects of a clandestine government experiment involving alien DNA.* **Classic Sound Bite:** *"You know for a holy man, you've got a knack for pissing people off."* **Background Check:** *Originally planned as a crossover episode with the CBS series* Picket Fences, *Mulder was to have traveled to Rome, Wisconsin, to investigate the phenomenon of cows giving birth to human children, believing it would provide information* *on the "Red Museum" X-File. Ultimately, the investigation would have proven fruitless when the truth turned out to involve a doctor using cows as surrogate wombs for couples with fertility problems. Both episodes were ultimately produced, but with Mulder absent on* Picket Fences.

"Red Right Hand" The Nick Cave and the Bad Seeds song Duane Barry was listening to on the car radio as he drove Scully to the abduction site at Skyland Mountain, Virginia. ("Ascension")

Regan, Lt. One of the firefighters who responded to Dr. Saul Grissom's 911 call for help when he saw flames outside his apartment door. Lt. Regan found no evidence of a fire in the sixth-floor hallway nor in Grissom's apartment, where the sleep disorder specialist was found dead near a spent fire extinguisher. ("Sleepless") *The actor who played Lt. Regan was uncredited.*

Rempulski, Det. (Rob Freeman) Alexandria, Virginia, police detective who met Scully at Mulder's apartment and asked her to positively identify her partner's corpse after he allegedly shot himself in the head. ("Gethsemane")

REM-sleep behavior disorder The malady Assistant Director Skinner received treatment for at the Bethesda Sleep Disorder Center during the three month period prior to the mysterious murder of prostitute Carina Sayles, of which he was suspected. Skinner complained that he had been experiencing dreams in which an old woman suffocated him. Scully hypothesized that Skinner could have killed Sayles in his sleep without realizing it. ("Avatar")

Repairman (Garvin Cross) A Telus phone company employee who fell to his death from atop a line pole in the Alberta, Canada, countryside after he was attacked by a swarm of killer bees. Five identical blond-haired teenage boys from The Project's nearby farm community inspected the repairman's body before returning to their work as drones. ("Herrenvolk")

Reticulans According to Mulder, an alien race of gray-skinned beings notorious for the extraction of terrestrials' livers due to iron depletion in the Reticulan galaxy ("Squeeze"). Scully jokingly accused Reticulans of being responsible for an experiment that heightened the existing phobias and violent impulses of the residents of a small Pennsylvania farming community. ("Blood")

📁 **"Revelations"** Written by Kim Newton. Directed by David Nutter. File number 3X11. *First aired December 15, 1995. Mulder and Scully track an assassin responsible for a series of religiously motivated murders in which each of the victims displayed inexplicable wounds similar to the crucified Christ.* **Classic Sound Bite:** *"How is it that you're able to go out on a limb whenever* *you see a light in the sky, but you're unwilling to accept the possibility of a miracle even when it's right in front of you?"* **Background Check:** *After realizing that the episode was "D.O.A." and "on the operating table . . . with life support," the producers called back Kevin Zegers (the boy who played Kevin Kryder), filmed some new footage, added new dialogue, and then re-cut and re-structured the episode so that it made sense. The end result was a season three high point, which online X-Philes consistently listed as one of their favorites.*

Rich (Fred Henderson) FBI agent and "advisory commander" who was in charge of resolving the hostage situation in Marion, Virginia, involving escaped mental patient and former federal agent Duane Barry and the four people he had abducted. ("Duane Barry") *Fred Henderson also portrayed Agent Thomas in "Beyond the Sea."*

Richard, Mrs. T. A recently deceased resident of the Excelsis Dei Convalescent Home in Worcester, Massachusetts. ("Excelsius Dei")

Richardson, Sen. Member of the Senate Select Subcommittee on Intelligence and Terrorism. During a hearing convened to investigate the mysterious death of a man outside Assistant Director Skinner's apartment, Sen. Richardson was noticeably quiet while Senators Romine and Sorenson questioned Scully concerning the whereabouts of Mulder. ("Tunguska/Terma") *The actor who portrayed Sen. Richardson was uncredited.*

Richmond, Dr. Janice (Catherine Lough) The Baltimore hospital physician on call who treated Eugene Tooms' facial injuries allegedly sustained from a beating by Mulder. The serial killer had marred his own face with a shoe he stole from Mulder's apartment in an attempt to frame the agent for assault. ("Tooms")

Richmond Train Station Richmond, Virginia, railway terminal where scientist Dr. Chester Ray Banton spent most of his days and nights after an experiment in dark matter turned his shadow into a black hole that split molecules into component atoms, effectively reducing matter to pure energy. The devastated Banton insisted on soft lighting rather than darkness and the train station's diffused fluorescent lights kept Banton's shadow from being cast. He unintentionally vaporized two police officers in an alley outside the station when they approached him and touched his shadow. ("Soft Light")

Richter, John (Ken Kirzinger) A respected geologist and team captain of the Arctic Ice Core Project in Icy Cape, Alaska. A week after sending a jubilant transmission regarding their depth record for ice-sheet drilling, Richter showed signs of extreme mental imbalance; his last video message included the cryptic words: "We are not who we are." Project teammate Campbell attacked him, and then they faced off with guns aimed at each other before turning the guns on themselves and firing. Autopsies conducted on the other three members of the Arctic Ice Core Project evidenced strangulation. ("Ice") *Ken Kirzinger is* The X-Files *stunt coordinator.*

Riddock, Helene Housewife in Braddock Heights, Maryland, who imagined she saw her husband committing adultery with a young blond woman in a backyard hammock and mistakenly shot her next door neighbor to death with a rifle. Mrs. Riddock was one of several townsfolk in the suburban community who became a psychotic killer after being subjected to subliminal messages transmitted covertly through their TV sets. ("Wetwired") *The actress who portrayed Mrs. Riddock was uncredited.*

Riddock, Victor Bearded husband of Helen Riddock. A long-haul trucker, Riddock had been on the road for ten days when his wife imagined seeing him in a backyard hammock with a shapely blond and mistakenly killed their neighbor. ("Wetwired") *The actor who portrayed Riddock was uncredited.*

Ride-Rite Rent-a-Truck Two-ton truck rental company that Alex Krycek favored for the transportation of numerous bags of highly explosive ammonium nitrate. ("Tunguska/Terma")

Ridgeway Elementary School Loveland, Ohio, school attended by Kevin Kryder, who began to bleed from his hands while writing on a classroom chalkboard. ("Revelations")

Ridley, Dr. Joe (Robin Mossley) Former physician who operated on inmates at Pennsylvania's Tashmoo Federal Correctional Facility in an experimental effort to reverse the aging process. Dr. Ridley had previously worked at the National Institute of Health in Bethesda, Maryland where he performed secret, unauthorized human experimentation on children suffering from progeria, a disease that causes rapid aging. Associates secretly gave him the derogatory nickname "Dr. Mengele" for his Nazi-like disregard of his patients as nothing more than human guinea pigs. Dr. Ridley had his medical license revoked by the state of Maryland in 1979 for research malpractice and misuse of a government grant. After leaving Tashmoo, he disappeared from sight, working in Belize, Mexico, and other Central American countries until John Barnett, a former Tashmoo inmate who was believed to have died in prison, stole his documentation and notes. Dying from a cerebral vascular disease caused by his own aging reversal experiment, Ridley showed up at Scully's door, telling her that the government had sponsored his work. ("Young at Heart") *Robin Mossley also portrayed Dr. Randolph in "Our Town" and Dr. Kingsley Looker in "Terma."*

Right Fielder (Lachlan Murdoch) One of several boys who discovered a hideously deformed baby buried in a shallow grave while they played a game of sandlot baseball in a vacant field next to the reclusive Peacock family's farmhouse. ("Home")

Right Hand, The Radical paramilitary group led by ex-Marine Denny Markham, whose stated aim was "violent revolution" and the empowerment of the "individual over a corrupt and corrupting federal government." The Right Hand's compound was located in Demeter, Virginia. ("Unrequited")

"Ring the Bells" A song by the band James, which was the last number on the jukebox heard by stocky off-duty pizza deliverer, Jack Hammond, before he was killed by an electrical surge outside a Connerville, Oklahoma, strip-mall video arcade. ("D.P.O.")

Ritual of Separation An Old World Romanian rite intended to divide the soul of a living child from the spirit of a dead twin. When Maggie Holvey's son, Michael, was stillborn, she refused to allow her mother to perform the ritual, which ultimately led to a demonic entity taking the place of Michael's soul. The malevolent force followed Charlie, Michael's living twin, until it was exorcised by a Ritual of Separation performed by the Calusari holy men and assisted by Mulder. ("The Calusari")

Rivers, Chief (Allan Lysell) Lexington, Tennessee, chief of police who held Ranheim in jail on a weapons-firing charge. The uncooperative Rivers released the truck driver when Mulder tried to question him. ("E.B.E.") *Allan Lysell also played Dr. Gardner in "End Game."*

Rob (Andrew Airlie) A handsome and divorced tax lawyer who dated Scully only once after she was introduced to him at her godson's birthday party. Although Scully tried to have some semblance of a personal life, as opposed to the obsessive dedication that Mulder had toward his work, she opted to diligently pursue X-File cases with Mulder and turned down a subsequent date with Rob even though he tempted her with Cirque du Soleil tickets. ("The Jersey Devil") *Andrew Airlie also portrayed Dr. Harrison Lloyd's defense attorney in "Sanguinarium."*

Robbins, Officer Uniformed officer on duty at the Desmond, Virginia, police forensics lab when Skinner impersonated Agent Mulder and switched a vial containing the blood of a recent bee attack victim with another, identical container. ("Zero Sum") *The actor who portrayed Officer Robbins was uncredited.*

Roberto Young janitor at the Idaho Mutual Insurance Trust in the town of Fairfield, who witnessed the effects of an invisible behemoth as it rampaged down the city street, causing the windows at the front of the bank building to shatter. ("Fearful Symmetry") *The actor who portrayed Roberto during the pre-credits sequence was uncredited.*

Roberts, Terri (Lisa Robin Kelly) Attractive blond cheerleader and senior at Comity's Grover Cleveland Alexander High School, who, along with her best friend, Margi Kleinjan, possessed strange telekinetic powers due to "a rare planetary alignment of Mars, Uranus, and Mercury." Two people born at the same time on January 12, 1979 (as were Terri and Margi) would be under the influence of "a grand square," when "all the energy of the cosmos would be focused" on them. After a series of murders, the two girls finally turned on each other in a telekinetic rage. Mulder locked the girls in the same small room until 12:01 a.m., when they were no longer the focal point of unseen galactic forces beyond their grasp. ("Syzygy")

Roche, John Lee (Tom Noonan) One the first serial killers Mulder profiled during his assignment to the Bureau's Violent Crimes Unit. Roche, a remorseless sociopath, culled his victims, all pre-adolescent girls, from the families of people to whom he sold vacuum cleaners door-to-door. Between 1979 and 1990, Roche abducted girls between the ages of eight and ten from their homes, strangled them with electrical cord, and cut a heart-shaped piece of fabric from their nightclothes as a trophy. After Mulder's profile led to Roche's capture, the serial killer confessed to thirteen murders scattered across the eastern seaboard and was sentenced to life in prison. In 1996, however, Mulder experienced a vivid dream which led to the site of an unmarked grave, where the agent unearthed the skeletal remains of a missing girl, Roche's fourteenth victim. When the child was identified, it proved that the murderous child molester began his heinous serial crimes as early as 1975. Another clue from his dreams helped Mulder locate Roche's vehicle, in which he hid the cloth hearts that were never discovered at the time of his capture. There were sixteen hearts, and Roche convinced Mulder that one of the two unidentified victims was Samantha Mulder. Without notifying Scully or Skinner, Mulder temporarily secured Roche's release from prison and escorted him back to Martha's Vineyard (the site of Samantha's abduction), where the agent was forced to kill Roche after he took another young girl hostage. ("Paper Hearts"). *Actor Tom Noonan, who portrayed Roche, also played the villain in* RoboCop II, *the Frankenstein creature in* Monster Squad, *and the murderer Francis Dollarhyde in the movie* Manhunter, *which was based on Thomas Harris' novel* Red Dragon: The Pursuit of Hannibal Lecter.

Rocky and Bullwinkle Long-running cartoon series recounting the adventures of an intrepid squirrel and moose. Scully surmised that Vsevlod Pudovkin's account of two crashed UFOs in the Bering Sea was nothing more than a poorly-veiled synopsis of a *Rocky and Bullwinkle* episode. ("Never Again") *The reference to* Rocky and Bullwinkle *was a nod to one of the Internet newsgroups that had consistently noted numerous similarities between Mulder and Scully and* Rocky and Bullwinkle.

rohypnol Also known as the "date-rape drug," a powerful tranquilizer that causes loss of inhibition and memory when taken in high dosages. Scully hypothesized that homely janitor Eddie Van Blundht may have used rohypnol to incapacitate four married women and impregnate them. ("Small Potatoes")

🗁 **"Roland"** Written by Chris Ruppenthal. Directed by David Nutter. File number 1X22. *First aired May 6, 1994. When several aeronautical scientists are killed at a jet propulsion laboratory, the finger of suspicion points to an autistic janitor, not to mention a dead scientist whose brain is preserved cryogenically.* **Classic Sound Bite:** *"Let's just say Roland isn't exactly a rocket scientist."* **Background Check:** *Actor Zeljko Ivanek (pronounced Zel-ko Eve-on-ek) was actually the first person to audition for the role of the mentally challenged janitor. Although ten others read for the part, the producers considered Ivanek's strong performance perfect for outweighing what they considered a "weak" and "frail" script.*

Rolston (John Oliver) Member of a Canadian survey team that discovered the frozen remains of a gray alien in a block of ice in the St. Elias Mountains of the Yukon Territory. Rolston was shot and killed by conspiracy assassin Ostelhoff when he left the discovery site to meet the helicopter carrying Mulder and forensics anthropologist Arlinsky from the Smithsonian Institution. ("Gethsemane")

Roman à Clef The weekly magazine that serialized the Jack Colquitt spy novel *Second Chance* by Raul Bloodworth (a *nom de plum* for the Cigarette-Smoking Man) in 1996. CSM, whose dream was to become a published author, was bitterly angry to discover that the magazine was nothing but a cheap salacious rag whose editors even altered the ending to his story. The incident was based on Lone Gunman Frohike's speculative and possibly dubious dossier on the life of the Cigarette-Smoking Man. ("Musings of a Cigarette-Smoking Man") *When CSM was looking for a recent copy of Roman à Clef at a magazine stand, the audience got a quick peek at a periodical whose cover stories included: "Where the hell is Darin Morgan?" The brother of writer/ co-executive producer Glen Morgan, Darin wrote some of The X-Files' most memorable installments (not to mention portraying the title characters in "The Host" and "Small Potatoes").*

Romine, Sen. (Campbell Lane) Chairman of the Senate Select Subcommittee on Intelligence and Terrorism. During a hearing convened to investigate the mysterious death of a man outside Assistant Director Skinner's apartment, Sen. Romine demanded to know the whereabouts of Agent Mulder. When Scully refused, claiming that the revelation could possibly endanger her partner's life in the field, the Senator warned her that as an FBI agent her response was not "optional." Mulder's eventual presence put the subcommittee's attention back on its original purpose, but when Scully offered to provide documents and interviews as evidence of a wide-ranging conspiracy to control a lethal biotoxin that was, in fact, extraterrestrial in origin, Sen

Romine abruptly adjourned the subcommittee until the "evidence could be properly evaluated." Referred to as an "honorable" man by the Well-Manicured Man, it appeared that the Senator was influenced to some degree by the Shadowy Syndicate. ("Tunguska/Terma") *Campbell Lane also played Margaret Hohman's father in "Miracle Man" and one of the Romanian holy men in "The Calusari."*

Roosevelt, Dr. Carl (Alan Robertson) American archaeologist who was killed in his tent by the jaguar spirit of a female shaman after a sacred Amaru urn was unearthed during a dig in the Ecuadorian highlands. ("Teso dos Bichos")

Roosevelt, Eleanor Former First Lady of the United States and highly respected historical figure. After discussing Eddie Van Blundht's apparent shapeshifting abilities, Mulder asked Scully who she'd like to become if she could choose to be any person for a day. She thought about the question for a moment and then responded with "Eleanor Roosevelt," to which Mulder snapped back, "It can't be a dead person." ("Small Potatoes")

Roque, Sammon (Bokeem Woodbine) Eastpoint State Penitentiary convict who supposedly possessed executed prisoner Napoleon "Neech" Manley's enemy list naming the five men who would die "to avenge all the petty tyranny and cruelty" he suffered before his death. Roque privately told Mulder that he'd overheard Manley giving another convict, John Speranza, the names of the intended victims. Roque offered to exchange the list for a transfer out of the prison, but Warden Brodeur insisted he wouldn't make the deal. Brodeur later beat Roque to death in the prison showers while demanding he reveal the names on the list. Roque defiantly asked, "How's it feel to be on death row, Warden?" ("The List")

Rosen, Tracy (Kerry Sandomirsky) A mentally-retarded friend of Roland Fuller's at the Heritage Halfway House. Roland was romantically interested in the young woman. ("Roland") *Kerry Sandomirsky also played Joanne Steffen, a friend and neighbor of Ellen Kaminsky in "2Shy."*

Ross, Caitlin (Carly McKillip) Little girl on whom convicted child murderer John Lee Roche fixated during a flight from Washington, D.C. to Boston. After Roche escaped from Mulder's custody (stealing the agent's gun and badge in the process), he obtained her name from the airline passenger manifest and tracked her down to a daycare center. Mulder, whose profile of Roche led to his original capture and imprisonment, pursued them to a mass trolley bus graveyard. Although Roche sat at the back of one of the buses with Mulder's stolen handgun pointed toward Caitlin's back, the agent was able to secure the fatal shot that saved the girl's life. ("Paper Hearts")

Roth, Walden New York publisher whose Pivotal Publications purchased the serialization rights in 1996 to the Tom Clancy-esque spy novel *Second*

Chance by Raul Bloodworth (the pseudonym for the Cigarette-Smoking Man). The incident was revealed in Frohike's dubious dossier on the life of CSM. ("Musings of a Cigarette-Smoking Man") *Walden Roth was named for Dana Walden, head of drama at Twentieth Century Fox Television, and Peter Roth, one of Fox's network heads.*

rubes Term used by circus and sideshow performers to describe outsiders. ("Humbug")

"Running Fox" Native American name suggested to Mulder by Ish because he was supposedly more open to Indian belief than some Native Americans. The FBI agent was agreeable as long as it wasn't "Spooky Fox," a reference to the disparaging nickname Mulder earned at the FBI Academy because of his belief in the paranormal. ("Shapes")

Ruxton Chemical Plant Powhatten Hill facility where Eugene Tooms hid one of the victims of his 1933 killing spree. Sixty years later, a professor at the Smithsonian Institution's Forensic Anthropology Lab examined the skeletal remains discovered by Scully and retired Baltimore detective Frank Briggs at the Ruxton Chemical Plant and matched the skull to a photo of the missing murder victim. ("Tooms")

Ryan, Det. Kelly (Kate Twa) Scheming and manipulative Richmond, Virgina, police officer and one of Scully's Academy students, who requested her former teacher's assistance in her first assignment as a detective: to investigate three cases of apparent abduction. Ryan died when Banton reluctantly stepped toward her, sucking her into his destructive shadow force, the only person the scientist intentionally killed. ("Soft Light") *Kate Twa also played the "female" Marty in the "Genderbender" episode from the first season.*

S

Skinner

Sacks, Dr. (Malcolm Stewart) Government exobiologist assigned to the NASA Goddard Space Flight Center in Greenbelt, Maryland. Dr. Sacks believed that a rock Mulder and Scully intercepted in a diplomatic pouch was, in fact, over four billion years old, and possibly of Martian origin. When he attempted to drill into the artifact to retrieve a core sample, black oil emerged that congealed into small, leech-like worms and penetrated his skin. Scully and Agent Pendrell, appropriately protected in contamination-suits, investigated the deadly enigma and discovered that Dr. Sacks (although not breathing) remained comatose in some type of biostatsis. Tests revealed a black vermiform organism attached to the pineal gland of Sacks' brain. A few hours later, Vassily Peskow, a former KGB assassin called out of retirement, injected the exobiologist with an amber fluid. The worms quickly emerged from various orifices in Sacks' body, and then Peskow disconnected his life support, effectively killing him. ("Tunguska/Terma") *Malcolm Stewart also played Dr. Glass in the pilot episode, Commander Carver in "3," and Agent Bonnecaze in "Avatar."*

Sagan, Dr. Carl Noted astronomer, educator, author, and pioneer of exobiology who participated in a NASA symposium at Boston University on November 20, 1972 to discuss the possible existence of extraterrestrial life. Mulder was watching a videotape of the conference when he allegedly killed himself with a gunshot to the head. ("Gethsemane")

Sai Baba An Indian guru whom digital imaging expert Dr. Charles Burks claimed to have witnessed create a feast from thin air during his hippie days in 1979, an act accompanied by the production of vibuti or "holy ash." ("The Calusari")

Saint Elias Mountains Tundra plain in the arctic regions of Canada's northwest Yukon Territory. A St. Elias Mountains survey team discovered in a cave the alleged corpse of a gray alien entombed and perfectly preserved in a block of ice. ("Gethsemane")

Saint Ignatius According to Roman Catholic tradition, the saint was recognized as being able to appear in two places at once. Kevin Kryder was compared to Ignatius after he inexplicably performed the same feat by creating an illusionary double of himself. ("Revelations")

Saint John's Burn Center Philadelphia hospital where Ed Jerse was rushed for treatment after thrusting his arm inside an incinerator in attempt to burn off his murderous "Betty" tattoo. Doctors at the medical facility found the psychosis-inducing ergot parasite in his bloodstream, which allegedly caused Jerse to experience aural and visual hallucinations. ("Never Again")

Saint Matthews Medical Center Arlington, Virginia, hospital where nine-year-old Charlie Holvey was taken after suffering a seizure. Mulder and the Romanian Calusari performed the Ritual of Separation in the boy's room, an exorcism rite that successfully divided the souls of Charlie and the malevolent demonic force that took the spirit form of his stillborn twin brother. ("The Calusari")

Sakaguchi, Naofomi One of four Japanese doctors murdered by gas-masked soldiers during an "alien autopsy" aboard an unmarked train car in Knoxville, Tennessee. ("Nisei") *The actor who portrayed Sakaguchi was uncredited.*

Sakurai, Kazuo (Yasuo Sakurai) Allegedly a high-ranking Japanese diplomat, whom Mulder apprehended as he tried to flee from the scene of Steven Zinnzser's execution-style murder in Allentown, Pennsylvania. Sakurai's body was later found floating in the C & O (Chesapeake & Ohio Railroad) Canal after he was murdered by the Red-Haired Man. ("Nisei")

Sal (Debis Simpson) A half-man, half-woman food server employed at Phil's Diner in Gibsonton, Florida, a town populated by former circus performers and sideshow acts. ("Humbug")

Salinger, Beatrice (Lisa Ann Beley) No-nonsense hospital night-shift nurse in Kenwood, Tennessee, who said she and others witnessed the deceased faith-healer Samuel Hartley walk out of the morgue. ("Miracle Man") *Lisa Ann Beley briefly appeared as an FBI cadet in "Little Green Men."*

Sanders, Owen Nineteen-year-old African-American whose body was found at a Philadelphia construction site. The fourth black man to have disappeared in three months, the discovery of his pigment-depleted corpse prompted the Centers for Disease Control to suspect that the men had been victims of some unknown but fatal pathogen. After the CDC's Philadelphia office called in Scully to unravel the medical mystery, her autopsy revealed that Sanders' total lack of pigmentation was due to the fact that his hormone-producing pituitary gland had been necrotized. Sanders was a victim of West African immigrant Samuel Aboah, a metamorphic ghost creature. ("Teliko") *The actor who portrayed Sanders' albino-like corpse and subsequently the subject of Scully's autopsy, was uncredited.*

Sandwich Man (Bill Finck) Present at the office food cart at FBI headquarters when Agent Jerry Lamana, Mulder's old partner in the Violent Crimes Section, surprised Mulder and Scully. ("Ghost in the Machine")

Sanford, Capt. Kyle (Richard Hersley) Commander of the submarine *Zeus Faber* which was sent to locate a sunken plane after World War II. Officer Christopher Johansen led a mutiny against Sanford after several of the crew died of radiation sickness, allegedly caused by the plane's cargo, an atomic bomb bound for Japan. One of *Zeus Faber*'s dying crewmen told three young government agents at the Pearl Harbor Navy Hospital that Capt. Sanford was possessed by "an enemy that was killing us" until they knocked him unconscious and a black oil oozed out of him and down a grate into the lower depths of the submarine. ("Piper Maru/Apocrypha")

Sanford, Dr. Sally (Marie Stillin) Physician who interviewed and hired cosmetic surgeon Dr. Hartman at a Los Angeles hospital. Dr. Sanford was thoroughly impressed with Hartman's professional credentials, unaware that he was a sorcerer, or that in Chicago, under the name Jack Franklyn, he had used black magic and the blood sacrifices of patients to transform his own appearance beyond the limits of surgery. ("Sanguinarium")

📁 **"Sanguinarium"** Written by Vivian Mayhew and Valerie Mayhew. Directed by Kim Manners. File number 4X06. *First aired November 10, 1996. Agents Mulder and Scully investigate a series of bizarre murders at a Chicago cosmetic surgery clinic after a doctor claims he was a victim of demonic possession.* **Classic Sound Bite:** *"There's magic going on here, Mulder. Only it's being done with silicon, collagen, and a well-placed scalpel."* **Background Check:** *The episode title comes from "sanguinary," meaning bloodthirsty or murderous; and "sanguinaria," which is an herb that stanches blood, also called bloodroot.*

Satin (Kathleen Duborg) A street-walking prostitute in Minneapolis whom escalating death fetishist Donne Pfaster picked up and took to his apartment. She grew alarmed upon seeing a collection of funeral wreaths decorating his bedroom. Pfaster killed her and took various tokens from her body, including her fingers. Satin was his first murder victim. ("Irresistible")

Saunders, Ms. (Veena Snood) Mysterious CIA agent who, along with her partner, Webster, requested Mulder and Scully's assistance after it was obvious that their investigation into HTG Industrial Technologies had turned up a potential X-File connection. ("Shadows")

Savalas, Cindy (Jen Forgie) Ex-wife of handsome Philadelphia stockbroker Ed Jerse, and mother of two small children. ("Never Again")

Sayles, Carina (Amanda Tapping) A former secretary for a Washington, D.C.-based law firm, she was fired for moonlighting as a high-priced prostitute in a call-girl ring. Assistant FBI Director Skinner picked her up in the Chesapeake Lounge bar at the Ambassador Hotel and later took her to a room, only to awaken from a nightmare to discover her nude, lifeless body. Scully determined that the cause of death was a crushed spinal cord and noted a phosphorescent glow around the dead woman's nose and mouth. ("Avatar")

Scanlon, Dr. Kevin (Sean Allen) Physician at the Allentown-Bethlehem Medical Center who treated Scully's inoperable brain tumor by attacking a gene known as p53, which Dr. Scanlon believed had mutated and caused Scully's cancer. Mulder later discovered that the physician was an active member of the Shadowy Syndicate's Project, and under the pretense of cancer treatment had accelerated the deaths of Betsy Hagopian, Penny Northern and the other female members of the Allentown MUFON group who claimed they had been abducted by aliens. ("Memento Mori") *Sean Allen also appeared briefly as a customer in "War of the Coprophages."*

Schaeffer, Lt. Jack (Michael Dobson) Air Force officer who, along with Maj. Robert Vallee, attempted to abduct and interrogate Klass County, Washington, teenagers Harold Lamb and Chrissy Giorgio while disguised as gray-skinned extraterrestrials. Mulder later encountered a nude Schaeffer wandering down a road saying, "This is not happening!" The Air Force lieutenant told Mulder that he and his partner were piloting a UFO as part of a covert government operation when they were abducted themselves by a real alien named Lord Kinbote. Shortly after Sgt. Hynek took Schaeffer into custody, his body was found at the crash site of a top-secret military plane. ("Jose Chung's 'From Outer Space'") *Actor Michael Dobson also made brief appearances in "Duane Barry" as an FBI marksman and in "The Field Where I Died" as a BATF agent. Lt. Schaeffer was named after paranormal and UFO author Robert Schaffer.*

Schalin, Scott A prisoner jailed in the cell adjoining Eugene Tooms'. ("Tooms")

Schiff-Immergut Lumber Company A logging company in the Pacific Northwest. Thirty of Schiff-Immergut's loggers had mysteriously vanished in the remote Olympic National Forest practically overnight. The company's security chief suspected eco-terrorists were behind the disappearances. ("Darkness Falls")

Schilling, Kaye (Jillian Fargey) Ed Jerse's downstairs neighbor in his Philadelphia apartment building. Believing that the taunting voice he heard was Schilling, he beat repeatedly on the floor of his apartment. In response, she only turned up the volume on her stereo. The voice in his head eventually drove Jerse to madness and in a blind rage he knocked Schilling's door down, murdered her, and dragged her body to the basement, where he stuffed it inside an incinerator. ("Never Again") *As an in-joke by episode writers Glen Morgan and James Wong, the character was named after Mary Kaye Schilling, the senior editor in charge of the November 1996 special* X-Files *issue of* Entertainment Weekly. *Supposedly, Morgan and Wong were infuriated with the magazine's reviews of some of their previously penned episodes, particularly "The Field Where I Died," which* EW *called "stultifyingly awful."*

Schnablegger, Dr. Glenna (Jill Teed) County coroner at the Atlantic City morgue who confirmed to Mulder and Scully that Roger Crockett, a dead vagrant, had been found with parts of his body eaten and bite marks on his mutilated corpse that appeared to be human. Mulder theorized that the legendary Jersey Devil man-beast was responsible for the brutal murder. ("The Jersey Devil")

Schnauz, Gerald Thomas Father of Gerald, Jr., the North Michigan dentist was brutally beaten by his son in 1980 after his daughter confided to her brother that he had molested her. He was confined to a wheelchair, until his death; as a recipient of a Bronze Star during the Korean War, he was buried with full military honors. ("Unruhe") *The actor who posed for the computer-enhanced photo of Gerald T. Schnauz, Sr. was uncredited.*

Schnauz, Gerald Thomas, Jr. (Pruitt Taylor Vince) Paranoid-schizophrenic with shifty eyes who attacked his father with an axe-handle so severely that he spent the remaining years of his life in a wheelchair. Instead of being incarcerated for the violent assault, Schnauz was institutionalized in a Michigan mental hospital for six years. Turning kidnapper, he began abducting young women and conducting primitive lobotomies on them with an icepick in an attempt to "save" them from the "howlers" in their heads that apparently made his sister tell him about the incestuous molestation by their father. Although Schnauz was eventually apprehended, he escaped and kidnapped Scully, on whom he planned to perform the same procedure. Mulder shot and killed him with hardly a moment to spare. After Schnauz's death, a diary was found among his personal belongings. Written in the second person and apparently intended as an open letter to his father, the journal included the names of his victims, the women he desired to "save," including Scully. ("Unruhe") *Pruitt Taylor Vince co-starred in the six-hour series finale of* Murder One, *in which he portrayed the "street sweeper," an unrepentant serial killer of seventeen violent criminals whose prison sentences and plea bargains didn't meet his notion of justice. Vince has also appeared in* Big Girls, Natural Born Killers, JFK, Mississippi Burning, Red Heat, *and* Angel Heart, *but he's best remembered for his movie roles in* Nobody's Fool *with Paul Newman and* Heavy *with Liv Tyler. And, yes, Vince really does have shifty eyes, which were caused by a birth defect.*

Schneider, Andy MUFON (Mutual UFO Network) member and friend of eccentric Minneapolis FBI agent Moe Bocks, who consulted Schneider in regards to possible UFO activity in the area. Bocks was convinced that a recently mutilated corpse was the work of grave-digging aliens. ("Irresistible")

School Nurse (Selina Williams) Nurse at Ridgeway Elementary School who treated fifth-grader Kevin Kryder with Bactine after he began to bleed from his hands while writing on the classroom chalkboard. When she took his temperature, the mercury rose rapidly and then the thermometer popped. ("Revelations")

Schumann Resonance The radio wave frequency emitted by flashes of lightning at eight cycles per second. ("D.P.O.")

Schwartsky, J. Crowley High School student who had previously checked out M.R. Krashewski's *Witch Hunt: A History of the Occult in America* from the library. ("Die Hand Die Verletzt")

scopolamine A controlled drug, which in quantities above 2mg. changes from motion sickness remedy to hallucinogenic anesthetic. Scully discovered traces of the drug in the blood of one of the teenage "victims" of the rural religious cult, Church of the Red Museum. ("Red Museum")

Scott A young boy who became a favorite of cult leader Vernon Ephesian. Scott was later physically abused and beaten after Ephesian decided that the boy was "not a child of God." ("The Field Where I Died")

Scully, Charles Younger brother of Dana Scully who played boyhood games with his tomboy sister, Dana. ("One Breath") *The young actor who portrayed Charles Scully in the flashback scenes of "One Breath" was uncredited. During the third season episode "Wetwired," X-Philes were disappointed when family photos on Margaret Scully's nightstand did not include Dana's two brothers. By the end of the fourth season, Bill Jr. made an appearance but no mention had been made of Charles, his profession or his whereabouts, although in the episode "Home" Dana remarked to Mulder that she had baby-sat her nephew over the weekend. Did this mean that one of her elusive brothers lived in the Washington/ Baltimore area?*

Scully, Dana Katherine (Gillian Anderson) FBI badge number: JTT0331613. Current address: 3170 W. 53 Rd. #35, Annapolis, Maryland. Dana was born on February 23, 1964, the middle child of William (d. December 1993), a U.S. Navy captain, and Margaret, a homemaker. She has one older brother, William "Bill Jr.," and one younger, Charles ("Born Again"). Her older sister, Melissa ("One Breath"), was killed in 1995 in a bungled attempt on Dana's life ("Paper Clip"). As a child, the tomboyish

Scully was, and presumably still is, afraid of snakes ("One Breath"), although interestingly enough as an adult she permanently distinguished herself with a tattoo on her lower left back of a snake eating its own tail ("Never Again"). Growing up, she was transferred from one naval base to another due to her father's military duty ("Piper Maru"). In 1986, Scully obtained a bachelor's degree in physics from the University of Maryland ("Jersey Devil"), her senior thesis was titled: "Einstein's Twin Paradox: A New Interpretation" ("The X-Files: Pilot" and "Synchrony"). Scully subsequently earned a medical degree with a residency in forensics and then disappointed her father by joining the FBI directly from medical school in 1990 ("Beyond the Sea"). For two years she was an instructor at the Bureau's training academy in Quantico, Virginia, where she maintained a year-long, open relationship with Agent Jack Willis ("Lazarus"). In 1992, Scully was recruited by Section Chief Scott Blevins to the X-Files unit with the intent to properly assess the quantitative value of Fox Mulder's work, while observing the agent's general deportment and state of mind and with her more "traditional" scientific approach, attempt to discredit Mulder's paranormal explanations. On their first case together, Scully realized how unique her fellow agent's instincts were in these type of cases, but held firmly to her belief that most supposedly paranormal phenomena actually had logical explanations ("The X-Files: Pilot"). Through their years working together, however, the usually no-nonsense and obsessively skeptical Scully has become more open-minded to extreme possibilities.

When the X-Files unit was closed in mid-1994 and Scully was reassigned to the Quantico Academy, she continued to advise Mulder unofficially on violent crime cases ("Little Green Men," "The Host," "Blood," and "Sleepless"). In October 1994, she was abducted by mental patient and former FBI agent Duane Barry under unexplained circumstances ("Duane Barry/Ascension"). A month later, she was discovered in a deep coma in the Intensive Care Unit of North Georgetown University Hospital, suffering from the afteraffects of genetic experimentation. No witnesses or records of her admission to the medical facility could be found ("One Breath"). She recovered and was reassigned as Mulder's partner after the X-Files were reopened, although she claims to have no memory surrounding the events of her abduction. Placed on mandatory leave and forced to surrender her badge and service weapon in the aftermath of Mulder's disappearance in 1995, she was obliged to go through the metal detector at the front of the FBI headquarters in Washington, D.C., whereupon she discovered a small piece of metal, resembling a computer chip, implanted in her neck ("The Blessing Way"). It was later discovered that the Japanese-designed subcutaneous mechanism functioned both as a tracking device and a memory retrieval unit ("731").

For several years, Scully has been something of a lapsed Catholic ("Miracle Man" "Revelations," and "Gethsemane"), even though she still wears a small gold crucifix on a chain around her neck, which she lost when she was abducted by Duane Barry but was later returned to her by Mulder

("Ascension" and "One Breath"). In early 1997, her religious faith was a great source of strength and consolation after an MRI X ray indicated an inoperable cancerous mass on the wall between her sinus and cerebrum. Instead of requesting a leave of absence, Scully opted to fight the disease and continue her work ("Memento Mori"). At the time of this writing, however, the tumor had metastasized and she has begun to suffer more frequently from sporadic nosebleeds. Scully was informed by Michael Kritschgau, who claimed to have run the Department of Defense's agitprop arm for a decade, that shadowy conspirators within the government had planted the cancer in her in an effort to ensure Mulder's belief in their campaign of propaganda about extraterrestrials and UFOs ("Gethsemane").

In 1997, as either a witting or unwitting part of an elaborate hoax, Scully appeared before an FBI review board chaired by Section Chief Scott Blevins and stated that the purpose of the current meeting was to report on the illegitimacy of Agent Mulder's work in the X-Files unit. Struggling to maintain her composure, she revealed to the officials present at the meeting that her partner had died of an apparent self-inflicted gunshot wound to the head ("Gethsemane"). *Gillian Anderson's resume includes a guest appearance on* Class of '96 *(TV) and theatrical films such as* The Turning, The Mighty, *and* Hellcab. *Young actress Tegan Moss played Dana Scully in the flashback scenes of her childhood in "One Breath" and "Apocrypha."*

Scully, Margaret (Sheila Larken) Mother of Dana and called "Maggie" by her husband, William, a captain in the U.S. Navy. Margaret once told her daughter that Capt. Scully proposed to her immediately after his return from the Bay of Pigs invasion in 1961. "Their song" was "Beyond the Sea," which was played at their wedding. Their marriage seemed happy in every way and Margaret spent the next thirty years as a homemaker and mother, raising four children: William Jr., known as "Bill Junior," Melissa, Dana, and Charles. Margaret was fifty-eight at the time of her husband's sudden death from a coronary during the Christmas holidays in 1993 ("Beyond the Sea"). She confessed to Mulder that she had had a premonitory dream about Dana's abduction by escaped mental patient Duane Barry, but was too embarrassed to tell her daughter about it. A devout Catholic, she gave her daughter a gold crucifix necklace for her fifteenth birthday, which Mulder later found in the trunk of Duane Barry's car after Dana's disappearance from atop Virginia's Skyland Mountain. When Mulder attempted to return it to Margaret, she told him hopefully to "give it to Dana . . . when you find her" ("Ascension"). Margaret was the executor of Dana's living will, which directed that life-support be ended once her Glasgow Outcome Scale reached a certain level. Margaret, who always respected her daughter's independence of mind (even when it went against her Catholic faith), came uncomfortably close to having to adhere to Dana's wishes after the FBI agent was discovered comatose in a Washington, D.C., hospital ("One Breath"). Although Dana recovered, Margaret returned to another Washington medical facility a few months later when her older daughter, Melissa, was shot by the Cigarette-

Smoking Man's lackeys, Alex Krycek and Luis Cardinal. Although Margaret prayed constantly and maintained a nonstop bedside vigil, Melissa eventually succumbed to her gunshot wounds ("Paper Clip"). Margaret's warm yet commanding presence and motherly concern always seemed to draw Dana home when there was a crisis in her life ("Gethsemane"). After Mulder's apparent death in the New Mexico desert, she visited her mother and broke down, crying ("The Blessing Way"). When Dana began to suffer from the dementia-inducing effects of a mind-controlling video signal and became violently paranoid, she hid in Margaret's home where her mother calmed her down before she was hospitalized ("Wetwired"). Dana left Margaret "in the dark" about her inoperable cancer diagnosis, however, which emotionally devastated the woman. When she visited her in an Allentown, Pennsylvania, hospital, the usually soft-spoken Margaret was visibly angry and dispirited ("Memento Mori"). A few months later, Margaret invited a longtime friend of the Scully family, Catholic priest Father McCue, to a dinner party at her house for the purpose of discussing Dana's faith at a time when her health was at great risk due to the brain tumor ("Gethsemane"). *Sheila Larken is the real-life wife of* X-Files *co-executive producer and frequent director, R.W. Goodwin. She co-starred as attorney Deborah Sullivan in* The Storefront Law-yers/Men at Law, *and was a prolific TV actress before semi-retiring in the 1980s to pursue a master's degree in social work.*

Scully, Melissa (Melinda McGraw) Dana's older sister (family nickname "Missy") who resembled her slightly, with red hair and hazel eyes. A New Age believer in miracles and crystals and apparently a psychic, she claimed that her comatose sister was deciding whether to live or die, and told Mulder that he was "in a very dark place," darker than Dana's ("One Breath"). Melissa tried to comfort Dana after Mulder's apparent death and convinced her sister to undergo hypnosis in an effort to recall her "lost" abduction time. In a case of mistaken identity, Melissa was shot in the head by renegade agent Alex Krycek and the Hispanic Man ("The Blessing Way"). Melissa died some time later after undergoing cranial surgery, but a grimly determined Dana vowed to bring her sister's killer to justice ("Paper Clip"). Five months later, the Hispanic Man shot Assistant Director Skinner at close range in a Washington, D.C., coffee shop after he appealed the Bureau decision to make Melissa's murder case "inactive." DNA testing confirmed that the Hispanic Man, a Nicaraguan mercenary named Luis Cardinal, was the shooter of both Melissa and Skinner. As promised, Dana brought her sister's murderer to justice when she arrested Cardinal during his second attempt on Skinner's life ("Piper Maru/Apocrypha"). *The producers originally toyed with the idea of creating an unlikely romance between Melissa and Mulder, but eventually decided against it. Actress Melinda McGraw met then-boyfriend Nicholas Lea (Alex Krycek) on the Vancouver-filmed series* The Commish, *in which she played Chief of Detectives Madison for two seasons and Lea played Officer Caruso. Future* X-Files *producers and frequent writers Glen Morgan and James Wong had helmed that show and specifically wrote the part of Melissa*

Scully with McGraw in mind. Christine Viner played the young Melissa Scully in Dana's flashback scenes in "Piper Maru."

Scully, William (Don Davis) Dana Scully's father, a retired captain in the U.S. Navy who participated in the Bay of Pigs invasion in 1961. Although he could be formal and reserved, he called his youngest daughter "Starbuck" after the character from the seafaring literary classic *Moby Dick* and she called him "Ahab." Although he disagreed with Dana's decision to join the FBI rather than pursue her medical career, he was still very proud of his daughter. His sudden death from a massive coronary during the 1993 Christmas season was emotionally devastating to Dana. When she saw a ghostly apparition of her father a short time later, the usually skeptical Dana questioned her lack of belief in the paranormal ("Beyond the Sea"). Attired in a crisp Navy dress uniform, Captain Scully reappeared during Dana's near-death experience with a message of hope and love ("One Breath"). *Don Davis is best remembered as Maj. Briggs on* Twin Peaks, *in which David Duchovny played transvestite Dennis/Denise. In 1997, Davis had a small but classic movie moment, as a driver who experienced something worse than bird-droppings on the windshield of his car in the blockbuster film* Conair.

Scully, William "Bill Jr." (Pat Skipper) Elder brother of Dana Scully who played a great deal with his hoyden sister, Dana, when they were growing up ("One Breath"). On leave from his Navy vessel in 1997, Bill Jr. confronted his sister and berated her for not telling him that she was suffering from an inoperable brain tumor. Dana claimed her cancer was too personal to share with her family and she didn't want sympathy. Her brother demanded to know why she was still working. What was she trying to prove? And where was her partner, Mulder, when she needed him? ("Gethsemane"). *A confrontational scene between Dana and Bill Jr. was filmed for "Memento Mori" but cut, which dealt mostly with their sister Melissa and her death being caused by Dana's job with the FBI. The young actor who portrayed the boyhood Bill Jr. in the flashback snake-killing scene in "One Breath" was uncredited.*

Seaboard Air Airline Mulder used to transport federal prisoner John Lee Roche from Washington to Boston (Flight #1650). Without notifying Scully or Assistant Director Skinner, Mulder escorted the convicted serial killer back to his childhood home on Martha's Vineyard to test Roche's "memory" of Samantha Mulder's abduction. ("Paper Hearts")

Sears, Tessa (Shelley Owens) Allegedly a friend of missing teenager Ruby Morris, she secretly met with Mulder and Scully at the public library. Sears told the agents that Ruby had run away with her boyfriend, Greg Randall, who had gotten her pregnant. After Randall's body was discovered in a shallow grave, however, Sears confessed that she was the one pregnant by Randall and that she murdered him out of jealousy because of his involvement with Ruby. ("Conduit")

Secare, Dr. William (Simon Webb) A fugitive who fled from police by leaping into the Ardis, Maryland, harbor, leaving behind a trail of green blood. Dr. Secare had escaped from a government facility that was conducting human experiments with extraterrestrial viruses. ("The Erlenmeyer Flask")

Secona Ecuadorian Indian tribe that practiced ancient shamanistic rituals and protested to the U.S. State Department after a sacred Amaru urn was unearthed from the Ecuadorian highlands and shipped to Boston's Museum of Natural History. ("Teso dos Bichos")

Second Chance A Tom Clancy-esque spy novel written by the Cigarette-Smoking Man under the pen name of Raul Bloodworth. The Jack Colquitt action-adventure novel detailing alien assassinations was bought by Pivotal Publications in 1996 for serialization in one of their magazines, *Roman à Clef.* The incident was based on Lone Gunman Frohike's questionable version of the Cigarette-Smoking Man's life. ("Musings of a Cigarette-Smoking Man")

Sefer Yezirah, The Also known as the "Book of Creation," the earliest known Hebrew text on "man's mystical communion with the Divine." After the body of murdered Hasidic Jew Isaac Luria was exhumed by the racist teenagers who had killed him, Mulder and Scully discovered a leather-bound copy of *The Sefer Yezirah* tucked beneath his burial shroud. When Mulder touched the ancient text, it spontaneously combusted. Luria's betrothed, Ariel, had placed the book inside his coffin in her attempt to re-create her dead lover as a golem, which according to tradition could only be brought to life by the power of certain, secret letter combinations found in *The Sefer Yezirah.* ("Kaddish")

Seizer, Dr. (Paul Batten) Physician at the San Diego naval hospital who treated the horribly burned and irradiated crewmen of the French salvage ship, the *Piper Maru.* Dr. Seizer stated that such radiation levels didn't exist in nature, or as Mulder commented, "not on this planet." ("Piper Maru") *Actor Paul Batten also played the Kindred's Brother Wilson in "Genderbender."*

Senate Select Subcommittee on Intelligence and Terrorism. Body that convened a congressional hearing to investigate the mysterious death of a man found outside Assistant Director Skinner's high-rise apartment. Scully was jailed for contempt of Congress after refusing to provide Mulder's whereabouts, explaining to Skinner that someone with a secret agenda was deliberately obfuscating the case: focusing on a missing FBI agent, rather than the existence of a toxic biohazard of extraterrestrial origin and the deaths (such as of the man who fell from Skinner's balcony) of those connected to it. ("Tunguska/Terma")

Serios, Ted SEE: **thoughtography**

Seth County Morgue Dudley, Arkansas, temporary holding facility for the physical remains of Paula Gray, who suffered from the rare, noncommunicable Creutzfeldt-Jakob disease and was much younger than her birth records indicated. ("Our Town")

731 Referred to as Unit 731, a Japanese medical corps complement that conducted heinous experiments on humans, both civilians and prisoners of war (including American POWs), at a germ warfare research station in Manchuko (Japanese–occupied Manchuria). Mulder obtained a World War II photo picturing some of the slain Japanese scientists from the "alien autopsy" train car in Knoxville, Tennessee, who were part of the 731 unit decades earlier. ("Nisei/731")

☐ **"731 (Part 2 of 2)"** Written by Frank Spotnitz. Directed by Rob Bowman. File number 3X10. *First aired December 1, 1995. Mulder is trapped aboard a speeding, bomb-laden train with a government assassin and a mysterious quarantine subject who may or may not be a human/alien hybrid. Meanwhile, Scully's investigation of a secret West Virginia research facility leads to the discovery of massive graves filled with what appears to be the same type of mutants as the one incarcerated on the train with Mulder.* **Classic Sound Bite:** *"As an employee of the National Security Agency, you should know that a gunshot wound to the stomach is probably the most painful and slowest way to die. But I'm not a very good shot, and when I miss, I tend to miss low."* **Background Check:** *Episode writer Frank Spotnitz's inspiration for "731" was an article in* The New York Times *about Chinese war crimes and the exposure of prisoners of war to bacterial agents.*

☐ **"Shadows"** Written by Glen Morgan and James Wong. Directed by Michael Katleman. File number 1X05. *First aired October 22, 1993. The discovery of two terrorists' corpses in Philadelphia leads Mulder and Scully to a frightened young secretary whose boss has recently committed suicide. Further investigation involves the two FBI agents in a tangle of Middle Eastern religious extremism, a possible poltergeist and an ambiguous relationship between the forlorn secretary and her dead employer.* **Classic Sound Bite:** *"I would never lie. I willfully participated in a campaign of misinformation."* **Background Check:** *"Shadows" was written specifically for the Fox network, which had requested an episode about Mulder and Scully helping to save a "relatable character" from a ghost.*

Shadowy Syndicate Cabal of mysterious power-brokers who "predict the future, and the best way to predict the future is to invent it." A consortium representing "global interests," the group convenes periodically in a smoke-filled, private club on 46th Street in New York City where they control the conspiracy that continues to affect the lives of Mulder and Scully. The

Cigarette-Smoking Man is apparently the Shadowy Syndicate's "Washington associate," but he is obviously answerable to higher-ranking members such as the 1st Elder and the Well-Manicured Man, whom CSM deeply resents. The group has always handled the FBI "internally" (through the Cigarette-Smoking Man) and can sway, but not seemingly control, federal judges. They have links to other branches of the U.S. government, especially the CIA and the military, as well as a web of equally nefarious international cohorts. The Syndicate typically utilizes one of two methods to terminate an enemy: one or two men commit the murder with an unregistered weapon, which they leave at the scene (and with false documents immediately leave the country); or somebody the victim trusts kills him, at an unscheduled meeting. The Well-Manicured Man seems to think such killings unnecessary or, at least, that they have been poorly handled in the past by the Cigarette-Smoking Man and his lackeys (Alex Krycek and Luis Cardinal). From experiments seeking to create a human/alien hybrid immune to genetic warfare ("Anasazi/The Blessing Way/Paper Clip") to systematically suppressing evidence of the existence of extraterrestrials ("The Blessing Way/Paper Clip," "Apocrypha," and "Tunguska/Terma") to a joint colonization project with alien lifeforms seeking a new master race ("Talitha Cumi/Herrenvolk" and "Zero Sum"), the Shadowy Syndicate has been involved in all matter of malevolence since the end of World War II.

Shamrock Women's Prison Facility Correctional institution where former Aubrey, Missouri, police detective B.J. Morrow was incarcerated in a psychiatric cell after an attempted self-abortion. ("Aubrey")

Shannon, Dr. Theresa (Arlene Mazerolle) Physician at the Aesthetic Surgery Unit of Chicago's Greenwood Memorial Hospital. A colleague of devil-worshipping cosmetic surgeon Dr. Jack Franklyn, she was almost killed when he teleported several surgical instruments into her intestines. ("Sanguinarium")

📁 **"Shapes"** Written by Marilyn Osborn. Directed by David Nutter. File number 1X18. *First aired April 1, 1994. Montana rancher Jim Parker is only interested in the boundaries between his land and a neighboring Indian reservation until he shoots a wild animal and ends up with a naked Native American corpse— with fangs. Mulder and Scully's investigation leads them all the way back to the very first X-File on record, which also involved a werewolf.* **Classic Sound Bite:** *"They told me that even though my deodorant is made for a woman, it's strong enough for a man."* **Background Check:** *"Shapes" was written to satisfy the request of the network, which was demanding a traditional vampire or werewolf "monster show."*

shark fin An exotic Chinese medicinal described to Scully by San Francisco police detective Glen Chao. It was usually prepared in soup or a tea. ("Hell Money")

Sheherlis, Sarah (Susan Bain) Agent assigned to the FBI's Sci-Crime Lab. ("Grotesque") *Susan Bain also played a county coroner in "El Mundo Gira."*

"SHE IS ME" Words scrawled in blood at the scene of visionary encounters with the apparitions of a serial killer's young female victims moments after they died. Mentally-challenged Harold Spuller also anonymously phoned 911, claiming that one of the murdered women's last words were "She is me," even though her larynx had been severed, making it impossible for her to utter dying words. ("Elegy")

Sherman Crater Section of the active volcano at Washington State's Mount Avalon. ("Firewalker")

Shima-Tsuno, Mrs. (Marilyn Chin) Stockbroker Ed Jerse's supervisor at the Philadelphia investment firm of Fuller & Siegel. Mrs. Shima-Tsuno was forced to fire Jerse after he went into a rage and verbally assaulted two female co-workers conferencing in the office cubicle next to his. ("Never Again")

Shimizu, Matanaru One of four Japanese doctors murdered by gas-masked soldiers during an "alien autopsy" aboard an unmarked train car in Knoxville, Tennessee. ("Nisei") *The actor who played Shimizu was uncredited.*

Shove Park The wooded region near Minneapolis where psychic Clyde Bruckman led Mulder and Scully in search of the body of Claude Dukenfield, another victim of the Puppet serial killer. ("Clyde Bruckman's Final Repose") *Eagle-eye viewers will easily recognize the clearing in the forest as the same one surrounding Iowa's Lake Okobogee from the "Conduit" episode.*

Sidney SEE: **Ephesian, Melissa Riedal**

Sierra Pacific Railroad The railway company that at one time operated the train refrigeration car that teenager Eric Hosteen discovered buried in a New Mexico quarry. Mulder found what appeared to be alien corpses stacked to the ceiling of the boxcar. ("Anasazi")

silicon-base lifeform A previously unknown subterranean organism discovered alive inside the active Mt. Avalon volcano in Washington State. The volcanic-exploration robot, Firewalker, brought the new lifeform to the surface from deep within the Earth's core, where it proceeded to fatally infect the research team. After Mulder and Scully were rescued and quarantined, the military confiscated all specimens and field notes, and sealed off access to Mount Avalon. ("Firewalker")

Silver Streak The name of the boat Jeremiah Smith and Mulder used to make their escape from the alien Bounty Hunter after their confrontation with the relentless extraterrestrial on Bond Mill Road. ("Herrenvolk")

Simmons, Claudia The deceased mother of eight-year-old Teena Simmons. Claudia died of ovarian cancer in 1991. ("Eve")

Simmons, Jennifer A young Minneapolis woman with long, blond hair who had recently died. Mortuary worker and death fetishist Donnie Pfaster was fired by the Janelli-Heller Funeral Home director for cutting off locks of hair from her corpse. ("Irresistible")

Simmons, Joel Father of eight-year-old Teena Simmons. An FBI autopsy report stated that his death was caused by hypovolemia after seventy-five percent of his blood was drained from his body. Mulder noted that the wounds and blood-removal resembled those of "alien" cattle mutilation. Teena, speaking in a strangely adult manner, told Mulder and Scully that "men from the clouds" came for her father and "wanted to exsanguinate him." ("Eve")

Simmons, Scott (Russell Porter). A basketball player at Grover Cleveland Alexander High School in the small town of Comity. The blond duo of Terri Roberts and Margi Kleinjan were responsible for the violent deaths of Simmons and his girlfriend, Brenda. ("Syzygy")

Simmons, Teena (Sabrina Krievins) Eight-year-old Greenwich, Connecticut, girl who led Mulder to believe that aliens had been somehow involved in her father's murder. In actuality the little girl had committed the brutal crime herself. Dr. Sally Kendrick, a specialist in biogenetics, had cloned herself to produce Teena, but was later poisoned by the psychotic child. Teena was captured by Mulder and Scully and incarcerated in the Whiting Institute for the Criminally Insane. ("Eve")

Simpson, Homer Yellow-skinned and slow-witted popular prime-time cartoon character. When the black ops unit burst into The Thinker's apartment looking for the stolen MJ documents, the screen-saver on the Lone Gunman's computer displayed Homer Simpson mowing the lawn of his Springfield, Illinois, home ("Anasazi"). After the young boys at the Linley temporary shelter described Kevin Kryder's strange-looking abductor, Mulder commented that the kidnapper (Owen Jarvis) apparently looked like "Homer Simpson's evil twin." ("Revelations")

Sinclair, Sparky Trenton, New Jersey, landfill worker who discovered the corpse of Kenneth J. Soona, a.k.a. The Thinker, the Lone Gunman hacker who stole the top secret MJ files and gave Mulder a DAT copy. ("The Blessing Way")

Sioux City Public Library Where Mulder and Scully secretly met Tessa Sears, who was supposedly a friend of missing teenager Ruby Morris. Sears provided the agents with misinformation about Morris' mysterious disappearance. ("Conduit")

Sistrunk, Rev. Calvin (Linden Banks) Scranton, Pennsylvania, antiabortion activist who was arrested for the arson murder of Dr. Landon Prince. Sistrunk denied involvement, despite being arrested with a newspaper clipping of the doctor's photo in a classified ad: "Have you seen this man?" The right-wing fundamentalist was subsequently released after providing an alibi. ("Colony") *Linden Banks also portrayed Joseph Patrick in "Wetwired."*

Skinner, Sharon (Jennifer Hetrick) Wife of Assistant Director Walter Skinner. Following seventeen years of marriage she filed for divorce because her husband had built emotional barriers to keep everyone out of his life. After he was framed for the murder of a prostitute, Sharon visited her husband at his apartment and shortly thereafter she was forced off the road and seriously injured by someone driving his car. Mulder requested that FBI lab technicians analyze the vehicle's airbag, which revealed the face of the actual assailant. After Sharon recovered from a coma, her husband took a leave of absence from the FBI to spend time with her. ("Avatar") *Jennifer Hetrick played Capt. Picard's love interest, Vash, on* Star Trek: The Next Generation.

Skinner, Walter Sergei (Mitch Pileggi) Assistant FBI Director and Mulder and Scully's stern and demanding immediate supervisor. A by-the-book ex-Marine, Skinner has little patience with Mulder's unconventional investigative methods and irreverent manner, which constantly puts them at odds. Repeatedly he has warned Mulder and Scully that their inquiries were crossing into dangerous areas, and once shut down the X-Files unit on "orders from above" ("Little Green Men") After Agent Alex Krycek disappeared in the wake of the Duane Barry incident and the disappearance of Scully, Skinner was angry enough to defy his superiors and reinstate the X-Files section on his own authority. "That's what they fear most," he told Mulder without clarifying who *they* were ("Ascension"). The assistant director also gets frequent visits from the enigmatic Cigarette-Smoking Man, but the true nature of their relationship is equivocal at best. It's never clear whether Skinner is on the side of truth or conspiracy, or whose orders he takes, but his efforts on behalf of Mulder and Scully "through unofficial channels" demonstrate that he is truly concerned about his independent X-Files agents and their investigations ("End Game"). Obviously, Skinner walks a fine line between supporting Mulder and obeying the people who want the unorthodox agent out of the way permanently. After Scully was discovered in a Georgetown hospital in a coma, a guilt-ridden Mulder tendered his resignation, but Skinner rejected it as "unacceptable" and related a grim story about an out-of-body experience he had during his tour of duty in Vietnam: "I am afraid to look beyond that experience, Agent Mulder. You . . . you are not" ("One Breath"). The Assistant Director found his patience pushed to the extreme, however, after Mulder physically attacked him, not realizing that Mulder had been poisoned by the shadowy forces out to discredit or destroy him ("Anasazi"). Skinner covertly assisted Scully by taking the encyrpted DAT containing the stolen MJ files into his own custody, while publicly joining in the FBI's official censure of her for "direct disobedience" ("The Blessing Way"). Skinner refused to surrender the digital tape to the Cigarette-Smoking Man after Mulder returned from his own near-death experience in the New Mexico desert, but Alex Krycek and his accomplices ambushed the Assistant Director in a hospital stairwell and confiscated it. The Cigarette-Smoking Man later met with Skinner in his office, telling him that the tape was missing and that his own life may be in jeopardy. "This is where you pucker up and kiss my ass," Skinner snapped back, saying that Navajo code-talker Albert Hosteen had memorized the tape's contents and related it to twenty other men in his tribe's narrative tradition ("Paper Clip"). Five months later, Skinner appealed the Bureau decision to classify the investigation into Melissa Scully's murder "inactive," only to be shot himself by Shadowy Syndicate assassin Luis Cardinal (who had also participated in the death of Scully's sister) while eating lunch in his favorite coffee shop ("Piper Maru"). After recovering from his injuries, Skinner was framed for the murder of a prostitute and the attempted murder of his estranged wife, Sharon, by the same conspirators who had attempted to have him killed a few months earlier. Mulder theorized that Skinner's dismissal from the Bureau was an organized effort to put the two X-Files agents "in check . . . You remove Skinner and you weaken us." With Mulder and Scully's investigative assistance, Skinner was cleared and took a leave of absence from the FBI to spend some time with his recuperating wife and try to put his marriage back together ("Avatar"). After Scully was diagnosed with inoperable brain cancer, Mulder approached Skinner and attempted to arrange a meeting with the Cigarette-Smoking Man. But the Assistant Director refused, insisting that CSM only dealt in lies. Nonetheless, Skinner secretly enlisted the Cigarette-Smoking Man's help on his own in an effort to have Scully cured ("Memento Mori"). As part of his "deal with the Devil," Skinner obstructed justice and covered up the murderous attack of a smallpox-carrying swarm of bees. To insure his participation, a Virginia police detective was shot to death with Skinner's stolen gun. Skinner, angry at being framed and increasingly uncomfortable with his actions as dictated by the Cigarette-Smoking Man, confronted the nefarious operative with a pointed gun. After CSM alluded to the fact that only he could save Scully's life, Skinner backed down and fired several close shots over the Cigarette-Smoking Man's shoulder into the wall, leaving him visibly shaken ("Zero Sum"). *Mitch Pileggi, the actor who portrays Walter Skinner, has stated in several interviews that he based his stern, but caring, character on his father, Vito, an operations manager for a Defense Department contractor, who died shortly after* The X-Files *premiere. Pileggi's acting resume includes the television shows* China Beach, Doctor Doctor, Hooperman, *and* Alien Nation. *He also appeared in the theatrical films* Vampire in Brooklyn, Dangerous Touch, Basic Instinct, Guilty as Charged,

Brothers in Arms, Shocker, Return of the Living Dead: Part II, Three O'Clock High, Death Wish 4: The Crackdown, *and* Mongrel.

Skip The name of the previous delivery-person on Donnie Pfaster's Ficiecello Frozen Foods route. ("Irresistible")

skullcap root An exotic Chinese medicinal described to Scully by San Francisco police detective Glen Chao. It is considered to be an excellent tonic for the nervous system, which makes it good for insomnia. ("Hell Money")

Skyland Grill The restaurant (closed for the summer) located high atop Skyland Mountain, Virginia, where Mulder interrogated Duane Barry about the whereabouts of Scully. Mulder, losing control, started to choke the escaped mental patient, then walked out of the room to calm down. He returned to find Alex Krycek with the prisoner, and moments later Barry died, allegedly from asphyxiation, but Mulder suspected he was poisoned. ("Ascension")

Skyland Mountain A tourist attraction near Rixeyville, Virginia, off the Blue Ridge Parkway, whose prophetic advertising slogan was "Ascend to the Stars." At the mountain, Mulder took an aerial tram hoping to beat Duane Barry to the summit, but his new partner Alex Krycek killed the operator, stranding Mulder, who wriggled out of the tram and took off on foot. Reaching the mountaintop, Mulder found Barry's car empty except for a necklace that belonged to the kidnapped Scully. Under questioning, Barry insisted that he traded Scully to "them," referring to the shadowy MIBs standing in the hallway. ("Ascension")

Skywalker, Luke The legendary *Star Wars* Jedi Knight whose incredible adventures were chronicled in the classic swashbuckling space opera. Single mother and *Star Wars* fan Amanda Nelligan told Mulder and Scully that the father of her newborn was Luke Skywalker. In reality, Nelligan was unknowingly impregnated by shapeshifter Eddie Van Blundht. ("Small Potatoes")

Slash Killer, The Serial killer in 1940s Aubrey, Missouri, who raped and razored the word SISTER into the chests of three female victims, ranging in ages from twenty-five to thirty. Although The Slash Killer was never officially caught, the murders stopped after Harry Cokely was convicted of the rape and attempted murder of a woman in 1945. ("Aubrey")

Slaughter, Dr. Ruth (Meredith Bain-Woodward) U.S. Navy pathologist who performed an autopsy on Duane Barry and showed Mulder evidence of his asphyxiation. She refused, however, to provide the agent toxicological results unless he went through military channels. Quantico, Dr. Slaughter explained, was under military jurisdiction and there "wasn't an FBI patholo-gist available this morning." Her report did not address Mulder's suspicion that Barry was poisoned by Alex Krycek and that the results were being covered up by the military. ("Ascension") *Meredith Bain-Woodward also played Robert Modell's defense attorney in "Pusher."*

📁 **"Sleepless"** Written by Howard Gordon. Directed by Rob Bowman. File number 2X04. *First aired October 7, 1994. While investigating a series of bizarre deaths, Agent Mulder and his new partner, Alex Krycek, discover evidence of a covert military-controlled "sleep eradication" experiment to create the perfect soldier, but with deadly and unexpected side effects.* **Classic Sound Bite:** *"The truth is still out there. But it's never been more dangerous."* **Background Check:** *With the deadline for actual filming quickly approaching, a panic-stricken episode writer, Howard Gordon, couldn't sleep for three nights and came up with the idea, "What if somebody hadn't slept in twenty-five years?" In twenty-four hours Gordon hammered out the complete script.*

"Sleepy Fox" Native American name suggested to Mulder by Ish. The FBI agent was agreeable as long as it wasn't "Spooky Fox," a reference to the disparaging nickname Mulder earned at the FBI Academy because of his belief in the paranormal. ("Shapes")

📁 **"Small Potatoes"** Written by Vince Gilligan. Directed by Clifford Bole. File number 4X20. *First aired April 20, 1997. After five women give birth to babies with four-inch tails, Mulder and Scully discover that the newborns' father is a shapeshifter possessing the ability to change into anyone's image.* **Classic Sound Bite:** *"Did he have a lightsaber?"* **Background Check:** *"Small Potatoes" was the first episode directed by Clifford Bole, another alumnus of* Star Trek: The Next Generation, *along with* X-Files *producers, writers, and directors Rob Bowman, Kim Manners, and R.W. Goodwin, among others.*

Smallpox Eradication Project (SEP). Successful World Health Organiza-tion program which led to the worldwide eradication of the contagious disease through the standardized vaccination of hundreds of millions of people. Under the guise of the vaccination program, Operation Paper Clip retrieved DNA samples from every human born after 1954 and injected them with a minute DNA tag. Each "donor" received a Smallpox Eradication Project (SEP) number for cataloguing purposes, ostensibly for post-apocalyptic identification, the details of which were stored in the Social Security computer system ("Paper Clip"). Alien shapeshifter Jeremiah Smith, one of many duplicate extraterrestrials working in the Social Security Administration's regional offices, was assigned to track the Paper Clip subjects using their SEP numbers. ("Talitha Cumi")

Smirnoff, Yakov. Russian immigrant whom Mulder suspected of possessing valuable UFO information. He asked that Scully confirm Smirnoff's identity by conducting an INS and criminal background check and conduct surveillance of Smirnoff and his compatriots while in Philadelphia. ("Never Again"). *The character's name was a joking reference to the popular Russian comedian and occasional television and movie actor.*

Smith, Detective (Ian Robison) Plainclothes Philadelphia police detective who, along with his partner, questioned Scully as to the whereabouts of Ed Jerse, the man in whose apartment she had spent the previous night. The detectives revealed that Jerse's downstairs neighbor was missing, and that a blood type different from her own was found inside the apartment. When they learned that she was a doctor, the two policemen also showed Scully a breakdown of the chemical abnormalities that were discovered in the blood samples. ("Never Again")

Smith, Jeremiah (Roy Thinnes) Shapeshifting alien clone who displayed miraculous healing powers after a shoot-out at a Virginia fast-food restaurant. The messianic Smith, who seemingly changed his appearance in the blink of an eye and disappeared from the crime scene, was quietly captured by the Cigarette-Smoking Man's henchmen at a regional Social Security Administration building and confined in a prison cell for interrogation. CSM challenged Smith's loyalty to "the greater purpose" of The Project, asking the extraterrestrial if he realized the consequences of his actions. Startling CSM, the alien clone morphed into the likeness of Deep Throat and William Mulder, and asked how many must die "to preserve" the Cigarette-Smoking Man's "stake in The Project." Smith then told CSM that he was dying of lung cancer, prompting the nefarious chain-smoker to allow Smith to heal him and escape before the murderous alien Bounty Hunter arrived ("Talitha Cumi"). Mulder and Smith were pursued to a farm in Alberta, Canada, an apparent nursery for drones—both bees and mute child clones—where the extraterrestrial showed Mulder genetic replicas of his sister, Samantha. Meanwhile, Scully discovered that there were several identical clones all named Jeremiah Smith and that the real purpose of their work at regional Social Security Administration offices throughout the country was to catalogue millions of people using their Smallpox Eradication Project (SEP) numbers. After the relentless alien Bounty Hunter arrived at the farm in Alberta, he terminated Smith ("Herrenvolk"). *Ironically, actor Roy Thinnes was the star of the short-lived 1967–68 UFO/conspiracy series* The Invaders, *which Chris Carter has acknowledged as an inspiration for* The X-Files.

snake An exotic Chinese medicinal described to Scully by San Francisco police detective Glen Chao. It was usually prepared in soup or a tea. ("Hell Money")

Snorkel Dude (Terrance Leigh) Diver who was suddenly struck and pulled under the water by a mysterious creature residing in Heuvelman's Lake, while drug-abusing teenagers Stoner and Chick watched dumbfounded from the dock. After blood filled the water, Snorkel Dude's head bobbed slowly to the surface. According to Scully, the mutilation death could be attributed to a boat propeller. ("Quagmire")

Soames, Ray Twenty-year-old schizophrenic who was the third victim of the mysterious killer in Bellefleur, Oregon. Soames had confessed to the first two youth murders and was confined to a mental hospital, but then went missing for seven hours one day, and died of exposure although it was the middle of July. Mulder and Scully exhumed Soames' body, only to discover a non-human, almost simian dwarf-like carcass inside the coffin with a small, gray, metallic device lodged in its nasal cavity. ("The X-Files: Pilot") *Observant X-Philes will notice that in the second season episode "Irresistible" Ray Soames' headstone appears in the Montifiore Cemetery in Minneapolis where Mulder, Scully and Agent Bocks examine the mutilated corpse of Catherine Terle.*

Social Security Administration Government agency where six Jeremiah Smith alien clones were employed as clerks in regional satellite offices. Scully discovered that the shapeshifting Smiths had used the agency's computer system to collect data on millions of people tagged with genetic markers through smallpox vaccinations. ("Talitha Cumi")

📁 **"Soft Light"** Written by Vince Gilligan. Directed by James Contner. File number 2X23. *First aired May 5, 1995. An investigation into a series of disappearances in which the only clues are burn marks on the ground leads Mulder and Scully to a physicist who has been transformed into a human black hole because of his bungled experimentation with dark matter.* **Classic Sound Bite:** *"As a favor, we just handed over an A-bomb to the Boy Scouts."* **Background Check:** *Writer Vince Gilligan's original idea for the episode focused on an entirely different kind of shadow: Dr. Banton's girlfriend, who was "zapped into oblivion" during a linear accelerator accident and ended up living in Banton's shadow and feeding on human flesh.*

Son, The (Frank Military) One of the vampiric serial Trinity Killers (real name: John) who firmly believed that he would live forever so long as he continued to drink human blood. After Mulder arrested the violent sociopath at the Hollywood Blood Bank (where he was employed as a security guard), the agent left him in an open cell hoping that fear of sunlight would frighten him enough to supply the real names of "The Father" and "The Unholy Spirit." Although Mulder assumed the suspect's beliefs were delusional, The Son shriveled up and died horribly from severe epidermal burns. He returned from the dead, however, to rejoin his Trinity compatriots, but was finally destroyed when Kristen Kilar drenched the house with gasoline and set it ablaze. ("3")

Soona, Kenneth J. SEE: **Thinker, The**

Sophie (Jody St. Michael) Lowland gorilla at the impoverished Fairfield, Idaho, Zoo. Naturalist Willa Ambrose had rescued Sophie from black market smugglers ten years earlier and raised the ape herself, teaching her American Sign Language. The gorilla was capable of "speaking" six hundred words and understanding a thousand. After Ambrose was successfully sued by the Malawi government for Sophie's return, she arranged to have the gorilla kidnapped before she was shipped back to her homeland. When Mulder was locked in a room with the panic-stricken ape, she charged him. Dazed, he saw Sophie disappear in a blinding bright light, evidently the target of alien conservationists who wanted to harvest her embryo. Sophie reappeared miles away and was killed by a car. ("Fearful Symmetry") *Mime Jody St. Michael, hidden under a great deal of special-effects makeup in this episode, previously played a simian in the film* Gorillas in the Mist.

Sorenson, Sen. Albert (Fritz Weaver) Member of the Senate Select Subcommittee on Intelligence and Terrorism. When Scully offered to provide evidence of a wide-ranging conspiracy to control a lethal biotoxin that was, in fact, extraterrestrial in origin, the subcommittee hearing was abruptly adjourned. Mulder and Scully's investigative report and collaborating evidence were delivered to Sorenson who, in turn, gave the incriminating documents to the Cigarette-Smoking Man. ("Tunguska/Terma")*Fritz Weaver has appeared in numerous TV shows and motion pictures for over forty years, including the original* Twilight Zone, *mini-series such as Ray Bradbury's* The Martian Chronicles, *and theatrical movies such as* Creepshow, Black Sunday, Marathon Man, Demon Seed, *and* Fail-Safe.

Southern Crescent Designation of the NATO surveillance-station in Hakkari, Turkey. ("E.B.E.")

Southern Serpent, The SEE: **Big Blue**

🗁 **"Space"** Written by Chris Carter. Directed by William Graham. File number 1X08. *First aired November 12, 1993. When NASA's latest space shuttle launch is beset by numerous minor acts of sabotage, mechanical failures and irregularities, the finger of suspicion points to Lt. Colonel Marcus Belt, supervisor of the shuttle program and a former astronaut possessed by a spirit-like alien entity.* **Classic Sound Bite:** *"You make the front page today only if you screw up."* **Background Check:** *After the series had exceeded its budget on some of the first season's earlier episodes, "Space" was designed to be inexpensive by utilizing actual NASA footage. The construction of the Mission Control set, however, made the show the most expensive episode of the first season and, unfortunately, one of the least-liked by Chris Carter and the fans.*

Sparks, Addie Little girl kidnapped from her Pennsylvania home in 1975 by serial child killer John Lee Roche. A vivid dream directed Mulder to her shallow grave in a Manassas, Virginia, city park. Scully was able to identify the remains from data records maintained by the Center for Missing and Exploited Children. ("Paper Hearts")

Sparks, Robert (Byrne Piven) Father of murder victim Addie Sparks. Mulder and Scully visited the bearded widower at his home in Norristown, Pennsylvania, to get a positive identification of a pocket from the nightclothes found on a recently unearthed child's skeleton. A teary-eyed Mr. Sparks confirmed that the pocket, with its distinctive dollar sign, was where he used to place a quarter whenever it was time for the Tooth Fairy to make an appearance. ("Paper Hearts")

Sparks, Wendy According to Cleveland, Ohio, detective Cross, she was the police department's liaison with the FBI. ("2Shy")

Spencer Jehovah's Witness who accompanied Hannah when she knocked on Ed Jerse's apartment door. They hurried away after the hallucinatory man began ranting and raving about his downstairs neighbor. ("Never Again") *The actor who portrayed Spencer was uncredited.*

Spencer, Jim (John Cygan) Venago County sheriff who told Mulder that the small farming community of Franklin, Pennsylvania, had suddenly turned violent and dangerous, with twenty-two murders committed by seven different people in six months. The town had previously reported only three homicides "since colonial times." ("Blood")

Speranza, John (John Toles-Bay) A death-row inmate at Florida's Eastpoint State Penitentiary. He was convinced that executed prisoner Napoleon "Neech" Manley had made good on his promise to return from the dead and kill five people who had wronged him. ("The List") *John Toles-Bay wrote the screenplay for the film* A Rage in Harlem, *which featured a performance by Badja Djola, the actor who portrayed Neech Manley in this episode.*

Spiller, Nancy (Gillian Barber) FBI Academy forensics instructor, secretly nicknamed "The Iron Maiden" by her students. Special Agent Spiller was in charge of the investigation into the electrocution death of Eurisko CEO Benjamin Drake, a friend of the U.S. Attorney General. ("Ghost in the Machine") *Gillian Barber portrayed Beth Kane in "Red Museum" and Penny Northern in "Nisei" and "Memento Mori."*

Spinney, Doug (Titus Welliver) Eco-terrorist who warned Mulder and Scully of a swarm that came out at night and devoured people alive in a remote Pacific Northwest forest where loggers were mysteriously disappearing. Spinney was engulfed and killed by the swarm of prehistoric mites, which entered his Jeep through the air vents. ("Darkness Falls")

"Spirit is the Truth, The" Scripture (I John 5:07) that Dana Scully's mother, Margaret, had engraved on her daughter's headstone after she was abducted and believed dead. ("One Breath")

Spitz, Bob (Garry Davey) The principal at Grover Cleveland Alexander High School in the small town of Comity. He interrupted the funeral service of murdered student Jay "Boom" DeBoom, ranting and raving about satanism. ("Syzygy") *Garry Davey also played Hunter in "Eve," Dr. Keats in "Roland," and a ship captain in "End Game."*

Spitz, Dr. Joel (Leslie Carlson) A regression hypnotherapist whose treatment of eight-year-old Michelle Bishop convinced Mulder that the girl was the reincarnated spirit of a murdered policeman. ("Born Again")

Spitz, Dr. Joel Listed as one of the "doctors on call" at the Lombard Research Facility when Mulder and the Lone Gunmen infiltrated the building in hopes of discovering the origin of Scully's inoperable cancer. ("Memento Mori")

spontaneous human combustion The sudden, virtual destruction of a human body by fire, apparently from the inside out and leaving the victim's surroundings left untouched. Mulder originally considered spontaneous human combustion a possibility when a strange blotch (possibly residue from burnt flesh) was discovered on the carpet of missing businessman Peter Newirth's hotel room ("Soft Light"). Mulder, who was afraid of fire and had never previously encountered spontaneous human combustion, was finally able to witness not just one instance but two, when a young Jason Nichols fought with his time-traveling older self from the future. ("Synchrony")

"Spooky" Derisive nickname given to Mulder by fellow students at the FBI Academy because of his unusual beliefs in the paranormal and extraterrestrials ("The X-Files: Pilot"). After Mulder covertly journeyed to Puerto Rico to a possible alien contact site, Scully attempted to determine his whereabouts by gaining access to his personal computer, at first unsuccessfully trying the password "Spooky." ("Little Green Men")

"Spooky Fox" The only Indian name Mulder didn't want tribal elder Ish to call him, a reference to the disparaging nickname the agent earned at the FBI Academy. ("Shapes")

spree killing A type of murder perpetrated in public in which the killer has a total and complete indifference to personal safety or anonymity. A number of spree killings were committed in the small suburban farming community of Franklin, Pennsylvania, at the instigation of mysterious digital readouts in appliances. ("Blood")

Spuller, Harold (Steven M. Porter) Voluntary resident at the New Horizon Psychiatric Center in Washington, D.C. The autistic Spuller worked at Angie's Midnight Bowl, which was near the scene of several serial killings of young, blond women. After a fourth victim was discovered, Mulder found Spuller holed-up in a dimly-lit cubicle accessible from the bowling alley, the walls of which were covered with hundreds of score sheets and thousands of names, including those of the victims. Mulder then realized that Spuller had met each of the murdered women at the bowling alley. What he didn't know was that Spuller had repeatedly encountered the ghosts of the murdered young women and "just wanted to be left alone." Although Spuller was the chief suspect in the brutal murders, Mulder and Scully later discovered that the actual serial killer was Innes, a drug-addled registered nurse on staff at New Horizon Psychiatric Center. After Innes was apprehended, Spuller was found face-down in an alley only a few blocks from the mental hospital, dead from respiratory failure. A few moments later, Scully saw Spuller's apparition in the rearview mirror of her car. ("Elegy")

📁 **"Squeeze"** Written by Glen Morgan and James Wong. Directed by Harry Longsteet. File number 1X02. *First aired September 24, 1993. A Baltimore murder is hauntingly similar to a number of unsolved cannibalistic crimes that took place in 1903, 1933 and 1963. The search leads Agents Mulder and Scully to Eugene Victor Tooms, an immortal mutant who can stretch and flatten his body and awakes from hibernation every thirty years with an unsavory taste for human livers.* **Classic Sound Bite:** *"Is there any way I can get it off my fingers quickly without betraying my cool exterior?"* **Background Check:** *Doug Hutchison, the actor who played the monosyllabic liver-eating Tooms, has stated in interviews that he was inspired by Anthony Hopkins' performance as Hannibal Lecter in* Silence of the Lambs, *"because he had a grasp on stillness in that film which was incredibly powerful."*

"SRSG" Initials that the dying Mr. X wrote in his own blood, leading Mulder to the U.N.'s Special Representative to the Secretary General, and his new, enigmatic ally, Maria Covarrubias, the Special Representative's assistant. ("Herrenvolk")

Stans, Lt. Col. Victor (Don Thompson) Gulf War veteran and psychiatric patient at the military hospital in Ft. Evanston, Maryland, where he attempted suicide three times in three weeks. He told a staff physician that a phantom soldier wouldn't let him die. Left alone, Stans went to the hydrotherapy room, where, holding weights, he leapt into a scalding whirlpool bath. An alarm went off and a manually bolted door mysteriously opened, allowing

Stans to be saved despite being horribly burned. Stans told Mulder and Scully that the phantom figure had murdered his wife and children three months earlier and continued to torment him. The disfigured Stans later suffocated quadraplegic Leonard "Rappo" Trimble, an unspeakably evil veteran who was able to project his spirit out of his body and become the murderous "phantom soldier." ("The Walk") *Don Thompson also played NSA agent Holtzman in "Conduit" and war veteran Henry Willig in "Sleepless."*

Starbuck Navy Captain William Scully's pet name for his daughter Dana, in honor of Capt. Ahab's able lieutenant in Herman Melville's seafaring classic *Moby Dick*. ("Beyond the Sea")

Stay 'n Save Motor Inn Motel in Sioux City, Iowa, where Mulder and Scully stayed while investigating the possible alien abduction of teenager Ruby Morris. ("Conduit")

Stealth Man SEE: **Camouflage Man**

Steen, Dr. Larry (Robert Thurston) Mycology professor at California State University in Fresno who isolated an enzyme that made a common fungal infection grow at an alarming and fatal rate. It was his opinion that if the carrier, an illegal Mexican immigrant named Eladio Buente, was not quarantined and the highly contagious pathogen was allowed to escape into the environment, there would be a biological hazard of disastrous proportions. Dr. Steen was a member of the hazmat team that established a perimeter containing the lethal lichen within the area surrounding the San Joaquin Valley migrant workers' camp. ("El Mundo Gira") *Robert Thurston also played Jackson Towes, the funeral home supervisor who fired Donnie Pfaster in "Irresistible."*

Steffan, Gen. Jon (William Nunn) A high-ranking military officer who was gunned down in his Pentagon office by Nathaniel Teager, a seemingly invisible assassin. Teager, who had been declared killed in action, returned home to carry out death sentences against the men he perceived had abandoned him in a Vietnamese prison camp for twenty-five years. Gen. Steffan was one of the officials who had signed Teager's death certificate. ("Unrequited")

Steffan, Joanne (Jo) (Kerry Sandomirsky) Friend and neighbor of Ellen Kaminsky who dissuaded her from going out on a date with "Timid" after Mulder and Scully issued a localized Internet warning. "Timid" was the online handle for serial killer Virgil Incanto. ("2Shy") *Kerry Sandomirsky also played Tracy Rosen in "Roland."*

Stefoff, Val Name on the phony "Level 5" security pass used by Scully to gain entrance to a government facility that was apparently holding an E.B.E. (extraterrestrial biological entity). The fake credentials were courtesy of the

Lone Gunmen. ("E.B.E.") *The name on Scully's bogus security pass was an in-joke aimed at Vladimir Stefoff, a frequent second assistant director on* The X-Files.

Steinberg One of the agents assigned by Bruskin to canvass the three square miles around Washington County Regional Airport in an effort to find the kidnapped Scully. ("Lazarus")

stereotypy Stress-related syndrome from which Scully theorized former military test pilot Jim McLennen was suffering. ("Deep Throat")

Steve (John Tench) One of two escaped prisoners from Cumberland State Correctional Facility in Virginia. The convicted murderers hijacked a vacationing family's motor home in an attempt to flee the area, killing the father in the process. Steve inadvertently infected Elizabeth, the girlfriend of his fellow escapee, before he died from the plaguelike *F. emasculata* contagion. ("F. Emasculata")

Stevens, Jerry (Franky Czinege) One of four Crowley High School students who unintentionally summoned the demon Azazel to the small New Hampshire town of Milford Haven. Stevens' mutilated corpse was later found in the woods with the eyes and heart cut out. ("Die Hand Die Verletzt") *Per episode dialogue this character was called Jerry Stevens, but end-credits listed him as "Jerry Thomas." He was named after Jerry Jones, a.k.a. "FoxxMulder," co-host of the AOL* X-Files *forum.*

stigmata The spontaneous appearance of wounds similar to those inflicted upon Jesus Christ on the cross. Wounds of this sort were first described by St. Francis of Assisi in the year 1224 after a seraph appeared to him in a vision. Since then the devout of the Catholic church in particular have regarded their appearance as an outward sign of saintliness. To this date, approximately 300 cases have been recorded, including Italian priest Padre Pio, who reportedly suffered stigmata on his hands, feet and chest for over fifty years. Ten-year-old Kevin Kryder was considered a genuine stigmatic and was stalked by demonic industrialist Simon "Millennium Man" Gates, who wanted to sacrifice the boy "for the New Age to come." According to Catholic tradition, there are twelve true stigmatics in the world at any one time, representing Christ's original twelve apostles. ("Revelations")

Stodie, Mrs. (Micole Mercurio) Director of the Colson, Washington, Heritage Halfway House for the mentally challenged, where Roland Fuller resided. ("Roland")

Stoner (Alan Buckley) Drug-abusing teenager who, along with his friend Chick, witnessed Dude hack himself to death with a razor blade during a cockroach attack in Miller's Grove, Massachusetts ("War of the

Coprophages"). While hanging out on the Heuvelman's Lake dock in the Blue Ridge Mountains of Georgia, Stoner and Chick saw a diver in snorkel gear suddenly pulled underwater and mutilated by a mysterious lake creature. Stoner was searching for a certain type of frog that produced a hallucinogen that could be licked off the amphibian's back ("Quagmire")

Stratego Board game Mulder and his sister Samantha were about to play when she disappeared in November 1973 ("Little Green Men," "Paper Hearts" and "Demons"). When a grown "Samantha" inexplicably returned to the Mulder home on Martha's Vineyard, she jokingly asked her brother if he wanted to play the game of Stratego they were about to start twenty-two years earlier. ("Colony")

Strautcher Publishing Publisher of *Poeti Italiani Del Novecento,* a book of obscure sixteenth-century Italian poems, sent via the FedEx-like Transcontinental Express to fat–sucking vampire Virgil Incanto. ("2Shy")

Stress Man (David Bloom) Dark-suited courier for the Shadowy Syndicate traveling on a U.S. diplomatic visa. While returning to the United States from the Republic of Georgia, he was detained by U.S. Customs officials at the Honolulu Airport, ostensibly for a "random check" of his personal property. Although Stress Man contested that the purpose of his trip was "government business," he was subjected to a strip and full body search after refusing to provide the combination to his briefcase. When a Customs agent forced it open, Stress Man warned him not to open the two enclosed canisters because they contained biohazardous material. Nevertheless, the official ignored his admonition and then carelessly dropped one of the cylinders, leading to an attack by a black oil that congealed into small, leech-like worms. ("Tunguska")

Stroman, Dr. Henry (Colin Cunningham) Washington, D.C. psychiatrist allegedly appointed by the court to diagnose Joseph Patnick, who murdered five people believing that he was slaying the same Bosnian war criminal over and over again. Mulder discovered that Dr. Stroman was an active participant in a conspiracy involving mind control through television signals that was responsible for a series of murders in the small town. Dr. Stroman was shot to death by Mr. X, evidently on orders from the Cigarette-Smoking Man. It was later learned that the real Dr. Henry Stroman died in 1978 in Falls Church, Virginia. *Colin Cunningham also played the leper Escalante in "731" and Lt. Wilmer in "End Game."*

Strughold Mining Company Abandoned coal mining facility in West Virginia where Mulder and Scully found an incongruous set of security doors with numeric-keypad locks. When they punched in the first five digits of Napier's Constant (a clue given to them by former Nazi Victor Klemper), the doors opened. Inside were countless rows of file cabinets containing medical files, including one for Scully and another for Mulder's missing sister, Samantha; Mulder noticed that her name had been pasted over his own. Diminutive aliens inhabited some areas of the massive underground facility, but may have been evacuated by a majestic spacecraft sighted by Mulder. ("Paper Clip")

succubus A youthful and seductive female demon that offers infernal sexual pleasures to human males during their sleep, sometimes killing other women out of jealousy. Mulder theorized that Assistant Director Skinner's recurring dream of an old, hag-like woman was in reality a succubus. ("Avatar")

Sullivan, Judge One of three Maryland state judicial officials presiding over Eugene Tooms' commitment review and sanity hearing. ("Tooms") *The actor who portrayed Judge Sullivan was uncredited.*

Summerfield, Brenda Jaycee (Gabrielle Miller) A student at Grover Cleveland Alexander High School in Comity and the girlfriend of basketball player Scott Simmons. At a birthday party for Terri Roberts and Margi Kleinjan, Brenda asked a Ouija board who she was going to marry; to her horror, it spelled out "S-A-T-A-N." She ran to the bathroom, where she found Terri and Margi chanting. Brenda died quickly when she was impaled by flying glass from the bathroom mirror. ("Syzygy") *Actress Gabrielle Miller also played Paula Gray, the youthful granddaughter of Walter Chaco in "Our Town."*

Summers, James (Jim) (Chad Willett) Nineteen-year-old student at Jackson University in North Carolina. He and his girlfriend, Liz Hawley, were kidnapped and tortured by psychotic criminal Lucas Jackson Henry. Summers was rescued by Scully just as Henry was about to kill him with an ax at the Blue Devil Brewery. ("Beyond the Sea")

sunflower seeds Mulder's favorite snack food ("The X-Files: Pilot"). As a boy, he used to have nightmares that he was the only person left alive, and when he awoke his father would always be in the study eating sunflower seeds. ("Aubrey"). When an examination of the late Dr. Lewton's intestines revealed he had been eating the seeds, Mulder commented, "A man of taste." ("Teso dos Bichos")

Sun, Linda Memphis murder victim of the vampiric Trinity Killers. Mulder linked her death to the cult because her last name was a soundalike for "Son," a member of the murderous trio who really believed he was one of the undead. ("3")

"Superstar!" Inscription on a red cap that Eddie Van Blundht's court-appointed therapist strongly suggested he wear while incarcerated at the Cumberland Reformatory, in a therapeutic attempt to bolster Eddie's low self-esteem. He told Mulder he received a new Superstar! cap every week, however, because other inmates repeatedly beat him up and stole them. ("Small Potatoes")

Superstars of the Super Bowl Videotape gift Mulder presented to a hospitalized Scully after she awoke from a coma. ("One Breath")

Surnow, Dr. Ronald (Matthew Walker) Research scientist who worked on the top-secret Icarus Project at the Mahan Propulsion Laboratory. For four years Dr. Surnow and other team members had been attempting to create the next generation of jet engines by breaking Mach 15. He was killed when he was locked into a wind tunnel and sucked into an experimental jet engine. He was the second of four researchers involved in the Icarus Project to die within six months. ("Roland") *Michael Walker also played forensics anthropologist Arlinsky in the fourth season episode "Gethsemane."*

Svengali 1931 movie about a maleficent hypnotist starring John Barrymore. The black-and-white film was playing on Robert Modell's television when FBI agents raided his apartment. Like Svengali, Modell also possessed the ability to persuade and force others to do his bidding. ("Pusher")

Svo, Comrade (Bill Croft) Russian immigrant who operated a tattoo parlor in Philadelphia, Pennsylvania. Believing that a permanent body mark was a physical reflection of a person's soul, Svo's motto was "everybody gets tattoo they deserve." After downing too many drinks at a bar across the street from the Russian's sleazy establishment, Ed Jerse selected a Betty Page-like design, whose maniacal voice subsequently taunted him into committing murder. Although Jerse warned Scully to "think it over" when she expressed a desire to get her own tattoo, she nevertheless had Svo etch the image of an ouroboros (a snake eating its own tail) on her lower back. She and Jerse both suffered the hallucinatory effects of a parasite found in the rye that Svo used in his tattoo ink. Svo's parlor was shut down and the Russian was investigated for having criminal connections to another immigrant, Vsevlod Pudovkin. ("Never Again") *Bill Croft also played one of the woody wagon-driving Romanian holy men in "The Calusari."*

Swaim, Jeffrey SEE: **Blockhead, Dr.**

Swarthy Man (Lee Serpa) Courier for the Shadowy Syndicate, who was intercepted at Dulles International Airport by Mulder and Scully after being tipped off by Alex Krycek. Although Swarthy Man escaped, the agents recovered the red diplomatic pouch he was carrying, which contained a rock of extraterrestrial origin. He later fell to his death after struggling with Alex Krycek on the balcony of Assistant Director Skinner's high-rise apartment. ("Tunguska")

swastika SEE: **gammadion**

Swenson, Karen A victim of the mysterious youth murders in Bellefleur, Oregon. After her corpse was discovered in the woods with two small, pink, circular marks on her lower back, Mulder theorized that Swenson had been a human subject of alien experimentation. ("The X-Files: Pilot") *The actress who played Karen Swenson was uncredited.*

Sylvia Scully's high school friend. During a double-date with Scully and Marcus, the "twelfth grade love" of Scully's life, Sylvia and her "idiot" boyfriend let a campfire get out of control. The four teenagers were forced to ride back to town on a fire department pumper-truck. Scully told the faux-Mulder (shapeshifter Eddie Van Blundht) about the disastrous date while relaxing with a bottle of wine at her apartment one evening. ("Small Potatoes")

synchrony Something happening, existing or arising at precisely the same time, which is exactly what occurred when an older version of MIT cryobiologist Jason Nichols came back from the future to stop himself and others from developing the very technology that would make time travel possible. ("Synchrony")

📁 **"Synchrony"** Written by Howard Gordon and David Greenwalt. Directed by Jim Charleston. File number 4X19. *First aired April 13, 1997. A technologically-advanced rapid freezing compound is the focal point of three deaths, one of which is predicted by an elderly man whose ability to foresee the future is explained, according to Mulder, in Scully's graduate thesis.* **Classic Sound Bite:** *"You were a lot more open-minded when you were a youngster."* **Background Check:** *The Fox network originally issued an official press release stating that fan-favorite Charles Nelson Reilly ("Jose Chung's 'From Outer Space'") would make a cameo appearance in the episode, which never happened.*

Syracuse Hancock International Airport Syracuse, New York, airport where Mulder claimed Max Fenig's knapsack containing the third interlocking piece of alien technology. The agent was forced to use an employee exit to elude several MIBs who desperately wanted the extraterrestrial device. ("Max")

syzygy An astronomical term for the alignment or conjunction of three celestial objects, such as the sun, the Earth, and the moon or a planet. Astrologer Madame Zirka was convinced that the odd behavior of the Comity townsfolk, including Mulder and Scully, was attributable to Earth entering a planetary alignment with Mars, Mercury, and Uranus. Syzygy is also a Greek word roughly translated to mean "two things (objects, people, etc.)

that are part of a larger whole, in that to reach completeness they must be together." ("Syzygy")

📁 **"Syzygy"** Written by Chris Carter. Directed by Rob Bowman. File number 3X13. *First aired January 26, 1996. Mulder and Scully are called to the small community of Comity by a semi-hysterical police detective to investigate several high school students' murders as rumors of a Satanic cult whips the normally placid townsfolk into a panic.* **Classic Sound Bite:** *"I was just never sure your little feet could reach the pedals."* **Background Check:** *The episode originally aired during an actual syzygy of Mars, Mercury and Uranus, although, Chris Carter said, January 9th had the best alignment of the planets.*

T

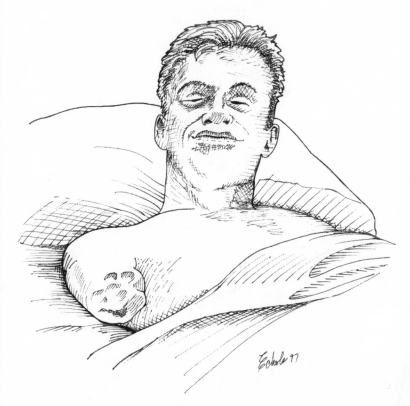

Trimble

Taber, Gary (John Harris) Claustrophobic real estate salesman in Franklin, Pennsylvania. In an elevator at the town's civic center, he saw an electronic readout saying NO AIR, CAN'T BREATHE, and finally, KILL 'EM ALL. The forty-two-year-old Taber murdered four people with his bare hands before being killed by a security guard. A greenish-yellow residue on Taber's fingers, of an unidentified, nontoxic chemical compound found on plants, led Mulder to suspect a chemical cause. ("Blood")

Tabernacle of Horror Artist Hepcat Helm's description of the funhouse he operated in Gibsonton, Florida, a town populated by former circus performers and freaks. Helm wanted customers of the Tabernacle of Horror to be frightened and took offense at Sheriff Hamilton's reference to the place as a "funhouse." ("Humbug")

Tablers Community Hospital Medical facility in the small town of Martinsburg, West Virginia (pop. 15,000), where five babies born with four-inch vestigial tails had been delivered over the course of three months. Human shapeshifter Eddie Van Blundht locked Mulder in the hospital's basement boiler room while he impersonated the agent and tried to romance Scully. ("Small Potatoes")

Take a Chance Title of the Cigarette-Smoking Man's first Tom Clancy-esque novel, according to Lone Gunman Frohike's version of the enigmatic chain-smoker's life. Written under the pseudonym Raul Bloodworth, *Take a Chance* was a political potboiler featuring spy Jack Colquitt. ("Musings of a Cigarette-Smoking Man") *The title of the novel was an in-joke from Glen Morgan and James Wong's canceled sci-fi series* Space: Above and Beyond. *The phrase, "Take a chance," was the motto of that show's AIs (Artificial Intelligence silicates), humanoid-shaped computers programmed by a renegade scientist to treat everything as a gamble.*

Takeuchi, Shigeru One of four Japanese doctors assassinated by black-clad soldiers during an "alien autopsy" aboard a secret government train car in Knoxville, Tennessee. ("Nisei") *The actor who portrayed Takeuchi was uncredited.*

Talapus According to the Lone Gunmen, a salvage vessel registered out of San Diego which had been searching several months for a Japanese submarine sunk during World War II. The sub was allegedly carrying a cargo of gold bullion. Satellite photos retrieved by Mulder tracked the *Talapus* through the Panama Canal to a Naval shipyard in Newport News, Virginia. Although a Coast Guard official told Mulder that the DEA refused to allow the *Talapus* into port, the agent discovered an unmarked ship dockside with a *Talapus* jacket inside. When a contingent of black-suited and armed men suddenly arrived and began searching the boat, Mulder was forced to dive into the water. Climbing out, he peeped through the window of a shipyard warehouse where he discovered what appeared to be a large UFO recovered by the *Talapus* ("Nisei"). Several months later, the French salvage ship *Piper Maru* limped into port in San Diego, its crew suffering from radiation burns after being at the same coordinates as the *Talapus* when it retrieved the UFO. ("Piper Maru")

Talbot, Det. (Timothy Webber) Baltimore, Maryland, policeman who brought Eugene Tooms to a hospital emergency room after finding him unconscious in the street, beaten and kicked in the jaw. Tooms accused Mulder of the assault. ("Tooms") *Timothy Webber also portrayed Jess Harold in "Our Town" and Dr. Farraday in "Quagmire."*

talitha cumi Aramaic (ancient language in which the Bible was written) for "little girl, arise." Jesus speaks the words in the New Testament to a twelve-year-old girl whom he raised from the dead. The story is refashioned and retold (and the very same phrase used) in the Grand Inquisitor chapter of Dostoyevsky's *The Brothers Karamozov*, when the Messiah returns and raises a young girl in Seville. This chapter formed the basis of the conversations between the Cigarette-Smoking Man (substituting for the Grand Inquisitor) and his prisoner, Jeremiah Smith (standing in for the Messiah). ("Talitha Cumi")

🗁 **"Talitha Cumi (Part 1 of 2)"** Written by Chris Carter (based upon a story by David Duchovny and Chris Carter). Directed by R.W. Goodwin. File number 3X24. *First aired May 17, 1996. The life of Agent Mulder's mother hangs in the balance as the X-Files team races against time to save a renegade extraterrestrial clone with healing powers from the Cigarette-Smoking Man and the alien Bounty Hunter. This cliff-hanger episode was the third-season finale and typically created more questions than it answered about the mythology's complex tapestry.* **Classic Sound Bite:** *"You live in fear. That's your whole life."* **Background Check:** *Extras who appeared in the pre-credits Brothers K fast-food restaurant scene included cinematographer John Bartlett's daughter, first assistant director Tom Braidwood's daughter, key grip Al Campbell's daughter, and three of stunt coordinator Tony Morelli's children.*

Tall Man (Grai Carrington) New York businessman seduced by a plain-looking woman in a bar. Later, in a Germantown, Maryland, motel room, they engaged in a wild, passionate bout of sex, after which Tall Man choked and painfully died. Though a woman clearly entered the room, a man was seen exiting. ("Genderbender")

Tanaka, Peter (Hiro Kanagawa) Systems analyst on the Cascade Volcano Research Team. Tanaka was infected with an unknown subterranean organism, which manifested itself as a snakelike matured spore bursting out of his throat. Mulder noted that Tanaka's lungs contained sand (silicon dioxide), the theoretical waste product of silicon-based lifeforms. ("Firewalker") *Actor Hiro Kanagawa portrayed Dr. Yonechi in "Synchrony."*

Tanner, Albert SEE: **Betts, Leonard**

Tanner, Elaine (Marjorie Lovett) Mother of Albert, a.k.a. Leonard Betts, a highly-evolved genetic mutant who needed to ingest cancerous tissue to survive and regenerate. Mrs. Tanner loved her son unconditionally, telling Mulder and Scully, "God put him here for a purpose. God means for him to stay even if people don't understand." She demonstrated her undying devotion by allowing him to cut open her chest and remove a tumor, which he needed to sustain his existence. ("Leonard Betts")

Tapia, Donald "Deke" (Dean Norris) Federal marshal leading the manhunt for two escaped prisoners from Virginia's Cumberland State Correctional Facility. Although he initially told Mulder to stay out of his way during the pursuit of the fugitives, he grudgingly accepted the agent's assistance in the case. ("F. Emasculata")

Tarot Dealer (Alex Diakun) Professional prognosticator murdered by the Puppet, a serial killer who preyed upon fortune-tellers. In his haste to meet true psychic Clyde Bruckman at the Le Damfino Hotel, the Puppet neglected to remove the Tarot Dealer's eyeballs, as he had done in previous killings. However, he did leave a salad fork in his eye. ("Clyde Bruckman's Final Repose")

Tashmoo Federal Correctional Facility Prison in Pennsylvania where infirmary physician Dr. Joe Ridley conducted aging reversal experiments on John Barnett and other inmates. ("Young at Heart")

tasseography The ancient art of predicting the future by reading tea leaves. The Doll Collector, one of the Puppet's serial murder victims, was an amateur tasseographer. ("Clyde Bruckman's Final Repose")

Taylor, Barbara (Judith Maxie) Wife of Home, Pennsylvania, sheriff, Andy Taylor. Although she hid under the bed while the deformed Peacock boys "went caveman" and bludgeoned her husband to death in their house on Sweetgum Lane, she was eventually unable to stifle a small cry and in turn suffered the same fate as her husband. ("Home")

Taylor, Cpl. Bryce (Bret Stait) Military officer stationed at the U.S. Space Surveillance Center in Cheyenne Mountain, Colorado, who alerted Col. Henderson to a downed UFO near Lake Michigan. Cpl. Taylor ordered Crew Chief Karen Koretz to file a report, but was countermanded by Henderson, who told her to record the UFO sighting as a meteor and the radar findings as "instrument malfunction." ("Fallen Angel") *Bret Stait also played militia leader Terry Edward Mayhew in "Tunguska/Terma".*

Taylor, Sheriff Andy (Tucker Smallwood) Sheriff of the tiny town of Home, Pennsylvania. He called the FBI office in Pittsburgh when a terribly malformed newborn was found callously buried in a shallow grave. After describing the victim to the Bureau's regional office, they recommended Sheriff Taylor request Mulder and Scully and the X-Files unit. A gentle, peace-loving man who treasured the idyllic existence of his "quiet" town, Sheriff Taylor didn't even wear a gun or lock the doors of his house or office. The wholesome apple pie facade of the community was shattered, however, when Taylor issued warrants for the arrests of the reclusive Peacock boys. Taylor and his wife, Barbara, were clubbed to death in the bedroom of their unlocked home by the feral and murderous clan while the cheerful Johnny Mathis song "Wonderful! Wonderful!" played loudly on the Peacocks' car radio. ("Home") *Tucker Smallwood portrayed Commodore Ross on episode writers Glen Morgan and James Wong's short-lived sci-fi series,* Space: Above and Beyond. *He also portrayed a mission controller in the 1997 film,* Contact.

Teager, Nathaniel (Peter LaCroix) A member of Green Beret detachment B-11, a squad known as the "Bloody Sabers" during the Vietnam War. Sgt. Teager, who was described as a "killing machine" because of his twenty-six confirmed solo Viet Cong executions, was officially reported killed when his chopper was shot down over enemy territory in 1971. In reality, though, Teager had been left to die in a Southeast Asia prison camp, abandoned by a government intent on maintaining its secret policy of denial regarding American POWs. In December 1995, the radical paramilitary group, the Right Hand, liberated Teager from a Vietnamese prison camp. He resurfaced two years later, determined to exact his revenge against the high-ranking military officers who had deserted him. Teager, a seemingly invisible assassin who had the ability to effectively erase himself from the visual field of human sight by manipulating a naturally-occurring "blindspot," was successful in shooting two generals to death at close range. A third high-ranking military official, however, survived two assassination attempts during the Vietnam Veterans Memorial rededication ceremonies, and Teager was shot when he tried to escape. As he lay dying, he repeated only his name, rank, serial number, and date of birth. The Pentagon later claimed that the dead man was Thomas Lynch, a Vietnam veteran who had been institutionalized several times in psychiatric hospitals. Mulder complained to Assistant Director Skinner that the government wasn't just denying Teager's life. It was even denying his death. ("Unrequited") *Actor Peter LaCroix appeared as Ranheim (a.k.a. Frank Druce), the trucker in "E.B.E.," and as the doomed Skyland tram operator, Dwight, in "Ascension."*

Teague, Steve Radical eco-activist who drove spikes into trees and sabotaged logging equipment. He was originally suspected of being involved in the mysterious disappearances of several loggers in the Olympic National Forest. According to fellow "monkey wrencher" Doug Spinney, however, Teague had been devoured by a swarm of prehistoric wood mites. ("Darkness Falls")

Ted's Bait & Tackle Ted Bertram's shop on the shores of Heuvelman's Lake in the Blue Ridge Mountains of Georgia. In addition to fishing equipment and bait, Bertram also sold souvenirs and other merchandise promoting the legendary lake monster, Big Blue, the Southern Serpent. Adorning the roof of the bait-and-tackle shop was an enormous facsimile of the prehistoric aquatic creature. ("Quagmire")

Tee-Totallers A golf-driving range where Robert "Pusher" Modell led Mulder and Scully. When FBI Agent Collins apprehended him there, Modell used his psychic powers to will Collins to set himself on fire. ("Pusher")

tegretol A prescription drug for the treatment of epilepsy. Scully found a bottle in Robert Modell's medicine cabinet during a search of his apartment. Mulder theorized that a brain tumor may have given Modell psychokinetic powers. ("Pusher")

Teliko According to West African folklore, an evil spirit of the air who emerges at night to suck the life and color out of its victim. Mulder suspected a Teliko was responsible for the deaths of a number of African-American men in Philadelphia whose bodies were found completely lacking color pigmentation. ("Teliko")

🗁 **"Teliko"** Written by Howard Gordon. Directed by James Charleston. File number 4X04. *First aired October 18, 1996. When several African-American men mysteriously turn up dead in Philadelphia with all the pigment drained from their bodies, Agents Mulder and Scully investigate the possible involvement of a ghost creature from West African folklore who could transmorgify into any size or shape.* **Classic Sound Bite:** *"All new truths begin as heresies and end as superstitions. We fear the unknown, so we reduce it to the terms that are most familiar to us, whether that's a folktale, or a disease, or a conspiracy."* **Background Check:** *"Teliko" was the first non-mythology episode to use an*

334 / James Hatfield and George "Doc" Burt

alternative opening tag line (Deceive Inveigle Obfuscate) and the second X-Files *installment in three weeks to substitute the usual "The Truth Is Out There."*

Teller, John (Ernie Lively) Johnston County, Oklahoma, sheriff who insisted that five recent lightning strikes (four fatal) in the area was not unusual. Mulder, however, wondered why the only victims were seventeen- to twenty-one-year-old males, adding to the bizarre nature of such a coincidence. The openly hostile sheriff declared that Mulder and Scully had a weak case against Darin Peter Oswald, and released the boy from custody. Teller was later killed by Oswald; the coroner ruled his death an accidental one, by lightning. ("D.P.O."). *Sheriff Teller was named for the magicians Penn & Teller, notorious skeptics who doubt all aspects of the paranormal, but who met with Chris Carter and asked to appear in an* X-Files *episode.*

Telus Canadian telephone company. One of Telus' line repairmen was attacked and killed in the Alberta countryside by a deadly strain of bees. ("Herrenvolk")

Temple of the Seven Stars A doomsday religious cult that preached reincarnation. From the sect's compound in Apison, Tennessee, which was once the site of a Civil War battle, its paranoid charismatic leader, Vernon Ephesian, dominated his followers with his extensive knowledge of Biblical text (especially the Book of Revelations), New Age channeling and skillful coercion. After one of the cult's members contacted the FBI to warn of child abuse and weapons stockpiling, the FBI joined BATF agents in raiding the compound, which ultimately led to the cultists' mass suicide. ("The Field Where I Died")

tempus fugit. Latin phrase meaning "time flies," which aptly describes the inexplicable loss of nine minutes on two separate commercial airline flights intercepted by alien spacecraft. ("Tempest Fugit")

"Tempus Fugit" Written by Chris Carter and Frank Spotnitz. Directed by Rob Bowman. File number 4X17. *First aired March 16, 1997. Mulder and Scully investigate the crash of a commercial airliner, possibly the result of interaction between the jet, the U.S. Air Force, and an alien spacecraft.* **Classic Sound Bite:** *"Once I got a quarter off the deep end at the Y pool."* **Background Check:** *Initially this episode was titled "Flight 549," but was changed to "Tempus Fugit" only days before it originally aired.*

Tepes, Vlad Fifteenth-century Romanian *voivode* (prince) of Wallachia, a province bordered by Transylvania. *Dracula* author Bram Stoker based his classic villain on this actual historical figure, who was also known as Vlad the Impaler. The after–sunset Club Tepes in Los Angeles, where Mulder met Kristen Kilar, was named after the bloodthirsty Romanian ruler. ("3")

Terle, Catherine Ann Young woman whose corpse was desecrated at the Montifiore Cemetery in Minneapolis. FBI agent Moe Bocks requested Mulder and Scully's assistance, believing that they were dealing with grave-digging extraterrestrials. The dates on Terle's headstone read: 1975–1995. ("Irresistible")

🗁 **"Terma (Part 2 of 2)"** Written by Frank Spotnitz and Chris Carter. Directed by Rob Bowman. File number 4X10. *First aired December 1, 1996. A former KGB assassin comes out of retirement to erase all connections to American experiments involving the lethal "black cancer," a toxic biohazard of extraterrestrial origin, and Scully is jailed for contempt of Congress when she refuses to reveal Mulder's whereabouts to a Senate subcommittee.* **Classic Sound Bite:** *"If you cannot get past this, then I suggest that this whole committee be held in contempt for ignoring evidence that cannot be refuted."* **Background Check:** *Many of the actors in the Russian prison sequence were actually from the former Soviet Union, but the menacing men on horseback were world champion riders from Calgary. Two scenes between the Cigarette-Smoking Man and the Well-Manicured Man were cut from the episode, including one in which the head of the Shadowy Syndicate was threatening to publicly expose the operation through Sorenson's Senate subcommittee, and CSM was challenging him to the stupidity of that idea.*

Terrel, Lisa Member of a girl scout troop that sighted and photographed a UFO in August 1967 near Lake Okobogee. ("Conduit")

teso dos bichos Archaic Brazilian Portuguese phrase meaning "burial mound of small animals." It was also the site of an archaeological dig that unearthed a female shaman's sacred remains (and her vengeful jaguar/cat spirit) in the Ecuadorian highlands. ("Teso dos Bichos") *Much to the chagrin of Fox network executives, the word "bichos" is slang for "balls" (as in "You have big bichos") in Colombia and Venezuela.*

🗁 **"Teso dos Bichos"** Written by John Shiban. Directed by Kim Manners. File number 3X18. *First aired March 8, 1996. Members of an archaeological expedition in the Ecuadorian Highlands begin dying mysteriously after they forcibly remove the remains of an Amaru, a female shaman. Agents Mulder and Scully investigate whether the string of baffling murders are part of the holy relic's vengeful curse involving a jaguar spirit or simply the result of political terrorism.* **Classic Sound Bite:** *"So what are we talking here, Mulder? A possessed rat? The return of Ben?"* **Background Check:** *An actor named Frank Welker, who had created voices and sound effects for numerous animated and science-fiction movies, provided all the animal sounds heard in this episode. "Teso dos Bichos" was rewritten twelve times before it was finally filmed.*

Tetra Meal D Fish-food flakes that Air Force pilot Col. Budahas sprinkled on his food at a dinner party. ("Deep Throat")

tetrodotoxin Powerful poison found naturally in a number of fish and toads. A medical report listed trace levels of the paralytic in Marine Pvt. John "Jack" McAlpin's bloodwork. Although Scully pointed out that tetrodotoxin was a delicacy in Japan, Mulder stated that Harvard ethnobotanist Wade Davis had discovered that the chemical, which could cause paralysis and depressed cardiorespiratory activity, was a part of zombification rituals in Haiti. ("Fresh Bones")

Texas School Book Depository Dallas employer of Lee Harvey Oswald who, according to Lone Gunman Frohike's conjectural dossier on the Cigarette-Smoking Man, was set up by the CSM to be the "patsy" for President Kennedy's assassination. While the CSM shot and killed JFK from a sewer in Dealey Plaza, Oswald was arrested for firing the fatal shots from his vantage point in a window of the Texas School Book Depository. ("Musings of a Cigarette-Smoking Man")

Texas Theatre, The Movie theatre in the Oak Cliff suburb of Dallas where Lee Harvey Oswald was apprehended only eighty minutes after the assassination of President Kennedy. When Dallas police officers converged on the theatre, the movie projector stopped and the house lights were turned up. After a brief struggle with the officers, Oswald was rushed to police headquarters. According to Lone Gunman Frohike's speculative case file on the Cigarette-Smoking Man, the shadowy operative was sitting in the back of the theatre and in the aftermath of his successful assassination of JFK, lit his first smoke (from a pack of Morleys Oswald left with him earlier in the day) and became the Cigarette-Smoking Man. ("Musings of a Cigarette-Smoking Man")

Therapist, The (Donna White) A middle-aged woman specializing in hypnosis, she regressed cult member Melissa Riedal Ephesian and Agent Mulder in an attempt to recover their memories of past lives. ("The Field Where I Died")

Thibodeaux, Ruby (Joy Coghill) Woman raped on her stairwell landing and almost murdered by Harry Cokely in Terrence, Nebraska, in 1945. She survived and Cokely was sent to McCallister Penitentiary for almost fifty years. Thibodeaux admitted to Mulder and Scully that she had a baby after the assault and put it up for adoption. The child grew up to become police officer Raymond Morrow, the father of pregnant detective B.J. Morrow. ("Aubrey")

Thinker, The (Bernie Coulson) A short-lived fourth member of the Lone Gunmen. After Byers uploaded Scully's patient chart to the computer hacking genius, he concluded that someone had experimented on Scully's DNA, compromising her immune system ("One Breath"). The Thinker, a.k.a. Kenneth Soona, also hacked into the Defense Department computer system, effectively penetrating the MJ documents which contained everything the government had compiled about UFOs since the 1940s. The Thinker, "an anarchist and snoop," covertly met with Mulder and gave him a digital audiotape (DAT) of the top-secret files, which were encrypted in Navajo. The Thinker was later captured by a multinational black ops unit and murdered, execution style. According to a newspaper article, the body of Kenneth J. Soona was discovered April 16 in the Trenton landfill by worker Sparky Sinclair. Soona was raised in Youngstown, Pennsylvania, and went to college on an academic scholarship. He was survived by his mother, Jane, sisters Isabel and Elsbeth, and brother Mike. ("Anasazi/The Blessing Way"). *The Thinker was named after the highly knowledgeable X-Phile Yung Jun Kim, whose online handle is "DuhThinker."*

3rd Senior Agent (Chris Carter) One of four mysterious, high-ranking members of an FBI panel who interviewed Scully and threatened her with dismissal without chance of reinstatement when she refused to shed light on Mulder's activities after the MJ files were stolen. ("Anasazi") *X-Files creator and executive producer Chris Carter appeared as the senior FBI agent in an uncredited cameo.*

Thomas, Agent (Fred Henderson) An FBI agent present when rescued kidnap victim Liz Hawley positively identified a mug shot of Luther Jackson Henry as her abductor. ("Beyond the Sea") *Fred Henderson also played FBI Agent Rich in "Duane Barry."*

Thomas, Det. Ray (Fred Keating) Police detective in Desmond, Virginia who E-mailed Mulder crime scene photographs of a young mail sorter who died after being attacked by a swarm of bees in an overnight delivery company's employee rest room. As part of a deal brokered with the Cigarette-Smoking Man in an attempt to save Scully from terminal cancer, Skinner intercepted and deleted Thomas' E-mail file from Mulder's computer. Identifying himself as Fox Mulder, Skinner then visited the police forensics lab in Virginia, where he switched a vial containing the victim's blood with another identical container. As he was leaving, Skinner was approached by Det. Thomas (who thought he was actually talking to Agent Mulder), but Skinner disappointed the detective by telling him that the evidence did not warrant his further involvement in the case. Upon orders from the Cigarette-Smoking Man, the Gray-Haired Man neutralized "a potentially compromising situation" by shooting Thomas in the head and leaving his body to be found near the precinct. To insure Assistant Director Skinner's continued cooperation in the cover-up, the weapon used was Skinner's government-issued handgun. ("Zero Sum")

Thomas, Gerd (Paul Sand) The Kanes' "Peeping Tom" landlord in Delta Glen, Wisconsin, who admitted that he had abducted several children in the town. Thomas stated that Dr. Larson, a local physician, had conducted secret chemical experiments on them, and inoculated cattle with the same drug. A check of the substance revealed synthetic antibodies of unknown origin, leading Mulder and Scully to theorize that the town was part of an experiment on the effects of extraterrestrial DNA. ("Red Museum") *Gerd Thomas was also the name of the famous original Peeping Tom of Coventry. Actor Paul Sand starred in the 1970s series* Paul Sand in Friends and Lovers *shortly after winning a Tony Award for the Broadway production of* Story Theatre. *The sympathetic hangdog Sand also played Dr. Michael Ridley on the NBC medical series* St. Elsewhere.

Thompson, Mike (Wayne Tippit) Police detective investigating the Atlantic City murders of several vagrants. Thompson resented the FBI's involvement in the case and tried to undermine Mulder and Scully at every opportunity, even at one point having Mulder arrested and held in the drunk tank until after the weekend, when charges were dropped. The police detective knew that the cannibalistic murders were the work of the legendary Bigfoot-like Jersey Devil and orchestrated a police cover-up, fearing that the truth would hurt tourism. ("The Jersey Devil")

thoughtography Paranormal ability to produce images on photographic film by concentrating on a mental image. During the investigation into the "psychic photos" left behind after Mary LeFante's kidnapping, Mulder related to Scully the true story of 1960s bellhop Ted Serios, who became somewhat famous for what he called "thoughtographs." Serios claimed that by concentrating on unexposed film negatives he could create a photograph representative of what he saw in his mind, including landscapes, cathedrals and even the Queen of England. ("Unruhe")

🗁 **"3"** Written by Chris Ruppenthal, Glen Morgan, and James Wong. Directed by David Nutter. File number 2X07. *First aired November 4, 1994. With the X-Files unit officially reopened, Mulder keeps his sanity after Scully's disappearance by investigating a series of apparent vampire-like homicides in Los Angeles that follow the pattern of the so-called Trinity Killers, a trio of murderers obsessed with blood rituals.* **Classic Sound Bite:** *"It's not who you are. It doesn't make you happy."* **Background Check:** *Episode writers Glen Morgan and Jame Wong's first draft of "3" was a much more "kinky and erotic episode" about the "sexual kick to ingest blood," but Fox's Standards and Practices department demanded changes.*

Tickle Me Elmo A very popular doll based on a character from the TV series *Sesame Street*. It was so popular during the 1996 Christmas season that a Tickle Me Elmo black market developed, with exorbitant prices charged by those who had one for sale. At the Syracuse Hancock International Airport, where Mulder claimed Max Fenig's knapsack containing the third inter-locking piece of alien technology, the agent was forced to use an employee exit to elude several MIBs who desperately wanted the extraterrestrial device more than "a Tickle Me Elmo" doll. ("Max")

Tiernan, Merv (John Cuthbert) Orderly at the Excelsis Dei Convalescent Home in Worcester, Massachusetts. When one of the patients, bolted from Tiernan, he pursued the surprisingly fleet-footed elderly man to the top floor where an invisible force knocked the attendant out the window and pried his fingers off the edge. Tiernan plummeted four stores to his death. ("Excelsius Dei")

Tillman, Lt. Brian (Terry O'Quinn) Married Aubrey, Missouri, chief of detectives who had an affair with detective B.J. Morrow and impregnated her. Tillman petitioned to adopt their unborn son after she attempted self-abortion and was held in a psychiatric cell on suicide watch. ("Aubrey") *Terry O'Quinn is best remembered as the titular human monster of* The Stepfa-ther *movies and in the recurring role of Peter Watts, the mysterious ex-FBI agent, on the Chris Carter series* Millennium.

"Timid" Online handle for mutant serial killer Virgil Incanto, which he used in the Internet chat-room "Big and Beautiful" to meet lonely and overweight women such as Ellen Kaminsky. ("2Shy")

Timmons, Penny Young, blond woman whose body was found in a parking lot across the street from Angie's Midnight Bowl in Washington, D.C., the third victim of a serial killer in as many weeks. Only moments before Tim-mons' body was discovered, her disembodied spirit was glimpsed in a bowling lane's machinery. ("Elegy") *The actress who played the ghostly Timmons in the bowling lane machinery was uncredited.*

Tippit, J.D Police patrolman who attempted to question Lee Harvey Oswald on a Dallas street only minutes after the assassination of President Kennedy. Oswald, who fit the description of the alleged gunman, shot and killed Tippit and then ran down the street into the Texas Theatre, where he was later arrested by other Dallas police officers. ("Musings of a Cigarette-Smoking Man") *The actor who portrayed Patrolman Tippit was uncredited.*

Tippy, Mr. Terri Roberts' pet Llasa Apso, whose bones were discovered by Comity townsfolk looking for a mass grave. ("Syzygy")

Toews, Jackson (Robert Thurston) Escalating death fetishist Donnie Pfas-ter's supervisor at the Janelli-Heller Funeral Home in Minneapolis, Minne-sota. He fired Pfaster for cutting off locks of hair from the corpse of a young woman. ("Irresistible") *Robert Thurston also played mycology professor Dr. Larry Steen in "El Mundo Gira."*

📁 **"Tooms (a.k.a. Squeeze 2)"** Written by Glen Morgan and James Wong. Directed by David Nutter. File number 1X20. *First aired April 22, 1994. With body-bending serial killer Eugene Victor Tooms released from a psychiatric hospital, Agents Mulder and Scully have to prevent him from making his fifth kill, which would allow him to begin his 30-year period of hibernation.* **Classic Sound Bite:** *"Can you determine the cause of death? My instinct tells me that burial in cement is murder."* **Background Check:** *The climactic scene, in which Mulder confronts Tooms in his nest under the escalator, was filmed with actor Doug Hutchison in the nude and doused head to toe with cake icing standing in for slime. Originally, this sequel to* Squeeze *was to contain several exterior scenes, but severe rain storms and uncooperative weather pushed the previous episode,* Darkness Falls, *over budget, forcing the production crew to rely on mostly interior shots for* Tooms.

Tooms, Eugene Victor (Doug Hutchison) Although he appeared to be in his early thirties, Tooms was a mutant serial killer capable of contorting and protracting his body in order to gain access to victims so that he could extract the livers which provided him with sustenance for a hibernation period of thirty years. Tooms' abnormally elongated eleven-inch fingerprints were found at seven of the nineteen Baltimore homicides linked to him, five every thirty years dating back to 1903. Mulder discovered that Tooms had resided at 66 Exeter Street, Room 103, for sixty years. Although Tooms was eventually captured at the condemned building and committed to the Druid Hill Sanitarium, he was released some months later, despite Mulder's dire warnings that the mutant needed to remain in custody for the safety of the public. After making his fifth present-day kill, Tooms built a nest under the escalator at the mall constructed on the site of his former residence at 66 Exeter. During a confrontation with Mulder, Tooms was crushed to death when the agent activated the escalator ("Squeeze" and "Tooms"). When Mulder and Scully were confounded by how tobacco company executive Patrick Newirth could vanish from a locked room, Scully glanced at the small heating vent. "You never know," Mulder remarked, an obvious reference to Tooms ("Soft Light"). *Actor Doug Hutchison also appeared in two of 1997's biggest summer movies:* Conair *and* Batman and Robin, *and in the 1996 films* All Points Between *with Moon Zappa, and the Joel Schumacher-directed movie version of John Grisham's novel* A Time to Kill, *in which he played a redneck gunned down by Samuel L. Jackson. Hutchison also starred in a failed pilot for Fox about a rock band called* Planet Rules *and had a recurring role in Glen Morgan and James Wong's short-lived sci-fi series,* Space: Above and Beyond.

Torrence, Bobby (Kim Kondrashoff) A prisoner at Virginia's Cumberland State Correctional Facility who received an overnight-mail package originally addressed to Dr. Robert Torrence. It contained a bloody pig's leg with a pulsating sore, wrapped in a Spanish-language newspaper, that was infected with the larvae of the *Faciphaga emasculata* parastoid. Eighteen hours later, Torrence was covered with grotesque boils and died shortly thereafter. At the prison incinerator, Scully found a body bag marked "001 Torrence," the first of several inmates whose highly infected remains were cremated. ("F. Emasculata")

Torrence, Dr. Robert (Bill Rowat) An entomologist who sought new rain forest species for drug applications, but instead fell victim to *Faciphaga emasculata,* a parasite carrier that secreted a dilating enzyme. In a Costa Rican jungle, he found the carcass of a wild boar with pulsating red sores. As he examined one of the repulsive boils, using surgical gloves, it burst open into his exposed face. Seven hours later, soldiers found him dead. ("F. Emasulata")

Townsend Y.M.C.A Recreational facility commandeered by the federal government to use as a relief center for the 12,000 evacuees of Townsend, Wisconsin, during the government's Operation Falcon quarantine from a "toxic cargo." ("Fallen Angel")

Tow Truck Driver (Dean Wray) Driver who stopped to offer assistance to child abductor Carl Wade, whose car was disabled on the side of the road after blowing a sidewall. A tire iron-weilding Wade chased the tow truck driver away because he had young Amy Jacobs in the trunk of his car. ("Oubliette")

Transcontinental Express Overnight delivery company that was responsible for shipping a package and its plague-inducing contents from Pinck Pharmaceuticals in Wichita, Kansas, to prisoner Bobby Torrence at the Cumberland State Correctional Facility in Virginia ("F. Emasculata"). The FedEx-like company also delivered a book of sixteenth-century Italian literature from Strautcher Publishing Company to serial killer, Virgil Incanto ("2Shy"). Jane Brody, a mail sorter at Transcontinental's routing center in Desmond, Virginia, was fatally attacked by a swarm of bees in the women's rest room. It was later discovered that the smallpox-carrying insects had escaped from a damaged overnight package in an adjoining room. ("Zero Sum")

transient SEE: **Fortean event**

transorbital lobotomy Also known as an icepick lobotomy, which paranoid-schizophrenic Gerry Schnauz conducted on young kidnapped women he wanted to "save" from the "unruhe" (German for "unrest" or "trouble") he believed was tormenting them. ("Unruhe")

Travel Time Travel Agency Richmond, Virginia, travel company visited by escaped mental patient and former extraterrestrial experiment subject Duane Barry, because he couldn't remember the site of his alleged abduction. ("Duane Barry")

Trego Indian reservation Browning, Montana, settlement being sued by neighboring rancher Jim Parker over grazing rights and a border dispute. Mulder and Scully traveled to the reservation to investigate deaths allegedly caused by a Manitou, an evil spirit capable of changing a man into a wolf-like beast. ("Shapes")

Trepkos, Daniel (Bradley Whitford) Visionary volcanologist who invented the robotic exploration device, Firewalker, which was capable of descending into the Earth's fiery core. The expedition leader of Mt. Avalon's Cascade Volcano Research Team, Trepkos discovered a silicon-based subterranean organism that could survive within the volcano. ("Firewalker")

Trimble, Sgt. Leonard "Rappo" (Ian Tracey) Quadruple amputee at the Fort Evanston military hospital in Maryland who was wounded by friendly fire during the Persian Gulf War. The bitterly obnoxious veteran exacted revenge against fellow soldiers and their commanding officers by using astral projection to unleash his murderous phantom soul. Lt. Col. Victor Stans suffocated Trimble with a pillow while his spirit was out of his body. Mulder noted that no physical evidence linked Trimble to the deaths at the military hospital but that his family's request for burial in Arlington National Cemetery was denied. His remains were cremated and his ashes interred at a Tannersville, Pennsylvania, graveyard. ("The Walk")

Trinity Killers, The A trio of vampiric serial murderers who called themselves The Father, The Son, and The Unholy Spirit. The trinity was responsible for deaths in Memphis, Portland, and Los Angeles, in which the victims were drained of blood and "Biblical" writings were scrawled on the walls of the crime scenes. The Trinity Killers' X-File case number was X256933VW. ("3")

Trios Gymnopedies Music by Erik Satie played (first movement only) at the funeral of a young woman named Jennifer. That night the funeral director found his assistant, Donnie Pfaster, taking locks of hair off the corpse. ("Irresistible") *The Satie piece was performed by Stu Charno, who played the Puppet serial killer in "Clyde Bruckman's Final Repose."*

Troisky, Dr. Kip (Les Carlson) Astronomer with the U.S. Naval Observatory in Washington, D.C., who gave Scully a list of SETI (Search for Extraterrestrial Intelligence) research locales. ("Little Green Men")

Trondheim, Henry (John Savage) Trawler captain who relocated from the United States to his presumed ancestral home, Norway, to pursue a fishing business. Trapped on the "ghost ship" USS *Ardent* when his ship, the *Zeal,* was stolen, Trondheim began to experience accelerated aging along with Mulder and Scully. After it was learned that the regular desalinated water had somehow become contaminated, the trawler captain barricaded himself inside the Sewage Processing Hold, the location of the only safe water on the Navy destroyer. Trondheim drowned, however, when the ship's hull corroded through and ocean water flooded the compartment. ("Dod Kalm") *John Savage is best known for his acclaimed performances in* The Deer Hunter, The Onion Field, Hair, Salvador, The Godfather: Part III, White Squall, *and* The Crossing Guard.

Trott, Officer (William MacDonald) North Michigan uniformed police officer who investigated the abduction of Mary Louise LeFante and the murder of Alice Brandt. After Gerry Schnauz confessed to the crimes, Officer Trott booked and fingerprinted the shifty-eyed killer at the police station. But when he took Schnauz's mug shot, the developed photograph was of Trott with a bullet hole in his forehead. When the police officer turned around in surprise, Schnauz grabbed Trott's handgun from the holster and shot him in the throat. Schnauz possessed the paranormal ability to create images on film with his mind. ("Unruhe") *William MacDonald also played the ER physician Dr. Oppenheim in "Fallen Angel," a federal marshal in "The Host," and Agent Kazanjian in "2Shy."*

"True Colors" Song sung by Ansel Bray, a photographer obsessed with capturing a picture of Big Blue, just before he was dragged into Heuvelman's Lake by either the aquatic serpent or a large alligator. ("Quagmire")

Truelove SEE: **Betts, Leonard**

Truitt, John (Stephen E. Miller) Substitute county coroner in Bellefleur, Oregon, who filled in for the regular medical examiner, Jay Newman. Truitt examined the body of Karen Swenson, a twenty-one-year-old woman found dead in the woods with two peculiar marks on her back. ("The X-Files: Pilot") *Stephen E. Miller also played a tactical commander during the "Duane Barry" hostage crisis.*

"Trust No One" The first alternate tag line to substitute for the usual "The Truth Is Out There," Deep Throat's dying words to Scully after being shot by the Crew-Cut Man ("The Erlenmeyer Flask"), and the inscription on the Cigarette-Smoking Man's lighter ("Musings of a Cigarette-Smoking Man"). *A scene from "Musings of a Cigarette-Smoking Man" was cut in postproduction, which showed CSM coming home on Christmas Eve and finding one present under his feeble little tree with a card saying, "Best wishes from Alex*

Krycek." Inside the wrapped box was the lighter with the words "TRUST NO ONE" inscribed on the side.

TRUSTNO1 Mulder's secret password for his personal computer files. Scully, seeking clues to Mulder's whereabouts, unsuccessfully tried the passwords SPOOKY and SAMANTHA before succeeding with TRUSTNO1. ("Little Green Men")

Truth About Aliens, The Title of a manuscript written by Roky Crikenson, a power company worker who witnessed an alien abduction in Klass County, Washington. Crikenson hand-wrote his "manifesto" in screenplay form in one sitting of forty-eight hours. ("Jose Chung's 'From Outer Space'")

"Truth Is Out There, The" The tag line that appears at the end of the opening credits of most *X-Files* episodes and effectively sums up the essence of Mulder's quest in life.

Tskany, Charlie (Michael Horse) Sheriff in Browning, Montana, whom Scully accused of attempting to destroy evidence when he forbade an autopsy of Joe Goodensnake's body. The sheriff, who was the tribal law for the reservation, stated that he had to live and work there and respected the Native American Indians' spiritual convictions; thus, in accordance with the tribe's customs, the corpse would be cremated on a pyre. ("Shapes") *Michael Horse played Deputy Hawk on* Twin Peaks *while David Duchovny was cast in the role of the transvestite Dennis/Denise Bryson.*

Tubu Shon Protective Chinese practice which, according to escape artist Dr. Blockhead, could be used to "train a man's testicles to drop into his abdomen." ("Humbug")

Tunguska Site in Central Siberia where a massive fireball crashed to Earth on June 30, 1908, igniting a series of cataclysmic explosions. The concussion from the blast, estimated at two thousand times the force of the bomb dropped on Hiroshima, decimated all life in an area nearly forty miles wide. Oddly enough, the detonation produced no crater nor other evidence of impact. Over the past several decades, dozens of explanations have been suggested—comets, black holes, nuclear explosions, antimatter, asteroids, and even extraterrestrial spacecraft. Mulder covertly traveled to the region after he and Scully intercepted a diplomatic pouch which contained a piece of alien-inhabited biohazardous rock from Tunguska. Once there, he discovered a gulag located at the site of the crash, its hard-laboring prisoners sentenced to mine the extraterrestrial rocks. ("Tunguska/Terma")

📁 **"Tunguska (Part 1 of 2)"** Written by Frank Spotnitz and Chris Carter. Directed by Rob Bowman. File number 4X09. *First aired November 24, 1996.*

When the X-Files team intercepts a diplomatic pouch containing a meteor fragment of extraterrestrial origin which crashed to Earth in Russia in 1908, Mulder becomes involved with two deadly lifeforms: one alien, the other his old nemesis Alex Krycek. **Classic Sound Bite:** *"You're full of crap, Krycek. You're an invertebrate scum-sucker whose moral dipstick is about two drops short of bone dry."* **Background Check:** *During the scene in which Krycek dangled over the balcony of Assistant Director Skinner's high-rise apartment, actor Nicholas Lea actually performed the stunt himself. Although he was very securely attached to the building by a harness and cables, there was nothing underneath him.*

turbellaria Large slug-like fluke or flatworm discovered by Scully during the autopsy of "John Doe," a body that turned up in the sewers of Newark, New Jersey. The agent noted that the fluke had attached itself to the bile duct and was feeding off the liver. Later, a sanitation worker who was pulled under the Newark sewage emerged with a strange wound on his back and complaining of a bad taste in his mouth. While taking a shower, the man began to convulse, coughing up a turbellaria that disappeared down the bathtub drain. ("The Host")

Turk, Hillary One of serial killer Virgil Incanto's forty-seven victims in five states. ("2Shy")

turmeric Spice used as a Chinese medicinal, as described to Scully by San Francisco police detective Glen Chao. The perennial plant, sold in ground form, is used as a mild aromatic stimulant and was once considered a cure for jaundice. ("Hell Money")

Twenty-First Century Recycling Plant Jerusalem, Ohio, facility owned by demonic industrialist Simon Gates (a.k.a. the Millennium Man). Gates, who had committed an international string of religiously motivated murders, took genuine stigmatic Kevin Kryder to the recycling plant to kill him "for the New Age to come." ("Revelations")

2400 Court The motel where Mulder and Scully stayed while investigating a series of bizarre murders in Braddock Heights, Maryland, a small town that had become the subject of mind control experiments involving television signals. After Scully began suffering from paranoid psychosis, she fired her gun at Mulder and the motel manager when they knocked on the door of her room. ("Wetwired")

Twilite Sleep A minor drug Gerry Schnauz's dentist father used on his patients to help them go to sleep. Schnauz concocted a stronger version of the drug which he used as a fast-acting anesthesia (twenty seconds or less) to immobilize his female kidnap victims. ("Unruhe")

2 Jays Café, The Diner in Roslyn, Long Island, where Vietnam vet and surviving J-7 squad member Salvatore Matola was employed. He told Mulder and Krycek that the special forces and recon squad had become a unit of killing machines during the Vietnam conflict, but the military lost control of them after they went AWOL and began to murder at random, finally massacring three hundred children outside Phu Bai. ("Sleepless")

Two Medicine Ranch Cattleman Jim Parker's ranch in Browning, Montana, which bordered on a local Indian reservation. ("Shapes")

"2Shy" Online handle mutant serial killer Virgil Incanto used to lure lonely, overweight women into his fat-sucking trap. ("2Shy")

📁 **"2Shy"** Written by Jeffrey Vlaming. Directed by David Nutter. File number 3X06. *First aired November 3, 1995. A series of dead bodies coated with a gelatinous fluid leads Mulder and Scully in search of an Internet chat room Cassanova who preys on lonely and insecure overweight women.* **Classic Sound Bite:** *"Yes, scorpions predigest their food outside of their bodies by regurgitating onto their prey, but . . . I don't know too many scorpions who surf the Internet."* **Background Check:** *The substance secreted by Virgil Incanto was devised by David Gauthier, after he "doctored up" a material called Ultra-slime, which was used in such movies as* Ghostbusters. *Some* X-Files *crew members nicknamed "2Shy" the "lick me—kill me" episode.*

Tynes, Mrs. (Nicole Robert) Fifth-grade teacher at Ridgeway Elementary School. Stigmatic Kevin Kryder began to bleed from his hands while writing on the chalkboard in her class. ("Revelations")

Tyson, Dennis (Roger Haskett) Kenwood County, Tennessee, deputy sheriff who was forced to detain his superior, Sheriff Daniels, in the fatal jailhouse beating of Samuel Hartley, a young faith healer. ("Miracle Man")

Tyvek A company that manufactured decontamination suits such as the ones used at the quarantined Cumberland State Correctional Facility during the prison's outbreak of a plaguelike illness. ("F. Emasculata")

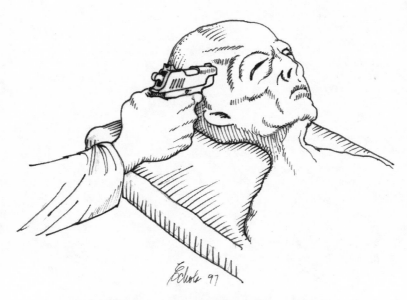

UN Security Council Resolution 1013

Ullrich, Dr. Jim (Paul Raskin) Florida state coroner who conducted an autopsy on Eastpoint State Penitentiary guard Fornier and discovered that his lungs were filled with the larvae of *Lucilia cuprina*, the green bottle fly. ("The List") *Paul Raskin also played cosmetic surgeon Dr. Eric Ilaqua in the fourth season's "Sanguinarium."*

U-Move Moving company from which spirit-protected Lauren Kyte rented a trailer to relocate from Philadelphia to Omaha, Nebraska. ("Shadows")

Ungar, Kenneth (David Wohl) Scholar associated with the Judaica Archives on the Upper East Side of Manhattan. Ungar was consulted by Mulder and Scully after the agents discovered the ancient Hebrew text, *The Sefer Yezirah*, tucked beneath Isaac Luria's burial shroud. Ungar explained that in observance of Jewish belief that with death came equality, a corpse was buried only in its shroud, with no personal symbols of class or position; *The Sefer Yezirah* should certainly not have been buried with the murdered Hasidic Jew. Mulder returned later to question Ungar about a golem, a creature from mystical text. He explained how early Kabbalists believed a righteous man could create a living being from the Earth itself, fashioned from mud or clay. ("Kaddish")

Unholy Spirit, The (Justina Vail) Female leader of a trio of vampiric serial murderers. She was impaled on a wooden post on a garage wall and her body destroyed when the house was doused with gasoline and set ablaze. ("3")

Unit 53 Firefighting unit that suffered casualties when it encountered a downed alien spacecraft and its semi-invisible occupant near Lake Michigan in Townsend, Wisconsin. ("Fallen Angel")

University of Maryland Institution of higher learning in College Park where Scully earned her B.S. in physics in 1986 ("The Jersey Devil"). During Mulder and Scully's investigation into Warren Dupre's possible reincarnation, Dr. Raymond Varnes of the university's biology department explained to the agents that in near-death experiences, the tremendous energy-release could cause profound personality changes ("Lazarus") The eccentric Dr. Charles "Chuck" Burks maintained a digital-imaging lab at the university. Mulder requested Burks examine a photo of two-year-old Teddy Holvey taken seconds before he was killed in a freak accident at a kiddie park. Dr. Burk's digital-imaging software raised an image of electromagnetic concentration, which Mulder interpreted as a ghost ("The Calusari"). A few years later, Dr. Burks examined a sample of Leonard Betts' decapitated head and by applying high-frequency electricity was successful in his attempt to photograph the genetic mutant's coronal discharge. ("Leonard Betts")

University Medical Center Hospital in Seattle, Washington, where fast-food worker and former kidnap victim Lucy Householder was rushed when she suddenly collapsed, bleeding from the nose, at exactly the same time another little girl was being abducted. ("Oubliette")

University of Pennsylvania Hospital Tissue Bank Medical facility where Mulder and Scully learned that the late Howard Graves' kidney was transplanted in Boston, his liver in Dallas, and his corneas in Portland; the dura matter of Graves' spinal column had been cryogenically preserved at the hospital. ("Shadows")

"Unmarked Helicopters" Soul Coughing song that was blaring on Max Fenig's stereo system while Mulder and Scully searched the UFOlogist's airstream trailer after his death aboard commercial airline Flight 549. ("Max") *"Unmarked Helicopters" is a track on the CD* Songs in the Key of X.

☐ **"Unrequited"** Written by Howard Gordon and Chris Carter. Directed by Michael Lange. File number 4X16. *First aired February 23, 1997. Mulder and Scully try to stop a phantom POW from killing the military brass who left him to die in Vietnam.* **Classic Sound Bite:** *"I found his story compelling, personally. But then again I believed the Warren Commission."* **Background Check:** *The scenes showing a mass of people at the Vietnam Memorial rededication ceremony was a visual "tiling effect" accomplished by taking 500 extras and duplicating them, effectively turning 500 into 5,000.*

unruhe German word meaning "unrest" or "trouble." The transorbitally-lobotomized victims of Gerry Schnauz endlessly repeated the word "unruhe." Scully identified Schnauz as a suspect by his terrified reaction to the word. ("Unruhe")

☐ **"Unruhe"** Written by Vince Gilligan. Directed by Rob Bowman. File number 4X02. *First aired October 27, 1996. Agents Mulder and Scully track* *a psychotic kidnapper/killer through psychic Polaroids ("thoughtography") left behind depicting nightmarish images of his terrified victims surrounded by demonic icons.* **Classic Sound Bite:** *"For truly to pursue monsters we must understand them. We must venture into their minds. Only in doing so we risk letting them venture into ours."* **Background Check:** *"Unruhe" was originally scheduled to be aired as the second episode of the fourth season, but was moved to become the first* X-Files *offering in the series' new Sunday night time slot.*

UN Security Council Resolution 1013 Ultra-secret pact that decreed any country that captured an E.B.E. (Extraterrestrial Biological Entity) was responsible for its immediate extermination. ("Musings of a Cigarette-Smoking Man")

Upshaw, Don (Paul Jarrett) Orderly at the Excelsis Dei Convalescent Home in Worcester, Massachusetts. Mulder discovered his body in the nursing home's basement, buried in the soil of orderly Gung Bituen's mushroom garden. ("Excelsius Dei")

Uranus Unlimited Investment firm that sold astrology-based marketing advice. The body of the company's owner, Claude Dukenfield, was discovered in the woods by Mulder and Scully with the assistance of reluctant psychic Clyde Bruckman. ("Clyde Bruckman's Final Repose")

U.S. Botanic Garden Washington, D.C., site of a clandestine meeting between Mulder and The Thinker (a.k.a. Kenneth Soona), a Lone Gunman computer hacker who broke into the Defense Department's system and penetrated the top-secret MJ files. ("Anasazi")

U.S. Coast Guard Headquarters Institution in Newport News, Virginia, where Mulder inquired about the salvage vessel *Talapus,* which had supposedly been searching for a gold-carrying Japanese submarine sunk during World War II. A Coast Guard official told Mulder that the DEA had refused to allow the *Talapus* into port. ("Nisei")

Usher, George (Terence Kelly) Businessman murdered by serial killer Eugene Tooms, who elongated and contorted his body in order to crawl through a six-by-eighteen-inch air vent in Usher's office. He was Tooms' third victim in 1993 and the one that captured Mulder and Scully's interest in the case. ("Squeeze")

U.S. Medical Research Institute of Infectious Diseases Medical facility where FBI agent Barrett Weiss' body was quarantined pending further examination after the pathologists who conducted the original autopsy became ill. ("End Game")

U.S. Space Surveillance Center Top-secret military installation located at Cheyenne Mountain, Colorado. One of the facility's radar observers detected an unidentified flying object entering the Earth's atmosphere off Connecticut's coast and tracked it to its impact point west of Lake Michigan near Townsend, Wisconsin. ("Fallen Angel")

V

Vallee

Vacation Village Motor Lodge Motel off I-90 in Germantown, Maryland, where Scully went into hiding after realizing that CIA Agent Ambrose Chapel wasn't who he appeared to be. Chapel, who was in actuality a shapeshifting extraterrestrial bounty hunter, tracked Scully to Vacation Village and, disguised as Mulder, took her hostage. ("Colony/End Game")

Valadeo, Danny Mulder's unseen but always helpful FBI friend who expedited fingerprint searches, test results, and other such quantitative data. Valadeo tracked down Linda Thibedeaux's son, police officer Raymond Morrow, whom she had put up for adoption as a baby after her 1940s assault and rape by The Slash Killer. ("Aubrey") *In an obvious continuity error, Danny Valadeo had the last name of Bernstein in the first season episode "Conduit."*

Valedespino, Dr. Peter (Allan Gray) Entomologist in Elsinore, Maryland, whom Skinner consulted in regards to a fatal bee swarm attack on a mail sorter at an overnight delivery company. Citing credibility problems and alleged sloppy work at the FBI lab in Washington, D.C., the assistant director asked Valedespino to examine a piece of honeycomb he took from the crime scene. Using larvae taken from the comb, Valdespino hatched more bees to identify the species. The insects unexpectedly swarmed the entomologist, killing him. After learning that Dr. Valdespino had died from a specially virulent strain of smallpox, Mulder hypothesized that someone had engineered a method of spreading the deadly contagion using bees. Mulder had consulted with the entomologist a few months earlier concerning a similar fatality. ("Zero Sum")

Vallee, Maj. Robert Air Force officer who, along with Lt. Jack Schaeffer, attempted to abduct and interrogate teenagers Harold Lamb and Chrissy Giorgio while disguised as gray-skinned extraterrestrials. An actual growling, red-skinned alien monstrosity, however, abducted all of them. After Vallee's costumed body was later discovered, an "alien autopsy" was videotaped by sci-fi fanatic Blaine Faulkner and edited so as to obscure the fact that the gray "alien" was in fact Maj. Vallee in disguise. ("Jose Chung's 'From Outer Space'") *Vallee was named in honor of author Jacques Vallee, the French astrophysicist and UFOlogist who, along with Allen Hyneck, wrote* The Edge of Reality: A Progress Report on UFOs.

Valley Woods High School Seattle, Washington, school attended by fifteen-year-old Amy Jacobs, who was later abducted by Carl Wade, the assistant to the school photographer. ("Oubliette")

V.A. Medical Center Military hospital in North Orange, New Jersey, where sleep-deprived patient Cpl. Augustus Cole was monitored for twelve years by Dr. Pilsson. Cole was discharged in 1994 with Pilsson's evidently forged or acquired signature. ("Sleepless")

Van Blundht Jr., Edward (Darin Morgan) Hopelessly romantic freak of nature with an anomalous muscular structure that allowed him to transform his physical appearance, including his height, weight, hair color and pattern, and even his voice. While working as a janitor at a medical park, Van Blundht (the "h" is silent) impregnated four women while impersonating their husbands. The shapeshifter also inseminated Amanda Nelligan, a dizzy single woman and rabid *Star Wars* fan, by morphing into the image of Luke Skywalker. All five women gave birth to babies with vestigial tails like their father, although in an attempt to live a normal life Van Blundht had had his removed. Taken into custody, Van Blundht escaped from the jail by metamorphosing into an exact duplicate of a deputy and, after locking Mulder in the boiler room of the community hospital, assumed the handsome visage of the FBI agent. Later, Van Blundht arrived at Scully's apartment with a bottle of wine, and was making headway in his seduction attempt until the real Mulder kicked in the front door just as their lips were about to meet. Van Blundht was incarcerated at the Cumberland Reformatory where he was regularly medicated with a muscle relaxant to deter his shapeshifting abilities. ("Small Potatoes") *Eddie Van Blundht was played by none other than Darin Morgan, who not only penned such* X-Files *classics as "Humbug," "Jose Chung's 'From Outer Space,'" and the Emmy-winning "Clyde Bruckman's Final Repose," but also played the repugnant sewer-dwelling Flukeman in season two's "The Host." Although Chris Carter asked Morgan to pen an episode for the fourth season, the burned-out* X-Files *writer declined the offer.*

Van Blundht Sr., Edward A former circus performer and sideshow act known as "Eddie the Monkey Man," who was born with a vestigial tail at the base of his spine. After his death from natural causes, his son Eddie Jr., hid the corpse in the attic of their Martinsburg, West Virginia, home so that he could continue to cash his father's Social Security checks. When Eddie Jr. escaped from police custody, Mulder and Scully questioned the man they believed was his father, until they realized he was, in fact, Eddie Jr. After Eddie Jr. ran out of the house and disappeared into the neighborhood, the agents searched the residence and discovered Edward Sr.'s mummified cadaver with its tail still intact in the attic. Scully's autopsy revealed an anomalous muscular structure (essentially the man's skin was muscle), which prompted Mulder to speculate that Eddie Jr. had inherited the same trait, thus explaining his unique ability to shapeshift. ("Small Potatoes") *The actor* *who played Edward Van Blundht, Sr. (or rather the actor who portrayed Eddie Jr.'s physical transformation of his father) was uncredited.*

Vance, Leonard (Dennis Lipscomb) Horribly burned man eight-year-old faith-healer Samuel Hartley brought back to life after he was killed in a 1983 automobile accident. The disfigured Vance, who later went to work as an aide for Hartley's evangelical Miracle Ministry, began poisoning people who came to the tent revivals as revenge for Hartley bringing him back from the dead to a life of anguish and deformity. After Hartley was beaten to death in jail, his spirit appeared to Vance and confronted him about his betrayal. After Hartley forgave him, Vance committed suicide by ingesting a cyanide derivative. ("Miracle Man")

Van Cleef, Laura Victim of the serial murderer "The Slash Killer," who raped her, carved the word SISTER into her chest with a razor and painted on the wall with her blood. Van Cleef, along with two other women, were murdered in Aubrey, Missouri, in 1942. The Slash Killer was never caught. ("Aubrey")

"VANITAS VANITATUM" Latin phrase translated to mean, "Vanity of vanities; all is vanity." Nurse Rebecca White, a practicing witch, scrawled the words in blood on the bathroom wall of Dr. Jack Franklyn's house, in reference to the sorcerer's sinful curse of vanity and his constant need for human blood sacrifices to transform his physical appearance over the years. ("Sanguinarium")

Varnes, Dr. Raymond (Jay Brazeau) Professor at the University of Maryland biology department consulted by Mulder and Scully during their investigation into possible soul switching between deceased bank robber Warren Dupre and wounded FBI agent Jack Willis. Dr. Varnes informed Mulder and Scully that in near-death experiences, the tremendous energy-release could cause profound personality changes. ("Lazarus") *Jay Brazeau also played Dr. Daly in "One Breath."*

Vase Man (Donald Fong) Older bespectacled Chinese immigrant in a dark suit whose job it was to pull the lottery tile from a jade vase in a smoke-filled gaming parlor in San Francisco's Chinatown. Although the betters drew tiles out of a vase in hopes of matching it and winning a jackpot that didn't actually exist, the losers had eyes, arms, legs, livers, and an assortment of other body parts surgically removed by the Hard-Faced Man, which were then sold on the lucrative black market. ("Hell Money")

VEGREVILLE The password that Mulder and one of the Kurt Crawford clones used to access the computer system at the Center for Reproductive Medicine and download a file directory containing the fertility clinic's patient list. Mulder noticed atop a desk a souvenir snowglobe etched with the word

VEGREVILLE and correctly guessed that it was the password to the computer terminal's protected files. ("Memento Mori") *The snowglobe shown in the episode originated from the real Vegreville in Alberta, Canada.*

Venable Plaza Hotel Elegant Boston hotel where a dinner party was to be held for Sir Malcolm Marsden, a British lord vacationing in Massachusetts. After a fire broke out on the fourteenth floor, pyrokinetic assassin Cecil L'ively (masquerading as Bob the caretaker) "rescued" the sleeping Marsden children. A room at the Venable Plaza had also been reserved by beautiful Scotland Yard Inspector Phoebe Green, an old flame from Mulder's student days at Oxford, who wanted to re-ignite their passion. ("Fire")

Venus According to the MIB who visited UFO witness Roky Crikenson, the planet most often confused with an alien spacecraft. ("Jose Chung's 'From Outer Space'") *Famous UFO debunker Philip J. Klass wrote in his book* UFOs Explained *the now familiar line, "No single object has been misinterpreted as a 'flying object' more often than the planet Venus." Klass County, the setting for* The X-Files *episode, "Jose Chung's 'From Outer Space,'" was a nod to the noted author.*

vever Haitian voodoo symbol. Self-proclaimed revolutionary Pierre Bauvais explained that the vever was a *loco-mirror* or "mirror of the soul." A vever adorned the tree into which Pvt. John "Jack" McAlpin slammed his car. ("Fresh Bones")

Vibuti Better known as "Holy Ash," a substance that supposedly materializes out of thin air during a paranormal event. Vibuti is created during either the presence of spirit beings or of bilocation, wherein a person's energy is transferred to a different place. After Steve Holvey was strangled to death in a garage-door mechanism, Mulder discovered the strange ash, which FBI lab technicians reported as containing nothing organic or inorganic. ("The Calusari")

Vietnam Veterans Memorial Also known as "The Wall," the Washington, D.C. monument, spanning nearly 240 feet in Constitution Gardens, that lists the more than 58,000 names of servicemen who died during the Vietnam conflict. While Mulder interrogated a witness at the famous memorial, Scully wandered away, seemingly preoccupied with a faded rose petal ("Never Again"). The 1997 rededication of the war memorial served as the site of an assassination attempt on the life of keynote speaker Maj. Gen. Benjamin Bloch by Nathaniel Teager, a former POW with phantom-like abilities. ("Unrequited")

Vikings vs. Redskins The professional football game Mulder missed attending after Minneapolis FBI agent Moe Bocks informed the X-Files team that two more desecrated corpses had been discovered. Mulder accepted the original grave mutilation case because he had a pair of forty-yard-line seats for the game at the Hubert H. Humphrey Metrodome. ("Irresistible")

Virtua Fighter 2 Darin Peter Oswald's favorite game at a strip-mall video arcade in Connerville, Oklahoma. An on-screen display alerted Mulder that the ten-game record-holder on Virtua Fighter 2 was initialed "D.P.O."— the only survivor in a series of fatal lightning strikes. ("D.P.O.")

Virtual Gambling A speculative stock that Philadelphia broker Ed Jerse recommended. Although the company's stock rose considerably in value as he predicted, Jerse was nevertheless fired for verbally assaulting two female co-workers at the investment firm of Fuller & Siegel. ("Never Again")

Vitagliano, Dr. (Barry W. Levy) Scientist associated with American University's paleoclimatology lab. Scully asked him to examine core samples taken from a cave in the Canadian Yukon Territory's St. Elias Mountains, where a survey team discovered the alleged corpse of an alien entombed in a block of ice. Dr. Vitagliano told Scully that the core samples consisted of numerous layers of sedimentation similar to the rings of a tree and contained hybrid cellular material within the matrix. ("Gethsemane") *Barry W. Levy also played a Navy doctor in "Apocrypha."*

Vitaris, Paul (Doug Abrahams) Coach at Crowley High School and a member of the town's secret occult religion in Millford Haven, New Hampshire. Thirty-five-year-old Vitaris was killed with a shotgun by demon-possessed school psychologist Pete Calcagni. ("Die Hand Die Verletzt") *The character was named after prominent online X-Phile Paula Vitaris, who has since written several articles about the series for leading entertainment magazines. Actor Doug Abrahams also appeared as a patrolman in "The X-Files: Pilot," an FBI agent in "Genderbender," Lt. Neary in "Hell Money" and ATF Agent Harbaugh in "The Field Where I Died."*

Volkischer Beobachter Nazi newspaper that blamed Jews for the type of ritual murders often blamed on occultists in modern times. Via the Internet, Scully accessed one of the publication's 1934 articles during the X-Files team's investigation into claims of occultism and Satan worship in the small New Hampshire town of Milford Haven. ("Die Hand Die Verletzt")

Von Drehle Air Force Reserve Installation Military facility located in Upstate New York, which recorded an unidentified radar blip enter commercial jet Flight 549's airspace and shadow the plane for ten minutes. Flight controllers then ordered a military fighter jet into 549's airspace on a mission to destroy the alien craft. Mulder was arrested and detained in the installations' brig on charges of interfering in the military investigation of a crash of a commercial airliner. ("Tempus Fugit/Max")

Vosberg (David Lewis) Member of the Cascade Volcano Research team assigned to the California Institute of Technology in Pasadena. ("Fire-walker") *David Lewis also played a police officer in "The Jersey Devil" and FBI agent Kreski in "Oubliette."*

Voyager The name of two unmanned space probes, launched August 20 and September 5, 1977. Each spacecraft carried a gold-plated copper record encased in a durable aluminum jacket. These multimedia presentations were meant for any intelligent extraterrestrial beings that might encounter the probes and included a greeting by then United Nations Secretary General Kurt Waldheim, fifty-four human languages, a detailed road map to our planet, hundreds of images of our populace, and various musical recordings, including Bach's *Brandenburg Concerto No. 2 in F* (which Senator Matheson played for Mulder in his Capitol Hill office). ("Little Green Men")

W

Well-Manicured Man

Wade, Carl (Michael Chieffo) Assistant to the school photographer for Valley Woods High in Seattle, Washington. When fifteen-year-old Amy Jacobs participated in the taking of her class picture, Wade fixated on the girl in an unhealthy way and was subsequently fired by his employer, Mr. Larken. That night, he crawled through a window and abducted Amy from her bedroom. In the 1970s, Wade kidnapped an eight-year-old girl named Lucy Householder and locked her in a cold, dark basement for five years before she escaped. Although Wade was never charged with the abduction, he was institutionalized for fifteen years for a bipolar condition. By the time the FBI raided Wade's cabin in Easton, Washington, he had already fled with Amy. Mulder shot him dead when he tried to drown the girl in a nearby river. ("Oubliette")

Waite, Rebecca (O-Lan Jones) Registered nurse who prepped patients at the Aesthetic Surgery Unit of Chicago's Greenwood Memorial Hospital. A practitioner of ritual magic, Nurse Waite placed pentagrams on or near patients undergoing cosmetic surgery, in an attempt to protect them from Dr. Jack Franklyn, a black magician, who transformed his appearance beyond the limits of surgery by using sorcery and the blood sacrifice of hospital patients. After several bizarre deaths, Dr. Franklyn tried to convince Mulder and Scully that Nurse Waite was a murderer, especially in light of the fact that she had worked at the hospital ten years earlier when similar deaths had occurred. After Nurse Waite was arrested for an unsuccessful knife attack on Dr. Franklyn, she died from the hemorrhaging caused by vomiting hundreds of straight pins. ("Sanguinarium") *The character of Nurse Rebecca Waite was named after Rebecca Nurse, one of the victims of the Salem witch hunts, and the popular Rider-Wait tarot deck. Actress O-Lan Jones played the organ-playing neighbor in Tim Burton's* Edward Scissorhands *and also appeared with Duchovny (although they didn't have any scenes together) in the movie,* Beethoven.

Waldheim, Kurt Former Secretary General of the United Nations whose recorded message was carried aboard the *Voyager* space probes: "I send greetings on behalf of the people of our planet. We step out of our solar system, into the universe, seeking only peaceful contact." ("Little Green Men")

walk-in Soul transference, in which enlightened beings take control of one's body. Per Mulder, Abraham Lincoln, Mikhail Gorbachev, and presidential advisor Charles Colson, were famous walk-ins. ("Red Museum")

"Walk, The" A single amputee's recurring dream about having two working legs. After talking about "The Walk," the man was berated by bitterly obnoxious quadruple amputee Leonard "Rappo" Trimble at a therapy session for wheelchair-bound war veterans at Fort Evanston's Army Hospital Psychiatric Ward in Maryland. ("The Walk")

🗀 **"Walk, The"** Written by John Shiban. Directed by Rob Bowman. File number 3X07. *First aired November 10, 1995. Another failed suicide attempt by a patient at a military hospital piques Mulder's interest with the talk of a "phantom soldier" who can walk where no man can walk, sees the Gulf War veterans no matter where they hide, and seems to know all their secrets.* **Classic Sound Bite:** *"Sometimes the only sane response to an insane world is insanity."* **Background Check:** *Episode writer John Shiban has stated that he got the idea for "The Walk" from watching an old Marlon Brando movie,* The Men.

Wallace, Carol Ailing woman who died shortly after Samuel Hartley tried to heal her with a laying on of hands. When Mulder, Scully and Sheriff Daniels attempted to exhume Wallace's body and conduct an autopsy, they were confronted by a threatening vigil of Hartley's flock. ("Miracle Man")

Wallace, Father Thomas Jesuit theologian who was slain in Memphis, Tennessee by the vampiric serial murderers, the Trinity Killers. ("3")

Wallenberg, Steve FBI agent who died during the 1989 apprehension of homicidal robber John Barnett. A videotape of his capture showed that Mulder hesitated in firing upon the armed Barnett, which allowed him the time to kill both his hostage and Agent Wallenberg. A remorseful Mulder blamed himself for the agent's death because he "screwed up" during his first case with the Bureau's Violent Crimes Unit. Wallenberg left behind a wife and two children. ("Young at Heart")

Waltos, Det. (Tom Mason) Washington, D.C. police detective assigned to the murder investigation of Carina Sayles, a prostitute whose body was found in FBI Assistant Director Walter Skinner's room at the Ambassador hotel. ("Avatar")

W.A.O. The Wild Again Organization, a group of anticaptivity activists dedicated to liberating circus and zoo animals. The W.A.O. and its spokesperson, Kyle Lang, asserted added pressure on the impoverished Fairfield, Idaho, Zoo to ensure its closing. ("Fearful Symmetry")

War of Northern Aggression, The Southern euphemism for the Civil War. During a conversation between Scully and Mrs. Peacock, the multiple amputee referred to "the War of Northern Aggression." ("Home")

📁 **"War of the Coprophages"** Written by Darin Morgan. Directed by Kim Manners. File number 3X12. *First aired January 5, 1996. While waiting out the fumigation of his apartment complex, Mulder investigates reports of UFO activity in a small Massachusetts town and discovers that killer mechanized cockroaches from outer space may be responsible for several recent deaths.* **Classic Sound Bite:** *"Her name is Bambi?"* **Background Check:** *Rather than the episode's dung-eating cockroaches (approximately 300 were used during the filming), Gillian Anderson was more horrified by the scene in which she gave Queequeg, her Pomeranian pooch, a bath in the kitchen sink of her apartment. "The dog had a wicked case of gas. I had to hold my breath while saying my lines," she recalled. "Something was dying inside of that dog." The title of the episode is Darin Morgan's play on H.G. Wells' Martian invasion classic* War of the Worlds, *as is the name of the town, Miller's Grove (Grover's Mill was the town in WOTW).*

Warren, Vernon SEE: **Ephesian, Vernon**

Washington County Regional Airport Small-craft airport near Lula Philips' hideout. Her phone call to the FBI demanding a $1 million ransom for Scully revealed the background noise of a small plane taking off was isolated, convincing agents to canvass the three square miles around the airport. ("Lazarus")

Washington Institute of Technology Site of the Mahan Propulsion Laboratory and the crime scene of several murders committed by retarded janitor Roland Fuller. ("Roland")

Washington National Airport Washington, D.C., airport where Skinner and Scully met Mulder's plane after it arrived from Syracuse, New York. Mulder had telephoned his partner from the aircraft, informing her that he had locked Agent Pendrell's assassin in the lavatory and instructing her to meet him at the airport when his flight landed. The killer was abducted, however, after the plane encountered a UFO in mid-air. ("Max")

Watergate Hotel & Office Complex Famous Washington, D.C., landmark whose underground parking lot was used as a secret meeting place for Mulder and Scully after the X-Files unit was disbanded and the two agents were reassigned. ("Little Green Men")

Waters, Bernadette Alleged alien abductee whose photo Mulder showed to Scully. Waters displayed a small V-shaped scar behind her left ear, as did NICAP member Max Fenig. ("Fallen Angel")

Watkins, Donna (Tina Gilbertson) Greenwich, Connecticut, resident who, while jogging with her husband, Ted, found eight-year-old Teena Simmons sitting stunned and unresponsive in her front yard, and her father, Joel, dead. ("Eve")

Watkins, Gina (Sheila Paterson) Clerk at the county hospital in Townsend, Wisconsin, who was unable to locate any records to prove that deputy sheriff Jason Wright had ever been treated at the medical facility. ("Fallen Angel")

Watkins, Richard Suspect in a series of heinous murders committed in the northwest region of the U.S. in 1946, in which the victims were ripped to pieces and eaten. After police cornered and shot a vicious animal, which they believed was responsible for the cannibalistic deaths, the lupine yet humanoid creature proved to be Watkins. The Trego Indians believed that Watkins had been attacked by what the Algonquians called the Manitou, an evil spirit that could turn men into beasts. The investigation into the mutilation murders was the first X-Files on record, initiated by J. Edgar Hoover himself. ("Shapes")

Watkins, Ted (David Kirby) With his wife, Donna, he discovered the mutilated body of his neighbor, Joel Simmons, sitting in a porch swing drained of seventy-five percent of his blood. Simmons' young daughter, Teena, sat dazedly near the corpse. ("Eve")

WDF Newscan/Channel 8 Television program that carried a live report on the Ardis, Maryland, police manhunt for a fugitive who leapt into the harbor, leaving behind a trail of green blood. Deep Throat telephoned Mulder at his apartment and told him to watch. The agent videotaped the report, and later printed out a frame-grab. ("The Erlenmeyer Flask")

Webster (Deryl Hayes) Mysterious CIA agent who, along with his partner, Ms. Saunders, requested Mulder and Scully's assistance after their investigation into Philadelphia-based HTG Industrial Technologies turned up a potential X-File connection. ("Shadows") *Deryl Hayes also played Agent Morris in "Little Green Men" and an army doctor in "The Walk."*

Weiss, Barrett (Andrew Johnston) FBI agent assigned to the Syracuse, New York, field office. Realizing that the abortion doctors assassin was following a geographic pattern, Mulder asked Weiss to go to the Syracuse residence of Dr. Aaron Baker, where he encountered the alien Bounty Hunter. When Weiss shot the menacing extraterrestrial, green fluid oozed from his wounds, causing the agent to collapse as if poisoned. Although no cause of death could be determined, Scully discovered polycythemia, an excessive production of red blood cells, which caused the agent's blood to curdle. Weiss's body was quarantined at the U.S. Medical Research Institute of Infectious Diseases where further examinations revealed a mysterious retrovirus present in his blood. ("Colony/End Game") *Andrew Johnston also portrayed military test pilot Col. Budahas in "Deep Throat" and a medical examiner in "Demons."*

Weiss, Jacob (David Groh) Caring and protective father of Ariel Luria, whose betrothed was brutally murdered in a Brooklyn market by three teenage racists. After the neo-Nazi youths were killed one by one, Scully suspected that Weiss, an ex-terrorist, was taking revenge in the guise of the mythical golem of ancient Hebrew text. The agent's background check on the Hasidic Jew revealed that at the age of ten he had survived a concentration camp massacre of 9,000 by the Nazis; immigrated to Israel after World War II, where he joined the Jewish military underground; and was arrested in 1959 by the British for a bombing that killed seven civilians. Weiss was nearly killed by the golem when he attempted to stop his daughter from marrying the monster-like "abomination." ("Kaddish") *Actor David Groh is best remembered for his role on the seventies' comedy series,* Rhoda.

Well-Manicured Man (John Neville) Suave, distinguished-looking older Englishman to whom the Cigarette-Smoking Man has to answer. The Machiavellian power-broker is a high-ranking member of the Shadowy Syndicate, the conspiratorial "consortium representing global interests" who meet at a smoke-filled, luxurious private club on 46th Street in New York City. At the funeral service for William Mulder, he told Scully that he and his colleagues "would be extremely threatened" by the contents of the stolen MJ documents being leaked. He also informed her that Mulder was dead and that she herself was marked for death in one of two ways: shot at her home with an unregistered weapon or by someone close to her, at an unscheduled meeting. Well-Manicured Man's motives were not benevolent: he merely felt that her death would draw problematic attention to him and his associates. When Scully asked what his business was, he replied, "We predict the future, and the best way to predict the future is to invent it" ("The Blessing Way"). After Alex Krycek and Luis Cardinal killed Scully's sister by mistake, the Well-Manicured Man berated the Cigarette-Smoking Man for his bungling and demanded that he produce the missing digital tape containing the MJ files. Shortly thereafter, the Well-Manicured Man met with Mulder and Scully at the greenhouse of the recently deceased Victor Klemper, a former Nazi scientist. He didn't deny complicity in Klemper's death and admitted to being in a photograph that Mulder found of his father, Deep Throat, and the Cigarette-Smoking Man. After the 1947 Roswell UFO crash, he explained, Klemper and other Nazi scientists were granted amnesty under Operation Paper Clip and brought to the U.S. to conduct experiments in creating an alien-human hybrid. During the Cold War, men like William Mulder collected genetic material from millions of people through smallpox vaccinations, and William—having threatened to expose the eugenics program—was kept silent via the abduction of his daughter, Samantha ("Paper Clip"). The Well-Manicured Man once again chastised the Syndicate's "associate in Washington" after the Cigarette-Smoking Man threatened their

"Project's future" by attempting to assassinate FBI Assistant Director Skinner. The Well-Manicured Man met with Mulder in Central Park after the agent obtained his secret telephone number, and confirmed that a UFO was downed by American pilots during the final days of World War II. Complications arose during the salvage operation, and a cover story about a third A-bomb bound for Japan was concocted. At the close of their meeting, Mulder told the Well-Manicured Man that the renegade Alex Krycek possessed the stolen DAT containing the MJ files and had been selling its secrets. In exchange for this information, Mulder received a warning that the hospitalized Skinner was still in danger of another assassination attempt ("Apocrypha"). The Well-Manicured Man, who openly disdained the way the Cigarette-Smoking Man resorted to overt violence, was forced to turn to CSM and his unique "capabilities" after his personal physician (and implied lover) was executed by a former KGB assassin at his horse farm in Charlottesville, Virginia ("Tunguska/Terma"). *John Neville is a noted Shakespearean actor who was awarded the Order of the British Empire in 1965. A former member of the prestigious London Old Vic Company, he has a long and distinguished career on stage. Onscreen, Neville's credits include* The Fifth Element, Dangerous Minds, Little Women, Crime and Punishment, *and the starring role in* The Adventures of Baron Munchausen. *For fun, Neville recites the complete works of Sir Francis Bacon from memory.*

Wells, Ms. (Christine Upright-Letain) Employee of the Fairfield County Social Services Hostel in Greenwich, Connecticut, who took care of eight-year-old Teena Simmons after her father, Joel, was murdered. ("Eve")

Werber, Dr. Heitz (Jim Jansen) Conducted Mulder's hypnotic regression therapy sessions on June 16, 1989, an audiotape of which Scully found in the X-File (X-42053) on Samantha Mulder's 1973 disappearance ("Conduit"). The hypnotherapist also interviewed psychiatric hospital patient Billy Miles, who recalled memories of an eerie light that took him to a "testing place," where he was told to gather others for experiments ("The X-Files: Pilot")

Werner, Mr. (Paul Joyce) Serial killer Eugene Tooms' fourth present-day victim. The 100-plus-year-old mutant crawled through an air vent into Werner's suburban Baltimore home by elongating his body. ("Squeeze")

Westin One of the FBI agents Bruskin assigned to canvass the three square miles around Washington County Regional Airport in search of Scully and her kidnapper, Lula Phillips. ("Lazarus")

Westward Inn Motel from which Kevin Kryder was kidnapped by Simon Gates (Millennium Man) while taking a bath. Mulder and Scully broke open the bathroom door to find the young boy missing, the wrought-iron bars on the window smoldering and bent outward. ("Revelations")

📁 **"Wetwired"** Written by Mat Beck. Directed by Rob Bowman. File number 3X23. *First aired May 10, 1996. Mulder and Scully's partnership is tested to the extreme when they uncover a clandestine conspiracy behind a bizarre series of seemingly unrelated murders involving tweaked cable-TV signals in a suburban Maryland community.* **Classic Sound Bite:** *"Bet all you guys were officers in the audio-visual club in high school, huh?"* **Background Check:** *"Wetwired" was penned by Mat Beck, the special effects producer for* The X-Files, *who left the series shortly after the episode originally aired to supervise the visuals on 20th Century Fox's disaster movie,* Volcano. *Beck was replaced by Area 51, the group that created the FX for* Space: Above and Beyond.

"whammy, the" Mulder's description of what happened to one of the victims of Robert "Pusher" Modell's psychic powers of persuasion. Scully's response was a typical, "Please explain to me the scientific nature of 'the whammy.'" ("Pusher")

Wharton, Col. Jacob (Daniel Benzali) Grim Marine commandant in charge of the Folkstone INS Processing Center, which housed 12,000 Haitian refugees. When self-proclaimed revolutionary Pierre Bauvais warned the colonel that the Marines stationed at the camp would have their souls taken one by one if the refugees weren't repatriated, Wharton responded by ordering his soldiers to beat the Haitians. An eventual victim of zombification, Col. Wharton was buried alive in a coffin. ("Fresh Bones") *Baldheaded Daniel Benzali starred as the high-profile L.A. lawyer Ted Hoffman on ABC's* Murder One *during the series' freshman year and as the seemingly nefarious head of White House security in the 1997 theatrical thriller* Murder at 1600.

white buffalo According to Native American Albert Hosteen, a rare animal whose birth was "a powerful omen," meaning that "great changes were coming" ("Paper Clip"). *Unable to use an actual white buffalo for this episode,* The X-Files *crew was forced to photograph a very light-colored calf and bleach it optically in post-production.*

White, Det. Angela (Dana Wheeler-Nicholson) Attractive police detective in "the Perfect Harmony City" of Comity who suspected a satanic cult was responsible for a series of high school students' deaths. Eventually it was discovered that an odd planetary alignment known as a "syzygy" was the catalyst for the population's out-of-character behavior, including a drunken Mulder, who suggested that Det. White help him "solve the mystery of the horny beast." ("Syzygy")

White, Kate One of four Crowley High School students who unintentionally summoned the demon Azazel to the small New Hampshire town of Milford Haven. ("Die Hand Die Verletzt") *The young actress who portrayed Kate White went uncredited.*

Whiting Institute Highly-secure medical facility for the criminally insane which housed a straitjacketed grown-up Eve 6 in cellblock Z. Eight-year-olds Teena Simmons and Cindy Reardon were incarcerated at the Whiting Institute after Mulder apprehended them for the murders of their "fathers" and Dr. Sally Kendrick. ("Eve")

"whopper" Word NTSB chief investigator Mike Millar used to describe Mulder's explanation for the cause of commercial airliner Flight 549's crash in Upstate New York, which claimed the lives of 133 passengers and crew. Although Millar seemed open-minded to extreme possibilities, he found Mulder's theory of UFOs, alien abductions, and "tractor beams" somewhat difficult to believe. ("Max")

Wicca Pre-Christian religion of occult witches. Wiccan beliefs are unstructured, but usually have an environmental bent marked by ritual worship of the earth and the changing seasons. Wiccans also take great pains to distinguish their worship from Satanism and black magic. ("Die Hand Die Verletzt")

"wiggy" Scully's non-medical description of Joseph Patnick after he saw a Bosnian war criminal on the cable news channel at a psychiatric hospital and became hysterical. ("Wetwired")

Wilczek, Brad (Rob LaBelle) Computer genius and founder of the high-tech Eurisko Corporation in Crystal City, Virginia. Forced out of the company by CEO Benjamin Drake (with a golden parachute of $400 million), Wilczek was adamantly against any use of Eurisko's software in military or "immoral government" applications, especially his pet project, the Central Operating System (COS). After Wilczek "disappeared," Deep Throat informed Mulder that the government had learned that he had developed an AI (artificial intelligence) "adaptive network," essentially a learning computer, and was holding Wilczek in an effort to retrieve his research. ("Ghost in the Machine")

Wilkes, Michele (Jennifer Clement) Emergency Medical Technician (EMT) who raced an ambulance through the streets of Pittsburgh as her partner, Leonard Betts, attended to a patient's life with his extraordinary ability to diagnose cancer. Wilkes lost control of the vehicle while speeding through an intersection and a massive wreck ensued, decapitating Betts. Later, Wilkes recognized Betts' voice transmitting over the ambulance radio. After she located him outside of Allegheny Catholic Hospital, a sincerely apologetic Betts (now going under the name Truelove) injected her with a lethal dose of potassium chloride in order to protect his secret—that he was a highly-evolved lifeform that possessed the ability to regenerate his body parts. ("Leonard Betts")

Wilkins, Nurse (Lorena Gale) Intensive care nurse who ministered to a comatose Scully at Northeast Georgetown Medical Center. When Scully regained consciousness, she asked Wilkins for Nurse Owens, who had spoken to her and encouraged her during her coma. Wilkins said she had worked at the hospital for ten years and she had never heard of a Nurse Owens. ("One Breath") *Lorena Gale also played Ellen Bledsoe, the Philadelphia county medical examiner, in "Shadows" and Harold Spuller's defense attorney in "Elegy."*

Willig, Henry (Don Thompson) One of the subjects of Dr. Saul Grissom's Vietnam-era secret military experiments to obtain the ideal soldier by eradicating the need for sleep. Willig was a Marine assigned to Special Forces and Recon Squad J-7 and one of three survivors out of thirteen, the other two being Cpl. Augustus D. Cole (a.k.a. Preacher) and Salvatore Matola, who was previously believed to have died in combat. When Cole visited Willig in his run-down Brooklyn apartment, Willig was seemingly gunned down by a vision of bloodied Vietnamese while watching a home-shopping channel. Mulder theorized that Cole, who hadn't slept in twenty-four years, had developed the psychic ability to create dreams so real they could kill. ("Sleepless") *Actor Don Thompson also played NSA agent Holtzman in "Conduit" and the tormented Lt. Col. Victor Stans in "The Walk."*

Willis, Jack (Christopher Allport) FBI agent assigned to the Violent Crimes Unit who spent a year in the obsessive pursuit of latter-day Bonnie and Clyde bank robbers Warren James Dupre and wife/accomplice Lula Philips. Willis, who was Scully's former Academy instructor and boyfriend, was seriously wounded when the two agents investigated a robbery tip, before Scully downed Dupre with three shots. In the hospital emergency room, Willis (who had been technically dead for thirteen minutes) was revived after much defibrillation while a dead Dupre, lying unseen, reacted to the final two jolts. Willis survived and began to take on the criminal's persona, which included severing three of Dupre's fingers to get his wedding ring, becoming left-handed, abducting Scully, declaring his undying love for Lula, manifestating Dupre's tattoo, and forgetting such important details as his birthday (which he shared with Scully) and the fact that he was diabetic. Scully attributed Willis' profound personality change to his near-death experience, combined with post-traumatic stress, but Mulder believed Dupre had returned from the dead in Willis' physical body. He later died of apparent hyperglycemia, complication of diabetes, after shooting Lula Philips, who refused to give him insulin injections. Mulder later retrieved Willis' personal effects from the morgue, and gave Scully a watch inscribed "HAPPY 35th Love D," which she had given Willis three years earlier. Since Willis was an only child and his parents died while he was in college, Scully said she would give his belongings to a Parklawn youth for whom Willis had served as a Big Brother. Scully noted that Willis' watch had stopped at the exact time he went into cardiac arrest, but wasn't sure what to make of it. "It means," Mulder remarked compassionately, "whatever you want it to mean." ("Lazarus")

Wilmer, Lt. Terry (Colin Cunningham) The lone survivor of the USS *Allegiance*, a U.S. Navy submarine stranded in Arctic ice. He claimed that a man came aboard, sealed most of the crew below without air, and executed the rest. Wilmer supposedly had survived by hiding under the chief petty officer's body. After Mulder handcuffed himself to Wilmer, the lieutenant morphed into the familiar form of the alien Bounty Hunter. ("End Game") *Colin Cunningham also played Escalante in "731" and Dr. Stroman in "Wetwired."*

Wilton, Brother (Paul Batten) Kindred member who angrily denounced Mulder and Scully at a communal dinner when they asked the reclusive group to identify suspects in a videotape filmed by a hotel security camera at the scene of a murder. ("Genderbender") *Paul Batten also played Dr. Seizer in the third season episode "Piper Maru"*

Winston (Jude Zachary) Prison guard at the Cumberland State Correctional Facility in Virginia who delivered an overnight-mail package to convict Bobby Torrence. Inside was a bloody pig's leg that was infected with larvae from the parastoid *F. emasculata*. ("F. Emasculata") *Jude Zachary also had a bit part in "Musings of a Cigarette-Smoking Man."*

Winston, Bonnie Member of a girl scout troop that sighted and photographed a UFO in August 1967 near Lake Okobogee. ("Conduit")

Winter, Larry (George Touliatos) Venango county supervisor in Franklin, Pennsylvania. Winter insisted that no "stealth" helicopter was spraying an experimental insecticide in the suburban farming community, but under pressure changed his story and stated that the chemical had been proven safe to him, though he wouldn't say by whom. He eventually agreed to stop the spraying and to test the blood of all those exposed. ("Blood") *George Touliatos also portrayed Dr. Katz in the first season's "Eve."*

Winters, Dr. (Garrison Chrisjohn) Veterinarian who performed the autopsy on the dog belonging to Mona Wustner, a graduate student working at Boston's Museum of Natural History. Dr. Winters determined that the canine died from eating a cat that had eaten a poisoned rat. ("Teso dos Bichos")

Witch Hunt: A History of the Occult in America Book by M.R. Krashewski borrowed from the Crowley High School library by teenager Dave Duran. He and his friend Jerry Stevens ventured into the New Hampshire woods with their dates to read a prayer to Satan from the book in order to scare the girls and get them drunk. As Duran read an incantation, spectral voices murmured and rats appeared at their feet. Although Duran and the girls fled, Stevens's body was later discovered with his eyes and heart cut out. ("Die Hand Die Verletzt")

witch's pegs Three-pronged stakes driven into the ground to ward off evil spirits in the Ozarks. Mulder and Scully discovered witch's pegs in a field in Dudley, Arkansas, but Sheriff Tom Arens dismissed them as a leftover superstition. ("Our Town")

Withers, Jack (Michael Cavanaugh) Sioux City, Iowa, sheriff who told Mulder and Scully that missing teenager Ruby Morris was a problem girl and likely just ran away. He also considered the girl's mother, an alleged former alien-abductee, "a flake." Sheriff Withers investigated Greg Randall's murder after Mulder and Scully discovered his shallow grave in a wooded area of the Lake Okobogee National Park. ("Conduit")

Wolf Industries Manufacturer of high-tech surveillance electronics. NICAP member and UFO-conspiracy theorist Max Fenig referred to Wolf Industries as a "CIA supplier" and owned several sophisticated spy gadgets produced by the electronics firm, including the Wolf's Ear 200 listening device. ("Fallen Angel")

Women's Care Family Services and Clinic Scranton, Pennsylvania, abortion clinic where Dr. Landon Prince was killed by the alien Bounty Hunter with a stiletto-like weapon. After the extraterrestrial burned the building to the ground, police arrested Rev. Calvin Sistrunk, a local right-wing antiabortion extremist who had previously threatened Dr. Prince. ("Colony")

Women's Health Services Clinic Seemingly deserted Rockville, Maryland, abortion clinic where Mulder encountered several more adult clones of his sister, Samantha, and discovered that he had been manipulated. The alien Bounty Hunter knocked Mulder unconscious before the clones could tell him the location of the real Samantha. He awoke later to find the clinic burning and all the genetic replicas missing. ("End Game")

"Wonderful! Wonderful!" The reclusive and inbred Peacock family's favorite song. The cheerful Johnny Mathis tune was playing on the radio of their ancient Cadillac while they committed their gratuitously vicious murder of Sheriff Taylor and his wife. ("Home") *When the Johnny Mathis version of the song proved to be too expensive for its limited use in the episode, the producers turned to soundalike singer Kenny James.*

Wong Rottweiler belonging to the groundskeeper at the Folkstone Municipal Cemetery. ("Fresh Bones") *The dog's name was an in-joke reference to X-Files producer and frequent writer James Wong, who with partner Glen Morgan had scripted the previous episode, then left the series to create the short-lived Space: Above and Beyond.*

Wong, Cheryl Alleged alien-abductee whose photo Mulder showed to Scully. Wong displayed a small V-shaped scar behind her left ear, as did NICAP member Max Fenig. ("Fallen Angel")

Woo Shing Wu Heroin-peddling Triad gang officially suspected in the Chinatown mutilation killing of Buffalo, New York, narcotics police detective Charlie Morris. Eight-year-old Michelle Bishop, the reincarnated spirit of the murdered cop, later proved that his real killers were larcenous fellow police officers, including his partner. ("Born Again")

Woosley, Scott Boy Scout leader who mysteriously disappeared after wandering off to relieve himself along the shore of Heuvelman's Lake in Georgia. The lower torso of Woosley's body was discovered two weeks later when a fisherman snagged the mutilated corpse line on his line. ("Quagmire")

Workman, Jennifer (Suzy Joachim) Roommate of Lauren Mackalvey, one of serial killer Virgil Incanto's lonely, overweight victims. Workman revealed that MacKalvey had met her charming and attractive final date via the Internet three months earlier. She gave Mulder copies of 2Shy's E-mail which included lines from obscure sixteenth-century Italian poems found only in controlled-circulation academic libraries, prompting Mulder to conclude that the murderer had a scholarly background. ("2Shy")

World Weekly Informer Tabloid newspaper Robert "Pusher" Modell picked up while standing in the checkout line in a Loudoun County, Virginia, supermarket. On the cover was an artist's rendition of the sewer-dwelling Flukeman next to the announcement that his body had washed ashore on Martha's Vineyard ("Pusher"). *A separate headline in the right corner of the tabloid announced "Depravity Rampant on Hit TV Show" and featured an inset photograph of* X-Files *props master Ken Hawryliw with a strip-o-gram artist, taken on his birthday.* An April 1997 issue of the *World Weekly Informer* showcased a mutant child on the cover with the glaring headlines: "Monkey Babies Invade Small Town . . . Did West Virginia Women Mate With Visitors from Space?" That particular edition of the tabloid caught Mulder's attention, compelling the X-Files team to investigate the births of five babies with vestigial tails over the course of three months—all within a town of less than 15,000 residents. ("Small Potatoes")

wormholes Theoretical portals where matter interfaces with time at an accelerated or decelerated rate. Mulder believed these wrinkles in time were used in the 1944 Philadelphia Experiment, and erroneously believed they would explain the disappearance of the USS *Ardent* and nine other ships in the 65th-parallel area over the years. ("Dod Kalm")

"Wow!" signal SEE: **Ehman, Jerry**

Wright, Belinda (Freda Perry) Widow of Jason Wright, a deputy sheriff killed while investigating the crash of a UFO near Lake Michigan in Townsend, Wisconsin. Mrs. Wright told Mulder and Scully that the government refused to release her husband's severely burnt body, and threatened to withhold his pension if she protested. The widow was the mother of a three-year-old son. ("Fallen Angel")

Wright, Jason (Alvin Sanders) Young deputy sheriff in Townsend, Wisconsin, site of a downed UFO. He sustained fifth- and sixth-degree burns over ninety percent of his body when he investigated a bright light that appeared to be a forest fire near the town. Wright later died of his injuries and the government whisked away his body before an autopsy could be performed. ("Fallen Angel") *Alvin Sanders also played the bus driver in "F. Emasculata."*

WSM 650 Radio station tractor-trailer operator Ranheim (a.k.a. Frank Druce) was listening to while driving his rig. WSM 650 was broadcasting country-and-western music from Nashville's Grand Ole Opry, sponsored by Goody's Headache Powder. ("E.B.E.")

Wustner, Mona (Janne Mortil) Graduate student working at the Hall of Indigenous Peoples of Boston's Museum of Natural History. Her death was one of several unsolved mutilation murders potentially linked to the unearthing of an ancient Ecuadorian artifact, an Amaru urn reputed to hold the remains of a female shaman and its jaguar spirit curse. ("Teso dos Bichos")

WXDL/Channel 11 Television station whose correspondent reported from the Jet Propulsion Laboratory in Pasadena, California, on the first *Viking* Orbiter pictures from Mars, revealing a face-like land formation. ("Space")

Wysencki, Margaret A sixty-six-year-old widow and retired production-line worker with Laramie Tobacco company, where she was employed for approximately thirty-six years. She was the second unintentional victim of Dr. Chester Banton's shadow, which reduced matter to pure energy. ("Soft Light")

Echols 97

X (Steven Williams) Also known as Mr. X, he was Deep Throat's successor as Mulder's informant. To initiate contact, the FBI agent used masking tape to form an "X" on his apartment window. The middle-aged black man was a shadowy character who worked for the Cigarette-Smoking Man, but obviously had his own self-serving agenda ("Wetwired"). Whereas Deep Throat was trying to atone for past deeds by giving Mulder enough information to further Mulder's search for the truth, X was much more ambiguous about his motivations and certainly more reluctant and cryptic in providing information. The ruthless X appeared to be edgy and even paranoid during his encounters with Mulder, more than once admitting that he was afraid of meeting the same fate as his predecessor. Mr. X literally went head-to-head with Walter Skinner in an elevator and warned the Assistant FBI Director that he had "killed men for far less" ("End Game"). He calmly and methodically executed an operative dispatched to steal a vial of Scully's blood ("One Breath") and ruthlessly killed the Red-Haired Man execution-style before helping Mulder escape from a bomb-laden train car ("731"). X and two "paramedics" abducted scientist Dr. Banton from Mulder and Scully's protection and turned him over to the very government researchers Dr. Banton feared most. Angrily, Mulder told X he wanted nothing more to do with the man, and the informant warned him, "You're choosing a dangerous time to go it alone" ("Soft Light"). The two men later engaged in a brutal confrontation for possession of the alien stiletto-like weapon before going for their handguns ("Talitha Cumi"). After years of covertly trying to undermine the Shadowy Syndicate's activities, Mr. X was identified as a traitor by the 1st Elder and the Cigarette-Smoking Man and was shot to death at close-range by the Gray-Haired Man in the hallway of Mulder's apartment house. During the last moments of his life, X crawled to the agent's apartment where he wrote in his own blood "SRSG," four initials that would point Mulder in the direction of his next informant, Marita Covarrubias, the assistant to the U.N.'s Special Representative to the Secretary General ("Herrenvolk"). Was the complex and devious Mr. X a player or a pawn? Was he a source of disinformation or was he Mulder's facilitator for the truth? With his violent death, X created more questions than he answered. *The role of X was originally played by actress Natalia Nogulich (Vice-Admiral Alynna on* Star Trek: The Next Generation), *who actually filmed one episode ("Sleepless"). After series creator Chris Carter reviewed the dailies, however, he decided the scenes didn't* *work out the way he had intended with a female contact and recast Steven Williams in the role of the shadowy informant. The actor has appeared in numerous movies and TV shows over the years, but he is best remembered for his five-year stint as Capt. Fuller on the hit Fox series* 21 Jump Street, *which was produced by the future X-Files creative team of Glen Morgan and James Wong.*

X-Files Division of the FBI that investigated unexplained and paranormal cases outside the Bureau mainstream. The first X-File, initiated by Director J. Edgar Hoover himself, stemmed from a series of murders in and around the northwest in 1946, in which the victims were shredded and eaten by a half-animal/half-man suspect. Although he was cornered and killed by police that year, similar murders occurred in 1954, '59, '64, '78, and '94 ("Shapes"). Agent Fox "Spooky" Mulder, an Oxford-educated psychologist known to be the Bureau's best crime investigator, persuaded his superiors to transfer him to the X-Files division's basement office at FBI headquarters in 1991. The next year, Dana Scully, a medical doctor who had spent two years in the FBI teaching at Quantico Academy, was asked to become Mulder's partner and report on his investigations of the highly unorthodox X-Files cases ("The X-Files: Pilot"). In 1994 the X-Files division was shut down and agents Mulder and Scully reassigned after "word came down from the top of the executive branch" ("The Erlenmeyer Flask"), only to be re-opened by a frustrated and angry Assistant Director Skinner a few months later ("Ascension"). *The pilot episode was preceded by text claiming "The following is inspired by actual documented events," although the teaser, according to series creator Chris Carter, was never meant to mislead viewers into believing there actually exists a paranormal investigative FBI division such as the X-Files.*

📁 **"X-Files, The: Pilot"** Written by Chris Carter. Directed by Robert Mandel. *First aired September 10, 1993. FBI Special Agent and medical doctor Dana Scully is assigned by her Washington superiors to keep an eye on the activities of fellow agent Fox Mulder, a withdrawn loner who has a tendency to trawl through the X-Files—paranormal cases that are both inexplicable and unsolved. Although a skeptic at heart, Scully finds herself drawn into Agent Mulder's latest X-File investigation: the murder of several high school classmates in an Oregon forest, all of them displaying the tell-tale signs of victims of alien experimentation.* **Classic Sound Bite:** *"Agent Mulder believes we are not alone."* **Background Check:** *Set decorator Shirley Inget and her staff combed through science magazines and used bookstores, gathering cast-off documents from police departments and UFO societies to fill Mulder's cluttered office in the basement of FBI headquarters with "anything that's weird, wacky, and a little bit puzzling." A close-up of the bulletin board next to the* I WANT TO BELIEVE *flying saucer poster would reveal articles on gamma rays, crickets, suicide, the "Murphodynamics of Toast," and crop circles.*

Yappi

Yaje (pronounced "YAH-hay") Hallucinogenic fluid often referred to as "the Vine of the Soul" by the Secona Indian tribe of Ecuador. Dr. Alonso Bilac of the Boston Museum of Natural History drank the yellowish liquid in large quantities in an attempt to open himself up to possession by the jaguar spirit of a dead female shaman. ("Teso dos Bichos")

Yaloff Psychiatric Hospital Mental health facility in Piedmont, Virginia, where Mulder and Scully placed "human black hole" Dr. Chester Banton to safeguard him. Mr. X manipulated Mulder to discover the whereabouts of Banton and abduct him from the hospital. ("Soft Light")

Yamaguchi, Dr. The pathologist who performed the autopsy on murdered Buffalo, New York, police officer Charlie Morris. Det. Sharon Lazard tracked down the retired Dr. Yamaguchi in Palm Beach, and asked him to fax a missing page of the autopsy report, which revealed that Morris had drowned in sea water before being mutilated. ("Born Again")

Yappi, The Stupendous (Jaap Broeker) Famous eyebrow-endowed TV psychic (1–900–555-YAPP) summoned by the St. Paul, Minnesota, police department to assist them in their investigation of a string of prognosticator murders. Yappi asked a skeptical Mulder to leave the crime scene of the Doll Collector's murder because the agent's negative energy was "blocking" his "psychic readings." In addition to his regularly published predictions in the tabloid *Midnight Inquisitor,* the publicity-hungry Yappi also served as narrator for the "alien autopsy" video. ("Clyde Bruckman's Final Repose" and "Jose Chung's 'From Outer Space'") *The comic-relief role of The Stupendous Yappi was written by Darin Morgan specifically for David Duchovny's stand-in, Dutch-born actor Jaap (pronounced "yapp") Broeker.*

Yonechi, Dr. (Hiro Kanagwa) Well-respected Japanese scientist who was murdered by the time traveling Jason Nichols, in an attempt to stop Yonechi and others from developing the technology that would make time travel possible. Although Nichols' present-time girlfriend, cryobiologist Lisa Ianelli, along with Scully and a team of medical personnel, successfully resuscitated Yonechi from the effects of a rapid freezing agent, his body temperature abruptly and rapidly began to increase, until finally he spontaneously combusted. ("Synchrony") *Actor Hiro Kanagawa portrayed systems analyst Peter Tanaka in the second season episode "Firewalker."*

📁 **"Young at Heart"** Written by Scott Kaufer and Chris Carter. Directed by Michael Lange. File number 1X15. *First aired February 11, 1994. A homicidal robber whom Mulder helped convict years earlier, and who supposedly died in prison, suddenly begins stalking the FBI agent and committing a new string of crimes after undergoing prison experiments to reverse the aging process.* **Classic Sound Bite:** *"Maybe John Barnett has found the perfect disguise— youth!"* **Background Check:** *The script for this episode began as a freelance effort by Chris Carter-acquaintance Scott Kaufer, the former editor of* California *magazine and head of Warner Bros. comedy development. Carter's rewrite added, among other things, Barnett's regenerative humanoid salamander hand. "Young at Heart" was also the first episode in which Mulder killed anyone.*

Yung, David (Richard Yee) An acquaintance of Kristen Kilar, a mysterious woman Mulder met at Club Tepes in Los Angeles. Mulder followed Kilar and Yung to a nearby restaurant, Ra, where the man was attacked and murdered by The Father and The Unholy Spirit, two members of the vampiresque Trinity Killers. ("3")

Z

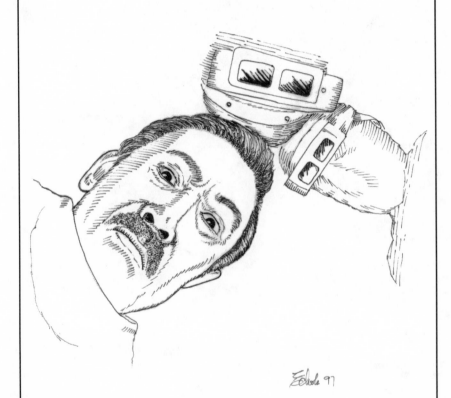

Zama

Zama, Dr. Shiro (Robert Ito) Adopted name of Dr. Takeo Ishimaru, a Japanese scientist who was a member of a World War II medical corps, 731, that performed horrible experiments on human subjects. Scully recalled seeing Zama hover over her during her abduction experience and believed he was responsible for the monitoring chip implant in her neck. Zama was traveling incognito on a train boarded by Mulder and was later murdered in the lavatory by the Red-Haired Man. The Cigarette-Smoking Man came into possession of Zama's meticulously-written journal and had it transcribed from its original Japanese. ("Nisei/731") *Robert Ito played assistant coroner Dr. Sam Fujiyama on Jack Klugman's* Quincy, M.E.

Zeal Henry Trondheim's fifty-ton, double-hulled Norwegian trawler. It was stolen by the crew of pirate whaler, Olaffson, effectively stranding Mulder, Scully and Trondheim aboard the "ghost ship" USS *Ardent*. ("Dod Kalm")

Zelma, Madame (Karin Konoval) Phony prognosticator consulted by the Puppet serial killer before he murdered her and gouged her eyes out with the shards of her crystal ball. Insurance salesman and reluctant psychic Clyde Bruckman found her mutilated body in the trash dumpster outside his apartment complex in St. Paul, Minnesota. ("Clyde Bruckman's Final Repose") *Canadian actress Karin Konoval also portrayed Mrs. Peacock in "Home."*

Zenzola, Dr. Jo (Gabrielle Rose) Middlesex County Hospital physician in Sayreville, New Jersey, who examined a sewer worker who had been pulled under the water and emerged with a strange wound on his back. The man suspected he was grabbed by a python, except that the wound had four points. ("The Host") *Actress Gabrielle Rose also played Anita Budahas in "Deep Throat."*

📁 **"Zero Sum"** Written by Howard Gordon and Frank Spotnitz. Directed by Kim Manners. File number 4X21. *First aired April 4, 1997. Agent Mulder's investigation into the unexplained death of a mail sorter at an overnight delivery company is hindered by his superior, Assistant Director Skinner, who appears to be the chief suspect.* **Classic Sound Bite:** *"A man digs a hole, he risks falling into it."* **Background Check:** *This is the only episode other than second season's*

"3," in which Scully did not make an appearance. Gillian Anderson was on-location filming The Mighty, *her major motion picture debut in a leading role starring opposite Sharon Stone, Harry Dean Stanton, and Gena Rowlands. Mitch Pileggi (Walter Skinner) dedicated "Zero Sum" to the "loving memory" of his late father, Vito J. Pileggi.*

Zeus Faber U.S. Navy submarine assigned to guard a UFO, a so-called "Foo Fighter" downed during World War II. Complications arose during the salvage operation, and a cover story about a bomber carrying a third A-bomb destined for Japan was concocted. An alien lifeform—one that existed in an oil medium—took possession of the captain, Kyle Sanford, causing most of the crew members to die of radiation sickness until Executive Officer Christopher Johansen led a mutiny and locked the alien-possessed Sanford below decks with the sick men. Only 7 of 144 crew members survived. ("Piper Maru/Apocrypha")

Zeus Storage Pandora Street warehouse used for secret experiments combining human DNA with extraterrestrial viruses. The Maryland facility, which Deep Throat claimed was the site of the first human/alien hybrids, housed five terminally ill men floating in immense, fluid-filled tanks. ("The Erlenmeyer Flask")

Z-14 filter Device used by FBI technicians to isolate background noise and hone in on Scully's location after Lula Philips telephoned the Bureau demanding a $1 million ransom for the agent's release. The Z-14 filter revealed the sound of a small plane taking off, which convinced law enforcement agents to canvass the area around Washington County Regional Airport. ("Lazarus")

Zhirinovsky, Vladimir Leader of the Russian Social Democrats, who, according to the Lone Gunmen, was being put into power by the CIA, "the most heinous and evil force in the twentieth century." ("E.B.E.")

Zinnzser, Steven MUFON member who videotaped an alleged alien autopsy from an intercepted satellite transmission and sold it via mail order through his Allentown, Pennsylvania-based company, Rat Tail Productions. Zinnzser was murdered execution-style by a high-ranking Japanese diplomat. ("Nisei")

Zirinka, Madame (Denalda Williams) Astrologer and pragmatic business-woman who was convinced the strange behavior of the townfolk in Comity, including Mulder and Scully, was being caused by "a rare planetary alignment" of Mars, Uranus, and Mercury. The sign on her business read: ASTROLOGY, NUMEROLOGY, RUNES, READINGS. ("Syzygy") *Denalda Williams also appeared in the episode "Irresistible" as Marilyn Mandas,* *an employee of Ficicello Frozen Foods who interviewed death fetishist Donnie Pfaster for a delivery-person job.*

Zoe (Lalainia Lindejerg) Teenage girl who covertly entered the grounds of Ellens Air Force Base through a fence-hole to neck with her boyfriend, Emil, to "watch the air show" of two airborne balls of light. The teenage couple helped Mulder infiltrate the base, which was rumored to be one of six sites where parts of the 1947 Roswell UFO crash wreckage were taken. ("Deep Throat")

APPENDIX A: EPISODE LISTS WITH WRITER AND DIRECTOR CREDITS

The authors of this book wish to acknowledge the writers and directors of The X-Files *television episodes, from whose work this document has been derived.* **NOTE:** *The weekly episodic installments are numbered in the order in which they were filmed. For example, "Never Again" (4X13) was shot before "Leonard Betts" (4X14), although it was aired afterward. Also, "Unruhe" (4X02), which was the second episode shot during the series' fourth season, was aired fourth because Chris Carter and the network wanted a strong standalone to be shown for the first Sunday night viewing after the series made the move from Fridays.*

SEASON 1 (FIRST AIRED 1993–1994)

"The X-Files: Pilot." Written by Chris Carter. Directed by Robert Mandel.

1X01. "Deep Throat." Written by Chris Carter. Directed by Daniel Sackheim.

1X02. "Squeeze." Written by Glen Morgan and James Wong. Directed by Harry Longstreet.

1X03. "Conduit." Written by Alex Gansa and Howard Gordon. Directed by Daniel Sackheim.

1X04. "The Jersey Devil." Written by Chris Carter. Directed by Joe Napolitano.

1X05. "Shadows." Written by Glen Morgan and James Wong. Directed by Michael Katleman.

1X06. "Ghost in the Machine." Written by Alex Gansa and Howard Gordon. Directed by Jerrold Freeman.

1X07. "Ice." Written by Glen Morgan and James Wong. Directed by David Nutter.

1X08. "Space." Written by Chris Carter. Directed by William Graham.

1X09. "Fallen Angel." Written by Alex Gansa and Howard Gordon. Directed by Larry Shaw.

1X10. "Eve." Written by Kenneth Biller and Chris Brancato. Directed by Fred Gerber.

1X11. "Fire." Written by Chris Carter. Directed by Larry Shaw.

1X12. "Beyond the Sea." Written by Glen Morgan and James Wong. Directed by David Nutter.

1X13. "Genderbender." Written by Larry Barber and Paul Barber. Directed by Rob Bowman.

1X14 "Lazarus." Written by Alex Gansa and Howard Gordon. Directed by David Nutter.

1X15. "Young at Heart." Written by Scott Kaufer and Chris Carter. Directed by Michael Lange.

1X16. "E.B.E." Written by Glen Morgan and James Wong. Directed by William Graham.

1X17. "Miracle Man." Written by Howard Gordon and Chris Carter. Directed by Michael Lange.

1X18. "Shapes." Written by Marilyn Osborn. Directed by David Nutter.

1X19. "Darkness Falls." Written by Chris Carter. Directed by Joe Napolitano.

1X20. "Tooms" (a.k.a. "Squeeze 2"). Written by Glen Morgan and James Wong. Directed by David Nutter.

1X21. "Born Again." Written by Alex Gansa and Howard Gordon. Directed by Jerrold Freedman.

1X22. "Roland." Written by Chris Ruppenthal. Directed by David Nutter.

1X23. "The Erlenmeyer Flask." Written by Chris Carter. Directed by R.W. Goodwin.

SEASON 2 (FIRST AIRED 1994–1995)

2X01. "Little Green Men." Written by Glen Morgan and James Wong. Directed by David Nutter.

2X02. "The Host." Written by Chris Carter. Directed by Daniel Sackheim.

2X03. "Blood." Written by Glen Morgan and James Wong. Directed by David Nutter.

2X04. "Sleepless." Written by Howard Gordon. Directed by Rob Bowman.

2X05. "Duane Barry (Part 1 of 2)." Written by Chris Carter. Directed by Chris Carter.

2X06. "Ascension (Part 2 of 2)." Written by Paul Brown. Directed by Michael Lange.

2X07. "3." Written by Chris Ruppenthal, Glen Morgan, and James Wong. Directed by David Nutter.

2X08. "One Breath." Written by Glen Morgan and James Wong. Directed by R.W. Goodwin.

2X09. "Firewalker." Written by Howard Gordon. Directed by David Nutter.

2X10. "Red Museum." Written by Chris Carter. Directed by Win Phelps.

2X11. "Excelsius Dei." Written by Paul Brown. Directed by Stephen Surjik.

2X12. "Aubrey." Written by Sara Charno. Directed by Rob Bowman.

2X13. "Irresistible." Written by Chris Carter. Directed by David Nutter.

2X14. "Die Hand Die Verletzt." Written by Glen Morgan and James Wong. Directed by Kim Manners.

2X15. "Fresh Bones." Written by Howard Gordon. Directed by Rob Bowman.

2X16. "Colony (Part 1 of 2)." Written by Chris Carter (based upon a story by David Duchovny and Chris Carter). Directed by Nick Marck.

2X17. "End Game (Part 2 of 2)." Written by Frank Spotnitz. Directed by Rob Bowman.

2X18. "Fearful Symmetry." Written by Steven DeJarnatt. Directed by James Whitmore, Jr.

2X19. "Dod Kalm." Written by Howard Gordon and Alex Gansa. Directed by Rob Bowman.

2X20. "Humbug." Written by Darin Morgan. Directed by Kim Manners.

2X21. "The Calusari." Written by Sara Charno. Directed by Michael Vejar.

2X22. "F. Emasculata." Written by Chris Carter and Howard Gordon. Directed by Rob Bowman.

2X23. "Soft Light." Written by Vince Gilligan. Directed by James Contner.

2X24. "Our Town." Written by Frank Spotnitz. Directed by Rob Bowman.

2X25. "Anasazi (Part 1 of 3)." Written by Chris Carter (based upon a story by David Duchovny and Chris Carter). Directed by R.W. Goodwin.

SEASON 3 (FIRST AIRED **1995–1996**)

3X01. "The Blessing Way (Part 2 of 3)." Written by Chris Carter. Directed by R.W. Goodwin.

3X02. "Paper Clip (Part 3 of 3)." Written by Chris Carter. Directed by Rob Bowman.

3X03. "D.P.O." Written by Howard Gordon. Directed by Kim Manners.

3X04. "Clyde Bruckman's Final Repose." Written by Darin Morgan. Directed by David Nutter.

3X05. "The List." Written by Chris Carter. Directed by Chris Carter.

3X06. "2Shy." Written by Jeffrey Vlaming. Directed by David Nutter.

3X07. "The Walk." Written by John Shiban. Directed by Rob Bowman.

3X08. "Oubliette." Written by Charles Grant Craig. Directed by Kim Manners.

3X09. "Nisei (Part 1 of 2)." Written by Chris Carter, Howard Gordon, and Frank Spotnitz. Directed by David Nutter.

3X10. "731 (Part 2 of 2)." Written by Frank Spotnitz. Directed by Rob Bowman.

3X11. "Revelations." Written by Kim Newton. Directed by David Nutter.

3X12. "War of the Coprophages." Written by Darin Morgan. Directed by Kim Manners.

3X13. "Syzygy." Written by Chris Carter. Directed by Rob Bowman.

3X14. "Grotesque." Written by Howard Gordon. Directed by Kim Manners.

3X15. "Piper Maru (Part 1 of 2)." Written by Frank Spotnitz and Chris Carter. Directed by Rob Bowman.

3X16. "Apocrypha (Part 2 of 2)." Written by Frank Spotnitz and Chris Carter. Directed by Kim Manners.

3X17. "Pusher." Written by Vince Gilligan. Directed by Rob Bowman.

3X18. "Teso Dos Bichos." Written by John Shiban. Directed by Kim Manners.

3X19. "Hell Money." Written by Jeffrey Vlaming. Directed by Tucker Gates.

3X20. "Jose Chung's 'From Outer Space.'" Written by Darin Morgan. Directed by Rob Bowman.

3X21. "Avatar." Written by Howard Gordon (based upon a story by Howard Gordon and David Duchovny). Directed by James Charleston.

3X22. "Quagmire." Written by Kim Newton. Directed by Kim Manners.

3X23. "Wetwired." Written by Mat Beck. Directed by Rob Bowman.

3X24. "Talitha Cumi (Part 1 of 2)" Written by Chris Carter (based upon a story by David Duchovny and Chris Carter). Directed by R.W. Goodwin.

SEASON 4 (FIRST AIRED 1996–1997)

4X01. "Herrenvolk (Part 2 of 2)." Written by Chris Carter. Directed by R.W. Goodwin.

4X02. "Unruhe." Written by Vince Gilligan. Directed by Rob Bowman.

4X03. "Home." Written by Glen Morgan and James Wong. Directed by Kim Manners.

4X04. "Teliko." Written by Howard Gordon. Directed by James Charleston.

4X05. "The Field Where I Died." Written by Glen Morgan and James Wong. Directed by Rob Bowman.

4X06. "Sanguinarium." Written by Vivian Mayhew and Valerie Mayhew. Directed by Kim Manners.

4X07. "Musings of a Cigarette-Smoking Man." Written by Glen Morgan. Directed by James Wong.

4X08. "Paper Hearts." Written by Vince Gilligan. Directed by Rob Bowman.

4X09. "Tunguska (Part 1 of 2)." Written by Frank Spotnitz and Chris Carter. Directed by Rob Bowman.

4X10. "Terma (Part 2 of 2)." Written by Frank Spotnitz and Chris Carter. Directed by Rob Bowman.

4X11. "El Mundo Gira." Written by John Shiban. Directed by Tucker Gates.

4X12. "Kaddish." Written by Howard Gordon. Directed by Kim Manners.

4X13. "Never Again." Written by Glen Morgan and James Wong. Directed by Rob Bowman.

4X14. "Leonard Betts." Written by Frank Spotnitz, John Shiban, and Vince Gilligan. Directed by Kim Manners.

4X15. "Memento Mori." Written by Chris Carter, Frank Spotnitz, John Shiban, and Vince Gilligan. Directed by Rob Bowman.

4X16. "Unrequited." Written by Howard Gordon and Chris Carter. Directed by Michael Lange.

4X17. "Tempus Fugit (Part 1 of 2)." Written by Chris Carter and Frank Spotnitz. Directed by Rob Bowman.

4X18. "Max (Part 2 of 2)." Written by Chris Carter and Frank Spotnitz. Directed by Kim Manners.

4X19. "Synchrony." Written by Howard Gordon and David Greenwalt. Directed by Jim Charleston.

4X20. "Small Potatoes." Written by Vince Gilligan. Directed by Clifford Bole.

4X21. "Zero Sum." Written by Howard Gordon and Frank Spotnitz. Directed by Kim Manners.

4X22. "Elegy." Written by John Shiban. Directed by Jim Charleston.

4X23. "Demons." Written by R.W. Goodwin. Directed by Kim Manners.

4X24. "Gethsemane (Part 1 of 3)." Written by Chris Carter. Directed by R.W. Goodwin.

BIBLIOGRAPHY

Abbot, Jon. "The X-Files Guide." *The Dark Side,* September 1995: 23–33.
Bacal, Simon. "The NeXt Millennium." *Starburst,* March 1997: 10–12.
Bash, Alan. "Fox Looks to its Bold Beginnings for a Route to No. 1 in Ratings." *USA Today,* 5 December 1996: Sec.3:D.
Bash, Alan. " 'X-Files' Cliffhanger: Will it End in 1998?" *USA Today,* 14 January 1997:Sec.3:D.
Bernstein, Abbie. "The Scripting Secrets of The X-Files." *Fangoria,* June 1997:44–48.
Bonario, Steve. "Opening the X-Files." *Sci-Fi TV Fall Preview,* October 1995:42–49.
Bonario, Steve. "X-Files: A Mid-Life Crisis?" *Sci-Fi Channel Entertainment,* April 1996:44–47.
Brick, Scott. "Closer X-amination." *Sci-Fi Invasion,* 1997 Special Publication: 88–93.
Brick, Scott. "Nothing But the Truth." *Sci-Fi Invasion,* 1997 Special Publication: 94–97.
Brooks, James. "Field of Dreams." *Xpose,* May 1997:36, 39, 41.
Brooks, James. "Identified." *Xpose,* February 1997: 36–39.
Bush, Alan. "More Paranormal Programming Sighted in Prime Time." *USA Today,* 4 October 1994: Sec. 3:D.
Calcutt, Ian. "Skin Deep." *Starburst,* March 1997:4.
Calcutt, Ian. "The X-Files: Tunguska." *Starburst,* March 1997: 13.
Cinescape Presents The X-Files & Conspiracy Television, Special Collector's Issue, Fall 1996.
Cinescape's 1995 Science Fiction Television Yearbook, Fall 1995.
Coleman, Loren. "The Truth Behind the X-Files." *Fortean Times,* August 1995: 22–28.
Cooney, Jenny. "Gillian in Alien Territory." *TV Week,* May 25, 1996: 8–9; 14.
Cooney, Jenny. "Just Your Average Paranormal Guy!" *TV Week,* September 2, 1995:12–14.
Cornell, Paul, Martin Day, and Keith Topping. *X-Treme Possibilities.* Virgin Publishing, London: 1997.
DeMain, Bill. "Fear's Accomplice." *Starlog,* April 1997:52–55.
Edwards, Ted. *X-Files Confidential: The Unauthorized X-Philes Compendium.* Little, Brown, and Company, Boston: 1996.
Emery, Gene. "X-Files' Coriolis Error Leaves Viewers Wondering." *Skeptical Inquirer,* May/June 1995:5.

Eramo, Steven. "Somewhere in Time." *Xpose,* May 1997: 40–41.

Flaherty, Mike, A.J. Jacobs, Mary Kaye Schilling, and Ken Tucker. "Veneration X." *Entertainment Weekly,* November 29, 1996: 24–58.

Flaherty, Mike. " 'X' and the Single Girl." *Entertainment Weekly,* April 25, 1997:53.

Fretts, Bruce. "A Genuine X-centric." *Entertainment Weekly,* December 2, 1994:32.

Fretts, Bruce. "Television: The Week." *Entertainment Weekly,* January 31, 1997:47.

Fretts, Bruce. "The X Lexicon." *Entertainment Weekly,* March 10, 1995:22.

Genge, N.E. *The Unofficial X-Files Companion.* Crown, New York: 1995.

Genge, N.E. *The Unofficial X-Files Companion II.* Avon Books, New York: 1996.

Gliatto, Tom, and Craig Tomashoff. "X-ellence." *People,* October 9, 1995: 72–78.

Goldman, Jane. *The X-Files Book of the Unexplained, Volume One.* HarperPrism, New York: 1996.

Gross, Edward. "Homeward Bound." *Cinescape,* June 1996: 74–75.

Gross, Edward. "Mister FiX-it." *Cinescape,* May 1996: 74–75.

Gross, Edward. "The X-Files Mystery Tour." *Cinescape,* August 1995.

Gross, Edward. "X-Files: The Truth Is Here." *Cinescape,* November 1994: 34–45.

Hatfield, James, and Burt, George "Doc." *The Unauthorized X-Files Challenge.* Kensington Publishing Corp., New York: 1996.

Hatfield, James. "An X-traordinary Series on the Brink of Becoming a Modern Television Classic." *Southwest Entertainment Guide,* January 1997: 22–26.

Hill, Annette. "Alternative Realities." *Starburst,* January 1997: 16–18.

Hill, Annette. "Home Is Where the Heart Is." *Starburst,* April 1997: 33–36.

Hughes, Dave. "Keepers of the Truth." *Fangoria,* April 1997: 20–22; 24–25; 82.

Hughes, Dave. "No Butts About It." *Fangoria,* April 1997: 23.

Idato, Michael. "Scully X-Posed." *The Sunday Telegraph TV Extra,* 16–22 June 1996: 4–6.

Jacobs, A.J. "Parting Shots." *Entertainment Weekly,* May 10, 1996: 39.

Kahn, Sheryl. "Sci-Fi Mama: *The X-Files'* Gillian Anderson." *McCalls,* June 1996: 52–55.

Kennedy, Dana. "The X-Files Exposed." *Entertainment Weekly,* March 10, 1995: 18–24.

Killick, Jane. "The X-Files: Report #1." *Starburst,* March 1996: 25–40.

Killick, Jane. "The X-Files: Report #3." *Starburst,* May 1996: 25–40.

Krantz, Kathy. "X-Boss." *Starlog,* August 1997: 4–5.

Lee, Julianne. "Mutants, Psychics & Freaks." *Starlog,* May 1996: 52–54.

Lovece, Frank. *The X-Files Declassified: The Unauthorized Guide.* Citadel Press, Secaucus, New Jersey: 1996.

Lowry, Brian. *The Truth is Out There: The Official Guide to the X-Files.* HarperPrism, New York: 1995.

Lowry, Brian. *Trust No One: The Official Third Season Guide to the X-Files.* Harper-Prism, New York: 1996.

Maccarillo, Lisa. "Trust No One." *Sci-Fi Entertainment,* December 1994: 74–77.

MacNeill, Ian. "Going to X-tremes." *TV Week,* 13–19 July 1996: 4–6.

Mansfield, Stephanie. "Gillian Looks Like a Million." *TV Guide,* 6–12 July 1996: 6–14.

Marin, Rick. "Alien Invasion." *Newsweek,* July 8, 1996: 48–54.

Martin, Ed. "Confronting the Millennium." *Fangoria,* November 1996: 24–28.

May, Caroline. "The X-Man." *Xpose,* February 1997: 12–15; 17–21.

McDonald, David. *Starlog's Science Fiction Heroes and Heroines.* Crescent Books, New York: 1995.

Meisler, Andy. "Inside 'The X-Files' With a Deadline to Meet." *New York Times,* 26 May 1996.

Melcombe, Lynne. "Supernatural SuXXess." *BC Woman,* October 1995. 10–13.

Miller, Leslie. "X-Files' Flirts with its Fans." *USA Today,* 26 April 1996: Sec 2:D.

Mitchard, Jacquelyn. "Mom was an X-Phile." *TV Guide,* 23–29 May 1996:60.

Mundy, Chris. "Duchovny & Anderson." *Us,* May 1997: 44–52; 112.

Nazzaro, Joe. "David Nutter Directing the X-Files." *Starburst,* July 1996: 14–15.

Nazzaro, Joe. "Fantasies in Dark & Light." *Starlog,* June 1996: 70–73.

Nazzaro, Joe. "Frank Spotnitz Editing the X-Files." *Starburst,* July 1996: 10–11.

Nazzaro, Joe. "Jeffrey Vlaming Never 2Shy 2Write." *Starburst,* May 1997: 33–36.

Nazzaro, Joe. "Kim Manners X-Files Second Unit Director." *Starburst,* July 1996: 12–13.

Nazzaro, Joe. "Sleepless Nights." *Starburst,* September 1996: 21–24.

Nazzaro, Joe. "The Agony & The Ecstasy, Part One" *Starlog,* June 1997: 44–49.

Nazzaro, Joe. "The X-Men." *Starburst,* January 1996: 27–30.

Nazzaro, Joe. "Truth & Consequences, Part Two." *Starlog,* July 1997: 72–75.

Nollinger, Mark. "The David Duchovny X-perience." *TV Guide,* 21–27 December 1996: 18–28.

Nollinger, Mark. "X Posed: 20 Things You Need to Know about The X-Files." *TV Guide,* 6–12 April 1996: 18–24.

The Official Map of the X-Files. HarperPrism, New York: 1996.

O'Neill, John J. "Is the Truth Still Out There?" *Sci-Fi Entertainment,* October 1996: 68–70; 92.

Perenson, Melissa. "The X-Files Season Four Episode Guide, Part One." *Starburst,* April 1997: 30–32.

Perenson, Melissa. "The X-Files Season Four Episode Guide, Part Two." *Starburst,* May 1997: 29–32.

Perez, Dan. "The Good, the Bad, and the Scary: Horror Writers on *The X-Files*." *Realms of Fantasy,* April 1997: 20–24.

Reed, Craig Dr. "The FX Are Out There." *Sci-Fi Entertainment,* April 1997: 52–57; 59; 61; 63–64; 102.

Reed, Craig Dr. "The Next X: Chris Carter Speaks Out." *Sci-Fi Entertainment,* December 1996: 78–81.

Rickard, Bob. "A Fortean Guide to the X-Files." *Fortean Times,* February/March 1996: 33–34.

Rose, Aiexia. "X-Files: The Truth is in Here." *Star!,* August 1996: 19–26.

Roush, Matt. "An Exciting Weekend Sweeps In." *USA Today,* 7 February 1997: Sec.3:D.

Roush, Matt. "An Out-There 'X-Files' Writer." *USA Today,* 12 April 1996: Sec.3:D.

Roush, Matt. "Listening for Gems Between the Lines." *USA Today,* 27 December 1996: Sec.3:D.

Roush, Matt. "'Murder' and Mayhem Reign as Season Draws to a Close." *USA Today,* 17 May 1996: Sec. 3:D.

Roush, Matt. "Smoke Clears from an 'X-Files' Mystery." *USA Today,* 15 November 1996: Sec.3:D.

Roush, Matt. "Television: A Year of Few Noteworthy Newcomers." *USA Today,* 30 December 1996: Sec. 3:D.

Roush, Matt. "X-Files Earns its Shivers with Style." *USA Today,* 4 October 1996: Sec.3:D.

Roush, Matt. "'X-Files' Lets Some Light Peek Through." *USA Today,* 22 April 1997: Sec. 3:D.

Russo, Tom. "Gillian Anderson: X-Files." *Us,* March 1996: 52–54.

Schiff, Laura. "Smoke & Mirrors." *Starlog,* August 1997: 24–27.

Schindler, Rick, and Stephanie Williams. "An X-Files Encyclopedia From A to X." *TV Guide,* 17–23 May 1997: 20–30.

Schuster, Hal. *The Unauthorized Guide to the X-Files.* Prima Publishing, Rocklin, CA: 1997.

Sexton, Jim. "No Rest for the Eerie." *USA Weekend,* May 12, 1995.

Spelling, Ian. "Deadly Enigma." *Starlog,* August 1997: 28–30.

Spelling, Ian. "The Mythology Guy." *Starlog,* August 1997: 34–37.

Spelling, Ian. "X-Factors." *Starlog,* December 1996: 43–46.

Starlog Presents The X-Files & Other Eerie TV#1, December 1995.

Stevens, Kevin. "Declassifying the X-Files." *Sci-Fi Universe,* September 1996: 40–56.

Svetkey, Benjamin. "No Wonder He's Called Fox." *Entertainment Weekly,* September 29, 1995: 20–26.

Swallow, James. "American Skeptic." *Starlog Yearbook,* August 1996: 38–41.

Swallow, James. "X-aminations." *Starlog,* December 1995: 30–33; 64.

Thomas, Mike. "The X-Files: The Story So Far . . . " *Starburst,* October 1995: 12–15.

Vitaris, Paula. "X-Files: The Truth is Out There." *Cinefantastique,* October 1996: 16–41; 62.

Wagner, Chuck. "X Marks the Spotnitz." *Infinity,* December 1996: 48–50.

Watson, Bret. "A Gillian to One." *Entertainment Weekly*, February 9, 1996: 18–21.

Watson, Bret. "Fox's Den." *Entertainment Weekly*, September 27, 1996: 40–51.

Watson, Bret. "Sunday Marks a New Spot." *Entertainment Weekly*, September 13, 1996: 36–40.

Watson, Bret. "X-tra Credits: A Guide to the X-Files Supporting Players." *Entertainment Weekly*, February 9, 1996: 22–25.

Wild, David. "The X-Files Undercover." *Rolling Stone*, May 16, 1996: 38–41; 74.

Williams, Stephanie. "Queasy Writers." *TV Guide*, 21–27 December 1996: 22.

X-Files Official Magazine, Winter 1996.

X-Files Official Magazine, Spring 1997.

ALL DONE.

BYE BYE.

VISIT THE AUTHORS' WEBSITE AT:
www.omegapublishing.com